The Book of Field and Roadside

Open-Country Weeds, Trees, and Wildflowers of Eastern North America

John Eastman

Illustrated by Amelia Hansen

STACKPOLE BOOKS

Published by
STACKPOLE BOOKS
5067 Ritter Road
Mechanicsburg, PA 17055
www.stackpolebooks.com

Printed in the United States of America

10 9 8 7 6 5 4 3 2 1

First edition

Cover design by Mark Olszewski and Wendy Reynolds
Cover art by Amelia Hansen

Library of Congress Cataloging-in-Publication Data

Eastman, John (John Andrew)
    The book of field and roadside : open-country weeds, trees, and wild-flowers of eastern North America / John Eastman ; illustrated by Amelia Hansen.—1st ed.
        p.   cm.
    Includes bibliographical references and index (p.).
    ISBN 0-8117-2625-8
    1. Weeds—East (U.S.)—Identification.   2. Trees—East (U.S.)—Identification.   3. Wild flowers—East (U.S.)—Identification.
I. Title.
SB612.E28 E27   2003
581.974—dc21   2002008825

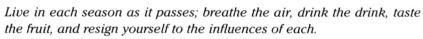

Live in each season as it passes; breathe the air, drink the drink, taste the fruit, and resign yourself to the influences of each.
—Henry D. Thoreau

Long live the weeds and the wilderness yet.
—"Inversnaid," Gerard Manley Hopkins

Contents

v

Acknowledgments

Black-and-white illustrations can often provide far more accurate representations of an organism than color photos and drawings, for the simple reason that none of nature's colors can be accurately duplicated, either by chemical toner or palette mixture; whereas the detailed line drawing can accurately be translated by talented eye and hand from actual scene to viewer's perception without futile attempts to re-create hues, to picture necessarily false if well-intentioned impressions. Such is the artistic talent of Amelia Hansen, to bring nature alive on the page without waiving an admission fee, the payment of attention. Her vision and mastery of images from the natural world have added immeasurably to the interest and utility of our 5 previous book collaborations as well as this one. I am grateful to her.

Several expert reviewers have graciously read and commented upon the plant accounts herein. I thank Dr. Heather L. Reynolds, plant ecologist at Indiana University in Bloomington; Dr. Gwen A. Pearson, entomologist at Michigan State University in East Lansing; and ecologist and land conservancy authority Dr. Richard Brewer, my former teacher, now professor emeritus, of Western Michigan University in Kalamazoo. Their valuable suggestions and advice have been most helpful, and I appreciate their time and contributions. All errors and expressed opinions are my own.

I also thank my friend, naturalist and teacher Jacqueline Ladwein, for solid help in locating various specimens and for loaning some of her excellent photographs for illustrative purposes. Her consistent interest and aid in my field projects have also been invaluable.

Other contributors of time, expertise, or both have included Derek Artz, Joyce Bond, Dr. Richard Fleming, Jan Mikesell, and Guy Sternberg. Editors Mark Allison and Amy Wagner of Stackpole Books have been consistently supportive.

Most of all I thank my loving companion of many years, Susan Woolley Stoddard, for the time, energies, and support she has contributed to this project, as to my previous books. Without her, none of them would exist.

Introduction

The natural world, to be seen truly, must be seen whole, even as a mosaic can be perceived only when its multiple fragments are joined. Once you have identified a plant, what other organisms might you expect to find in its company? What patterns reveal themselves when we look at the entire complex of organisms in, on, or around a plant?

The plants in this book typify the most common residents of open land—fields, roadsides, grasslands, sandy barrens, forest openings—in eastern North America, defined as all land areas east of the Mississippi. This book, third and last in a series of plant guides, follows the pattern of its predecessor volumes, *The Book of Forest and Thicket* (1992) and *The Book of Swamp and Bog* (1995). The focus of all 3 volumes is ecological; that is, the individual accounts deal not only with features of the plant itself, but also with its characteristics as a community hub, centering a mosaic of living organisms—other plants, invertebrates, birds, and mammals (including humans)—that a given plant may relate to or help support.

Plant and animal coactions—the effects of one species upon another—range through parasitic, commensal, competitive, and mutualistic relationships. Examples from all parts of this continuum abound in the following pages. Such a relational approach to plant observation, though hardly unique to the research realm, may offer something new to the everyday observer—an ecological focus that may enlarge one's perspectives in this environmentally conscious age. Aid to perception is the foremost aim of *The Book of Field and Roadside* and this 3-volume series.

This book focuses on 85 genera, including some of the plants most familiar to us. My selection has been arbitrary—another author's inclusions would probably vary somewhat from my own. Many of the plants herein belong to a single populous family, the world's second largest, after the orchid family—the asters, or composites. I have defined most technical botanical terms—though kept to a minimum—where they occur in the text; a list of recurring terms also appears in the Glossary. Latin names are given only for plant and invertebrate animal species, since the common English names (when they exist) for these organisms may often apply to more than one species. Both Latin and English names for plants rely upon Gleason and Cronquist's *Manual of Vascular Plants,* listed in the Bibliography, though occasionally, to facilitate arrangement of plant names, I have dropped one of the English-name hyphens beloved of these compilers. For insect names, my chief references have been the Entomological Society of America's *Common Names of Insects and Related Organisms* (edited by Joseph J. Bosik) and Arnett's *American Insects,* also listed.

Molecular biology, specifically the advent of DNA testing and analysis, has brought about a virtual revolution in the biological sciences, especially in the realm of classification and systematics, or taxonomy. Many plants and other organisms thought to be unrelated under the old systems are now revealed to share genetics closely in common—and some long classified as near relatives have been discovered to bear physical resemblances only. The new findings are analogous to an artillery barrage of monkey wrenches being thrown into the conventional, long-accepted plant classifications, wreaking havoc in the evolutionary shrubs. "The traditional plant classifications that have been used for a hundred years or so," as botanist Walter Judd has stated, "are being dramatically altered. We've probably learned more about the evolutionary relationships of plants in the last ten years than in the previous 100." When all the revisions are in—a process that may take years if not decades—the new plant systematics will give us a biologically more accurate, and much different, picture of plant relationships than the one our botany teachers taught us. It will confirm that physical resemblances between plants may in many instances result from convergent evolution of nonrelated species, producing unreliable indicators of genetic kinship.

In the meantime, a book such as this one must deal with systematics as they are, in the process of change but not yet finalized. Although the necessity of using taxonomic systems that are rapidly becoming obsolete does not present an ideal option, no other option is currently practicable. Thus, until the rigorous new systematics filter down to field range, to the usable levels of plant manuals and field guides, we use the old classifications.

Many if not most of the plants presented in this book are unpopular residents. Some have become invasive nuisances. One word categorizes these plants, a word generally synonymous with undesirable—*weed*.

Weed definitions abound. "I have heard it said that there are sixty definitions," wrote naturalist Donald Culross Peattie; "for me, a weed is a plant out of place." Such a definition, of course, presumes another one, that of a human-defined place of propriety from (and to) which the plant has escaped. One may also argue that some weeds become highly successful at making their own place. To Ralph Waldo Emerson, always the Unitarian optimist, a weed was a plant whose virtues hadn't yet been discovered. To Thoreau, the contrarian often quoted in this book, weeds were subjects of interest in the here and now. "I sympathize with weeds perhaps more than with the crop they choke, they express so much vigor," he wrote; "they are the truer crop which the earth more willingly bears."

Farmers and persons who depend upon crops for a living would, of course, vehemently disagree with Emerson and Thoreau. Weed-fighting industries of ever more complex herbicidal chemistry have grown and spread like radiating rhizomes throughout the agricultural landscape. "Weed science" has become a fully accredited adjunct of agriculture, sprouting its own professional curricula, journals, doctorates, and research organizations. Weeds feed a good many people in this country, and not just in salads or as cooked greens.

Today's American plant landscape reveals that a very high percentage of the plants we label as weeds—some 2,000 of them—are of alien (mostly Eurasian) origin. Not that "weed" and "alien" are necessarily synonymous, for numerous accounts of native American weeds also appear in the following pages; and alien plants, as we know, form almost the entire basis of our agriculture. Also, the designations "native" and "alien" are, in a sense, as anthropocentric as the term "weed." Anthropologists tell us that the human inhabitants found here by the earliest European colonists were "native Americans" only by virtue of their much earlier arrivals—arrivals that no doubt also brought seeds of change that probably transformed aspects of the continent they found. Who can say what the pristine, "original" North America looked like? The oral traditions of Indian cultures have not revealed many environmental details. Colonial travelers and explorers left tantalizing bits of information, and modern paleobotanists and ecologists can make likely guesses—but nobody alive can authoritatively detail what the North American landscape looked like five hundred, one thousand, eight thousand years ago. No doubt vast stretches of today's rural and urban vistas would appear utterly foreign to the eyes of the first European settlers in America, though some of the vegetation might remind them of Old World fields left behind. Those peoples we call native Americans found their long-familiar landscape changing beneath their feet—or rather, beneath the feet of the European intruders, who seemed to transport entire fields of alien plants on their wagon wheels and boot soles. Those boots kick-started a global economy long predating the present one—the interchange on a massive scale of Old World plants to the New and vice versa. Weeds found their most efficient carriers yet in the motions of human enterprise.

In North America, changes in the plant components proceeded rapidly, mostly as accidental side effects of trade, settlement, wars, territorial acquisition, and discovery. Explorers not only mapped new territory but, in a sense, created it. Lewis and Clark, for example, brought back numerous pressed botanical specimens from their 1804 western expedition, but who knows how many seeds they had transported west on their boots and boats? Yet this botanical transformation of the continent did not occur all at once but came in waves, successive tides, from the 17th to 20th centuries. New England often (though not always) took the brunt of them, being Europe's frequent landfall in the New World; from there the immigrant plants often abutted against the Appalachian range, then gradually trickled through and rippled across the continent. Such tides increased plant diversity at the same time that, in many places, they threatened the native flora with their swamping, aggressive vigor.

Today, among botanists and naturalists, a spectrum of weed attitudes exists. Experts tell us, in so many words, that there are good weeds and bad weeds—even as, for some, there is good nature and bad nature. Value hierarchies and inconsistent attitudes abound in the weed world. Mildness toward dandelions can morph into raging fury at the sight of spotted knapweed or garlic mustard. The distinctions between "naturalized" and "invasive" often seem, more than anything, subjective assessments. Each alien plant, of course, has been equally invited—plants seldom go where conditions do not welcome them—by means of the generous sites and habitats we have created for them.

Yet, beyond the emotions that weeds evoke and our frequent efforts to get rid of them, certain aspects of weed ecology must stir the plant observer's interest. So many weeds, for example, can take advantage of almost any human agricultural practice—including, in some cases, herbicidal treatments. Conscientious tillage, while destroying some weed stands, simply opens up the ground for others, exposing their seeds to light and freeing them of significant plant competition during vital stages of germination. Dormant weed seeds, often capable of sprouting after years or even decades of burial, may be seen in some sense as reproductive analogues to the system of delayed implantation in certain mammals (seals, walruses, fruit bats, mink, otters, roe deer, among others), in which the fertilized egg attaches to the uterine wall some months after fertilization occurs, thereby delaying birth to an optimal season for the young. The weeds we see are as nothing compared to what waits beneath our feet for apt conditions to occur—exposure to the right temperature, moisture, light, and space. This so-called seed bank—the trove of living but dormant seeds buried in almost any piece of ground—often requires disturbance, a plow, even, to bring them up near the surface so that germination can occur. Thus, in addition to providing capacious repositories for human emotions plus their expert usage of human transportation facilities, weeds also present a survival metaphor, a picture of enduring faith in the future, as it were. If one admires persistence and survival, one must admire weeds. If one seeks an example of outright aggression in nature, one also has a fine model in weeds. And should one crave samples of complexity, nuance, difficulty, and color in the outdoor world, a nearby weed can easily provide them.

In raising a lawn, garden, or crop, of course, one's plant priorities are clear. But the global economy of weeds raises another crop of questions outside the interests of lawn keeping and agriculture. For example, should uncultivated land likewise become subject to massive weed control, as advocated by many naturists (naturalists with an agenda) and conservationists? Increasingly, the science of ecology is teaching us that the chemical or physical act of yanking a plant from the ground bears disruptive and complex side effects. It violates the subsurface side of things, the seamless webs and interfaces. "Above ground," as ecologist Richard Brewer wrote, "we can see the individual trees standing here and there and, beneath them, shrubs and herbs. Below ground the distinction between individual plants is much less clear," being interconnected by "a vast, fine fungal network."

The complex consequences of plant pulling occur in the communities of soil mycorrhizae, fungi, and invertebrates that animate the underground and make it a pulsing, viable medium and substrate of life. Few of us are qualified to judge the worth—or unworth—of a plant's presence against the value of a cohesive realm of organisms that underlies and supports the obscure boundaries of its being. This is taking the long view of things—the community view—the view called ecology. In this view, interference in the natural world, despite one's best intentions, seldom seems rectified by more interference. "The closest thing to a law of nature that I know of," wrote zoologist Bernd Heinrich, "is that those who try to run an ecosystem inevitably get the opposite results of those they intend." Author-birder Pete Dunne stated it another way: "That environment is maintained best which is juggled least." Though perhaps overgeneralized to some extent, such comments represent a line of current thinking.

Still, even though a weed may be an attitude of mind as well as a plant in the wrong place—and even though many weed problems may as accurately be labeled people problems resulting from poor land management and a lack of ecological insight, weeds can be and often are worrisome. Ecologically, it is not the roadside plant or the old-field invader, the alien claimer of disturbed soil and disrupted ground, that poses the greatest botanical threat to North America. It is not even the opportunist and gainer of footholds where humans have fragmented the native plant community. The most serious threats are those weeds so aggressive that they invade intact native ecosystems. These invasive aliens exhibit rapid growth and maturity; prolific seed production; highly successful seed dispersal, germination, and colonization; ability to outcompete native species; and high cost to remove and control. Often they are also free of the natural pests left behind in their native lands. Most of these characteristics also, of course, might fit many weeds deemed not so dangerous or possessing only potential threat.

Among the major alien threats to our flora, those described in this book include autumn olive, multiflora rose, birdsfoot-trefoil, spotted knapweed, garlic mustard, spurges, sweet clovers, and several others. They do not rampage uniformly, but worse in some places than in others. In addition to these ecosystem invaders, crop farmers often have their own lesser but nuisance plant intruders to contend with, and many of those plants are also included in the following accounts.

So the disruption of ecosystems—and, ironically, the reduction in biodiversity that often follows the introduction of species that turn aggressive in areas bereft of their native natural controls—is not an insignificant matter. Yet one of the lessons taught us by Charles Darwin is that evolution and revolution are not always mutually exclusive processes. Darwin forever destroyed the notion of a pristine Eden, of an ideal world as the way things "once were and ought to be." Evolution has shown us the random dynamism operating in massive floods or slow seepages of change, the results of which have always, in time, found their own levels within, and helped create, new biotic contexts. Change remains the key word to any comprehensive understanding of a forest, old field, or indeed, a roadside. Certainly it is hardly wrong or shortsighted to protect and try to preserve our native biodiversity as best we may and to fight the weed threats that truly jeopardize it. Necessary too, however, is awareness that the engine of adaptation does not stall, that epics of competition and accommodation describe the drama and final unity of life. The "perpetual flux of disturbance ecology," in the words of ecologist Seth R. Reice, remains the essential creative force in nature. Nature's true nature is ongoing change; such is the long view of the ecologist. Weeds—plain weeds—can make us mindful of this dynamic in each field and roadside we encounter.

Weeds, in short, often become catalysts of change. They are the disruptive stimuli, the pests that invade, shaking things up, changing the scenery (sometimes literally), shifting, rearranging, provoking the changes that drive the mechanisms of natural selection and evolution. It might even be said that, in biology, many if not most stimuli that bring about change are usually intruders (that is, weeds) in some sense. Presumably this has been so since life began.

Yet another side of the matter exists and should not be minimized. Biodiversity is the holy word of ecologists today, and rightly so. Thoreau, as usual, said it best: "In wilderness is the preservation of the world." Today alien plant invasions certainly threaten North American biodiversity, not only of native plants but of the many organisms that depend upon them. In the wise words of plant ecologist Heather L. Reynolds, "What is justifiably alarming about today's exotic species invasions is the orders of magnitude greater scale of temporal and spatial change. Alien invasive species are the second leading cause of biodiversity loss today, behind habitat destruction. . . . Can we really afford to take an across-the-board 'live and let live' approach?" Personally I would rather study weeds than pull them. In current biotic circumstances, however, I may not ethically have that luxury. One need not always be a committed "naturist" in order to enlist on the side of biodiversity and the actions it may entail.

Whatever the labels one may affix to forms of life, the primary aim of this book—to explore, observe, and describe—is job enough. Here we strive simply to focus on some common expressions of those forms. In so doing, we try to expose some new realms of experience—right outside the door.

Ailanthus *(Ailanthus altissima)*. Quassia family. This smooth-barked tree often looks crooked, has a divided trunk. Leaves are pinnately compound and alternate; the leaflet undersurface shows gland-tipped teeth at the base. Fruits are winged, spirally twisted samaras, occur in large, brownish clusters *(panicles)*.

Other names: Tree of heaven, copal tree, Chinese sumac, stinktree.

Close relatives: Ten *Ailanthus* species exist, all native to Asia or Australia. Other quassia family members (some 120 in all) include Surinam quassia *(Quassia amara)* and bitter wood or Jamaican quassia *(Aeschrion excelsa)*. The related shrub called crucifixion thorn *(Chaparro amargosa)* grows in the Sonoran desert of the Southwest and Mexico. All family members except *A. altissima* reside in tropical and subtropical regions around the globe.

Lifestyle: Once widely planted as an ornamental, now regarded as a fast-growing weed tree—"about as much loved as some other introductions such as starlings and gypsy moths," wrote botanist Edward G. Voss—ailanthus seldom grows more than 50 or 60 feet tall. It sprouts vigorously from stumps and roots as well as seed, may rise 6 to 12 feet in a single growing season.

Its sumaclike foliage, acrid smelling when crushed, appears late in spring, turns yellow in autumn or drops when, still green, the first frost touches it. Since branches do not appear until the tree is a few years old, the tree appears to lose all its "branches" (actually, its pinnate leaves) each fall for its first few years, spending its winters as a stick in the ground.

Yellowish green flowers, mostly unisexual on separate trees (occasionally bisexual on the same tree), appear after the leaves are full grown in late May and June. Male flowers smell foul. The female flowers, almost odorless, are insect-pollinated. Prolific seeds, centered in twisted papery sheaths called *samaras,* ripen in October, may number some 350,000 per tree. Most stems begin to produce seed at 10 to 20 years, occasionally much sooner.

Most reproduction, however, occurs vegetatively by sprouting from horizontal root extensions. The shoot establishes a taproot, sending out ropelike suckers that can raise sprouts up to 50 feet from the parent stem. Pulling up an ailanthus sapling from one's yard can be like retrieving a buried cable across the lawn. In just a few years, the tree may form dense, clonal thickets that invade adjacent meadows from forest edges or fencerows. Typically short-lived, the trees usually survive only 30 to 50 years, though sometimes considerably longer.

Associates: Ailanthus populates city alleys and vacant lots, also inhabits fields, fencerows, and railroad and river embankments, dump sites, trash heaps, just about any disturbed-soil site that is sunny. Shade-intolerant, the tree thrives near the reflected warmth of buildings, garden walls, wooden fences, billboards, and other structures. Ailanthus adapts to a wide variety of soils, moisture conditions, and temperatures. It resists air pollutants, insect pests, and disease.

1

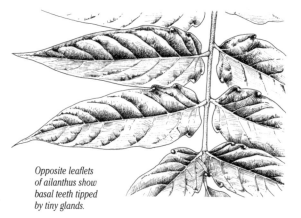

Opposite leaflets of ailanthus show basal teeth tipped by tiny glands.

Several fungi attack ailanthus. These include mushroom root rot, the fruiting body of which is called honey mushroom *(Armillaria mellea)*, plus various leaf spots, mildews, and twig blights.

Probably the best-known feeder on ailanthus is a large green caterpillar with black dots and bluish wartlike projections *(tubercles)* called the ailanthus silkworm *(Samia cynthia)*, also known as the ailanthus silkmoth and cynthia moth. Imported from China about 1861 as a possible silk producer on ailanthus trees, the insect never lived up to commercial hopes but spread across the country, feeding on ailanthus as well as several other trees and shrubs. Occasionally it becomes numerous enough to defoliate entire trees. Broods hatch in May through summer. The large adult silkmoth (6- to 8-inch wingspread), elegantly patterned in brown and pinkish, flies only in daytime. The large cocoon, from which a silk industry was supposed to hatch, resembles that of the promethea moth; suspended from a leaf midrib by a silken stem, it is easiest seen after leaflets fall in early autumn, often remaining on the tree through winter.

The ailanthus webworm moth *(Atteva punctella)*, an olive-brown ermine moth caterpillar, forms summer feeding colonies, creating loose webs on leaf surfaces. Adult moths, appearing in the fall, have colorful, yellow-spotted forewings. At rest they resemble sticks.

Little information exists on pollinators of ailanthus. Insects commonly found on the tree include syrphid flies (Syrphidae) and frit flies (Chloropidae), both of which probably pollinate the flowers; braconid (Braconidae) and ichneumon (Ichneumonidae) wasps; and green lacewings (Chrysopidae).

Birds seldom consume ailanthus seeds. In one study, however, meadow voles seemed to prefer them over seeds of white pine, in contrast to the preferences of white-footed mice. The leaves are reputedly toxic to livestock.

Lore: A tree that sprouts prolifically in city sidewalk cracks and beneath gratings, grows up to 12 feet tall in a year, and sends out numerous colonizing roots from its vertical taproot is undoubtedly "the ultimate urban tree," as some have labeled it. Unfazed by toxic fumes and smog, it thrives in cinders and grime. Its roots buckle sidewalks, damage foundation walls, and clog sewer lines. People who want everything in nature to be good for something usually find ailanthus good for nothing. Many of the tree's severest current critics are those urban foresters and landscapers who formerly encouraged its use in street and yard plantings. (Certain promoters of the tree in 1962 forecast that, by 1965, it would be "the most popular shade tree in America.") Pejorative labels abound: It is "oversexed," it is the "ashcan tree," it is the "tenement palm," "arboreal riffraff," "stink tree," and on into the night. Yet, were it not for the ubiquitous ailanthus, certain large urban areas would entirely lack any trace of tree greenery or shade. Novelist Betty Smith made ailanthus a symbol of urban perseverance and indestructibility in *A Tree Grows in Brooklyn* (1943).

Today ailanthus is planted nowhere in America, and it has few defenders. Yet it continues to plant itself just about anywhere that little else will grow. A small number of urban horticulturists and foresters see potential value for ailanthus as a hardy replacement for street plantings such as elms and maples that cannot survive urban fumes and the constriction of pavements. Some cities in Belgium and England have already begun using ailanthus for this purpose. From slag heaps in Pittsburgh to tenement slums in the Bronx, this tree represents nature to many urban dwellers. Most urban plantings are of female trees, which bear a less offensive odor and (lacking pollination from males) no seed clusters.

Introduced from China by Philadelphia horticulturist William Hamilton in 1784, the tree rapidly overran its plantings and quickly colonized the entire country. By 1875, it threatened to take over Washington, D.C., and the city declared it a "nuisance injurious to health." Today, in its native China, ailanthus continues to provide a pharmacopoeia of herbal medicines (mainly from the bark), as it has for thousands of years. Not tolerated as a haphazard volunteer there (China apparently permits the growth of few plants that can't be eaten, worn, or medicinally dosed), ailanthus is cultivated for homeopathic treatment of numerous ailments—diarrhea, dysentery, leukorrhea, tapeworm, and malaria, among others. Herbalists have prescribed it for everything from asthma to wet dreams. Large doses of the bark infusion may not be what the doctor ordered, however; the compound ailanthone may be toxic, can also cause skin rashes on persons allergic to the sap.

Ailanthone also accounts for the tree's tendency to inhibit seed germination and seedling growth of nearby tree species, a toxic effect called *allelopathy*. Soil microbial activity rapidly detoxifies the chemical substance, mainly exuded by the root bark, but its constant fresh pervasion of surrounding soil may cause herbicidal effects. Observers have noted that invasion of other shrubs and trees in stands of ailanthus, normal among most pioneering edge species, often occurs very slowly if at all, thus limiting or stalling plant succession in these places.

The word *ailanthus* originated as *ai lanto* in the Moluccan island of Amboina, Indonesia, meaning literally "tree of heaven," supposedly for its fast-gained height—which, in North America at least, is hardly imposing.

Alfalfa *(Medicago sativa)*. Pea family. Short spikes of blue flowers, 3-part (trifoliate) cloverlike leaves, and spiral seedpods identify this alien perennial forage plant. The terminal leaflet, turned upward, is longer than the 2 side leaflets, and leaflets are toothed only at their tips.

Other names: Lucerne, medick.

Close relatives: About 80 *Medicago* species exist, mostly in Eurasia. Other North American residents include black medick *(M. lupulina)*, smooth bur-clover *(M. polymorpha)*, and downy bur-clover *(M. minima)*. Legume kin include lupine, birdsfoot-trefoil, clovers, sweet clovers, common vetch, Canadian tick-trefoil, bush-clovers (all *q.v.*), and many others.

Lifestyle: Several alfalfa subspecies, forms, and hybrid varieties exist, but in eastern North America the plant typically consists of several stems and a taproot that may extend 10 to 15 feet down, occasionally farther. Like most legumes, alfalfa grows nitrogen-fixing nodules on its roots. *Rhizobium* bacteria in the nodules convert atmospheric nitrogen into substances that the plant uses in forming amino acids, also enriching the surrounding soil with nitrogen.

Another characteristic that alfalfa shares with many legumes is the trip mechanism of its flower, flinging pollen on the bodies of insect pollen or nectar collectors. Both male and female sex organs, held under tension by the basal keel petal of the flower, spring ("trip") when an alighting insect dislodges the keel petal. "The organs hit the bees on the lower portion of the head," as biologist Bernd Heinrich wrote, depositing pollen from the stamens, "while the female organ of the flower becomes dusted with pollen the bee has picked up at a previous flower." Tripping can also occur, however, when petal tissues become weakened by high or low temperatures, an event that usually results in self-pollination. Untripped flowers do not set seed. Fertilization—that is, when pollen tubes penetrate to the ovary—occurs about 24 hours after pollination. Seedpods, spiral in shape with 4 or 5 coils, contain several yellowish seeds.

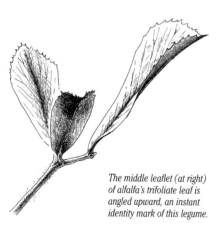

An alfalfa plant (unless harvested for hay) may live from 4 to 10 years or longer, increasing its root growth each year. Stems often become somewhat woody at the base as the plant ages.

Associates: Bushy, often half prostrate, alfalfa has flowered along with human agriculture and civilization from ancient times. Today it frequently overlaps its cropland borders, appearing in open areas everywhere. Alfalfa requires well-drained, limy soils.

The middle leaflet (at right) of alfalfa's trifoliate leaf is angled upward, an instant identity mark of this legume.

Numerous bacterial and fungous diseases affect alfalfa. Bacterial wilt, caused by *Corynebacterium insidiosum*, stunts and kills alfalfa plants and is widespread. An anthracnose disease, *Colletotrichum trifolii*, marked by stem lesions in summer, weakens the plant and kills crown buds. Fungous parasites include leaf invaders such as the rust *Uromyces striatus*, downy mildew *Peronospora trifoliorum*, stem and leaf spot *(Phoma, Ascochyta)*, *Fusarium* wilt and root rot, and several others.

Common dandelion *(q.v.)*, hoary alyssum *(q.v.)*, and cheat (see Brome-grasses) strongly compete with crop alfalfa growth at times.

A twining tangle of a plant parasite common on alfalfa and other legumes, attaching and tapping into their stems, is clover or legume dodder *(Cuscuta epithymum)*.

Like most crop plants raised in farm monocultures, alfalfa hosts numerous insect pests, which the uniformity of crop growth may allow in epidemic or plague abundance. Most of these pests are sap suckers that cause wilting and eventual death of the plant, but leaf and root feeders are also common. Many alfalfa pests appear endemic to the plant's western range, where it has been longest cultivated and remains a most abundant forage crop. The following paragraphs focus mainly on insect associates likely to be seen in eastern North America.

Common sap-sucking insects on alfalfa include the garden fleahopper *(Halticus bractatus)*, a shiny black bug that resembles aphids; the pea aphid *(Acyrthosiphon pisum)*, a green species introduced from Europe, often coating plants with honeydew and cast-off skins; the treehopper *Stictocephala bubalus;* the clover leafhopper (see Clovers); the potato leafhopper *(Empoasca fabae)*, wedge-shaped and green, migrating each spring to northern states from southern areas—it lays eggs in stems and leaf midribs of alfalfa plus other legumes and garden plants, and its larval feeding causes yellowing and loss of leaflet tips ("alfalfa yellows"); the meadow spittlebug *(Philaenus spumarius)*, nymph of a froghopper, which exudes masses of froth and feeds within them—according to the National Alfalfa Information System (NAIS), crop "alfalfa can support a tremendous population of spittlebugs without yield loss and they usually have no economic impact." The same cannot be said about plant bugs, which puncture plant tissues, causing leaves to pucker and crinkle. These include the tarnished plant bug *(Lygus lineolaris)*, brownish in color; the rapid plant bug *(Adelphocoris rapidus)*, dark brown; and the alfalfa plant bug *(A. lineolatus)*, a greenish European import. Plant bug nymphs are especially destructive, injuring buds and preventing flowering.

Foliage feeders include grasshoppers, probably alfalfa's most destructive insect pests. Most damage is inflicted by several grasshopper species, all of which hatch in late spring; these include the migratory grasshopper *(Melanoplus sanguinipes)*, two-striped grasshopper *(M. bivittatus)*, red-legged grasshopper *(M. femurrubrum)*, and clear-winged grasshopper *(Camnula pellucida)*.

Several butterfly and moth caterpillars commonly feed on alfalfa foliage. The Melissa blue *(Lycaeides melissa)*, a green caterpillar, is much attended by ants as it feeds; its 2 broods hatch in late spring and midsummer. Caterpillars of the alfalfa butterfly or orange sulphur *(Colias eurytheme)* are grass green with a white side stripe; a common predator on this caterpillar is *Collops vittatus*, a soft-winged flower beetle. The common or clouded sulphur *(Colias philodice)*, our most abundant yellow butterfly, also feeds on alfalfa as a larva. Among moths, the bilobed looper moth caterpillar *(Autographa biloba)* feeds on alfalfa, as does the corn earworm moth or bollworm *(Helicoverpa zea)*, the armyworm moth *(Pseudaletia unipuncta)*, and the fall armyworm moth *(Spodoptera frugiperda)*; armyworms often occur in irruptive, destructive abundance. Greenish yellow caterpillars may be alfalfa webworms *(Loxostege cerealis)* or garden webworms *(Achyra rantalis)*, both pyralid moths. Figured tiger moth caterpillars *(Grammia figurata)*, densely haired, plus a wide variety of dart moth and cutworm caterpillars (Noctuidae) also feed extensively on alfalfa.

A destructive beetle larva that skeletonizes leaves and also feeds on stems of young alfalfa plants is the alfalfa weevil *(Hypera postica)*, a European import. At first dark in color, it becomes bright green as it grows. The parasitic wasp *Bathyplectes curculionis*, imported from Italy in 1911, has become a well-established, effective biological control on this species.

Alfalfa stem feeders include the clover stem borer *(Languria mozardi)*, a beetle larva that tunnels in host plants. A nematode or roundworm, *Ditylenchus dipsaci*, also feeds in the stems.

Although many insects seek nectar and pollen from alfalfa flowers, relatively few are effective pollinators—that is, can trip the stamens, retrieve and carry the pollen, and cross-fertilize the plants with consistent regularity. These few are mainly bees of various genera—honeybees *(Apis mellifera)*, bumblebees *(Bombus)*, and alfalfa leafcutting bees *(Megachile rotundata)*. A pollen-collecting bee may visit 20 to 40 alfalfa flowers in a single trip from the hive, tripping most of the flowers it visits. Honeybees, however, favor pollens from other plants, visit alfalfa mainly for nectar. The aforementioned tripping mechanism sometimes traps nectar collectors, pinning them down. Most trapped bees manage to escape, though occasionally you can find a victim in the flower. Honeybees apparently learn to avoid this hazard by approaching flowers from the side of the keel petal, taking nectar without tripping the stamens (they "apparently do not like having their heads snapped at each flower visit," according to Bernd Heinrich). The conventional "front-door" approach, usually taken by inexperienced worker bees, usually results in tripped stamens, pollinated flowers, and sometimes a trapped bee. Bees that measure 3/8 inch or longer usually trip the flowers more consistently than honeybees.

Other, less reliable pollinators include such flower residents or visitors as thrips (Thysanoptera), tiny insects that nectar-feed in the flowers; blister beetles (Meloidae);

soldier beetles *(Chauliognathus);* and the aforementioned alfalfa butterflies *(Colias eury-theme,* also called orange sulphurs), displaying orange, brown-bordered wings.

Crinkled or aborted seedpods indicate infestation by tiny flies called alfalfa gall midges *(Asphondylia websteri).*

Larval alfalfa snout beetles *(Otiorhynchus ligustici)* feed just below the root crown in early fall; over winter, they hibernate deeper in the soil, then pupate during the following June. Tiny root-knot nematodes (roundworms), mainly *Meloidogyne* species, also parasitize the roots.

Probably alfalfa's foremost mammal feeder (excluding livestock) is the cottontail rabbit, though almost all vegetarian grazers (deer, rodents) also consume it. In the West, pocket gophers are the foremost alfalfa foragers. Foliage is also grazed by American coots, Canada geese, American widgeons, and sharp-tailed grouse. Sandhill cranes, ring-necked pheasants, and northern bobwhites consume the seeds. Alfalfa fields provide prime nesting habitat for ring-necked pheasants, but first mowing of the year may destroy many nests.

Lore: Many farmers rank alfalfa first among crop legumes. It is said to furnish more green forage, more pasture, and more dry hay per acre than any other hay or grass.

The quantity of atmospheric nitrogen fixed by *Rhizobium* bacteria in any given stand of alfalfa, though difficult to measure, is probably about 100 pounds per acre. Alfalfa may yield from 3 to 12 tons of hay per acre. This plant grows poorly, however, in soils not already rich in nitrogen. A successful alfalfa crop requires soil priming or preparation with manure or nitrogen fertilizers. Such inoculation enables nodule bacteria to produce all the nitrogen (and more) required by the plants, thus further priming the soil for the potential benefit of other crops. Yet, since an alfalfa stand may last 3 to 10 years or longer, many farmers do not rotate it with other crops, allowing it to regenerate each year until it loses vigor and declines. Somewhat offsetting its soil fertility value for other crops is deep-rooted alfalfa's tendency to lower the water table, especially in arid regions where it is grown, causing hardship for more shallowly rooted crops sown afterward.

Herbalists also set great store by this plant, claiming it as the source of 8 essential amino acids along with useful laxative, diuretic, and other medicinal properties. According to homeopathic lore, almost any ailment one might think of having can benefit from a swig of bland alfalfa tea steeped from leaves and flowerheads. Alfalfa provides a source of commercial chlorophyll and carotene as nutrition supplements, is rich in vitamins A, D, and K, also the antioxidant tricin. Alfalfa sprouts are widely marketed as salad items, and most honeys sold as clover or clover blend actually come from alfalfa. On the negative side, reports indicate that canavanine, found in alfalfa sprouts and seeds, may adversely affect lupus conditions. Alfalfa's main commercial use is cattle feed; overfeeding alfalfa, however, may cause a condition called bloat in livestock.

Alfalfa is said to be a native of Asia, but nobody really knows for sure—its place of origin is lost in time. Earliest mention may have been in Babylonian texts around 700 B.C. Alfalfa became the main forage for the horse cavalries of ancient Persia and Greece as well as Rome. Probably Roman farmers first planted it about 200 B.C. The Arabs, to whom we owe the plant's English name, called alfalfa the "father of all foods" for its hay forage value. Spaniards brought alfalfa to the New World in the 15th and 16th centuries, and it arrived in the southwestern United States about 1750. In 1793, Thomas Jefferson raised a field of it in Virginia. Even as late as 1900, however, only 1 percent of field alfalfa grew east of the Mississippi, and it remains a predominantly western crop. A new cold-hardy strain developed in 1858 by Minnesota farmer Wendelin Grimm (who called it "everlasting clover") enabled northern hay growers to raise alfalfa.

Today alfalfa remains widely cultivated (and widely escaped) throughout the country. After centuries of cultivation, horticultural tinkering, and deliberate hybridization with other *Medicago* species, it has also become a genetic mixture of characters far removed from those of earlier cultivated strains in both ancient and recent times—even farther from those of the original plant. Thus "pure" alfalfa is virtually nonexistent; the plant is as thoroughly domesticated as corn.

The word *alfalfa* is the Spanish modification of an Arabic word for the plant. *Medicago,* from the Greek word *medike,* probably refers to the region of Media in Persia, an early source of the plant.

Alyssum, Hoary *(Berteroa incana).* Mustard family. Common in summer, this white-flowered alien grows a foot or two high. Its 4-petaled flowers surmount the 2 or more erect branches that rise atop the main stem. The small petals are deeply notched, and the hairy seedpods, oblong with a beak at one end, stand erect close to the stem. A whitish bloom covers the plant.

Other names: Hoary false alyssum, hoary alison.

Close relatives: Five *Berteroa* species exist, all in temperate Eurasia. Hoary alyssum shows close resemblances to other mustards, notably the peppergrasses *(Lepidium)* and false flaxes *(Camelina).* Alyssums *(Alyssum)* and whitlow-grasses *(Draba)* are also closely related. More than 40 mustard genera occur in eastern North America; others in this book include garlic mustard and yellow rocket.

Lifestyle: Its frosted appearance—a gray-green coat of downy, star-shaped hairs, easily seen with a hand lens—immediately identifies this hardy mustard. Reproductively, it covers the gamut from annual and biennial to short-lived perennial life cycles, spreading mainly by seed.

Numerous stems rise from alyssum's deeply plunging taproot, which gives the plant drought resistance.

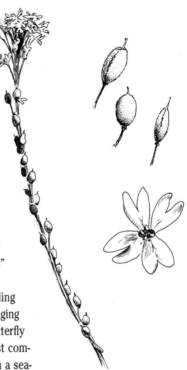

Associates: Hoary alyssum favors dry, sandy, or gravelly ground along roadsides and in old fields, pastures, gravel pits, disturbed ground. Drought and winter-kill in hayfields are said to increase invasive occurrences of this plant. It readily competes with crop alfalfa *(q.v.)* during conditions of drought.

The syrphid fly *Eristalis tenax,* also called hover fly or drone fly, is a known pollinator of this plant.

Flea beetles *(Psylliodes, Phyllotreta)*—many are black with yellow-striped wings—commonly feed on mustards, often producing tiny "shot holes" in the leaves.

A velvety green or greenish caterpillar feeding on the leaves may be one of several mustard-foraging white butterflies. The imported cabbageworm butterfly *(Pieris rapae),* introduced from Europe, is the most common species; it may produce 5 or 6 generations in a season, eating large holes in the foliage; its angular chrysalis or pupa often hangs by a silken belt from leaf or stem. Other alyssum-feeding whites include the checkered white *(Pontia protodice)* and the mustard white *(Pieris napi),* both native butterflies.

Alyssum's hairy seedpods hugging the stem and its 4 deeply notched petals are distinctive; flower development progresses upward.

Seeds of hoary alyssum are not widely consumed by wildlife. Probably some ground-feeding sparrows and finches occasionally eat them. Mammals rarely graze this plant.

Lore: While hoary alyssum does not rank as harmful in livestock forage as some other plants, it can cause toxic symptoms, especially in horses, when consumed in large quantity. Horses may suffer swelling of the lower legs. Cattle and sheep usually reject the plant.

The word *alyssum* originates from a Greek word for similar plants meaning "rabies cure." It doesn't and won't. The plant's native home is Europe; when or how it came to North America remains unknown.

Amaranths *(Amaranthus* species). Amaranth family. Most amaranths have large leaves and green flowers, the flowers occurring in dense, bristly spikes. Two of the most common species are *A. retroflexus,* called redroot or rough pigweed; and *A. hybridus,* smooth pigweed, known also as slim or smooth amaranth. Both annuals are native to tropical America. Seedling leaves often show bright red undersides.

　　Other names: Green amaranth, pigweed, careless weed. The unrelated lamb's quarters *(q.v.),* which resembles amaranth, is also called pigweed.

　　Close relatives: Some 60 species of *Amaranthus* exist, of which 45 or so are indigenous to Mexico and Central and South America. About 20 *Amaranthus* species reside in eastern North America. These include tumbleweed *(A. albus),* love-lies-bleeding *(A. caudatus),* and prince's feather *(A. hypochondriacus).* Family relatives include cock's comb *(Celosia argentea),* cottonweeds *(Froelichia),* and bloodleaf *(Iresine rhizomatosa),* among others.

　　Lifestyle: These 2 familiar "weed amaranths," or pigweeds, abundant in gardens and along roadsides, reproduce solely by seed each year.

　　Redroot flowers are distinctively surrounded by 3 to 5 spiny bracts; the plant's shallow taproot is pinkish or red. Smooth pigweed looks less coarse, darker green, has slender, bending flower spikes.

　　Both plants stand from 1 to 6 feet high or taller. Seeds, shiny black or brown, mature from late summer through fall in 1-seeded pods *(utricles)* that uncap to release the seed. Reputedly a single plant may produce more than 100,000 seeds, and amaranth seed may remain viable for at least 40 years. The bisexual flowers appear throughout summer, are pollinated by wind, and also commonly self-pollinate.

　　Most green plants transform raw materials into plant tissue by a process of photosynthesis known as the C3 carbon-fixation pathway. Amaranths, however, use a C4 carbon-fixation process. The chemistry is complex, but essentially the C4 process more efficiently absorbs atmospheric carbon dioxide; it also requires less water and adapts the plant for higher temperatures, brighter sunlight, and drier conditions. Since grain amaranths probably evolved in the Andes, benefits of the C4 adaptation for mountain habitats are obvious.

The bristly green flowerheads of redroot, a garden and roadside amaranth, produce prolific seed.

Associates: Redroot typically appears in bare ground soon after fire, rototilling, or other disturbance, but it thins out quickly as grasses and old-field herbs become established. Also chemically inhibited by the growth of curly dock *(q.v.)*, it is sometimes root-parasitized by branching broom-rape *(Orobanche ramosa)*. It may, however, become a major pest in corn and other field crops. Smooth pigweed also grows as a cosmopolitan weed of roadsides, vacant lots, and gardens.

Fungal parasites on amaranths include the rust *Albugo bliti,* leaf spots *(Alternaria),* fusarium wilt *(Fusarium oxysporum),* and stem rot *(Sclerotinia sclerotiorum),* as well as black root *(Aphanomyces cochlioides),* root rots *(Phymatotrichum omnivorum, Rhizoctonia solani),* and various others.

Also parasitic, mainly on roots, are several nematode or roundworm species, among them *Meloidogyne radicola* and *Aphelenchoides fragariae;* and *Conotrachelus* root weevils.

Redroot is an alternate host for the green peach aphid *(Myzus persicae),* and cowpea aphids *(Aphis craccivora)* also feed on the plants.

Other common feeders include nymphs of the tarnished plant bug *(Lygus lineolaris),* which hatch from eggs deposited in the flower spikes and leaves, and the flea beetles *Systena frontalis* and *Disonycha xanthomelas,* the spinach flea beetle. *Lygus* is the major pest of grain amaranth.

Several moth and butterfly caterpillars feed on amaranths, though none exclusively. A hairy, day-active caterpillar that curls into a ball when disturbed may be the agreeable tiger moth *(Spilosoma congrua);* the adult moth is white. An inchworm moth caterpillar called the somber carpet *(Disclisioprocta stellata)* also feeds on amaranth in its warmer southern range; the brown-winged adult moth strays northward in summer, however. The spotted beet webworm *(Hymenia perspectalis)* and the Hawaiian beet webworm *(Spoladea recurvalis)* both feed on amaranth as well as beet foliage, as does the related *Helvibotys helvialis.* All 3 species are pyralid moths. Other moth caterpillar feeders include the European corn borer *(Ostrinia nubilalis)* and the casebearer moth *Coleophora lineapulvella,* which feeds on amaranth seeds. Black cutworms, the noctuid larvae of the ipsilon dart moth *(Agrotis ipsilon),* also attack amaranth. Highly destructive southern armyworm moths *(Spodoptera eridania),* though more common in the South, may use amaranth as a primary host, especially in dense stands, then transfer to sunflowers *(q.v.).*

Common sootywings *(Pholisora catullus)* are skippers, a group of lepidopterans noted for rapid, erratic flight (though they are not classified as true butterflies, most manuals include them along with the butterflies). These caterpillars appear olive green with yellowish granulations. Sootywing caterpillars hibernate over winter in amaranth leaves they have tied together with silk.

Amaranth seeds often persist over winter in the dense spikes, providing one of the most important and nourishing winter foods for both gamebirds and songbirds. Northern bobwhites and ring-necked pheasants consume the seeds, as do mourning doves, horned larks, snow buntings, dark-eyed juncos, Lapland longspurs, common and hoary redpolls— plus many sparrows, especially chipping, field, grasshopper, savannah, song, American tree, vesper, white-crowned, and white-throated. (Migrant birds from the northeastern states feed on the plant in their southern wintering regions.)

Cottontail rabbits also feed on the plants. Redroot foliage has been rated for wildlife food value in several western states: Mule deer, white-tailed deer, and pronghorn all derived benefit from the plant for both food and cover.

Lore: Before the Spanish conquest of South America in 1519, an amaranth species (*A. caudatus,* known to the Aztecs as *kiwicha* and to horticulturists as love-lies-bleeding, a garden ornamental) was planted and harvested by both Aztecs and Incas as a grain crop; they cooked the seeds for cereal and ground them for flour. This crop may have provided the main agricultural base for the Aztec economy. The Spanish conquerors, aided by their priests, banned its growth and usage, apparently in the nervous belief that the food provided too much energy for a defeated people; also, its use in native rites and rituals made it anathema to the missionaries. Thus widespread amaranth cultivation disappeared from the New World for many centuries, though remote pockets in Andean and Mexican locales preserved the grain amaranth species from extinction. During the 1960s, the Rodale Research Center in Emmaus, Pennsylvania, led in the reintroduction of grain amaranth as an agricultural crop. Today in the United States, some 5,000 to 7,000 acres of amaranth are commercially grown, mainly in Nebraska.

The tiny seeds yield a protein content of some 16 percent, higher than that of wheat, corn, and rice. Large amounts of vitamins A and C plus calcium, iron, and potassium also make these plants nutritionally exceptional, as does the unusually high lysine content in the plant's amino acid balance.

The leaves, especially of young plants, also make edible cooked greens. These leaves concentrate nitrates, however—they are known to poison cattle and pigs that forage on the plants—so boiling to eliminate the toxic materials is essential. An astringent tea made from the leaves has served as a homeopathic treatment for external and internal bleeding, diarrhea, dysentery, and ulcers.

The word *amaranth* originates from a Greek word meaning "unfading" or "everlasting."

Apple *(Pyrus malus).* Rose family. A bushy, widely spreading tree, usually round-topped and 20 to 30 feet high, the apple has stubby, knotty spur branches and egg-shaped, slightly toothed leaves plus spectacular flowers and fleshy fruits.

Other names: Domestic, common, or garden apple.

Close relatives: About 60 *Pyrus* species, many of hybrid origin, exist in north temperate regions globally. Some of the most familiar ones in the northeastern United States include pear *(P. communis)* and several crab apples. Related rose family plants in this book include wild strawberry, common cinquefoil, multiflora rose, and hawthorns (all *q.v.*).

Lifestyle: To most of us, the apple fruit is much more familiar than the tree that produces it. Commercially grown apples are always rootstock fruits or cultivars; that is, they develop from scions of grafted buds. By contrast, the fruits of wild seedling trees are smaller, less sweet and eye-appealing, and they vary greatly in palatability and natural resistance to fungous and insect parasites. Old orchard trees, unattended by fertilizer or trimming for years, also tend to revert in fruit quality to ancestral types; thus the fruit *phenotypes* (observable physical traits) may change on the tree over time. Apple trees grow fairly slowly and live long. Most begin producing fruit at 4 to 5 years of age, and many thence bear fruit biennially (once every 2 years); others bear annually. Individual trees often fall into 1- or 2-year fruiting "habits" that they maintain.

Apple flowers, white or pinkish, appear in May. Each is 5-petaled, bisexual, and insect-pollinated. A mature apple tree may produce some 50,000 to 100,000 blossoms each spring. Look closely to observe that each petal is attached by a thin stalk. Most flowers appear in clusters of 5 or 6 on the spur shoots. The terminal flower in the cluster opens first, followed by the 2 basal flowers, then the ones in the middle. A single blossom survives 2 to 5 days, but pollen becomes viable only during a 3- or 4-hour period during that time. Pollen ripening is accompanied by the release of ethyl acetate aroma that attracts insects up to 1,000 feet away. Individual apple varieties and flowers from the same tree are self-incompatible—that is, a Red Delicious cannot fertilize another Red Delicious but requires another apple variety for effective cross-pollination. The fruit of any tree bears true to the maternal stock in form, color, taste, and hardiness, regardless of the fertilizing pollen. Only the seeds bear combined genetic characteristics of both parent trees.

Relatively few apple blossoms—only 2 to 5 percent of the total on a tree—ever set fruit that develops to maturity. Even a 20 percent fruit set of a tree's flowers would so deplete the tree's energy resources that it would probably die. Apple trees thus resort to 2 major thinning mechanisms. The first occurs soon after flowering, in which all unpollinated flowers—some 65 to 75 percent of the total—drop off the tree, along with petals and stamens of the pollinated blossoms. Self-pollinated flowers also fall in a following wave of blossom drop. The second major thinning occurs as the tree aborts undernourished fruitlets from the developing fruit clusters—an event called the June drop. One can plainly observe this casting-off process by inspecting the ground beneath an apple tree around mid-June.

The terminal flower, having a longer lifespan than its cluster siblings, produces the *king fruit* of the cluster and usually survives, producing abundant seeds. These developing seeds in turn produce hormones that draw carbohydrates and amino acids from nearby leaves (development of a mature apple requires about 30 leaves). This period ends with only a few side fruits left in the cluster—king fruits produce the main apple crop. The fleshly green fruit with a papery core, called a *pome,* ripens by late summer, usually becoming reddish skinned. Apple fruits stop producing new cells when they measure about an inch in diameter, usually in July. All subsequent fruit growth results from the expansion of cells already present and the air spaces between them. Flesh of the fruit, mainly starch and malic acid (which causes apple tartness), converts to sugars soon after a partition layer of cells cuts off the stem from receiving further nutrients. The red pigment anthocyanin gradually colors the skin; sunlit days produce more coloration than overcast ones.

Apple fruits serve to transport the seeds via ingestion by animals, and they also protect the seeds from premature germination during winter warm spells. The fruit goes on living long after it falls or is picked from the tree—sometimes for months, if stored correctly. It continues to respire and produce energy from its stored sugars. In time, however, its sugars run out and the flesh deteriorates, producing an overripe and eventually rotten apple. Apple seeds require 3 months or so of afterripening before they can germinate. The seeds may remain viable for 2 to 3 years.

Associates: Apple trees require well-drained soil, tolerate neither "wet feet" nor severe drought. As orchard escapees (often dispersed by human-discarded cores), they frequently appear on roadsides, in fields, along railroads, and in other open areas.

Uniform orchard stock tends to host the spread of apple pests and parasites, whereas a lone "wild" tree often escapes some of the more common woes that beset the cultivated trees. A study in Canadian apple orchards revealed that insect parasites of pest mites and of other insects numbered 4 to 18 times higher in orchards that included many wildflowers in the ground cover. Such parasites include long-legged flies (Dolichopodidae), insidious flower bugs *(Orius insidiosus),* mullein bugs *(Campylomma verbasci),* and assassin bugs *(Acholla).* Grass ground cover plays an ambivalent role in orchards. Many grasses are toxic *(allelopathic)* to apple roots, though not severely so, and many orchardists cultivate grass growth to inhibit the widespread extension of apple roots as well as to compete for nutrients and thus incite fruiting at the expense of shoot growth.

Blackened, wilted leaves, curled twig tips, branch cankers—and ultimately, dying trees—may indicate fire blight, a devastating disease caused by the bacteria *Erwinia amylovora,* which is often vectored by nectar-seeking bees. It also enters the tree through breaks in the bark caused by storm damage.

Various fungi grow frequently on apple trees. Apple scab *(Venturia inaequalis)* gives fruits a scabby, knotty, misshapen appearance; brownish lesions *(conidia)* may first appear on leaf undersurfaces. Another destructive fungus is cedar-apple rust *(Gymnosporangiam juniperi-virginianae),* which parasitizes alternate host trees—apple and red cedar *(q.v.)*—to complete its life cycle. On apple trees, the rust creates yellow-orange pustules *(pycnia)* on leaf upper sides or on developing fruit; a month or two later (usually in late summer), tube-like structures *(aecia)* develop on leaf undersides. The aecia release spores that can travel on wind up to 2 miles, infecting red cedar trees. *Basidiospores,* released the following spring from red cedar, usually infect apple trees during rainy periods. Orchardists try to avoid, when possible, the proximity of red cedars to their apple trees.

Nectria cankers, caused by the fungus *Nectria galligena,* appear commonly on trunks of apple, as of many hardwood trees. Also called target canker, nectria resembles a concentric target eaten into the tree. It enlarges in cool weather, eventually weakening or girdling the tree.

Finely brown-stippled leaves, often covering entire trees, may indicate feeding of a common apple pest, the European red mite *(Panonychus ulmi),* which appeared in North America about 1911. Brick red in color, it hatches into 6-legged larvae just as apple blossoms begin to mature, feeding on leaf undersides and transforming to adult, 8-legged mites through several moltings. Two-spotted spider mites *(Tetranychus urticae),* red with large black spots, also turn leaves bronze, sometimes causing them to drop prematurely. Natural predators of these mites include other spider mites, notably *Neoseilus fallacis.*

A host of insects feed on apple foliage, flowers, and twigs. Foliage feeders include several true bugs. The apple redbug *(Lygidea mendax)* is orange-red; the dark apple redbug *(Heterocordylus malinus),* reddish black. Signs of both include curled leaves covered with dark sunken spots. White-spotted or bleached leaves may indicate feeding of white apple leafhoppers *(Typhlocyba pomaria),* pale jumping homopterans that hold their wings rooflike over the back. Apple leafhoppers *(Empoasca maligna),* greenish white, cause similar effects in late summer and fall. Curled leaves, deformed fruits, and many ants on the tree may signal presence of the rosy aphis or rosy apple aphid *(Dysaphis plantaginea),* dark or orange-yellow in color; their honeydew secretions attract ants, also feed growth of a black, crusty, sooty mold fungus *(Fumago vagans)* on leaves and twigs. Frequent aphid predators include two-spotted lady beetles *(Adalia bipunctata);* golden-eyed lacewings *(Chrysopa oculata),* greenish, delicate, lacy-winged, golden-eyed insects—their eggs, laid on leaves, stand on long stalks; brown lacewings *(Hemerobius humlinus);* and the flat, wrinkled larvae of syrphid flies *(Syrphus torrus).*

Beetle foliage feeders include rose chafers *(Macrodactylus subspinosus)*, yellowish tan with long, spiny legs. Apple flea weevils *(Rhynchaenus pallicornis)*, leaping insects, mine the leaves as larvae; as adult insects, they chew tiny "shotholes" through leaves.

Butterfly caterpillars seen on apple foliage in spring include the viceroy *(Limenitis archippus)*, a humped, mottled greenish and gray larva with 2 long, hornlike projections rising like antennae. Apple leaves host many more moth than butterfly caterpillars, however. Eastern tent caterpillars *(Malacosoma americanum)* construct large colonial webs in forks and crotches of the tree, moving out in daytime along the branches, sometimes defoliating entire trees; these hairy, brownish caterpillars appear irruptively, widely prevalent one year, virtually disappearing the next. Red-humped caterpillars *(Schizura concinna)*, also gregarious, show a conspicuous bright red hump and head; the plain adult moths lay massed eggs on leaf undersides. A prominent orchard pest is the fruit-tree leafroller moth *(Archips argyrospila)*, which rolls several leaves together with light webbing and lives inside the enclosure; the caterpillars are pale green. Sphinx moth caterpillar feeders (most are bright green and show a projecting rear horn) include the apple sphinx *(Sphinx gordius)*, Clemens' sphinx *(S. luscitiosa)*, wild cherry sphinx *(S. drupiferarum)*, twin-spotted sphinx *(Smerinthus jamaicensis)*, and white-lined sphinx *(Hyles lineata)*. The cecropia or robin moth *(Hyalophora cecropia)*, a large, green, spined caterpillar, feeds on apple as well as many other trees and shrubs, as does the large tolype caterpillar *(Tolype velleda)*, striped and densely hairy. Several dagger moth *(Acronicta)* species, hairy caterpillars that often show tufted "pencils" of longer hair, feed on apple leaves, as do a number of dart moth species, including the dingy cutworm *(Feltia jaculifera)*. Dart moth caterpillars characteristically curl head to tail when resting or disturbed. Green fruitworms *(Lithophane antennata)* begin by eating leaves, then transfer to the developing fruits.

Other leaf-feeding moth caterpillars include the many-dotted appleworm *(Balsa malana)* and the tufted bird-dropping moth *(Cerma cerintha)*, both noctuid moths; the latter adult moth, at rest, mimics a bird dropping.

Apple leaf miners form an entire guild of apple tree dwellers, feeding between epidermal layers of the leaf; they create a variety of linear, serpentine, or blotchlike dead areas *(mines)*, the mine shapes depending on species. Most of the 10 or so species are tiny gracilariid moth caterpillars. *Phyllonorycter* species—notably P. *crataegella*, the apple blotch leaf miner—are at times abundant. Others include *Bucculatrix* and *Lyonetia* species, lyonetiid caterpillars that make serpentine mines; and coleophorid (casebearer) moth caterpillars. The appleleaf trumpet miner *(Tischeria malifoliella)*, a tischeriid moth larva, creates trumpet-shaped mines.

Leaf skeletonizers feed on leaf tissue, leaving only a shredded network of veins. A common caterpillar is *Choreutis pariana*, greenish with brown head, called the apple-and-thorn skeletonizer, a choreutid moth. Another larva, the appleleaf skeletonizer *(Psorosina hammondi),* is brownish green. Caterpillars of the eye-spotted budmoth *(Spilonota ocellana)* feed on apple buds in early spring before or just as they open; they create small, silken nests attached to twigs and buds; in summer, the brown caterpillars skeletonize leaves from silken cases on leaf undersides.

A large variety of other moth caterpillars—the complete list would require several pages—also feed on apple foliage. Winter's leafless season is the best time to look for insect cocoons and egg masses on apple trees. Large, baglike cocoons attached lengthwise to twigs are probably those of the aforementioned cecropia moth. Gray, horseshoe-shaped egg masses, deposited by the aforementioned fruit-tree leafroller, overwinter on twigs. Shiny, brown-varnished bands of insect eggs encircling twigs near their ends are the wintering egg masses of the eastern tent caterpillar, also mentioned.

Fly larvae of apple leaf midges *(Dasineura mali),* natives of Europe, attack developing leaves; adult midges deposit eggs on leaf margins, and larval feeding results in a characteristic gall, a tight roll toward the leaf center.

Apple blossoms attract hosts of nectar and pollen collectors. Pollinators are mainly bees—honeybees *(Apis mellifera),* hives of which are often brought into orchards during pollination season, plus bumblebees *(Bombus),* andrenid and halictid bees (Andrenidae, Halictidae), leaf-cutting bees *(Osmia),* and carpenter bees *(Xylocopa).* Syrphid and anthomyiid flies (Syrphidae, Anthomyiidae) also pollinate the flowers, as do ants, often attracted by aphids, whose honeydew they consume. Numerous butterfly and moth species also come for a nectar course.

Twig and bark sap suckers include woolly aphids and scale insects. Woolly apple aphids *(Eriosoma lanigerum),* purple colored and covered by white, cottony wax, feed on elm buds for 2 generations; the winged third generation migrates to apple and other fruit trees, feeding in trunk and branch wounds and on the roots, causing root cankers that may kill the tree. Two common scale insects that encrust apple twigs and branches are the oystershell scale *(Lepidosaphes ulmi),* so named from its shape; and the San Jose scale *(Quadraspidiotus perniciosus),* gray-black and circular in shape. Long, threadlike mouthparts of these wax-exuding insects suck plant juices.

Two borers attack weakened, diseased, or storm-injured trees: the flat-headed apple-tree borer *(Chrysobothris femorata),* a buprestid beetle, bronze-metallic in color; and the round-headed apple-tree borer *(Saperda candida),* a long-horned beetle, brown with white stripes. The larvae tunnel into bark and sapwood, emerging as adults in spring. *Chrysobothris* feeds for a year inside the tree, then emerges as an adult through elliptical holes cut through the bark. *Saperda* feeds and pupates inside the tree for 3 years, cutting round exit holes. Larvae of the eyed click beetle *(Alaus oculatus),* at an inch or more long the largest click beetle (elater), reside beneath the bark and prey on other insect larvae.

Twigs with leaves still attached that litter the ground beneath apple trees indicate the work of twig pruners *(Elaphidionoides)*. The ends of the fallen twigs, inside which the long-horned beetle larvae grow, are smoothly cut. The apple twig borer *(Amphicerus bicaudatus)*, a bostrichid beetle, feeds as a larva in dying branches of apple.

Apple fruits host a roster of insects, some of them extremely injurious to commercial apple production. Growers use the term *catfacing* for fruit surface injuries caused by insects. Catfacing insects include a variety of true bugs and others (some of which reside on alfalfa *[q.v.]* as an alternate host plant), but the most destructive pests are certain moth caterpillars. Probably the foremost apple pest is the codling moth *(Cydia pomonella)*, a tortricid moth native to Eurasia. Holes in the sides and blossom end of the fruit indicate the caterpillar's presence inside the apple, where it feeds for only 3 weeks; then it emerges and pupates beneath the tree bark. Several of the pinkish, brown-headed caterpillars may occupy a single fruit. Adult moths are brownish, inconspicuous.

Other fruit pests include several species of green fruitworms *(Lithophane)*, green-and-white-striped noctuid moths (the grayish adults are called pinion moths), and the aforementioned apple flea weevils. Fallen apples with shallow pits eaten in them indicate fruitworm presence; apples attacked later in the season do not drop, but the eaten-out pits become filled with a corky material, rendering them unfit for market. The adult moths appear light brown.

Apple maggot flies (Rhagoletis pomonella), *frequently seen on the ripening fruits, also center their mating and egg-laying activities here, a recently evolved association.*

Next to the codling moth, the most destructive apple pest is probably the apple maggot *(Rhagoletis pomonella)*, a white fruit fly larva that tunnels winding galleries in the fruit, emerging after the ripe apple drops to the ground. It pupates in the soil for a winter or for up to 3 years, finally emerging in midsummer as a white-striped fly. The females lay eggs on developing apples; tiny specks on the fruit surface indicate punctures of the needle-sharp ovipositor. These native insects have enabled some interesting studies in evolutionary biology, for their association with apples dates only from the middle 19th century; originally their ancestors fed on hawthorn *(q.v.)* fruits. New species often originate by means of geographical isolation, but studies of the apple maggot indicate that speciation may also occur by ecological isolation; that is, a race or subspecies of the insects adapts to a new host fruit, thereby isolating it reproductively from its ancestral relatives that still feed on the original host fruit. Mating occurs on the fruit itself, the male flies apparently summoned not by female *pheromones* (chemical attractants) but by the odor of the fruit, which also attracts the egg-laying female insect.

Another, less common fruit pest is the plum curculio *(Conotrachelus nenuphar)*, a snout weevil, dark brown with humped wing ridges. Its deep, circular or crescent-shaped egg scars on the fruit indicate its presence; together with round feeding holes of the adult insects, these injuries cause the fruit to drop, and the white, grublike larvae feed inside the fallen apples. Signature of the similar apple curculio *(Anthonomus quadrigibbus)* consists of more numerous puncture marks on the fruit skin.

"Young trees may be the best for apples, but old trees are sure to bear the most birds," wrote naturalist John Burroughs. A frequent consumer of apple flower petals is the cedar waxwing. Several bird species frequently nest in apple trees and orchards—mourning doves, eastern kingbirds, American robins, and Baltimore orioles, among others. Cavities in old apple trees may host owls, European starlings, house wrens, and eastern bluebirds, as well as tree frogs and wild honeybees.

Numerous birds and mammals consume apples in fall and winter. Apples are a choice food of ruffed grouse, red-bellied and red-headed woodpeckers, yellow-bellied sapsuckers, tufted titmice, European starlings, cedar waxwings, gray catbirds, evening and pine grosbeaks, and purple finches. Less frequent consumers include ring-necked pheasants, hairy woodpeckers, American crows, northern mockingbirds, common grackles, Baltimore orioles, American robins, northern cardinals, and eastern towhees. "Blue jays feed on apples in distinct fashions," wrote naturalist Mark Elbroch. "While the fruit is ripe and still hanging on the tree, jays feed on the flesh, leaving obvious gouges in the sides of the apples. Jays also peck at the rotting windfalls below the tree, feeding only on the seeds in the core." A variety of birds and mammals also consume fruits rotting on the tree or ground. Black bears, red foxes, porcupines, raccoons, squirrels, mice, and white-tailed deer relish apples, mainly fallen ones. Red squirrels sometimes store them in middens, and opossums, striped skunks, and wood rats also devour them. Apple seed eaters include American crows, pine grosbeaks, and red crossbills. And apple bud eaters during winter include ruffed grouse, ring-necked pheasants, and northern bobwhites. Apple is one of the main sap-feeding trees of the yellow-bellied sapsucker; its regular rows of drilled holes that exude sap are easily recognized. Meadow and pine voles frequently cause damage to young orchard trees by chewing bark and inner tissues of roots and lower trunks, mainly in autumn and winter. White-tailed deer consume apple foliage in summer and twigs and buds year-round.

Lore: Some 7,000 varieties of apples have been named and cultivated in the United States alone. The Red Delicious, noted more for looks and shelf durability than taste, heads the roster of commercial varieties. People who prefer apples with distinctive flavor must search harder these days than in the past, since most commercial growers (if not consumers) value an apple's appearance and long storability over its flavor.

Apples do not "breed true," and apple variety results from cross-pollination between 2 genetic strains; the seedling offspring produces yet a third variety, unique in genetic makeup. To maintain this unique variety requires grafting of scions from the desired tree onto rootstocks of mature "mother trees." Apple taxonomy is a genetic mélange, impossible to trace in precise detail owing to several millenia of horticulture plus both deliberate and natural hybridization among *Pyrus* species. "The apple genus itself, after some three thousand years of human meddling," biologist Rebecca Rupp wrote, "is a confusing network of incestuous interrelationships." Not all apple genes produce edible apples—some turn out quite bitter. And none except several crab apple species are native to North America. Early settlers brought seeds from Europe, and pioneer orchardists and wanderers like the fabled John Chapman ("Johnny Appleseed")—with the ample help of birds and mammals, to be sure—spread apples across the continent. (Unmentioned in most of the schoolbook Johnny Appleseed lore is the fact that his popularity mainly stemmed from the often sole frontier use of apples for making hard cider.) Each apple seedling parented a new variety—and if it turned out worth eating or selling, each scion on a rootstock reproduced it.

Where did apples originate? Not in the Garden of Eden, apparently. Opinions differ, but a fairly convincing case can be made for eastern Kazakhstan, a country once contained in the former Soviet Union. Here on the lower slopes of the Tian Shan range near the city of Almaty ("father of apples"), vast apple forests stood in grovelike acres over this hilly region. (They are about 90 percent gone today, owing to recent building development.) Here the first apple "fell to the ground long before the authors of Genesis had learned to read or write or tell the story of Paradise," wrote author Frank Browning. That original apple was probably *Malus sieversii,* ancestor of all present apple fruits and still growing in Kazakhstan. Because the apple "survived so long on these slopes, and because until recently it has been undisturbed by man," wrote Browning, "it has retained rich genetic diversity." Horticulturists and orchard specialists still come here from many countries to check out ancestral varieties and obtain scions for propagation, so the region continues to provide new apple gene combinations to the world. From here or elsewhere, apples spread across Europe in prehistoric times, but those fruits were mostly small, bitter, and uncultivated. Roman invaders planted orchards across Gaul and Britain, raising sweet, pale yellow apples—and after the Romans, monastery gardens preserved the sweet-apple genes for European (and ultimately American) posterity.

Sources differ as to time and origin of the first cultivated apples in the New World. Some say that Puritan governor John Endecott brought the first ones, others that the first French colonists in early 17th-century Quebec raised the first North American apples. Anglican clergyman William Blaxton apparently raised the first named American variety of apple—the Yellow Sweeting—on Beacon Hill in Boston about 1640. "New Englanders grew apples not so much for eating as for animal feed and cider making," wrote naturalist Sue Hubbell. The oldest apple *variety* surviving today is probably the Pomme d'Api, a small yellow or red fruit that originated in ancient Rome, known today in North America as the Lady or Christmas Apple.

Besides repertoires of flavor and genetic characteristics, apples carry a heavy freight of symbolic lore—more than the eagle or the rose or any other life form. Throughout history and folklore, 2 apples have emerged: the good apple and the bad apple. The apple tree sheltered both the serpent in paradise and a mystical, implicit promise of immortality ("an apple a day keeps the doctor away"). Both Merlin and the Buddha sat beneath apple trees.

The good apple symbolized fertility and eternal life in Greek, Celtic, Persian, and Christian mythology. *Paradise* as a word originated as a description of Persian walled fruit gardens, and apple as the universal fruit. Golden apples of the sun vie with sacred apple trees of life in the ancient tales (though biblical apples may actually have been apricots). "Them apples," as in "how do you like," and "apples," as in "comfort me with," stand for aspects of life, even as the "Big Apple" represents the largest and busiest center of human life in North America—New York City. A falling apple (reputedly a Costard variety) bopped Sir Isaac Newton on the head at Woolsthorpe Manor in England, according to Voltaire, thereby inspiring Newton's theory of gravitation. Protestants in England embraced the apple as spiritually superior to the Roman Catholic grape—thus transportation of apple trees to the New World looked somewhat beyond an exclusively secular matter of fruit culture.

The apple's diabolical side is seen in the "forbidden fruit" consumed by Eve; the bewitching apple offered Snow White—beautiful outside, poisonous inside; the enchantment and erotic imagery of Venus and Aphrodite in its shape; the pentagram of its 5-sided core vastly meaningful in sorcery and magic. Residues of too many rotten apples—perhaps the worst residues of all—lie today in the topsoil of abandoned orchards that become subdivisions and residential property, where decades of pesticide applications have sometimes made the subsurface toxic to human health.

The food benefits of apples are well known—or at least well alleged. Naturalist John Burroughs probably overstated the case when he claimed the apple as "the natural antidote of most of the ills the flesh is heir to." But only after the Prohibition era, with its abundant usage of apples for making ciders with a kick, did the apple health promoters take over in a widespread way. The fruits are high in carbohydrate (pectin), relatively high in phosphorus, potassium, and vitamins A and C. Yet compared to most other fruits or to lettuce, apples rank relatively low in nutritive values and substances. The best part of an apple, healthwise, is apparently the skin. Apples have been recommended (by separate polishers) as effective remedies for both constipation and diarrhea. Recent research suggests that the aroma of unripe apples may chemically affect a person's perception of area, increasing one's sensation of space; people plagued by feelings of claustrophobia, recommended a scientist at Chicago's Smell and Taste Treatment and Research Foundation in 1995, may carry a green apple to sniff in claustrophobic places or situations. Most homeopathic claims, however, rely on prescriptions of regular cider and vinegar dosages. Cider production—both sweet and hard—as well as Calvados, the brandy distilled from it, are major industries in themselves, especially in Europe.

Which variety is the "best apple"? Color and size have long supplanted taste as the criteria for apple quality. Fruit gourmets and plant conservators universally deplore the disappearance of numerous once-familiar varieties, each with distinctive traits of taste and appearance. Requirements of mass marketing and storage have virtually wiped out all but the reddest, easiest sold, most pesticide-sprayed and banal varieties—apples that "have no real *tang* nor *smack* to them," in Thoreau's words. All *Pyrus* species readily hybridize, another factor accounting for the richness of the apple gene pool. The current trend of commercial apple growing, however, is to reduce that gene pool so that increasingly the lesser known (and in many cases, most desirable) varieties have declined in availability or altogether disappeared.

Thus many living persons have never tasted an apple of true apple taste and distinction. The names of these old apples haunt the overgrown orchards of upstate anywhere: the Winter Banana, the Spitzenburg, the Greening, the Russet, the Red Astrachan, the Newton Pippin, the Yellow Bellflower, the Pearmains. Many apple lovers judge the Northern Spy, its production now rapidly declining, as the best apple currently available (some say the best ever grown) in the United States. Thoreau thought wild apples by far the best. Yet, "it is remarkable," he confessed in "Wild Apples," one of his last and best essays in *Excursions,* "that the wild apple, which I praise as so spirited and racy when eaten in the fields or woods, being brought into the house, has frequently a harsh and crabbed taste. . . . sour enough to set a squirrel's teeth on edge and make a jay scream." Such fruits, he insisted, should be labeled: "To be eaten in the wind."

Apple provides a desirable firewood; the wood was also traditionally favored for rocking-chair rockers and wooden flutes. Such uses are uncommon today.

Two states—Arkansas and Michigan—have adopted the apple blossom as their official flower.

Asters *(Aster* species). Aster family. Aster flowerheads consist of aggregate flowers, as do those of daisies, sunflowers, and all other members of its family; another name for the family, descriptive of flowerheads, is composites. Numerous ray flowers surround a central disk of tubular flowers. Field and prairie asters, most standing 2 to 5 feet tall, include both white-flowered and blue-flowered species. Common white-flowered ones include calico or goblet aster *(A. lateriflorus);* heath, wreath, or white prairie aster *(A. ericoides);* owl or frost aster *(A. pilosus);* and panicled aster *(A. lanceolatus).* Blue asters include arrow-leaved aster *(A. sagittifolius);* New England aster *(A. novae-angliae);* clasping or spreading aster *(A. patens);* smooth aster *(A. laevis);* long-stalked or bushy aster *(A. dumosus),* sometimes white flowered; and stiff aster *(A. linariifolius).* All asters are perennials.

Other names: Wild aster, Michaelmas-daisy, fall-rose, frostweed, starwort.

Close relatives: Some 66 native *Aster* species reside in eastern North America; more than 200 species exist worldwide. The aster family, second largest in the plant kingdom, consists of more than 1,000 genera and some 20,000 species. Among asters' relatives are goldenrods *(q.v.)* and fleabanes *(q.v.),* among many other aster family plants in this book. The garden aster called Michaelmas-daisy *(A. novi-beglii),* a hybrid, derives from New England heath asters, among others. China aster *(Callistephus chinensis),* the familiar garden aster, is not closely related to our native asters.

Lifestyle: For the professional botanist, aster taxonomy poses tough quandaries; for the rest of us, the field manuals often (except for a few well-marked species) force highly tentative identification decisions. The genus *Aster* remains difficult to sort out or even define. Many taxonomists believe that the traditional aster classification scheme is incorrect and must be replaced by another arrangement based on chromosome number or DNA relationships. Most North American asters, many researchers suggest, belong in separate genera *(Ionactis, Oclemena, Seriocarpus, Symphyotrichum,* among others). "Polyploidy [sets of multiple chromosomes in plant cells] is frequent," botanist Edward G. Voss wrote, and "hybridization (with subsequent backcrossing) seems more frequent than in most genera." Also, much variation of visible characters exists within individual species. "None of the wild plants have read their job descriptions," observed Voss, "much less attempted to conform to them." Thus exceptions occur to almost any general statement one can make about any aster species.

In broad terms of their structure and form, however, all asters look enough alike to be lumped as loosely, if not closely, related. Meadow asters show a much greater proportion of flower clusters to stem and foliage, in contrast to the reverse situation seen in woodland asters. Such divergent ratios reflect the plants' concentration of energy in varying habitats; in meadow asters, the foliage, receiving more sunlight than the leaves of shaded woodland asters, becomes less vital to the plant's survival than its reproductive parts.

The flowerhead disk florets, often yellowish or reddish, center the 15 to 100 strap-shaped ray florets, depending on species—which appear white, pale lilac, or deeper blue (color in asters is not always a reliable identifier to species). The flowerheads, though bisexual as in all aster family species, are dominantly female in *Aster* species since the ray flowers bear only pistillate (female) flower parts (in many plant genera—as among organisms generally—the male sex is far more expendable than the female). The disk flowers bear both pistils and (male) stamens. A hand lens easily shows this flower arrangement (see Goat's-beards). Many asters exhibit so-called sleep movements, with the ray flowers closing around the disk at night.

Asters are usually *obligate outbreeders*—that is, they require pollination from other aster plants to produce seed. Some *Aster* species grow colonially, can clone from *rhizomes* (underground stems); others produce new shoots from the bases of old stems in spring. Most cloning asters survive for only 3 or 4 years.

From summer to fall, aster plants produce several rosette shoots—flat, leafy circles of growth at the plant base—from rhizomes or at the base of flowering stems. Rosettes remain green and dormant on the ground over winter, often beneath snow. In the spring, they produce erect shoots that become flowering stems.

Most wild asters flower after goldenrods *(q.v.)* in summer and fall. Individual flowerheads mature from the outside in—that is, the ray florets become pollen receptive before the disk florets open. As the asters in any given area are in multiple stages of development at any given time, opened disk flowers of some plants may be producing pollen before the disk flowers in other plants have opened. Also, asters begin flowering at their branch tips, the flowerheads nearest the stems blooming last. Depending on aster species and local weather conditions, insect-pollinated flowers remain pollen receptive for 5 to 10 days. A 1999 study on a yellow-centered aster species (*A. vimineus,* the small white aster) showed that as the disk flowers changed in color from yellow to red—either as the result of aging or of pollination—the flower's insect relations also changed. The younger, yellow disk flowers, which produced much more pollen than the later red flowers, attracted many more pollinating insects. Why, then, would the older red florets exist on the plant at all? The researchers suggested that the 2-toned floral display attracted more pollinator attention to a stand of the asters than would a single yellow hue.

Aster fruits consist of 1-seeded *achenes,* which mature a month or more after flowering ceases. Bristles (the *pappus* or "parachute") on the dry achene end curl and spread, catching air currents that disperse the seeds. *Cold stratification,* a period of freezing necessary to the germination of some plant seeds, though unnecessary for aster germination, nevertheless increases germination rate.

Associates: Most meadow asters favor open, sunny areas, including roadside, garden, and pasture habitats. Bushy aster sometimes associates with oaks and jack-pines. At least one wild aster species *(A. pilosus)* appears consistently associated with farm habitats. It invades abandoned fields, usually in the second year after field cultivation ceases; quickly becomes a dominant plant; and typically remains so for about 2 years in old-field plant succession.

Needle blister rust *(Coleosporium asterum)* appears as bright, orange-yellow pustules on leaf undersides. This club fungus parasitizes 2- and 3-needle pines as alternate hosts.

Parasitic dodder plants (often *Cuscuta cephalanthi,* the buttonbush-dodder) attach to asters and other plants, tapping into their stems by means of *haustoria,* or suckers.

Several species of gall midge larvae *(Rhopalomyia, Cecidomyia)* produce galls on flowers, buds, leaves, and stems. Aster blister galls, caused by *Asteromyia* and *Lasioptera* species, resemble yellowish oval fungous spots on leaves.

The aster leafhopper *(Macrosteles quadrilineatus),* greenish yellow with black spots, is a bane of produce farmers, for it is a vector of aster yellows, a mycoplasmalike disease that severely damages carrot, celery, and lettuce crops. The leafhoppers inoculate stems with the organism as they suck plant juices, and contaminated plants infect subsequent leafhoppers. Despite the insects' name, aster is not their predominant plant host. Mainly southern insects that cannot survive northern winters, they migrate northward each summer in variable numbers and frequency, infesting cropland and weeds alike as they travel.

Another common insect on asters is the buffalo treehopper *(Stictocephala),* which sucks plant juices.

Ambush bugs *(Phymata),* insect predators that lurk atop the flowerheads, frequently capture aster visitors. *Ellychnia* lightning bugs or fireflies (actually lampyrid beetles) are often seen on the flowers in autumn.

Moth caterpillar feeders include the lost sallow *(Eupsilia devia);* and the asteroid *(Cucullia asteroides),* omitted cucullia *(C. omissa),* and brown-hooded owlet *(C. convexipennis),* all flowerhead feeders. Other flower feeders include larvae of the white-dotted groundling *(Platysenta videns);* and the northern flower moth *(Schinia septentrionalis,* mainly on New England aster), the arcigera flower moth *(S. arcigera),* and the goldenrod flower moth *(S. nundina).* The sharp-stigma looper *(Agrapha oxygramma),* the unspotted looper *(Allagrapha aerea),* and the dark-spotted looper *(Diachrysia aereoides)* are also aster feeders. The burdock borer *(Papaipema cataphracta)* feeds in aster stems. All of these moth caterpillars are variably marked noctuid species; most feed on the plants at night.

Several inchworm moth caterpillars, also common on asters, include the dimorphic gray *(Tornos scolopacinarius);* the confused eusarca *(Eusarca confusaria);* the blackberry looper *(Chlorochlamys chloroleucaria)*, which feeds mainly on the ray flowers; and the soft-lined wave *(Scopula inductata)*.

Skeletonized leaves may indicate the presence of butterfly caterpillars that forage in groups on the plants. The silvery checkerspot *(Chlosyne nycteis)* has dark and orange stripes and barbed spines. The extremely common pearl crescent *(Phyciodes tharos)*, often found feeding on New England aster, appears spiny and black, with yellow dots and side stripes; also look for the adult butterfly's layered egg masses on the leaves. Yellowish green caterpillars of the painted lady *(Vanessa cardui)* feed singly on aster and other composites, building a silken web that may enclose some flowers.

Pollinators include a variety of insects. Anglewing butterflies *(Polygonia)* frequently visit aster flowers, as do yellows *(Eurema)*, sulphurs *(Colias)*, checkered whites *(Pontia protodice)*, common buckeyes *(Juonia coenia)*, plus the aforementioned painted ladies, several skippers, and south-migrating monarch butterflies *(Danaus plexippus)*. Adult butterflies and moths generally favor the blue and purple asters, whereas white asters are mainly pollinated by honeybees *(Apis mellifera)*, bumblebees *(Bombus)*, and flies. Most asters produce relatively low quantities of nectar. "But since the florets are massed," wrote researcher Bernd Heinrich, "the perching foragers, such as bumblebees, may achieve a relatively high rate of energy intake by extracting the food from large numbers of florets in a short time." Heath asters, by contrast, produce such abundant pollen and nectar that apiarists sometimes cultivate them, and honeybees seem to prefer this species over white clover.

Ruffed grouse and wild turkeys occasionally consume aster leaves and seeds, as do eastern chipmunks and white-footed mice. American tree sparrows eat the seeds, and I have watched American goldfinches foraging on New England aster seedheads. Cottontail rabbits and white-tailed deer also forage on asters. American goldfinches occasionally nest in tall asters. Asters do not, however, provide favored or frequent wildlife food resources. New spring shoots of heath aster may provide palatable and nutritious livestock forage, but the mature plants are rarely eaten.

Spectacular, densely bushy New England aster, one of autumn's most colorful wildflowers, may stand 5 feet tall, attracting many butterflies and moths.

Lore: The word *aster* comes from a Greek word meaning "star," as in *asterisk.* The flower was considered a sacred emblem in the pantheon of Greek divinities.

Early American botanist Asa Gray recognized "the great if not insuperable difficulties" of classifying asters. Anyone's identification of an aster species may, in short, be correct today and wrong tomorrow. The entire confusing situation indicates that this plant group is in a remarkable state of evolutionary flux, rapidly changing, branching, and blossoming in more than a floristic sense. The same applies, in greater or lesser degree, to the entire aster family—in part, at least, because so many of these plants thrive in disturbed, human-disrupted habitats, of which more exist today than ever before.

Asters have a long pedigree in ancient history and mythology. The "star-flower" or its images, sacred to various gods, adorned altars of every size. In one myth, asters are the goddess Astraea's grieving tears fallen and sprouted on Earth. An early English name for the flower was "starwort," and various species were named Michaelmas daisies because they flowered around St. Michaelmas day (September 29).

New England aster roots provided a tea for native tribal treatments of fevers and diarrhea, and various other asters were smudged, smoked, or steamed as tranquilizing inhalations. Aster roots, according to one anonymous source, "were crushed and fed to bees in poor health" (a statement that is worth a double take). Asters had no widespread medicinal usages, however.

Beach-grass *(Ammophila brevigulata).* Grass family. This tall (3 or more feet), pale yellow, native perennial grass of the sand dunes can be seen any time of year along the Atlantic coast and around the Great Lakes and Lake Champlain. Its foot-long, spikelike seedhead, rising above the long, narrow leaves, emerges only in midsummer.

Other names: American beachgrass, marram, or marram grass.

Close relatives: Only 2 *Ammophila* species exist; the other one is *A. arenaria,* European beach-grass, native to coastal Europe and north Africa. Closely related grasses include canary-grasses *(Phalaris),* reed-grasses *(Calamagrostis),* and bent-grasses *(Agrostis).* Other grass family members include bluegrasses, bluestem grasses, and brome-grasses (all *q.v.*).

Lifestyle: Those circles and arcs etched in the sand by the tips of blowing grass leaves are the signatures of beach-grass, expressions of its intimacy with the wind. *Ammophila* depends on the wind, not only for pollination of its flowers, but also for its own stability and growth in an ever-shifting environment. The plant depends upon recurrent burial, thriving in accumulations of up to a foot of new sand annually, sending out both horizontal and vertical *rhizomes* (underground stems) and root anchorages into the new sub-surface, additions of sand that actually stimulate budding and growth of new rhizomes.

The subsurface biomass of beach-grass—the underside of many beaches and dunes—holds unstable sand but also responds to its increase.

Enhanced mycorrhizal activity (see Associates) may also partially account for such rejuvenation. When sand pileup ceases, vigor and density of *Ammophila* decline, probably owing to aging and drying of plants and to nematode infestation, among other factors.

Beach-grass's underground growth occurs faster and has greater biomass than the comparatively small part of the plant we see atop the dunes; a single rhizome may extend 5 to 8 feet in a year. Horizontal rhizomes *(stringers)* may spread in a wagon-wheel pattern 20 feet or so, sending up clonal shoots *(tillers)* at the ends of rhizomes, which may later lengthen farther to produce more shoots. The year's old grass shoots die off in the fall.

As with bracken ferns *(q.v.)* and other cloning growths, distinguishing individual clones from one another is impossible by surface visual cues. Yet, although it depends upon unstable surfaces for survival, beach-grass's subsurface growth acts to stabilize, slow down, the shifting dune. The surface plant becomes a windbreak, fragmenting the wind surf, ultimately forming beach-grass meadows that provide the surface stability for germination of other plant species. Thus beach-grass, critical to dune formation and endurance, in many areas becomes vital to coastline protection. It begins the dune plant *succession,* which may ultimately result in dune and coastal forests.

Grass flowers have distinctive form and parts (see Bluegrasses). Each flower spikelet on beach-grass's long spike or inflorescence is bisexual, can both cross-pollinate and self-pollinate. But most reproduction is vegetative and clonal. The plant devotes little energy to fertilized flowers, and seed production is relatively slight. Seedling growth, even rarer, occurs mainly at driftlines and in moist hollows *(slacks)* in the dunes. Populations disperse by extending rhizomes toward the shoreline, where wave action tears and fragments them, transporting pieces laterally along the surf line. Where currents deposit them onshore at new locations, they often begin new beach-grass colonies.

Beach-grass tolerates salt spray, even immersion in seawater. Plant ecologists classify it, however, as a salt-resistant *glycophyte*, a plant growing in low-salt soils, rather than a *halophyte*, a plant tolerant of high-salt soils. Beach-grass also tolerates acid rain and acidic soils.

This plant exhibits several moisture-conserving adaptations in its dry, windy habitats. The long, narrow leaves with furrowed upper surfaces tend to curl and fold inward when exposed to hot sunlight and drying winds. Upper leaf surfaces, with their microscopic *stomata*, or pores, also tend to orient away from the wind stream. Conversely, during rainy or foggy weather, the leaf blades open up, exposing themselves to moisture and carbon dioxide absorption.

Associates: Beach-grass's native range in North America lies between 35 and 53 degrees N latitude. The plant colonizes foredune areas just above the flotsam line, the farthest reach of storm waves. Other plants that commonly occur as part of the beach-grass community include ryegrass *(Lolium perenne)*, sandburs *(q.v.)*, common wormwood *(q.v.)*, dune-willow *(Salix cordata)*, and sand-cherry *(Prunus pumila)*. Beach-grass tends to compete with American dunegrass *(Leymus mollis)* and, in the Midwest, with sand-reed *(Calamovilfa longifolia)*. It may itself be crowded out by the more aggressive European beach-grass *(A. arenaria)* where both species occur. On the landward side, beach-grass often tends to grade into stands of little bluestem grass (see Bluestem Grasses).

Fungi play a vital role in beach-grass growth and vigor—specifically, the several species of subsurface mycorrhizae that enable nutrient absorption by the grass roots. At least 17 species of these fungous associates have been identified (*Acaulospora, Glomus,* and *Scutellospora* species).

A destructive fungus on grasses, occasionally infesting the seed spikes of beach-grass, is ergot *(Claviceps purpurea)*, a sac fungus. This fungus displaces the seeds with black *sclerotia*, or masses.

Declining beach-grass populations are often found to be infested with the beach-grass root-knot nematode *(Meloidogyne sasseri)*, a roundworm parasite that feeds in the roots.

The beach-grass scale *(Eriococcus carolinae)*, a mealybug, sucks sap from stems and leaves. Unidentified aphids (Aphididae) also become numerous at times.

The gall midge *Mayetiola ammophilae* feeds as a larva in stem bases, causing rot and breakage.

Spring rose beetles *(Strigoderma arboricola)*, shining leaf chafers closely resembling Japanese beetles, sometimes devour the grass florets.

Seed feeders on beach-grass are relatively few. Probably the foremost consumer is the Ipswich sparrow, an Atlantic coastal subspecies of the savannah sparrow. Snow buntings also forage on beach-grass seeds. Other birds occasionally use beach-grasses for nesting cover and materials. Among these are short-eared owls, piping plovers, herring and laughing gulls, and vesper sparrows. Migrating horned larks and American pipits also frequent beach-grass areas. The only mammal grazers on the plant are probably the feral horses—the so-called Chincoteague ponies—that inhabit Assateague Island off the eastern seaboard.

Lore: *Ammophila* is Greek for "sand loving" (a genus of digger wasp also bears this name), and probably a more efficient sand binder and dune stabilizer than beach-grass does not exist. Coastal engineers and conservationists often plant it for this purpose. So successful have European beach-grass plantings been on the Pacific coast that it now competes with native beach vegetation in many areas, also threatening nesting habitat of the snowy plover. Stabilized land also leads to faster plant succession, and some West Coast environmentalists, now deploring too much of a good thing, are seeking control measures.

Although tolerant of strong winds and sand abrasion, *Ammophila* is vulnerable to heavy beach use, does not bear up well under foot and vehicle traffic on the dunes. Bending and breakage of stems seriously damage the plants, leading ultimately to their destruction and consequent dune destabilization.

DNA sequencing indicates that interior beach-grass populations (Great Lakes and Lake Champlain) originated from an Atlantic coastal *refugium* (unglaciated area) via the St. Lawrence Seaway following the last glacial retreat.

Beach-grass is not humanly edible and has no known medicinal uses.

Beard-tongues (*Penstemon* species). Figwort family. Recognize these native perennials by their tubular, stalked, unevenly lobed flowers—white, pink, lavender, or violet—surmounting the stem. Flower clusters rise from paired stalks; leaves are also paired but stalkless and toothed. Probably the commonest species in the Northeast are the foxglove or tall white beard-tongue *(P. digitalis)*, with white or pink-tinged flowers; hairy or northeastern beard-tongue *(P. hirsutus)*, with woolly stem and magenta-tinged white flowers; large or large-flowered beard-tongue *(P. grandiflorus)*, with pale bluish, 2-inch-wide flowers, mainly western in distribution; eastern beard-tongue *(P. laevigatus)* and slender beard-tongue *(P. gracilis)*, both with pale violet flowers. Most *Penstemon* plants stand 2 or 3 feet tall.

Other names: Pentstemons.

Close relatives: About 275 species of *Penstemon* exist, all endemic to North America. Only 11 of these reside in the Northeast. The garden beard-tongue *(P. hartwegii)*, red flowered and beloved of florists, is an import from Mexico. Close figwort kin include common mullein *(q.v.)*, butter-and-eggs *(q.v.)*, speedwells *(q.v.)*, painted cup *(q.v.)*, turtleheads *(Chelone)*, and figworts *(Scrophularia)*.

Lifestyle: The tonguelike, "bearded" sterile stamen rising amidst the 4 fertile, pollen-loaded ones gave these flowers their name. Beard-tongue's flower is technically bisexual but—as with many flowers—is actually sequentially unisexual. The flowers first become *staminate* (male), developing pollen on their anthers; when the stamens decline, the small (female) *pistil* matures, its sticky tip *(stigma)* curving down from the roof of the flower tube. Individual plants or flowers exhibit different phases of sexual sequencing at once, so that some are pollinating and others receiving pollen. A flower in the staminate phase drops pollen on a bee's hairy body as the insect jostles the anthers in seeking the nectaries at the base of the tube. A female-phase flower, on the other hand, partially blocks the insect's visit with its pistil, to which adhere grains of pollen snagged from the insect as it brushes past. Beard-tongue's sequential sex change, called *protandry*, helps ensure cross-pollination (as opposed to self-pollination, an added option for many flowers).

Most beard-tongues flower from May to July, some later. Many white-flowered beard-tongues show violet or purple lines radiating from the flower's center; these *nectar guides* may help lead pollinating insects to the nectaries.

Many *Penstemon* plants also have dense root masses and maintain a winter basal rosette of leaves, from which rises the new stem in spring. Fruit capsules, ripening in late summer or early fall, contain the seeds.

Associates: Look for beard-tongues in old fields, sandy outwashes, open woods. The many species vary considerably in their shade and moisture tolerances; some prefer fairly dry, sunny conditions, whereas others require more mesic soils, thriving as well in partial shade. Large beard-tongue favors very sandy soil.

Few genera show such wide diversity as *Penstemon* in flower form and adaptation for various pollinators. Some 15 western species are pollinated mainly by hummingbirds. In the East, a 1966 study discovered that 2 beard-tongues—the eastern white *(P. pallidus)* and the slender—are pollinated extensively if not exclusively by a single genus of mason bees *(Osmia)*, which depend upon

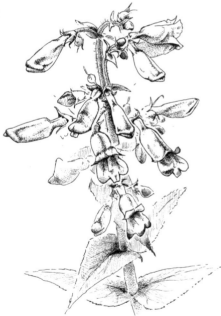

Beard-tongue flowers, tubular and lobed, attract bumblebee and other bee pollinators; the crosswise arrangement of opposite leaves enables maximum light exposure.

the plants for food (pollen and nectar). Since *Osmia* bees also frequently pollinate clovers *(Trifolium)*, research suggests that planting of *Osmia*-associated beard-tongues in clover fields might increase clover seed production. Hairy beard-tongue and Kentucky beard-tongue *(P. tenuiflorus)* are pollinated mainly by genera of *Hoplitis* bees, closely related to *Osmia*, and small carpenter bees *(Ceratina)*.

Foxglove and other beard-tongues attract some 6 species of bumblebees *(Bombus)*; pollinators of other *Penstemon* species include other bees plus wasps, butterflies, moths, and flies. As in many tubular flowers, wasps and bumblebees sometimes cut holes through the corolla (the petals, collectively) to the nectaries, bypassing the normal nectar-seeking (and pollination) route; this action is termed *nectar robbery.*

Penstemon plants provide only slight food value to larger wildlife, primarily in the West, where most beard-tongue species grow. The main seedeaters are small rodents, the foremost consumers being golden-mantled squirrels and kangaroo rats.

Lore: *Penstemon,* like the common name *beard-tongue,* refers to the plant's vestigial stamen; the original Greek words mean "almost a stamen."

Naturalist Thomas Nuttall, during western trips in 1810–11, collected and first described several *Penstemon* species. This complex genus, it is said, contains the most species of any flowering plant group restricted to North America.

Various *Penstemon* species hybridize readily, and this propensity has led to horticultural development of many garden ornamentals—notably, the common beard-tongue *(P. barbatus)* and garden beard-tongue *(P. hartwegii)*—of which many colors and cultivars exist. The American Penstemon Society distributes information to botanists and beard-tongue enthusiasts.

Beggar-ticks *(Bidens* species). Aster family. Mostly yellow-flowered herbs standing 1 to 3 feet tall, the many species of beggar-ticks show much variation. The 2 common field and roadside *Bidens* considered here are beggar-ticks *(B. frondosa)* and Spanish needles *(B. bipinnata)*. Both are native annuals, and both have yellowish flowerheads that somewhat resemble sunflowers with their ray flowers missing. Green, leafy bracts support the central disk of *B. frondosa.* Leaves are divided—3 to 5 toothed, compound leaflets in *B. frondosa,* much lobed and fernlike in *B. bipinnata.*

Other names: Sticktights, tickseeds, tickseed-sunflowers, bur-marigolds, pitchforks, devil's pitchfork, old ladies' clothespins, beggar-lice, stickseed, devil's bootjack; soapbush needles *(B. bipinnata).*

Close relatives: The genus *Bidens* consists of some 280 species, most of them native to Africa and the New World, the rest ranging throughout Eurasia and Polynesia. *B. bipin-*

nata is apparently native to both eastern Asia and eastern North America. Most of our 16 northeastern North American species inhabit wetland and moist areas. Family relatives include tickseeds *(Coreopsis)*, as well as asters, goldenrods, coneflowers, sunflowers, ragweeds, ox-eye daisy, common yarrow (all *q.v.*), and many others. The similarly named Canadian tick-trefoil *(q.v.)*, also producing adherent fruits, is unrelated.

Lifestyle: Plant guides often identify these 2 *Bidens* as rayless (that is, lacking ray flowers). Close inspection, however, reveals that yellowish ray flowers, though rudimentary and inconspicuous, are indeed present. Flowerheads in both species grow at the ends of long, sparsely leaved branches. Both plants reproduce entirely from seed. A single *Bidens* plant can easily produce more than 1,000 seeds.

Flowering from late summer into fall, beggar-ticks become most conspicuous to hikers after the flowers are gone. *Bidens* are pants pests; the barbed seed packages *(achenes)* hook onto one's clothing, hitchhiking there until removed by hand, brush, or comb. With trouser legs crusted and solidly armored by the achenes in October, "it is as if you had unconsciously made your way through the ranks of some countless but invisible Lilliputian army," wrote Thoreau, "which in their anger had discharged all their arrows and darts at you, though none of them reached higher than your legs." *B. frondosa* has 2-pronged flat achenes, allowing for wind distribution, whereas the black, long, and narrow Spanish needles have 4 short adherent barbs. Both kinds appear in central clusters protruding from the former flowerhead.

B. frondosa has a shallow, much-branched taproot; *B. bipinnata*'s taproot is thicker and plunges deeper, with numerous side branches.

Associates: Although these 2 *Bidens* annuals can rapidly colonize disturbed areas, they seldom compete for very long with perennial plants as old-field plant succession advances. These sun-loving plants help stabilize the soil after digging, erosion, or other disturbance.

Dodder *(Cuscuta,* often *C. coryli)*, a twining, yellow-stemmed plant, parasitizes *Bidens* along with many other plants.

Calligrapha elegans, a spotted, broad-bodied leaf beetle, feeds on *Bidens* foliage. Several noctuid moth caterpillars feed on the foliage of Spanish needles. These include the mobile groundling *(Platysenta mobilis)*, the confederate *(Condica confederata)*, and the goldenrod stowaway *(Cirrhophanus triangulifer)*. The bidens borer *(Epiblema otiosana)*, a tortricid moth caterpillar, bores into *Bidens* stems, as does the smartweed borer *(Ostrinia obumbratalis)*, a pyralid caterpillar.

Hairstreak butterflies (Lycaenidae)—especially the great purple hairstreak *(Atlides halesus)*—frequently visit the flowers of Spanish needles. Other butterfly nectar seekers include the gulf fritillary *(Agraulis vanillae)*, the pearl crescent *(Phyciodes tharos)*, and the sleepy orange *(Eurema nicippe)*, among others.

Bidens flowers often host ambush bugs *(Phymata),* predators on bee and butterfly visitors.

Cottontail rabbits consume *Bidens* foliage to some extent. *Bidens* seeds, though not a significant food for larger wildlife, are consumed by several waterfowl, gamebirds, and finches, primarily wood ducks, mallards, American black ducks, ring-necked pheasants, northern bobwhites, wild turkeys, purple finches, pine grosbeaks, common redpolls, swamp sparrows, and American goldfinches. *Bidens* seeds can be dispersed by almost any mammal or bird that comes into contact with the plant. Sheep wool, especially, often becomes matted with the achenes—these animals stand at just the right height to snag *Bidens* barbs in passing.

Lore: Drab and scrubby *Bidens* conveys some interesting items besides its sticktights. Since most (though not all) *Bidens* species are native plants, they provide refreshing exceptions to the idea that all our weeds are alien intruders. Also, the adaptation of barbs and hooks on seeds as a way of dispersal represents a complex level of evolution—that is, they are apparently adaptive to self-propelled life forms.

Four barbs at the tip of a Spanish needle achene snag onto clothing and animal fur, efficiently distributing this seed and plant wherever legs walk.

Without the later appearance on earth of fur and feathers, no impetus for the evolution of barbed or sticky seeds would have occurred. "How surely the *Bidens* . . . prophesy the coming of the traveller, brute or human," wrote Thoreau.

Native tribes and homeopathic practitioners found several medicinal uses for *B. bipinnata.* The Cherokee drank a tea of the leaves to expel worms, also chewed the leaves for sore throat. European doctors prescribed infusions of *Bidens* as astringents and cathartics and to induce sweating, menstruation, and urination. A strong infusion of *B. frondosa* was said to have effectively remedied croup in children. *Bidens,* like many herbal brews, serviced its patients by giving them the feeling they had been genuinely treated, if not cured.

The generic name, meaning "two teeth" (Latin *bis* and *dens*), refers to the prongs, or awns, on the achene.

Bergamot, Wild *(Monarda fistulosa).* Mint family. Its coarse appearance; roundish flowerhead *(cyme)* of pink, magenta, lavender, or pale lilac tubular flowers; opposite leaves; square stems; and pungent odor identify this summer native perennial. It stands 2 to 3 feet tall.

Other names: Purple bee-balm, lemon-mint.

Close relatives: Of the 15 native *Monardas* that exist in North America, 7 reside in the East. Some of the best known include horse mint *(M. punctata),* basil-bergamot *(M. clinopodia),* purple bergamot *(M. media),* and Oswego-tea or bee-balm *(M. didyma).* Closely related mints include hedge-nettles *(Stachys),* wood-mints *(Blephilia),* and sages *(Salvia).* Other family members include catnip *(q.v.)* and self-heal *(q.v.).*

Lifestyle: Variable in hue but consistently displaying color shades on the subdued edge of the red-blue spectra, bergamot florets bloom separately; part of the flowerhead often looks spiky or vacant. Past, present, and future florets may exist on any given head. Florets progressively develop from the center of the cyme outward, the color moving about the flowerhead as individual tubes "blink" on and off. The final stage is a bald central cyme ringed by a fringe of florets. Each cyme produces 20 to 50 florets over the July-August season, and each floret is bisexual, its color attracting long-tongued pollinators, especially butterflies. One problem experienced by many long-tubed flowers: Placement of the nectar reward deep within the tube summons insect entry and efficient pollination, but it also makes the floral tube vulnerable to a kind of thievery (nectar robbery) by certain insects that chew through the petals into the nectaries from outside the floret, thus circumventing the pollination route.

Close inspection of a floret reveals the lower of its two lobed lips as spreading and platformlike—an insect "landing stage." Note also the densely hairy interior of the calyx, or inner floret, and the protruding (male) stamens and (female) pistil, which not even a slender butterfly proboscis can avoid brushing against. The seeds are 4 small nutlets embedded in the base of each calyx tube.

Bergamot's pungent-smelling flowerhead consists of numerous individual florets that develop in a centrifugal progression.

Much of bergamot's strong odor—as in all mint-family plants—emanates from a system of hairlike epidermal cells called *trichomes*, which contain volatile oils.

Bergamot's root system is shallow, making the plant vulnerable to winter-kill by intense cold. Where well established, bergamot reproduces mainly by vegetative cloning from the roots. Over time, the plant spreads outward from the central root mass, which sometimes dies out, leaving its clonal progeny to encircle the parent plant site.

Associates: Wild bergamot favors open sandy ground, roadsides, and forest and thicket edges, tolerating light shade. It also tolerates a range of soils, from moist to moderately dry.

Yellowish raised spots on deformed stems and leafstalks may indicate spearmint rust *(Puccinia menthae),* a club fungus disease.

Bergamot's chief pollinators are bumblebees *(Bombus)* and butterflies; among the latter are pipevine swallowtails *(Battus philenor).* Spectacular sphinx moths—notably the hummingbird and snowberry clearwings *(Hemaris thysbe, H. diffinis)*—also visit bergamot flowers, as do syrphid or hover flies (Syrphidae). Examine the floret bases for punch holes, where solitary bees or wasps may have tapped the nectaries from outside. Other insects also come to feed at these wounds. An occasional pollinator is the ruby-throated hummingbird, whose needlelike bill easily inserts into the deep nectaries.

Foliage feeders include 2 moth caterpillars: the hermit sphinx *(Sphinx eremitus),* large and green with a rear-projecting horn; and the gray marvel *(Agriopodes teratophora),* a dagger moth. *Pyrausta orphisalis* and *P. acrionalis,* pyralid moth caterpillars, also feed on *Monarda* plants.

Burrower bugs *(Sehiris cinctus),* oval and shiny black with white margins, often feed on mints. An inconspicuous forager is the mint aphid *(Ovatus crataegarius),* mottled yellow-green, which causes curling and puckering of leaves. Gall gnat larvae *(Cecidomyia monardi)* sometimes produce round galls on stems. A common forager on bergamot flowerheads is the seed bug *Ortholomus scolopax.*

As attractive as this plant is to some insects, the oils (mainly thymol) that give the plant its characteristic odor apparently repel others. The dried and powdered leaves, sprinkled over meat or food, reputedly keep away flies.

Few records exist of seed consumption by larger wildlife. Field sparrows and American goldfinches perch on swaying stems and pick out the seeds. During winter in my own backyard *Monarda* clones, I sometimes observe dark-eyed juncos feeding on seedheads.

Lore: As with most mints, a decent tea may be brewed from bergamot leaves, or they may be mixed with other tea leaves. It is said that New England colonists used bergamot leaves as a tea substitute after the 1773 Boston Tea Party deprived them of the oriental brew. Bergamot has a long history of medicinal uses among native Americans, who drank the leaf tea for many ailments—colic, flatulence, colds and bronchial complaints, fever, stomachaches, nosebleeds, insomnia, among others. Bergamot is also diaphoretic, inducing sweating, and physicians once prescribed it to expel worms and gas. Bergamot became a popular yard flower in colonial gardens, also in England, where it was imported in 1637.

The name *bergamot,* applied to the plant by pioneer collectors in North America, originated from its supposed aromatic similarity to the unrelated Italian bergamot orange *(Citrus bergamia),* still a source of perfumes and cosmetics.

Bergamot itself is grown commercially for a modest market; its aromatic and antiseptic oil is used in perfumes, soaps, cosmetics, and as a source of oil of thyme.

Bindweed, Field *(Convolvulus arvensis).* Morning-glory family. Arrowhead-shaped, gray-green leaves and trumpet-shaped white or pinkish flowers borne in clusters of two identify this perennial vine. Its trailing stems climb, tangle, and mat upon other vegetation or sometimes form a dense ground cover. Two small bracts just beneath the flower distinguish this alien perennial species from other bindweeds.

Other names: Small or lesser bindweed, European bindweed, creeping jenny, wild or field morning-glory, corn lily, cornbine, barbine, bellbine, devil's guts, hedge bells, laplove, green vine, possession vine, and at least 80 others.

Close relatives: More than 200 *Convolvulus* species exist in mainly tropical and subtropical regions of Eurasia and Africa. Closely related are the *Calystegia* bindweeds, including hedge-bindweed *(C. sepium)* and Japanese bindweed *(C. hederacea).* Family relatives include morning-glories *(Ipomoea)* and wild potato *(I. pandurata).*

Lifestyle: Its roots sprawling almost as widely as the colorful trailing vine, field bindweed can send up new shoots many feet distant from the original plant, while its taproot plunges deep. Any root or rhizome fragment that gets detached, as by digging or plowing, can soon reproduce the entire plant. The twining aerial stem tips rotate about once every 2 hours, rapidly reaching until they find a support surface, usually another plant.

Visually similar plants include hedge-bindweed (see *The Book of Forest and Thicket*), black bindweed *(Polygonum convolvulus),* jimson-weed *(Datura stramonium),* and buckwheat *(q.v.);* size and form of lilylike *Convolvulus* flowers are, however, distinctive. Flowering typically begins near the center of the plant, then progresses along the lateral branches. Each spectacular flower, about an inch in diameter, lasts only about a day, closing when shaded and before nightfall, but the plant steadily produces bisexual flowers all summer. The 5 fused petals, forming a funnel-like corolla that produces nectar at its base, attract insects that pollinate the plant. Floral parts—female pistils and male stamens—mature simultaneously, but since the pistils are longer, they receive cross-pollinating insects before the insects brush against the pollen-loaded stamens. Bindweed can also self-pollinate.

Field bindweed reproduces 3 ways: by seed; by extension of underground stems, or *rhizomes;* and by budding from lateral roots. Oval seedpods usually contain 4 seeds. The seed, mature about a month after pollination, develops a hard, impermeable coat that requires a winter in the soil to break dormancy; it may, however, remain dormant and viable for up to 50 years or longer. An average bindweed plant produces more than 500 seeds per growing season.

Bindweed's extensive root system includes both vertical taproots, typically 4 or 5 feet long, though some may plunge 20 or 30 feet, and, extending from the taproots, shallow, cordlike lateral roots. It is by means of this lateral root system, which can angle downward at intervals and develop secondary vertical roots, that a single plant may radially spread 10 or 12 feet in a growing season, producing up to 25 clonal plants. The vigorous subsurface biomass not only helps propagate clonal vines, but also stores carbohydrates and proteins that may enable the plants to resprout despite several years of continuous mowing or removal of top growth.

Bindweed's pliable, aboveground stems twist counterclockwise, in contrast to most twining vines, and usually extend 1 to 4 feet. They have no tendrils or other means of holding or gripping a support, simply lodging and twining against a plant, post, or other available object. Failing that, they twist and tangle on the ground. "If the support is firm," wrote naturalist Anna Botsford Comstock, "it makes only enough turns around it to hold itself firmly; but if it catches to something as unstable as its own stems, the stems twist until they become so hard-twisted that they form a support in themselves." Frost kills all surface portions of the plant in the fall.

Field bindweed, an epiphyte, depends for support upon the strength and rigidity of other plants; here it twines around a grass stem.

Associates: Rare is the ground, moist or dry, where field bindweed cannot grow, though it favors fertile, disturbed soils (that is, crop fields). Ideal to field bindweed are other habitats that most resemble agricultural lands, sites that offer scant plant competition, strong sunlight, and moderate to low moisture. Owing to its massive root capacity, it easily tolerates periods of drought. Field bindweed thrives between 60 degrees N and 45 degrees S latitudes, thus encompassing several climates, including temperate and tropical. Wherever and as long as humanity tills the earth, field bindweed will sprout. It helps define, in a sense, the farmer.

Labeled one of the world's 10 worst weeds (12th worst, according to another source) because of its abundance, wide distribution, and economic impact, it also resists eradication. Few weeds evoke the venom that accompanies this plant's clones: "It is one of the most tenacious, vicious, aggressive, and downright obnoxious weeds," foamed a Utah State University horticulturist. Herbicide application "just makes the weed mad." It is "strong willed" and "evil," driving dispassionate scientists to spit canard. Its several reproductive options make it notably persistent once established. Bindweed competes with other plants not by hogging light, for it usually spreads low and is easily shaded, but by its extensive underground biomass, which reduces the amounts of soil moisture and nutrients available for other plants. Its trailing vines may also smother and dislodge crop plants and tangle in harvesting equipment. Thus, especially in North America's central states and provinces, bindweed's foremost unhappy associate is the farmer.

Field bindweed's strongest crop competitor is said to be closed stands of alfalfa, also rye, soybeans, and sorghum, which shade the plant, thereby forcing it into dormancy. Lawn grass—if a healthy, vigorous turf—is also said to crowd out bindweed growth.

Two fungal growths commonly infect field bindweed, in some cases attacking plants already weakened by insect or mite attack. Bindweed decline disease or fusarium wilt, caused by *Fusarium oxysporum,* infects roots and buds on the rhizomes, resulting in circular patches of blighted seedlings and stunted plants. Septoria leaf spot *(Septoria convolvuli)* affects bindweed foliage, causing spotted leaves and defoliation. Both fungous organisms survive in the soil and in bindweed plant debris. A few other rusts and leaf spots also attack bindweed. Increasing its reputation as the farmer's anathema, bindweed hosts several potato, tobacco, tomato, and blueberry viruses.

Bindweed's chief pollinators are bees, including halictids (Halictidae), honeybees *(Apis mellifera),* bumblebees *(Bombus).* Butterflies and moths also pollinate.

Insect foliage feeders include the argus tortoise beetle *(Chelymorpha cassidea),* a yellow to bright red insect with spots, resembling a miniature turtle in form. It feeds on many bindweed relatives as well, can defoliate entire plants, and offers some hope as a biological control species. Other tortoise beetle feeders include the golden tortoise beetle *(Metriona bicolor)* and *Plagiometriona clavata,* dark brown with translucent wing margins. Irregular holes eaten in the leaves indicate tortoise beetle presence.

In attempting to establish biological control of bindweed in North America, scientists have imported a noctuid moth and a gall mite from southern Europe, where they attack field bindweed, into Texas. Caterpillars of *Tyta luctosa,* the field bindweed moth, devour the plant's leaves; and the field bindweed mite *(Aceria malherbae),* an eriophyid, forms galls on buds and growing tips, resulting in clusters of stunted, twisted leaves. Since both insect and mite originated in bindweed's native Eurasia, researchers believed that good reason existed to hope for eventually successful biocontrol. The red imported fire ant *(Solenopsis wagneri)* soon interfered, however, with establishment of the field bindweed moth. A research team concluded that the "prospective biocontrol agents themselves are heavily parasitized, do not feed exclusively on one species, or simply do not cause sufficient damage to field bindweed."

Caterpillars of the common spragueia moth *(Spragueia leo),* a noctuid, also feed on the leaves. A slim-bodied moth with a T-shaped adult appearance when at rest is the bindweed plume moth *(Emmelina monodactyla),* another foliage caterpillar. Caterpillars of the straight-lined seed moth *(Eumestleta recta),* another noctuid, feed on seeds of bindweed and other morning-glories; the adult moths, yellowish and brown shaded, range mainly in the Southeast.

Although cattle and sheep will graze bindweed and hogs will eat the plant tops and root for underground parts, the plant is not a preferred forage, and toxic effects have been reported. It "has no feed value and may make stock vomit," according to an Australian agricultural agency. The plants also have little value for larger wildlife, though a variety of birds consume the seeds, which remain viable in the droppings. Indeed, next to farm implements, birds probably account for much of this plant's spread in North America. Seedeaters include ducks, geese, greater and lesser yellowlegs, killdeers, common ravens, European starlings, and northern mockingbirds. Probably ring-necked pheasants, northern bobwhites, and meadow voles also consume the seeds.

Lore: Much agricultural research attention has been lavished on this scourge of field and farmland, and with good reason: Its root complex can so reduce soil moisture that crop yields may decline 50 to 60 percent where bindweed invasion is dense. Much of the control research, as with most crop plants, focuses upon herbicides and their application. Although biological and chemical controls can check and restrain the plant's growth and reproduction, success in eliminating field bindweed remains virtually nil. Yet, incredibly, field bindweed has also had its friends, being occasionally reintroduced, under the rubric "wild morning-glory," as an ornamental ground cover and for hanging baskets.

This plant was well known to ancient Egyptian and Greek herbalists. The Romans called it *volucram majus,* "a large worm that wraps itself in vines." In an interesting prefocus on evolution, an English herbalist in 1562 claimed that "byndweed . . . is as it were an imperfect worke of nature learning to make lilies." Bindweed probably arrived in North America as a contaminant in grain. Virginia colonists first noticed it in 1739; a century later, it had covered the eastern seaboard states and also began to thrive in areas westward wherever migrants settled. A notable "bindweed plague" that infested Kansas in 1877 was traced to Ukrainian settlers who had brought wheat seed from their native land. Well established in California by 1890, bindweed was soon thereafter proclaimed the state's worst weed, a title soon awarded by several other western and plains states as well.

Bindweed roots are strongly purgative, and both European and Asian folk used various root, leaf, and flower infusions for laxative purposes. Although field bindweed came as a late addition to native American herbal usage, several tribes quickly adopted it. A leaf tea treated spider bites and, internally, was said to help reduce menstrual flow.

"Entwiner of fields," field bindweed's apt Latin name, derives from the same source word as *convoluted.*

Birdsfoot-trefoil *(Lotus corniculatus).* Pea family. This low, alien perennial legume exhibits yellow, pealike flowers and 3 cloverlike leaflets (actually 5, with 2 opposite leaflets at the base of the "trefoil" or triple leaflets; despite its name, this trefoil is the only legume with 5 leaflets). The plants often sprawl, though sometimes stand erect up to 2 feet tall.

Other names: Broadleaf trefoil, poor man's alfalfa.

Close relatives: More than 200 *Lotus* species exist worldwide. Some 40 western species are known as deer vetches. Two other northeastern species, likewise aliens, are narrowleaf trefoil *(L. tenuis)* and Spanish clover *(L. purshianus).* Pea family relatives include loco-weeds *(Oxytropis),* licorice *(Glycyrrhiza lepidota),* and crown-vetch *(Coronilla varia),* plus lupine, clovers, alfalfa, vetches, tick-trefoils (all *q.v.*), and others. *Lotus* is unrelated to American lotus *(Nelumbo lutea)* or the oriental sacred lotus *(N. nucifera),* both water plants of the lotus-lily family.

Lifestyle: Planted both as a nourishing forage for livestock and for erosion control—its extensive root system branching from a strong taproot binds loose soil effectively—birdsfoot-trefoil has received, like dandelions, an "OK status" from most of our plant guardians, though unquestionably it competes with native prairie vegetation. Like most legumes, it produces root nodules; *Rhizobium lupini* bacteria in the nodules convert atmospheric nitrogen to ammonia, enriching the soil and providing a usable form of nitrogen to plants. This self-supply eliminates the need for nitrogen fertilizer. Maximum nodulation occurs at soil pH 6 to 6.5. For raising hay crops of birdsfoot-trefoil, however, the seed must often be inoculated with the bacteria before planting.

Numerous branched stems rise from a basal clump, or *crown*. Four to 8 bright yellow, sweetpealike florets, sometimes tinged with orange or reddish striping, cluster at the ends of the flower stems *(peduncles)*. Each floret is bisexual and can self-pollinate, though the plant has a self-incompatibility mechanism that limits self-seeding, and most seeding results from cross-pollination between plants by insects. Pollen in this flower actually matures before the flower opens. Filaments push the loose pollen forward into the closed tip of the united lower petals *(keel)*, and pollination occurs when an insect's weight on the keel forces a ribbonlike mass of pollen from the keel opening, some of it adhering to the insect's underside. Further pressure as the insect seeks the nectaries causes the female stigma to slide onto the same contact area, where its stickiness may pick up pollen on the insect from another trefoil plant. Flowers

Its yellow, pealike flowers marked by nectar guides, birdsfoot-trefoil commonly appears in lawns and fields; despite its name, most of its leaves are 5-parted.

unvisited by pollinators remain open 8 to 10 days, but frequently visited flowers usually last less than 4 days as fertilization occurs. Inch-long seedpods, each containing 10 to 15 dark, tiny seeds, ripen about a month after pollination. The 5 or 6 pods attached at right angles to the peduncle somewhat resemble a splayed "bird's foot," accounting for the plant's name. They split and twist open spirally, scattering the seed, in a process called *shattering.* "On a hot, still day," wrote one observer, "anyone standing in a field of trefoil will be conscious of a rustling sound, often almost a steady undertone, as the ripe pods snap and the seeds patter on the foliage."

This is a so-called "long-day plant," requiring some 16 hours of daylight to flower. At night, the leaflets fold along the leaf stems, probably conserving moisture. The plant also reproduces vegetatively; although this species does not extend subsurface stems *(rhizomes)*, its roots can and do develop clonal shoots.

Associates: Fields, expressway medians, and roadside areas throughout North America display this bright yellow ground cover from late spring through summer. Birdsfoot-trefoil favors well-drained, acid-neutral soils, but it also tolerates acid, infertile soils, and periods of flooding and drought.

Grasses are common plant associates of birdsfoot-trefoil. For hay production, farmers often plant *Lotus* and forage grasses together. The erect grass stems reduce birdsfoot's weak-stemmed tendency to lean and become beaten down by rains or wind, a characteristic known as *lodging.*

Various crown, root rot, and flower blight fungi *(Phoma, Sclerotina, Fusarium)* afflict this plant, mainly in its southern, warmer, more humid range.

Many roundworm or nematode species parasitize birdsfoot-trefoil roots. These tiny creatures can be found in almost all birdsfoot plants; they may weaken but seldom damage the plants. They include *Pratylenchus, Meloidogyne, Heterodera,* and several other genera.

Pollinating insects are mainly honeybees *(Apis mellifera)* and bumblebees *(Bombus),* seeking both nectar and pollen. The latter bees are probably birdsfoot's most effective pollinators.

Several bug and homopteran species feed destructively on birdsfoot-trefoil. The tarnished plant bug *(Lygus lineolaris),* alfalfa plant bug (see Alfalfa), and trefoil plant bug *(Plagiognathus chrysanthemi)* are sap suckers, puncturing leaves and stems, creating a toxic reaction in the plant that causes flower buds to abort. Meadow spittlebugs (froghoppers), potato leafhoppers, and pea aphids (see Alfalfa for each) are also common sap suckers.

Larvae of the trefoil seed chalcid *(Bruchophagus platypterus),* a small, black eurytomid wasp, infest the seedpods, leaving hollow seeds.

Food data, mostly gathered from western states, show high usage rates by birds and mammals. Seeds are relished by ring-necked pheasants, northern bobwhites, mourning doves, and probably many ground birds, as well as mice and voles. Foliage consumers include cottontail rabbits, mule and white-tailed deer, and moose.

Lore: Hay farmers like to graze livestock on birdsfoot-trefoil and raise it for hay because, unlike alfalfa and some other hays, it does not cause bloat when consumed by animals and is more palatable. It also tolerates poor soil conditions and resists numerous legume-foraging insects. The wise farmer leaves this crop unharvested during late summer and fall, a procedure known as *stockpiling;* this allows the plant's root reserves to accumulate, improving its winter survival and spring growth. The plant can still be grazed as pasture forage in late fall since it holds its leaves after frosts.

A native of Eurasia and still cultivated there as a forage legume, birdsfoot-trefoil probably came to North America along with European livestock about 1900. It was first discovered growing wild in 1934 in New York.

Birdsfoot-trefoil honey is the only human food derived from this plant.

Blazing Stars (*Liatris* species). Aster family. These native perennials, most of them 2 or 3 feet tall, show magenta or purple (rarely white) flowerheads crowded on dense, wandlike spikes; the feathery, thistlelike flower rises from a scaly-bracted base *(involucre)*. Leaves are narrow, grasslike, alternate, and show resin dots. Most commonly seen are the northern or large blazing star *(L. scariosa)*; rough or lacerate blazing star *(L. aspera)*; dense or sessile blazing star *(L. spicata)*; prairie, tall, or thick-spike blazing star *(L. pycnostachya)*; cylindric or few-headed blazing star *(L. cylindracea)*; scaly or plains blazing star *(L. squarrosa)*; New England blazing star *(L. borealis)*; and dotted blazing star *(L. punctata)*.

Other names: Gay feather, liatris, colic-root, rattlesnake master, button snakeroot, devil's bit, prairie pine, throatwort.

Close relatives: About 30 *Liatris* species exist, all in temperate North America. Some 13 species inhabit the East. Other closely related family members include Joe-Pye-weeds *(Eupatorium)* and false boneset *(Kuhnia eupatorioides)*. Numerous related aster family plants appear in this book. Unrelated plants sometimes called blazing stars include *Chamaelirium luteum*, a lily; and *Mentzelia* species, a loasa genus also called stickleaf.

Lifestyle: "It has a general resemblance to thistles and knapweed," Thoreau noted, "but is a handsomer plant than any of them." *L. spicata* is probably our most commonly seen species, though *L. pycnostachya* is widely planted in gardens and frequently escapes to marshy fields. Some *Liatris* species readily hybridize with others, creating plants with intermediate characters. *Liatris* flowering may occur irregularly from year to year. Some plants may produce flower stalks as early as the second year, many (notably *L. aspera*) not until their eighth or ninth year.

Unlike many other plants with tall flower spikes, such as purple loosestrife or vervains, blazing stars begin flowering from the top of the spike, progressing downward as the summer season advances; look for developing seedheads above the flowering portion of the spike, unopened flower buds below it. Each flowerhead is an aggregate, consisting of many separate bisexual florets, as in all aster family plants (composites). The number of florets on each flowerhead varies with the species; *L. punctata* usually has only 4 to 6 per head, *L. scariosa* up to 80 per head. Florets are insect-pollinated and are *obligate outbreeders,* which means that they cannot self-pollinate.

Liatris flowers produce 1-seeded *achenes* with barbed or feathery bristles (depending on species) that aid seed dispersal. In winter, Thoreau observed, "the now bare or empty heads of the liatris look somewhat like dusky daisies surmounted by a little button instead of a disk." This "base on which its flowerets stood is pierced by many little round holes just like the end of a thimble. . . . It readily scales off and you can look through it."

Dotted blazing star has a long, slender taproot that can sink 15 feet, but most other *Liatris* species rise from a winter basal rosette of leaves atop a thick, rounded rootstock called a *corm.* *Liatris* corms may be aged by their cross-sectional rings, annually formed like tree rings. Typical corms may live 11 to 17 years; an extreme of 34 years has been recorded. The corms may be fire adaptive, for most *Liatris* species grow in frequent fire habitats, and corm food storage enables survival of the plant following ground burns.

Associates: *Liatris* species range across the continent. Frequent fires probably turned many presettlement prairies into summer vistas of phlox-purple blazing stars, visible as far as the eye could see. Today we see them more often as solitary stalks or small stands in a field or along a fencerow. Most *Liatris* species favor open, dry, sandy ground or roadsides; a few, including *L. spicata,* prefer wet meadows and sandy shores. *L. scariosa* often associates with bluestem grasses *(q.v.)* on northern rangeland. Although *L. spicata* often becomes a dominant forb in tall-grass prairie, on rangeland *Liatris* species are generally considered *decreasers,* transitory plant dwellers being replaced by less desirable rangeland species, resulting either from grazing pressure or

Blazing stars resemble knapweeds or spineless thistles; unlike many flowers, they begin flowering at the top of the stem, progressing downward.

plant succession. *L. spicata* also pioneers plant succession in strip-mined spoils and in old fields. Ordinarily, *Liatris* is easily outcompeted by grasses and other grassland herbs.

Chief pollinators include those of the long-tongued insect tribes—bumblebees *(Bombus),* butterflies, and bee flies (Bombyliidae, notably *Exoprosopa fasciata).*

The glorious flower moth *(Schinia gloriosa),* a noctuid, feeds as a well-camouflaged caterpillar on both flowers and seeds. Ants are common on *Liatris* during flowering, as are ladybird beetles (Coccinellidae).

Larvae (wireworms) of click beetles (Elateridae) sometimes feed in *Liatris* corms.

Neither seeds nor foliage of *Liatris* rank as an important wildlife food for birds or mammals. *L. scariosa* and *L. punctata* are palatable, nutritious livestock pasture forages, especially in early growth stages; the latter is especially relished by sheep. Some sources state that the hairy stems of some *Liatris* species make them unpalatable to white-tailed deer, thus maintaining the plants in heavily foraged deer areas. Voles often collect *Liatris* corms, storing them in their food caches.

Lore: Native Americans found *Liatris* useful for several medicinal purposes. The Chippewa called *L. scariosa* "elk tail," probably because of its tall flower spike. They drank the root tea for treatment of dysentery. Other tribes, as well as white settlers, used the infusion as a diuretic, a gargle for sore throat, and in poultices for snakebite. Plains tribes apparently ate the bulblike corms of *L. punctata,* said to have a carrot flavor, in early spring. Some tribes fed their horses *Liatris* corms and applied the tea externally to the animals before a race, claiming it improved their speed and endurance.

Almost all *Liatris* species have been cultivated and hybridized as popular native garden flowers. They also dry and preserve well as winter bouquets.

Resembling a grass in form except for its blue flowers, blue-eyed grass can easily be overlooked in its grassy habitats.

Blue-eyed Grasses *(Sisyrinchium* species). Iris family. Not grasses but so called because of their stiff, grasslike leaves and flat, wiry stems, these native perennials typically stand 4 inches to a foot tall. They exhibit 6-petaled, mostly blue-violet flowers with white, 6-pointed centers accented with golden yellow. Each blunt petal is tipped with a bristlelike point, an infallible identity mark. Flowers open solitarily at the end of branched or unbranched stems. *S. angustifolium* is probably the most common species.

Other names: Eye-bright, blue star.

Close relatives: About 75 blue-eyed grass species exist; most are New World natives, and few are distinguished by separate English names. Some 8 species, separated on the basis of technical characters, grow in the Northeast. Iris family kin include blackberry-lily *(Belamcanda chinensis),* irises or flags *(Iris),* crocus *(Crocus neapolitanus),* and gladiolus *(Gladiolus).*

Lifestyle: The apparent petals of iris family flowers are actually *tepals,* a term for both sepals and petals when they look alike and occur together in the flowerhead. In the blue-eyed grasses, 3 sepals alternate with 3 petals in each flower, but all resemble petals in color and form. Dark lines on the tepals serve as possible nectar guides, leading insect pollinators to the yellow center. Usually about 3 flower buds occur at the end of a stem, but buds open separately—often a day or so apart—and stay open for only a day or less; they never remain open at night. Time windows for cross-pollination—the chief transaction of most flowers—are thus very brief; but what an individual bisexual flower lacks in exposure time may be compensated for by the more or less constant flowering of the plant from May through midsummer or later. Blue-eyed grasses also reproduce vegetatively, rising from masses of fibrous *rhizomes,* subsurface stems that also store food. Seed capsules are round and 3-celled.

Associates: Blue-eyed grasses occupy both moist and dry open habitats, depending on species—meadows, sandy flats, gravel banks, grassy pastures. Thoreau noted that flowering blue-eyed grasses marked dry footing through wet fields: "You can cross the meadows dry-shod by following the winding lead of the blue-eyed grass, which grows only on the firmer, more elevated, and drier parts."

Pollinators are mainly bees. Prairie-chickens and wild turkeys are known to consume the seed capsules. Probably other ground-feeding birds and mammals do likewise.

Lore: *Sisyrinchium* lore is not large. The rhizomes provided a tea that native Americans drank for treating both diarrhea and constipation, say the sources; the leaves made a tea for stomach ailments.

Bluegrasses *(Poa* species). Grass family. Recognize bluegrasses by the tuft of cobwebby hairs at the base of each floret; by a parallel translucent line on either side of the leaf's central midrib; and by the abruptly incurved (not long-tapered) leaf tip resembling a boat prow in three-dimensional shape. Mature bluegrasses typically stand 2 or 3 feet tall. Most common of the 24 species in eastern North America are Kentucky-bluegrass *(P. pratensis),* Canada-bluegrass *(P. compressa),* and annual bluegrass *(P. annua);* all are probably alien plants.

Other names: June grass, speargrass *(P. pratensis);* wiregrass *(P. compressa);* six-weeks grass, low or dwarf speargrass *(P. annua).*

Close relatives: More than 200 *Poa* species exist worldwide. Tribal relatives (Poeae) include orchard-grass *(Dactylis glomerata),* brome-grasses *(q.v.),* fescues *(Festuca),* and lovegrasses *(Eragrostis).*

Lifestyle: Most bluegrasses are perennials. *P. annua,* however, usually exhibits an annual life cycle. Even this species, however, sometimes roots laterally at its lower leaf joints *(nodes),* a process called *tillering,* thus becoming a perennial in fact if not name.

The boat-shaped leaf tip said to be characteristic of bluegrasses can be a misleading cue, since several other grass genera exhibit leaf tips that could similarly be described; the *Poa* distinction, if any, is seldom made clear in most grass manuals. A better identity mark is the leaf blades' *rugosity,* referring to the crinkled or puckered area that runs across some blades about one-third the distance from the tip.

Unlike most other plants, grasses grow by lengthening from their stem joints, or nodes, instead of at the plant tip, or apex; this explains why the lawn always needs removing. Grasses have distinctive flower structures and a specialized vocabulary to describe them. In brief, the floral parts—pollen-bearing stamens, seed-producing pistils—are enclosed by scales instead of centering a radial or irregular arrangement of petals and sepals. As with all grasses, bluegrass flowers are bisexual and wind-pollinated. The flowers occur in tufts of spikelets, each of which contains several florets.

Shape of the *inflorescence,* the entire flowerhead of the plant, varies by *Poa* species. Kentucky-bluegrass shows an oval to pyramidal form of inflorescence, with flowering branches in whorls of 3 to 5; the Canada-bluegrass inflorescence appears narrower, with short branches in pairs and flat, wiry stems; and annual bluegrass has a low, spreading inflorescence rising from a densely tufted leaf mat. Annual bluegrass flowers early, late April to early May, also sometimes in late fall—unable to tolerate hot weather, it usually disappears in summer. Kentucky-bluegrass flowers in May and June, Canada-bluegrass mainly in June but extending into September.

Although all bluegrasses reproduce by seed, the foremost method of all but annual bluegrass is vegetative, mainly by tillering and subsurface stems *(rhizomes),* forming dense sods. Annual bluegrass forms dense, patchy tufts, dying down in hot weather. *P. pratensis* and *P. compressa* tend to spread rapidly into bare-soil areas, forming mats or patches sometimes highlighted by bluish green color. (Kentucky-bluegrass, however, can also look quite bluish in spring during pollination, when the flowerheads give the grass field a bluish purple cast.)

Kentucky-bluegrass exhibits distinct phases of growth activity, a pattern that varies only slightly in most other *Poa* species. The plant sprouts rhizome buds mainly in summer and fall; aerial shoots and tillers in spring and early summer; and inflorescences in spring and fall, when short days and cool temperatures provide optimum growth conditions. Soil moisture and temperature, day length, and soil nutrients may modify this

Note the rugosity, or crinkling, that often appears on bluegrass leaves, one of these grasses' chief identity marks.

sequencing. The plant becomes semidormant in summer heat, rejuvenating with cooler fall temperatures.

Associates: Bluegrasses thrive only on disturbed or previously plowed land. Kentucky-bluegrass adapts to many soil types but thrives best in open, sunny habitats and on well-drained, limestone-derived soils. Most of its plant associates in this country are those provided by farmers and lawn owners, either by design or neglect. For optimal pasturage, farmers often raise a mix of Kentucky-bluegrass with white clover. Canada-bluegrass grows best on dry, acid soils in cool climates, whereas annual bluegrass favors compacted, heavy soils but is highly adaptive.

Foremost bluegrass plant competitors are trees, as in yards and pastures. Tree roots generally derive most of their nutrients from the top 12 to 18 inches of soil, the same zone occupied by grass root systems. Grasses often come out the best in this contest if they receive adequate light and rainfall beneath the tree.

Numerous plant fungi parasitize bluegrasses. Among these are anthracnose *(Colletotrichum graminicola)*, brown patch *(Rhizoctonia)*, summer patch *(Magnaporte)*, dollar spot *(Sclerotinia, Puccinia)*, powdery mildew *(Erysiphe graminis)*, leaf eyespot *(Helminthosporium vagans)*, stripe smut *(Ustilago striiformis)*, and flag smut *(Urocystis agropyri)*. Most *Poa* fungi appear, if at all, in warm weather, but gray snow molds *(Typhula, Pellicularia filamentosa)* often coat matted-down grasses soon after snowmelt in early spring.

The list of *Poa* invertebrate residents is impossibly long to list here. Few such residents associate exclusively with bluegrasses; rather, they tend to occupy ecological niches and guilds created and maintained by grasses generally. Since *Poa* species are among our most abundant grasses, populous invertebrate communities occur where these grasses grow. A 1971 Minnesota study found that the variety of animal life in pasture bluegrass stands appeared extremely abundant for a pure stand crop; most monoculture plantings or crops, by contrast, support a very few species that sometimes have an excessively high number of individuals. The Minnesota researchers suggested that "close resemblance of the bluegrass stands to the original prairie biome" might account for these results.

Focusing on spiders, for example, the researchers found 41 species present, the most abundant being *Araneus* and *Erigoninae* genera and *Tetrognatha laboriosa*. Common too are the grass spiders *(Agelina, Agelenopsis)*, funnel weavers whose webs spread flatly across the grass, becoming most visible in late summer's morning dew.

A 1984 study in Kentucky confirmed the previous findings as related to numbers of predatory insect species present in bluegrass stands. The most abundant species were ants (9 species, with the turfgrass ant, *Lasius neoniger,* prominent); rove beetles (Staphylinidae, 41 species); and ground beetles (Carabidae, 27 species). Such varied predator populations indicate a vast array of prey organisms, mainly other insects and invertebrates.

Several aphid species that suck the sap of bluegrasses include *Acyrthosiphon chandrani,* *Anoecia haupti,* and *Schizaphis agrostis.* Meadow plant bugs *(Leptopterna dolabrata),* elongate and variably colored, are often numerous on bluegrasses, as are grass thrips *(Anaphothrips obscurus),* minute, barely visible scrapers of plant epidermis. Some common hemipteran species include *Litomiris debilis, Stenodema trispinosum, Capsus cinetus,* and several others.

Short-horned grasshopper species common in bluegrass fields include *Aeropedellus clavatus,* with clubbed antennae. Aster leafhoppers *(Macrosteles quadrilineatus)* suck the sap of bluegrasses as well as many other plants. *Poa* grasses also host the mycoplasmalike aster yellows disease, of which these leafhoppers are vectors (see Asters). Other *Poa* leafhoppers include *Dorycephalus platyrhyncus,* a flattened, brown species; and *Doratura stylata,* masked like a raccoon. Look for the pleated egg cases of mantids, foremost insect predators; eastern species are mainly European mantids *(Mantis religiosa)* and Chinese mantids *(Tenodera aridifolia).*

Beetle larvae (grubs) that feed on bluegrass roots and rhizomes include May beetles *(Phyllophaga),* bluegrass billbugs *(Sphenophorus parvulus),* green June beetles *(Cotinis nitida),* Japanese beetles *(Popillia japonica),* northern masked chafers *(Cyclocephala borealis),* and European chafers *(Rhizotrogus majalis).* Dead patches in bluegrass pastures and lawns indicate the presence of a grub species or possibly bluegrass webworms *(Parapediasia teterrella).* These webworms, pyralid moth larvae, spin webbing on the turf surface; the yellowish gray adult moths fly low above lawns during daytime hours. The annual bluegrass weevil *(Listronotus maculicollis)* is a common root feeder on *P. annua.*

Larval mines in bluegrass leaves may indicate the feeding of tiny elachistid moth caterpillars, *Cosmiotes illectella.* Other caterpillar feeders on bluegrasses include the common arugisa *(Arugisa latiorella),* the black-banded owlet *(Phalaenostola larentioides),* the glassy cutworm *(Apamea devastator),* and the armyworm moth *(Pseudaletia unipuncta);* all are noctuid moths.

A number of butterflies, mainly skippers (Hesperiidae), feed as caterpillars on bluegrasses. These include the least skipper or skipperling *(Ancyloxypha numitor),* the garita skipperling *(Oarisma garita),* several Hesperia species, and the common roadside-skipper *(Amblyscirtes vialis),* among others. Most grass-feeding skipper caterpillars are themselves grass green in color. Other butterfly caterpillars that feed on bluegrasses include the little wood-satyr *(Megisto cymela),* finely hairy and greenish brown, and the common ringlet *(Coenonympha tullia),* long and slender, with 2 short tubercles on the last abdominal segment; the olive-brown ringlet butterflies fly low over grassy meadows.

Insect seed feeders on *Poa* include a common seed bug species, *Phlegyas abbreviatus.* Plant bugs (Miridae) are also numerous at times. In early-summer fields, the small, bug-eyed *Labops brooksi* may often be seen. The capsus bug *(Capsus cinetus),* invading flowerheads, can be a major bluegrass pest; it causes a visible condition known as silvertop when large numbers of flowerheads in a field die, resulting in a silvery-topped appearance.

Earthworms abundantly reside in lawns (if not made chemically toxic by pesticides and herbicides) and pastures. Moles, primarily carnivores, devour both earthworms and grubs. Mole tunnels and mounds, though perhaps unsightly on a lawn, can indicate either healthy or unhealthy turf grass—healthy if it supports earthworms, not so good if it supports numerous root-feeding beetle grubs. Snails, slugs, crustaceans such as sowbugs, and millipedes are common invertebrate scavengers of dead plant materials in lawns and pasture grasses.

Bluegrasses rank high as food plants for birds and mammals. Foliage consumers include American coots, wild turkeys, ruffed grouse, cottontail rabbits, moose, and, in the West, elk, mule deer, and bighorn sheep. Common seedeaters are voles, wild turkeys, ring-necked pheasants, prairie-chickens, mourning doves, house sparrows, and field, savannah, chipping, vesper, and white-crowned sparrows, among others.

Bluegrass fields provide favored nesting cover for blue-winged teal and, in some areas, sharp-tailed grouse.

Lore: Livestock farmers and landscape designers give bluegrasses mixed marks. Kentucky-bluegrass is more valued for pasture forage in eastern North America than in the West because in areas of less precipitation, its summer dormancy makes it a less important range forage. Called the "king of the pasture lands," it thrives in limestone soils and areas of abundant rainfall. Minnesota and Kentucky claim it as an important seed crop, but it is rarely cultivated for hay. Its palatability and nutritional value, especially in early growth stages, rank high. As a lawn grass, it provides the basis for most turf seed mixtures. It also tends to invade native grassland; once established, it can withstand heavy grazing, rapidly replacing more desirable but less competitive forage grasses. Prescribed burning programs more often seem to inhibit this grass's growth than rejuvenate it, which can be good or bad from a livestock producer's point of view. The plant's dense, sod-forming, underground biomass also makes it useful for erosion control.

Canada-bluegrass and annual bluegrass are less desirable plants from the pasture or turf viewpoint; indeed, they are often considered weeds. Canada-bluegrass generally grows in poorer, more acidic soils than *P. pratensis,* is sometimes used in pasture mixtures. Annual bluegrass, lighter green in color than the other two, is the least popular turf grass because of its poor heat and drought tolerance, its vulnerability to disease and insect attack, and its invasiveness. Despite these problems, its easy maintenance has made it the dominant turfgrass of many older golf greens in the northern United States. Rarely planted, *Poa annua* usually establishes itself in such cultivated habitats by its aggressive competitiveness with other turf grasses at cutting heights below 1 inch; higher growth discourages the germination of annual bluegrass.

Some botanists think that native Kentucky-bluegrass populations may have existed. While many native *Poa* species do occur, however, most grass specialists believe that all 3 common bluegrasses in this account originated in Eurasia and northern Africa. Some accounts credit Pennsylvania colonist William Penn for planting the first *P. pratensis* in North America. It "took much root," he reported, "and held and fed like old English ground." (The gardens of Pennsbury Manor near Tullytown, where this epochal 1685 introduction allegedly occurred, may still be visited.) From Penn's garden, according to tradition, the grass spread rapidly across America wherever pioneers cleared and plowed land. Native Americans called it "white man's foot grass" because it seemed to mark the foreign invader's footprints, following closely on his heels. Yet "regardless of where Kentucky bluegrass originated in the northern hemisphere," as one account stated, "it had plenty of time to migrate to and become well established in the middle Great Lakes region and the Ohio Valley before the first explorers, traders, hunters, and French missionaries entered the territories." A century after Penn's success, at any rate, the grass grew abundantly throughout eastern North America.

Lawn turf is an ecology unto itself when pesticides and weed killers have not rendered the grass virtually as inert as a rug (the so-called "industrial lawn" beloved by so many suburbanites). A lawn withdrawn from its chemical sustenance may decline precipitously until it can reachieve a restorative community of supportive organisms. "Today's lawn is a sickly, chemically dependent space filler," one botanist wrote. About 1 percent of the U.S. landmass is now blanketed by residential lawns; golf courses, campuses, parks, and other tended lawns bring the figure to 2 percent. Fine lawns are an American institution, but many of them are veritable biological deserts.

Yet the typical lawn that remains unblasted by chemical loads—consisting of Kentucky-bluegrass and 1 or 2 fescue *(Festuca)* species, say—may host an amazing variety of organisms, ranging from snails, earthworms, and spiders to more than 100 insect species, most of them minute and many preying upon others. And other organisms arrive as well. I have often watched European starlings, American robins, and northern flickers *anting* near the few anthills in my yard—plucking up ants and quickly inserting them into their plumage, perhaps as a defense against skin parasites. Jungle dramas occur amid the sheet webs and predatory stalkers in the green grasses fertilized by a judicious attitude of live and let live—an ecological attitude.

The name *bluegrass* may have derived from Canada-bluegrass, with its bluish green shade; the name was in popular use by 1750. *Poa* derives from the Greek word for grass.

Today Kentucky-bluegrass is so naturalized, if not native, that its name identifies a popular style of American country music. Kentuckian Bill Monroe and his Bluegrass Boys originated their unique sound about 1938, but the musical term "bluegrass" did not become widely accepted until 2 decades later.

Bluestem Grasses (*Andropogon* species). Grass family. Bluestems, native perennials, are usually identified by technical characters of the spikelets (flower clusters). The 3 most common species, however, show distinctive features that can be easily recognized without a hand lens. Bluestems flower in summer and fall. They remain standing when dry, turning conspicuously straw yellow or other tan or reddish shades.

Big bluestem *(A. gerardi)* stands 6 or more feet tall. It has long, flowering *racemes* (flower stalks) that branch radially from the tip of the stalk. The bristles *(awns)* that project from the flowers are sharply bent, and the bases of lower leaf blades and sheaths are often silky haired.

Little bluestem *(A. scoparius)* usually stands 2 or 3 feet tall. It branches along the stem, with fuzzy flowers and wiry branches that extend beyond the leaves, which tend to fold; the spikelets each bear a long, projecting bristle. Clumps of dried stems in fall and winter show a distinctive orange color.

Broom-sedge *(A. virginicus),* the most common bluestem, resembles little bluestem but is leafier, its flowers more fuzzy and feathery and tucked inside the leafy bracts. From a distance, the downy spikelets, which grow on the upper stem portion, may appear silvery ("like frost on the plant," wrote Thoreau). Its color in fall and winter is bright straw yellow.

Other names: Beardgrasses, because of their conspicuous terminal awns; bunchgrasses, because of their frequently clustered growth habit; forked beardgrass, turkeyfoot, or turkey claw *(A. gerardi),* for its radiating racemes that resemble a bird's foot; broom or prairie beardgrass, broom, wiregrass, purple wood grass *(A. scoparius);* broom-sage (broom-sedge, *A. virginicus,* is obviously not a true sedge).

Close relatives: Some 100 *Andropogon* species grow in warm temperate climates worldwide. Of the 30 or so species native to North America, about 6 inhabit eastern fields and prairies. Closely related grasses include sorghums *(Sorghum)* and Indian grasses *(Sorghastrum).* Some botanists place little bluestem in a separate slot as *Schizachyrium scoparium.*

Lifestyle: Anything blue colored on these plants resides almost wholly in the eye of the beholder; the bluish green shoots that sprout mostly unseen in early summer are said to account for the name bluestem.

Like most grasses, bluestems are bisexual and wind-pollinated (see Bluegrasses for grass flower structure). *Andropogon,* however, is distinctive in the fact that its flower spikelets occur in pairs, one stalked and one unstalked *(sessile).* Also, *Andropogon* stems are solid or pithy, not hollow as in most grasses.

Impressive indeed is big bluestem; vast seas of this tall, splay-flowered prairie grass greeted American pioneers, revealed good soil, told them where to settle and plow. Fire-maintained big bluestem often stood taller than a man, and its sod, built through millennia of prairie growth, provided—and still provides—the rich loam soils that underlie America's heartland agriculture.

Big bluestem's imposing height is topped by its
so-called turkeyfoot, the radiating flower spikes.

Big bluestem has short, scaly underground stems *(rhizomes)* and fibrous roots that may plunge 12 feet deep. This grass grows in large clumps, new stems cloning from the rhizomes; its lower leaves curl up when dry. Little bluestem likewise propagates by short rhizomes, seed, and tillers or sprouts. Length of little bluestem's dense roots usually exceeds the plant's height, reaching 5 to 8 feet down. Broom-sedge roots are much shallower, densely fibrous. All 3 species exhibit a bushy growth form, but the dense sods created by big and little bluestems produced prairie grassland that only John Deere's steel plowshares could break. Broomsedge clumps, poor sod formers, tend to grow in isolated, single-plant patches.

Big and little bluestems produce seed irregularly, often do not develop abundant seed every year; indeed, some stands produce only once every 5 to 10 years. Requirements of these 2 species are surprisingly exacting. They apparently demand a combination of optimal conditions, including abundant moisture and moderate temperatures at flowering time, in order to produce seed. Most of their reproduction, in fact, occurs vegetatively by means of their rhizomes.

Much research has focused on the relationship of fire and bluestems. A 1968 study, which indicated that a maximum interval of 3 years between burnings maintained the most vigorous stands of big bluestem, is fairly representative of recent work. The rejuvenative effects of prairie fire on bluestem growth have long been noted, but exactly how the process operates remains largely speculative. What makes the plants fire adaptive consists mainly in their dense, subsurface root systems that can rapidly "green up" a grassland burn with new sprouts. The present consensus is that fire benefits, and causes a growth surge in, bluestem mainly by removal of dead grass litter, thus exposing the new sprouts to more sunlight and warmth—rather than by fire release of plant nutrients that fertilize the soil, as has also been theorized. Other studies suggest that heat of the fire itself evokes a flowering response by destroying a "heat-labile floral inhibitor" in the root crown of the plant at the soil surface.

The existence of such an inhibitor, wrote biologist Nancy J. Petersen, "is consistent with the observation that flowering does occur but at a lower frequency in the absence of fire." In a 1950 study, observers noted that in the autumn, the dying stems in a bluestem clump tend to fall in a radiating or sunburst pattern, thus opening the surviving central crown of the stem clump to direct sunlight, encouraging early growth in spring. The researchers found that in dense stands, where the radiating stem falls covered neighboring crowns, new spring growth lagged some 3 to 4 weeks. Fire in such stands would no doubt produce a considerable rejuvenating effect.

Associates: Big bluestem's main habitats are the moist, highly fertile loams of the central states and eastern Great Plains. Little bluestem tolerates drier, more gravelly soils, and it extends farther west than big bluestem. Big and little bluestems have broadly overlapping ranges, however, and often associate. Broom-sedge is the "poor relation"; an indicator of low-fertility soils, it grows throughout the eastern half of the continent, often invading sandy fields.

Prairie fire tends to restrict and revert plant successional communities (or *seral stages*). Lightning ignited most presettlement prairie fires, but native tribes also burned the grasslands for various reasons. Ecologically, big and little bluestem prairies are sometimes regarded as examples of *fire climax*—that is, a plant community that remains stable as a result of regular fire passage. Historically, the climax prairie communities were complex, containing some 250 plant species, but dominated by big bluestem. A major influx of biodi-

Broom-sedge tends to grow in isolated clumps, its straw yellow stems and feathery seed spikes frequently indicating worn-out, infertile land.

versity in the tall grass prairie, research reveals, resulted from natural interruptions of various sorts—ant hills, mammal burrow systems including badger dens and gopher mounds, and relict bison wallows—that disrupted the uniform bluestem growth and provided openings and space for other plant species. "The mosaic of disturbances of different size that characterize plant communities," one researcher has concluded, may be "one factor that maintains habitat diversity."

Fungi parasites on bluestems are many; most of them attack leaves and stems. They include leaf rusts, cattail disease (*Epichloe typhina*, a white fungus that surrounds the stems in a tight sleeve), leaf spots, and tar spot (*Phyllachora luteomaculata*, producing black, glossy spots on the leaves). One of the most destructive grass fungi, sometimes found in bluestem stands, is ergot *(Claviceps)*, a dark sac fungus that replaces and mimics the seed.

Insect feeders on bluestem leaves include several grasshoppers; *Pseudopomala brachyptera*, a slant-faced species, feeds on both big and little bluestems. A common leafhopper on little bluestem is *Laevicephalus unicoloratus.*

Butterfly caterpillars include the common wood-nymph or grayling *(Cercyonis pegala)*, yellowish green. Many skipper species feed on bluestems, among them larvae of the common branded skipper *(Hesperia comma)* and the cobweb skipper *(H. metea).* These caterpillars, like most skippers, have necklike constrictions behind the head.

Common animal associates in tallgrass prairie dominated by big bluestem include a variety of reptiles, birds, and mammals. Ornate box turtles, slender glass lizards, garter and ribbon snakes, and bullsnakes are common reptiles. Resident birds include upland sandpipers, greater prairie-chickens, ring-necked pheasants, red-tailed hawks, American kestrels, horned larks, western meadowlarks, red-winged blackbirds, bobolinks, dickcissels, and brown-headed cowbirds. Snow geese relish the rhizomes, and seedeaters include several small songbirds; big bluestem provides choice food for indigo buntings. "In an average year," wrote ecologist Richard Brewer, "tallgrass prairies run 120 to 140 territorial [bird] males per 40 ha (about 100 acres)." Since many resident prairie birds are polygynous (1 male mating with 2 or more females), total bird populations may more than double the singing male counts. Broom-sedge also supplies an important fall and winter food reserve for ground finches, including dark-eyed juncos and chipping, field, and American tree sparrows, which pluck off the feathery plumes before consuming the attached seeds. Prairie-chickens and wild turkeys are reported seed consumers in Texas, probably feed on bluestems elsewhere as well.

Tallgrass prairie mammals include thirteen-lined and Franklin's ground squirrels, deer mice, meadow and prairie voles, badgers, white-tailed deer, and bison. As bison specialist Heather Smith Thomas pointed out, "The grazing animal has a unique and complementary relationship with the grass." The periodic grazing pressure of nomadic bison herds before pioneer settlement probably stimulated and invigorated the growth of prairie grasses—possibly to a greater extent than fire. Some evidence seems to indicate that even bovine saliva—that is, drooling—may contain substances that aid plant growth.

Big and little bluestems make palatable, nutritious livestock forage, especially in their earlier growth stages. Farmers still plant them in some areas for pasture forage and hay. Broom-sedge, on the other hand, is coarser, not favored as forage; in pastures, it is usually regarded as a weed.

Lore: In late fall, the reddish or straw-colored tufts of bluestem grasses stand out in the landscape, lending a distinctive autumnal cast to fields and roadsides where it is present. Broom-sedge, the commonest bluestem, decorates even the poorest sandy acres with islands of rich, warm color. Thoreau wrote a passage to broom-sedges in his journal of late August 1858, noting his "sympathy with them because they are despised by the farmer and occupy sterile and neglected soil."

Today the once-endless tallgrass prairie with its vistas of majestic big bluestem is largely a panorama from the past. Less than 1 percent of some 222,000 square miles of pre-settlement tallgrass prairie remains. John Deere's plow took only about 25 years—from 1837, when Deere introduced it—to cut and tame the prairie. Tallgrass range has been largely converted to corn and soybean agriculture. Little bluestem range is today primarily the American wheat belt. Isolated stems, stands, and preserves of big and little bluestems exist today mainly along railroads and old fencerows, in country cemeteries and relict prairie patches, consigned like native Americans to roadsides and reservations.

Several American tribes found *Andropogon* roots and rhizomes beneficial for various ailments. The Chippewa used a decoction of big bluestem for digestive problems; the Catawba boiled broom-sedge as a treatment for backaches. The Cherokee drank a leaf tea of broom-sedge for diarrhea (apparently a common ailment among Indians, to judge from the number of herbal remedies they used for it); and they and other tribes also used *Andropogon* leaf teas as a skin wash for sores, rashes, and other irritations.

Andropogon means "man's beard" in Greek, indicating the characteristic long, feathery awns—certainly a more descriptive term than "bluestem."

Blue-weed *(Echium vulgare).* Borage family. Identify this coarse alien biennial by its stiff, bristly, spotted stem; its rough, hairy leaves; and its down-curved, 1-sided flower spikes on which a single blue, tubular flower blooms at a time. It stands 1 to 3 feet tall.

Other names: Viper's bugloss, viper's herb, snake-flower, blue-thistle, blue devil, blue or wild borage, Our Lord's flannel.

Close relatives: Some 50 *Echium* species exist, all Old World natives. Purple viper's bugloss *(E. plantagineum)*, a shorter species, often decorates gardens. Family relatives include puccoons *(q.v.)*, false gromwells *(Onosmodium)*, buglosses *(Anchusa)*, comfreys *(Symphytum)*, and borage *(Borago officinalis)*.

Lifestyle: Often mistaken for a thistle because of its bristling appearance, blue-weed extends a deep taproot. It produces only a flat basal rosette of leaves the first year (or sometimes in several successive years if disturbed or in unfavorable conditions) and the erect flowering stem the second. The insect-pollinated flowers may range in color between lilac, sky blue, blue-violet, even purple (rarely white or pink), usually all the same color on a single plant and typically appearing from June to September. The tightly coiled flower spike (termed a "scorpoid inflorescence" in old books because of its curl like a scorpion's tail) gradually unfurls, opening a single flower that runs a sex-change course from male to female. As it opens, it projects 4 conspicuously red, pollen-abundant (male) stamens upon which insects alight. Then, after the stamens are spent, the pinkish (female) pistil elongates, the stems dividing into 2 small horns that stickily greet the incoming, pollen-bearing insects. This type of bisexual sequencing is termed *protandry*, a common mechanism that hinders self-pollination and promotes cross-pollination. Then another flower opens on the spike, repeating the progression, and flowering continues through summer.

Blue-weed reproduction occurs only by seed. The seeds are flattened, angular nutlets, occurring in tangled groups of four. Blue-weed produces prolific seed—500 to 2,000 per plant—and seeds may remain viable for several years.

Associates: "There the blue bugloss paints the sterile fields," wrote English poet George Crabbe in *The Village* (1783). Blue-weed favors dry, rocky habitats where dense stands may occur. It is a *calciphile*, a plant favoring limestone soils. Often, though, it stands solitarily in disturbed, infertile areas—gravelly roadsides, railroads, fields, where it often seems to function as a vegetative dust-catcher; its fibrous coating seems to attract windblown silt, sometimes giving the plant a grayish

Blue-weed's scrubby, dusty aspect protects it from herbivores, but its intricate blue flowers attract numerous insects.

appearance. Along with such plants as common burdock *(q.v.)* and common ragweed *(q.v.),* it adorns vacant lots. In Canada, it often associates in rocky pastures with 2 related alien plants: hound's tongue *(Cynoglossum officinale)* and gromwell *(Lithospermum officinale).*

Blue-weed's abundant pollen and nectar production attracts many insects—at least 67 species, according to one older study. These include several species of bees.

In England, a common blue-weed habitat is at the base of seaside dunes, where the plant typically hosts several uncommon insects—2 *Ethmia* moth caterpillars (a tiny oecophorid micromoth genus) and the minute seed weevil *(Ceutorhynchus* species), among others. New World species of these genera may likewise reside on the plant.

Blue-weed in flower is also a good place to look for pipevine swallowtail butterflies *(Battus philenor),* which feed on the nectar of this and other flowers.

The plant's bristled surfaces preclude its use as forage by mammals, even discourage climbing ants from exploring this plant. Information on seed consumption by birds and rodents is virtually nonexistent; blue-weed is apparently an insignificant food source for larger wildlife.

Lore: Since blue-weed only reached North America about 1683 from England, little usage of the plant by native Americans occurred (it took about 200 years for blue-weed to reach Michigan from its Virginia landfall). A substantial Old World medicinal lore exists, however, much of it based on the antiquated *doctrine of signatures* theory: Plant parts or shapes were believed to signal, by their supposed resemblances to human body parts or other organisms, their intended curative uses. Thus, because blue-weed stems are "speckled like a snake or viper," according to William Cole's *Art of Simples* (1656), and the seeds resemble the shape of a snake's head, the plant revealed its God-ordained purpose as a remedy for snakebite; probably some unfortunates have died believing this.

A decoction of the seeds in wine was also said to "comfort the heart and drive away melancholy" (a treatment less effective, probably, without the wine). A leaf tea promoted sweating and calming, a tonic that reputedly relieved everything from fevers and headaches to the nervous nellies—"strengthens the lungs and sharpens the wits," according to one herbal prescription. Blue-weed roots contain allantoin, an oxidation product of uric acid that indeed promotes cell proliferation and healing. The roots also produce a red dye. The only humanly edible part of this plant is the flowers, which crystallized, may be added to salads. Examine the plant's bristly hairs; many of them have blisterlike bases, as if "loaded"—they are, with a toxic alkaloid that may cause a rash on skin contact.

In New Zealand, blue-weed honey has been found to contain natural antibacterial properties useful in the current development of antibiotics that are effectively resistant to bacteria.

The unappealing word *bugloss* often used for this plant refers to neither bugs nor their sheen; it derives from the Greek word *bouglossus,* meaning "ox-tongued," referring to the leaf shape.

Bracken Fern *(Pteridium aquilinum).* Bracken family. Recognize this fern by its dry, open habitats; its height (2 to 5 feet); and its leaves *(fronds)* divided into 3 leathery, pinnate blades, or branches.

Other names: Brake, eagle fern, hog brake, western bracken fern.

Close relatives: Some 350 bracken family species exist, mainly in the tropics. Bracken fern is the only *Pteridium* species. Although it grows worldwide, several distinct varieties occur (along with a few botanists who name them separate species). Hay-scented fern *(Dennstaedtia punctilobula),* in the same family, is a North American representative of about 70 species.

Lifestyle: Bracken fern survives year-round, as do all ferns, but it produces its leafy stage—the full-grown fronds—only in summer. Because bracken ferns are not seed plants, they occupy (along with common horsetail) a unique position in this book. In ferns and a few other nonflowering plants, reproduction occurs by means of *alternation of generations;* that is, the tiny bisexual gametophyte, or *prothallus,* that germinates from a spore produces the visible plant, or *sporophyte,* which is the asexual spore-producing generation.

But bracken actually reproduces mainly by vegetative means—by budding from lateral branches of its *rhizomes* (underground stems). Unlike most ferns, which produce fronds in clusters from a central compact base, bracken fronds rise individually along the horizontal subsurface rhizome. Thus a given clump of brackens often consists of a single plant, its many erect fronds branching from a rhizome that may spread underground over many square feet. Rhizomes, up to an inch thick, may lie several inches to several feet (sometimes up to 10 feet) deep, extending horizontally 15 or more feet. Bracken rhizomes usually exist in 2 horizontal tiers or levels—the smaller upper level, which gives rise to the fronds and dense meshes of fine roots descending at intervals; and the deeper level, which stores food and drives growth. Long vascular strands, rare in other ferns, extend inside the rhizomes. The rhizomes also produce side branches that sprout new frond buds. Dormant buds also exist along all portions of the rhizomes; these come to life and sprout following a fire or other soil disturbance. A single bracken clone can spread to 400 feet in diameter, though this is not a typical span. The rhizomes live long in optimal circumstances; bracken clones in certain fire-maintained habitats may survive more than 1,000 years. In the bracken country of northern Michigan, one may see fragments of unearthed black rhizomes thickly scattered atop and along the dirt roads, the broken threads of a vast subsurface meshwork.

The young fronds, called *fiddleheads* or *croziers,* rise in a coiled shape—little balled fists, silvery gray and fuzzy haired, unfolding like a raptor's talons. Bracken produces its spores in tiny fruit dots *(sori)* lined along the overlapping edges *(indusia)* of leaflet margins ("they look as if they were hemmed," wrote one observer). Not all leaflets show these

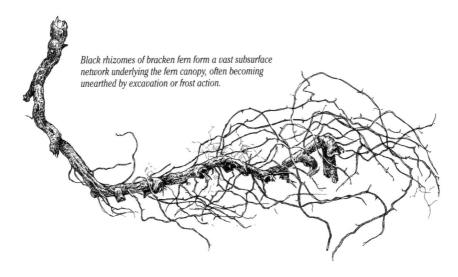

Black rhizomes of bracken fern form a vast subsurface network underlying the fern canopy, often becoming unearthed by excavation or frost action.

reflexed edges or produce spores, since spore reproduction is relatively rare in this fern, which proliferates mainly by clones and rhizomes. A single fertile frond may produce some 300 million spores annually, but spore production varies from year to year. Bracken spores germinate best on fire-scorched, sterile soils.

In northern regions, bracken fronds die back to the rhizome each fall, are replaced each spring. In some northern areas, however, observers have noted that fronds turn yellow and begin to die back before the first killing frost. Whether the yellowing is caused by maturity, soil moisture, changes in light values, or a critical temperature point inherent to the plant remains unknown. In autumn, the plants lie "fallen in their ranks," as Thoreau noted, paving the north country with a dry ground cover. The thick mat of dead fronds insulates the rhizomes from frost to some extent, also delays the rise in spring soil temperature and the emergence of frost-sensitive fiddleheads. In warmer regions, individual fronds may persist 2 or 3 years.

Another feature of bracken, uncommon in ferns as a group, is paired nectaries or glandular areas on the frond stalk *(rachis)* and leaflet stalk *(costa).* The hardly visible nectaries, located just beneath the branching point where the costa of each leaflet joins the rachis—and just beneath the point where the subleaflets *(pinnules)* join the costa—seldom exude visible droplets but make these surfaces slightly sticky.

Its deep-lying rhizomes protect bracken from extremes of heat, drought, freezing, and fire. Its fronds, however, are extremely vulnerable to freezing; the first touch of autumn frost turns the bracken seas brown. Even a quirky June frost rapidly kills the new fronds and fiddleheads, causing the rhizomes to activate dormant buds. Paradoxically, the emergent fiddleheads on open land, which appear sooner than in shaded areas because of the earlier-warming soil, often produce full fronds later than the shaded ferns, which usually emerge after frost danger is past. Thus the shaded sites often end up bracken-canopied earlier than the sunnier but frequently frost-stung open sites.

Associates: Bracken fern is a true citizen of the world, native to all continents except Antarctica. It is said to be one of the 5 commonest plants in the world; it is easily the most abundant wild fern in North America.

Sun-loving but highly shade-tolerant, bracken fern easily adapts to a variety of climatic and moisture conditions. Note the configuration of bracken fronds with the sun. In wide-open areas where sunlight blazes, they stand more or less straight up, arching over like elm boughs; but in shadier places, where brightness is scarcer, the fronds spread horizontally, presenting a tabled green surface for every photon. Bracken fern is one of the chief plant colonizers in eastern pine and oak forests following fire or land disturbance. In the northern burned-over timberlands and jack-pine plains, it covers acres, forming a waist-high green canopy in summer, a sea of frost-killed brown cover in the fall. Bracken spores seem to germinate best on recent burns. Sprouting fiddleheads are vulnerable to competition from other plants, but once the horizontal frond canopy spreads full-grown, bracken dominates the summer landscape—sometimes for decades, since its shade may hinder tree and shrub growth for many years. Bracken's *allelopathic* compounds (that is, plant chemicals that inhibit germination and growth of surrounding plants), released from both green and dead fronds, also help maintain bracken populations. Eventually, however, shrub and tree growth usually wins out and forest shade becomes denser, and the light-loving bracken finally declines and dies out.

Several conifer needle rust fungi—mainly of native fir species in western North America—inhabit bracken fern as an alternate host. The only fir-bracken rust that occurs to any extent in eastern North America is *Uredinopsis pteridis* on balsam fir *(Abies balsamea)*. It has a 2-year life cycle. Aeciospores produced on infected balsam needles infect bracken fiddleheads in spring. The infection produces urediniospores on fern fronds, and these spores blow to other bracken fronds, giving rise in late summer and fall to teliospores that overwinter in the dead fronds, germinating basidiospores the following spring. These wind-blown fourth-stage spores infect balsam needles in May and June, producing aeciospores the following spring.

Numerous other fungi also parasitize brackens, though none extensively. *Ceratobasidium, Mycosphaerella,* and *Puccinia* rusts, among others, occur. In Great Britain, where bracken fern is widely regarded as a pernicious weed, it invades pastures, also competes with and at times overwhelms such moorland plant associates as heather *(Calluna vulgaris)* and the rare moonwort fern *(Botrychium lunaria)*. Dense bracken growth is known to inhibit the growth of spruce and balsam fir seedlings—whether by shading or allelopathy remains uncertain—in areas of North America.

Despite its long-evolved toxic properties (see Lore), bracken fern hosts a large number and variety of insect consumers—more than 100 species worldwide. Owing to bracken's cosmopolitan distribution, however, the particular species of insect feeders vary widely. Most research on bracken associates has been done in Great Britain, where some 35 insect species are listed as bracken feeders. In North America, the number and diversity of insect bracken feeders apparently depend on climatic region.

The North American list includes short-horned and long-horned grasshoppers (Acrididae, Tettigoniidae); the western flower thrips *(Frankliniella occidentalis)*; stink bugs (Pentatomidae); delphacid planthoppers (Delphacidae); aphids *(Macrosiphum)*; and buprestid and leaf beetles (Buprestidae, Chrysomelidae). Noctuid moth caterpillars include the black arches *(Melanchra assimilis)*; the bracken borer *(Papaipema pterisii)*, which channels into the rhizomes; and fern moth caterpillars *(Callopistria)*, which feed on the foliage. Inchworm or geometer moth caterpillars include 2 *Petrophora* species and the pale homochlodes *(Homochlodes fritillaria)*. Fly larvae feeders include midges *(Chirosa, Dasineura)* and anthomyiids *(Anthomyia)*, among others. A few species of sawfly larvae *(Tenthredo livida* and others) also feed on bracken.

Insect predators on bracken include jumping spiders (Salticidae) and ladybird beetles (Coccinellidae). Bracken nectary feeders often include leafhoppers (Cicadellidae), ladybird beetles, flies, parasitic wasps, bumblebees *(Bombus)*, and honeybees *(Apis mellifera)*. Before I knew about the existence of the invisible nectaries, I used to watch bumblebees flying beneath the bracken canopy, bumping into the stalks as if hunting or foraging. I remained puzzled about this behavior for years, until I learned about bracken nectaries and that bees knew all about them. Foremost nectary feeders, however—and probably bracken's main animal associates—are ants. Some 18 species of 3 subfamilies—Dolichoderinae, Myrmicinae, and Formicinae—are known to climb and forage on bracken. Nectar secretion and ant activity are said to be highest in the late fiddlehead stage of frond development, just before the fronds fully open. Past researchers have sometimes defined this association as mutualistic—that is, with both fern and ants deriving benefit from it, the ants obtaining nourishment, the bracken obtaining protection by the ants from attack by caterpillar munchers and borers. Several more recent studies, however, have found scant evidence that ants deter herbivorous insects on bracken.

Bracken's height and density provide ample nesting and resting cover for a variety of creatures. One summer, during an irruption of forest tent caterpilars *(Malacosoma disstria)*,

Nectaries below the leaflet angles of bracken, though usually invisible, often attract ants and bees beneath the overhead frond canopy.

I noted an abundance of the moth cocoons attached to bracken foliage. In Britain, sheep ticks implicated as transmitters of Lyme disease inhabit dried bracken litter, but no direct association between ticks and bracken has been discovered elsewhere.

I have found indigo buntings nesting in bracken foliage, and chestnut-sided warblers occasionally build nests in the fronds as well. Birds that use dried bracken as nesting material include cuckoos, hermit thrushes, and white-throated sparrows.

Grazing mammals usually avoid bracken unless forage is extremely scarce. Elk and white-tailed deer graze infrequently on the bitter foliage, mostly on fiddleheads, and cottontail rabbits occasionally eat fronds and rhizomes. Goats are the only livestock that consume the plant with any regularity. Thoreau noted new fronds eaten off by rabbits or woodchucks, and I once watched a porcupine consuming a June fiddlehead from its furled top down. The mountain beaver, a burrowing rodent (not a true beaver) of the Pacific Northwest, is also one of the few mammals that regularly consume bracken, cutting and caching it. Passage of larger mammals through bracken stands can often be traced; bent or broken fronds mark the aislelike trails. Deer often bed down in high-standing bracken during daytime, and a variety of birds and mammals find shelter and cover beneath the dense canopy.

Lore: Most accounts agree that bracken foliage is toxic to humans and grazing mammals alike, but sources frequently differ as to degree, causes, and effects of bracken's toxicity. Alarmist reactions have occurred in Scotland, where the plant is rampantly spreading "out of control," according to one recent report. Scientists there worry about high levels of airborne bracken spores in late summer and fall; the spores, it seems, have caused respiratory cancers in laboratory rats. "It is a nasty plant with high toxicity and definite carcinogenic properties," concluded one researcher.

Bracken poisoning in any case is cumulative; dire effects appear only after the plants have been ingested over a period of time. Many sources list bracken as edible in its tender fiddlehead form; bracken fiddleheads and starch from the rhizomes are especially relished in Japan (some sources attribute Japan's relatively high rate of stomach cancer to this diet). Many native American tribes not only ate the fiddleheads, but also dug up bracken rhizomes in fall and winter, drying, roasting, and pounding them into flour for making dough cakes. Today, however, most wild-foods and forage experts caution against food use of the plant for humans and livestock at any time. Even the fiddleheads have been implicated in carcinogenic and mutagenic effects—mainly intestinal, bladder, and throat cancers—in humans and grazing mammals. Two culprit toxins have been identified: thiaminase, an enzyme that destroys B-vitamin reserves; and ptaquiloside, a cancerous compound that can be passed into milk from cows fed on bracken. Young fronds also release hydrogen cyanide when damaged.

Human usage of bracken fern has embraced many forms. Roofing thatch, fuel, livestock bedding, and green mulch and compost were its chief uses, some of which continue today. The plant became a kind of legal tender in some places during the Middle Ages, given and accepted in dry bulk as rent payment. Bracken ash became a source of potash for soap, bleach, and glass making until 1860. Rhizome substances tanned leathers and dyed wool yellow.

Ecologically, bracken performs important roles. It reduces plant competition by its production and release of allelopathic chemicals and by shading out lower or emergent plants; and it aids shade-tolerant plant growth by the shelter ("nursery") protection of fronds. Bracken rhizomes also perform a function similar to that of mycorrhizal fungi in enabling transformation of soil phosphorus into a form usable by plants. And because bracken ferns are extremely sensitive to acid rain, the plant is regarded as a useful indicator species for signaling this type of air pollution. Bracken growth not only succeeds ground fire, it also promotes it by producing a highly flammable layer of dried fronds each fall.

Bracken also serves another, more informal indicator function, one that cuts across the seasons. In the north-country summer, a full-grown bracken canopy stands about "snow-high," giving the observer an approximate idea of the winter snow depth past—and to come.

Brome-grasses *(Bromus* species). Grass family. Most of these large, coarse grasses, which stand a foot or more tall, include both annual and perennial species. Their visible identity marks are subtle. Leaf blades are flat, tapering to a sharp tip, often etched with a crinkled W mark crossing the leaf midpoint or higher. The flower- and seedheads *(panicles),* open and spreading, often droop to one side when mature. Florets of most species each terminate with a long or short bristle. The hard, enlarged area at the base of the floret is slightly hairy.

Our most common species include smooth brome *(B. inermis)*, an alien perennial with flowering branches angled slightly upward and very short floret bristles; cheat or chess *(B. secalinus)*, an alien annual showing seeds without bristles or with minute ones; and downy brome *(B. tectorum)*, another alien annual that has fuzzy leaves and flower scales, strongly drooping branches, and long floret bristles, a plant that tends to sprawl at its much-branched base.

Other names: Awnless brome, Hungarian brome, Austrian brome, Russian brome *(B. inermis)*; wheat-thief, Williard's brome-grass *(B. secalinus)*; junegrass, Mormon oats, downy chess, military grass, cheatgrass *(B. tectorum)*. The name "brome" refers mainly to the perennial species, "chess" or "cheat" to the annual bromes.

Close relatives: Some 21 of 43 *Bromus* species reside in eastern North America. These include rescue-grass *(B. wildenowii)*, soft chess *(B. hordaceus)*, hairy chess *(B. commutatus)*, Japanese chess *(B. japonicus)*, and ripgut-grass *(B. rigidus)*. Worldwide, brome-grasses, which mainly reside in temperate regions, number about 100 species.

Lifestyle: Bromes include several forage grasses that often escape to fields and road-sides plus a number of species widely regarded as weeds and invasive plant pests. Most bromes flower in spring, producing seeds in late spring and summer (see Bluegrasses for grass flower structure). Many annual bromes also develop sharp bristles *(awns)* on seeds, making them hazardous for livestock forage (hence the name ripgut-grass). Perennial bromes reproduce by sprouting from underground stems *(rhizomes)* and from seed; the annual species grow from seed alone. Individual rhizomes survive for about a year.

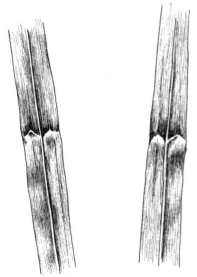

Smooth brome, flowering in late spring and early summer, has 4 to 10 florets on each spikelet. It produces a dense, durable sod owing to its spreading rhizomes. This grass survives periods of drought and flooding plus extremes of heat and cold; it becomes dormant in dry summer periods, rejuvenating in autumn coolness and moisture. Agronomists have developed numerous strains and cultivars for various regions where smooth brome is grown for forage, hay, and erosion control. Smooth brome, unlike many brome species, is reproductively self-incompatible, requires cross-pollination to produce seed. When the bisexual florets are pol-

A characteristic identity mark on brome-grasses is the crinkled W mark on the flat-bladed leaves.

linating, they cast visible clouds of pollen in the fields, cross-fertilizing and producing seed that may vary in abundance from less than 50 to more than 10,000 per plant.

Cheat, one of the most invasive annual grasses of grain fields and overgrazed landscapes, has a shallow, fibrous root. Spikelets contain 5 to 15 seeds. A prolific seed producer, cheat does not easily vacate agricultural land once it gains a foothold. According to weed botanist Ada E. Georgia, a professor at Cornell University sowed a pound of it "and reaped ninety-nine pounds of seed; and as they are quite small and light, there are nearly as many seeds in a pound as there are wheat kernels in a bushel." Cheat seeds may remain viable for several years.

Downy brome, so called because of its fuzzy leaf blades, has a spreading, extremely fibrous root system, typically extending about a foot deep and notable for its ability to extract soil moisture. A downy brome density of 50 plants per square foot can remove soil water to a depth of more than 2 feet, permanently wilting such plant competitors as winter wheat. Downy brome typically germinates in the fall, overwinters as a small seedling, then resumes growth in early spring. In order to flower, most bromes, including downy, require a period of cold exposure *(vernalization)*, whether in seed, seedling, or (in the case of *Bromus* perennials) rhizome-shoot stages. Downy brome, well adapted to cold, can rapidly extend its roots through winter at soil temperatures just above freezing. As downy bromes flower in heavy, drooping panicles, they assume a silvery, shiny look, maturing to reddish purple. Downy brome flowers are mostly self-pollinated and self-fertile *(autogamous)* clones; little or no outcrossing occurs. The long-awned seeds ripen in June and July, are simply shed from the plant, and may remain viable in the soil for 2 to 5 years.

Associates: The alien annual bromes compete both with field crops and with native grassland vegetation. Once the roots of any grass extend lower than about 20 inches, however, that grass becomes relatively free of dominance by the shallower-rooted annual bromes. Erosion, overgrazing, and worn-out land invite annual brome invasion, but it also intrudes into fields of winter wheat and alfalfa, into pastures and rangeland. Downy and Japanese bromes often associate, whereas neither of these annual bromes typically survives in stands of perennial smooth brome. Smooth brome, a much more desirable forage grass than the annuals, is frequently sown with a legume such as alfalfa or clover for hay. The nitrogen supplied by legume root nodules (see Alfalfa) nourishes brome productivity. Once established, the dense sod of smooth brome discourages shrub competition and invasion of annual plant species.

Bromes are subject to an array of parasitic fungi, most of which affect other grasses as well. One source listed 61 blight, powdery mildew, leaf-spot, smut, and rust fungi that exhibit a variety of leaf and stem spotting, flower infection, and lesions on brome-grasses. Common fungi include *Fusarium* (snow mold), *Helminthosporium* blights, *Puccinia* (leaf rusts), and *Ustilago bulleta* (head smut). Some of them, such as crown rust *(Puccinia coronata)* and stem rust *(P. graminis)*, require alternate hosts to complete their life cycles—buckthorns *(Rhamnus)* for crown rust, American and common barberries *(Berberis canadensis, B. vulgaris)* for stem rust. Probably the most dangerous fungus—one that makes affected grasses poisonous to livestock—is ergot, caused by *Claviceps purpurea*, a sac fungus that produces a sticky "honeydew" in the flowerheads that attracts flies and other insects; black growths *(sclerotia)* develop in place of seeds, later producing spore-bearing organs.

Mimicking fungal infection is halo blight, marked by streaks and haloed spots on leaves, caused by a bacterium *(Pseudomonas coronafaciens)*. The brome mosaic virus *(Marmor graminis)*, occurring on smooth brome, causes leaf lesions, yellow streaking, and eventual death of the plant. Nematodes (roundworms) of the genus *Xiphinema* are often vectors of the virus. Other nematodes found in smooth brome as root parasites include *Ditylenchus, Heterodera*, and *Meloidogyne*, among other genera.

Spider mites (Tetranychidae) and thrips (Thysanoptera) forage on brome leaves and flowerheads. Grasshoppers—especially the lesser migratory grasshopper *(Melanoplus sanguinipes)*—frequently feed on smooth brome. Another common grasshopper resident of brome fields is *Phoetaliotes nebrascensis*, the big-headed grasshopper. A common brown leafhopper found in brome fields is *Athysanus argentarius*.

The yellowish larva of a wheat pest, the wheat stem sawfly *(Cephus cinctus)*, bores into smooth brome stems as alternate hosts to wheat stalks. Wheat stem maggots *(Meromyza americana)*, the larvae of frit flies, also tunnel into brome stems. Glassy cutworms *(Apamea devastator)*, noctuid moth caterpillars, cut stems at or near ground surface.

Several wainscot moths *(Leucania)*, also noctuids, feed as caterpillars on bromes and other grasses. Feeders on maturing seeds include larvae of the bromegrass seed midge *(Stenodiplosis bromicola*, mainly on smooth brome), a gall gnat; the stink bug *Aelia americana*, brownish in color; and larvae of chalcid flies (Chalcididae). Harvester ants *(Pogonomyrmex)* collect brome seeds and store them in their nests.

Both seeds and foliage of bromes are widely consumed by bird and mammal species. Seedeaters include ruffed grouse, ring-necked pheasants, horned larks, savannah and vesper sparrows, plus chipmunks and

Numerous fungi parasitize brome-grass leaves, especially as the leaves age in summer.

mice. Canada geese devour brome seedlings; greater prairie-chickens, wild turkeys, cottontail rabbits, and white-tailed deer also forage on the plants.

Lore: A unique feature of grass anatomy in many species occurs inside the rigid, hollow stems, an adaptation to strong prairie winds. Thin, pliable disks stretch across the stem interior at regular intervals; they crumple when a high wind bends the stem, but once wind pressure abates, they spring back into circular shape, erecting the stem again. "Grass doesn't sway in the wind so much as it springs," biologist Carl Zimmer wrote.

Smooth brome, the "friendliest" brome to farmers, makes a fine forage for livestock, is widely planted for this purpose. Its rhizomes also bind soil effectively, making this grass useful for stabilizing roadside banks and other erosion control. This Eurasian native was unknown in America until 1884, when it was introduced (probably from Hungary) into California; plantings rapidly spread across the continent, but American interest in grasses as crops soon languished. The midwestern drought years of the 1930s brought smooth brome, the foremost alien grass survivor of drought-devastated landscapes, back into prominence as a hay and forage grass. It remains one of the main pasture grasses of North American northern and middle latitudes. Today about 34 smooth brome crop varieties ("cultivars") exist in the United States.

Downy brome, also a continentwide resident, has been a bane especially in the western Great Basin region, where years of overgrazing have invited its invasion and replacement of native grasses and sagebrush. As far back as 1940, conservationist Aldo Leopold wrote about this grass, which he called cheat: "The honey-colored hills that flank the northwestern mountains derive their hue not from the rich and useful bunchgrass and wheatgrass which once covered them, but from the inferior cheat which has replaced these native grasses. The motorist who exclaims about the flowing contours that lead his eye upward . . . is unaware of this substitution. It does not occur to him that hills, too, cover ruined complexions with ecological face powder." Downy brome, drying by late summer, clothes the landscape with a flammable tinder, ready to spark wildfires at far greater frequency than the native grasses. "It is impossible to fully protect cheat country from fire," Leopold remarked. Yet newly sprouted downy brome in the fall and early spring provides a suitable livestock forage; probably "the lamb chop you ate for lunch was nurtured on cheat during the tender days of spring," wrote Leopold. He also pointed out that "cheat reduces the erosion that would otherwise follow the overgrazing that admitted cheat." By summer, however, the yellowish mature plant with its masses of prickly awns has become a worthless forage. Downy brome entered North America from Mediterranean Europe during the mid-1800s, had spread throughout the continent by 1914.

Of the other brome called cheat *(B. secalinus),* someone once said that probably the first settler who planted wheat in America sowed some cheat with it (both plants are aliens). So suddenly abundant did cheat appear amid their wheat that some farmers added awe to the mixture, believing that some of their wheat stalks transformed into cheat as they grew. To avoid accidentally sowing cheat with wheat, smarter farmers stirred their wheat seed in a barrel of water; the cheat seeds floated and could thus be removed.

The word *bromus* is Greek for "oat"; superficial resemblances of these plants to oats *(Avena)* has often been noted.

Buckwheat *(Fagopyrum esculentum)*. Smartweed family. Recognize buckwheat by its arrowhead-shaped leaves attached in swollen joints to the reddish stem. Loose, branching clusters of dish-shaped, greenish white or pink flowers top this 1- to 2-foot-tall alien annual.

Other names: Brank, crap, corn-heath, duck-wheat, goose buckwheat, Indian-wheat, Saracen's-corn, Saracen's-wheat.

Close relatives: Some 15 Eurasian *Fagopyrum* species exist. India wheat or tartary buckwheat *(F. tataricum)*, along with buckwheat, is widely cultivated. Other relatives include knotweeds and smartweeds (both *q.v.*), including wild and false buckwheats; curly dock *(q.v.)*; and rhubarb *(Rheum rhabarbicum)*. Buckwheat is unrelated to wheat *(Triticum aestivum)*, a grass.

Lifestyle: Buckwheat, a crop plant that has widely escaped, has a long flowering season, from June into September, so plants in almost every stage of development may be seen throughout summer. Sprouting anew from seed each year, buckwheat forms a low ground canopy where sown as a crop, effectively shading out competing weed growth. This buckwheat species displays a floral form called *heterostyly,* consisting of flowers differing in length of their *styles* (the stalklike parts of the female pistils). Two types of flowers exist, both lacking petals: *pin*-type flowers, with long (female) pistils and short (male) stamens; and *thrum*-type flowers, with short pistils and long stamens. Such dimorphism in flowers induces self-incompatibility, increasing the likelihood of cross-pollination from other buckwheats. Buckwheat begins flowering 5 to 6 weeks after it germinates, and the insect-pollinated flowers can produce mature seed in about 2 weeks. The triangular, beechnutlike, 1-seeded fruits *(achenes)* protrude from the sepals, readily dropping when mature. Buckwheat's taproot, along with fibrous lateral roots, may extend 18 to 24 inches deep.

Buckwheat tends to *transpire* (that is, evaporate water from its leaves) so rapidly that it may wilt in the midday sun, recovering at night. Yet its water requirements are not large, and it tolerates a wide range of soil moisture and acidity. The plant may also *lodge* (lean over) or break in the wind and heavy rains. It is extremely sensitive to cold, so its entire life cycle occurs between the last spring frost and the first one of autumn.

Associates: Buckwheat thrives along roadsides, fencerows, railroads. It favors cool, moist climates for optimal growth.

Common fungal growths on buckwheat include ramularia leaf spot *(Ramularia)*, which causes a frosty or mildewlike spotting on leaf undersides and greenish spotting on upper leaf surfaces; downy mildew *(Peronospora ducometi);* and root rot *(Rhizoctonia soleni).* Other fungi include *Ascochyta* and *Phomopsis* blights, powdery mildew *(Erysiphe polygoni),* and leaf spot *(Phyllosticta polygonorum).*

Nematodes or roundworms are common root parasites, infiltrating the lateral fibrous root mass and inhibiting water uptake. Affected plants frequently die. The root lesion nematode *(Pratylynchus penetrans)* sometimes occurs in high density on buckwheat.

Numerous insects forage on the plant. Wireworms (larvae of click beetles, Elateridae) are common root feeders, and aphids (Aphididae) suck sap on the stems.

On the flowers, look for small, oval, flattened, black-and-white bugs; insidious flower bugs *(Orius insidiosus)* and minute pirate bugs *(O. tristicolor)* both prey on aphids, thrips, and mites. Especially attracted to buckwheat flowers are syrphid flies (Syrphidae), also called hover flies or sweat bees; species include *Allograpta obliqua, Syrphus* and *Tosomerus* species, and the drone fly *(Eristalis tenax).* Honeybees *(Apis mellifera)* are probably buckwheat's chief pollinators and nectar collectors. Wasp nectar feeders include thread-waisted wasps *(Sphex), Cerceris,* sand-loving wasps *(Tachytes),* spiny digger wasps *(Oxybelus),* potter wasps *(Eumenes),* paper wasps *(Polistes),* hornets *(Vespula),* and spider wasps (Pompilidae).

The tarnished plant bug *(Lygus lineolaris),* brownish and mottled, sucks juices from the leaves and flowers. Twiglike caterpillars of the cross-lined wave moth *(Calothysanis amaturaria),* an inchworm, feed on buckwheat and smartweeds. Most destructive to buckwheat is probably the Japanese beetle *(Popillia japonica),* which feeds en masse on many plants; on buckwheat, it mainly attacks the flowerheads.

White-tailed deer and cottontail rabbits graze on the plant. For many waterfowl, gamebirds, and songbirds, buckwheat seed is a choice food. Seed foragers include American black ducks, mallards, green-winged teal, northern pintails, American widgeons, ring-necked pheasants, wild turkeys, greater prairie-chickens, northern bobwhites, gray partridges, mourning doves (which favor the seeds at backyard bird feeders), American crows, horned larks, cardinals, and white-throated sparrows, among others. Fox squirrels also relish the seeds. Wildlife food patch plantings often include buckwheat as a nutritious seed source for birds.

Lore: Human usage of buckwheat consists mainly of flour ground from the seed, often an ingredient of pancake mixes and pastas. Most buckwheat grown in North America (mainly in New York and North Dakota) is exported to Japan, where it forms the chief ingredient of soba noodles, a diet staple. The groats (inner parts of the dehulled seed) are used in cereals or, roasted, as kasha in traditional Jewish and Polish dishes.

The plant produces high amounts of rutin, a flavenoid glycoside that reduces cholesterol and blood pressure in humans; of vitamins B1 and B2; and of lysine and iron. Some people, however, become allergic to buckwheat protein. A continuous diet of buckwheat cakes may produce skin rashes, and occupational asthma occurs among workers in Japanese soba shops. The other main food produced from buckwheat is honey; dark and distinctively flavored, it is prized by gourmets. One beehive per acre of buckwheat may produce up to 150 pounds of honey per year.

Other uses of buckwheat include livestock feed and green manure. Buckwheat hulls have been collected for mulches, pillow and mattress stuffing, and packing material. One of the plant's most important agricultural uses is as a smother crop for controlling weeds such as quack-grass, thistles, leafy spurge, and Russian knapweed. Decomposing buckwheat roots are apparently *allelopathic* to (that is, chemically inhibit) the germination of weed competitors. Buckwheat plants also acquire phosphorus from the soil by means of root exudates and transform it to a usable form for other plants.

Once a much more common crop and food than today, buckwheat was apparently one of the first plants cultivated by American colonists, who brought it to the New World. Its origins are obscure; perhaps a native of China, it was introduced into Europe about 1400. Foremost world producers today are Belarus, the Ukraine, and China.

Scots, it is said, coined the word *buckwheat* from the Anglosaxon *boc* ("beech") and *whoet* ("wheat"), apparently because of the achenes' resemblance to beechnuts.

Burdock, Common *(Arctium minus).* Aster family. Recognize this familiar alien perennial by its 3- to 5-foot height; its lavender, thistlelike flowerheads, which become round, adherent burs; and its large, untoothed, rhubarblike leaves.

Other names: Bur, cocklebur (a name that usually designates related *Xanthium* species), beggar's buttons, cockle buttons, cuckoo buttons, clotbur, bardane, wild rhubarb, many others.

Close relatives: Five *Arctium* species exist, all natives of Eurasia. In North America, common burdock's less common relatives include woolly or cotton burdock *(A. tomentosum)* and great burdock *(A. lappa).* Burdock kin also include Canada thistle *(q.v.)* and all other aster family plants.

Lifestyle: "Literally by hook or by crook," wrote naturalist Neltje Blanchan of burdock's round, prickly burs, "they steal a ride on every switching tail, every hairy dog and woolly sheep, every trouser-leg or petticoat." Closely examined, the burs show hooked bristles, actually bracts, seedcases well equipped to snag any passing hide or clothing. The burs typically remain on the dried flower stalks over winter, sometimes much longer. Each plant can produce more than 100 burs; each bur holds about 40 *achenes* (1-seeded fruits).

Although commonly designated a biennial (that is, a plant with a 2-year lifespan), burdock is actually a short-lived perennial that flowers only once in its life. Before that, however, it may produce its large-leaved basal rosette for several years in succession. Such plants are called *semelparous* (once-flowering) *perennials* or *facultative biennials.*

The key trigger for burdock flowering is size rather than age of the plant. The rosettes of basal leaves (each one "not infrequently long and wide enough to hold a baby," wrote weed lorist Pamela Jones) must reach a critical size before flowering can occur.

The size of common burdock's huge basal leaves determines whether the plant will produce a flower stalk in any given year.

(This size index can be figured by multiplying the total number of leaves by the centimeter length of the longest leaf blade; a product number in the range of 150 indicates imminent flowering.) Rosette size does not accurately indicate the plant's age, however, since competition and crowding from surrounding plants may slow rosette development considerably.

Unlike many flowers of the aster family, burdock has only tubular disk florets, no radiating ray florets as in daisies and sunflowers. Flowers appear from July into October. Burdock's tubular florets are bisexual and insect-pollinated. The half-inch disk becomes the hitchhiking bur.

Burdock produces heaps of biomass. One study indicated that amounts of above- and belowground biomass were about equal. The plant's large, fleshy taproot may descend 3 feet or so, and each rosette or lower leaf may extend more than a foot long and broad. The photosynthate energy stored in the taproot ultimately produces the flowering stems, a process called *bolting.* Burdock reproduces only by seeds, which remain viable for at least a year, probably longer. It often grows in small patches, resulting from seed dumping by parent plants that once grew at the site.

Associates: Burdock cannot be labeled a truly invasive weed, for it rarely intrudes into cultivated fields. Tilling usually controls and eradicates burdock populations. Its favored havens are the disturbed soils of roadsides, railroads, fencerows, vacant lots, and around sheds and old buildings. It tends to favor partially shaded sites over those in full sun. Especially in the rosette stage, when leaves are large and sprawl low to the ground, burdock covers and shades out competing plant growth. In later erect growth, the arrangement of leaves on the stem, with each level angled by its *petioles* (leaf stalks) and the upper leaves smaller than lower ones, results in a vaguely pyramidal form that allows maximum light exposure on each level.

Frequent plant associates include grasses such as smooth brome *(Bromus inermis, q.v.)* and quack-grass *(Elytrigia repens),* plus such common weeds as fleabanes, Canada thistle, Queen Anne's lace, common dandelion, common yarrow, yellow rocket (all *q.v.*), and white campion *(Silene latifolia).*

Pollinating insects include a roster of bees: honeybees *(Apis mellifera),* bumblebees *(Bombus),* leafcutting bees *(Megachile),* andrenid bees *(Andrena),* small carpenter bees *(Ceratina),* halictid bees *(Halictus),* and others. European cabbage butterflies *(Pieris rapae)* and soldier beetles *(Chauliognathus)* are also common pollinators.

Foliage feeders on burdock include several insects. Grasshoppers sometimes defoliate rosettes and flowering stems. Solitary caterpillars of the painted lady butterfly *(Vanessa cardui),* also known as the cosmopolite, create webbed nests on upper leaf surfaces of burdock and other aster family plants, sometimes binding several edges of a leaf together as it grows. The yellowish green, spiny caterpillar emerges from the nest to feed on green leaf tissue, eventually suspending itself from the plant in a pupa or chrysalis, from which it emerges as an orange-patterned adult butterfly. This butterfly raises 2 broods per year in the North; like the monarch butterfly, it is migratory.

Another foliage feeder is a leaf-mining fly larva, *Agromyza maculosa,* which channels mines in leaf tissue.

Several stem-boring moth caterpillars feed on burdock. The burdock borer moth *(Papaipema cataphracta),* the northern burdock borer moth *(P. arctivorens),* and the rigid sunflower borer moth *(P. rigida)* are the foremost stem borers, all noctuids. White, seed-eating gelechiid moth caterpillars, *Metzneria lappella,* introduced from Eurasia, bore into the flowerhead, cementing several seeds together to form silk-lined cavities. Adults of these so-called burdock moths emerge in midsummer.

Ring-necked pheasants, killdeers, European starlings, American goldfinches, and probably other finches and sparrows consume the seeds, though not a choice food. Livestock and ruminants do not relish the plant, but they probably account for much of its spread, carrying the matted seedheads in their manes, tails, or wool, dispersing them where the animals rub against fences, trees, or shrubs.

Lore: The name *burdock* derives from the Latin "burra," or lock of wool, presumably owing to the intimacy of sheep with the burry seedheads. Common burdock apparently arrived in North America with early English and French colonists. The burs are dangerous only when they lodge in skin, eyes, or ears of grazing mammals or pets or when ingested with other vegetation—if swallowed, the bur may form the core of a "hairball" mass in the digestive tract. Occasionally a small bird such as a hummingbird or kinglet becomes ensnared by a bur cluster, fatally exhausting itself in trying to pull loose.

Burdock's food, medicinal, and camp uses have long been known. The peeled, raw or boiled stem provides a nourishing, asparaguslike food (its flavor "a blend of celery and potato, with perhaps a soupçon of cucumber," according to one weed eater); roots and young leaves also become edible after boiling to remove their bitterness. Root and leaf teas, both taken internally and applied externally, treat a variety of ailments. The leaves make effective poultices for skin sores or rashes. Some sources say that native Americans used the plant extensively for medicinal purposes, but this seems unlikely, given its immigrant history.

The strongly adherent burs find practical use as substitute buttons or temporary patchwork devices for cloth or clothing. Indeed, it is claimed that the fabric fastener Velcro, invented by Swiss engineer Georges de Mestral in 1948, originated from his microscopic examination of burdock's spiny seedheads when he removed burs from his dog's coat following a hunt in the Alps.

Great burdock *(A. lappa),* a larger plant, is raised commercially, its roots harvested, dried, and packed as an organic food.

Bush-clovers *(Lespedeza* species). Pea family. All bush-clovers have untoothed trifoliate (3-leaflet) leaves and terminal, often bristly spikes. Otherwise, bush-clover species appear variable in size, lifestyle, and form. Some of these legumes are annuals and some are woody shrubs, though native lespedezas are all perennial herbs. Some trail and sprawl, though most stand erect 1 to 3 feet tall. Flowers vary from white and yellowish to purple and pink, depending on species. Bush-clovers also hybridize widely, so species identification is not always simple.

Native perennial bush-clovers include round-headed bush-clover *(L. capitata),* with cream-white bristly, knoblike flower clusters; slender bush-clover *(L. virginica),* with short purple flower clusters; violet bush-clover *(L. violacea),* with solitary purple flowers in loose terminal heads; and trailing bush-clover *(L. procumbens)*, with a reclining or trailing stem, downy stems and leaves, and purplish flowers. Sericea or Chinese bush-clover *(L. cuneata)* is an alien perennial forage plant with cream-yellow flowers. The 2 annual species, both Asian imports, are Korean bush-clover *(L. stipulacea)* and common or striate bush-clover *(L. striata)*; both plants show pinkish to purple flowers.

Other names: The names bush-clover and lespedeza are interchangeable for most species. Names of round-headed bush-clover or lespedeza include rabbit foot and dusty clover.

Close relatives: Some 25 *Lespedeza* species exist; about 11 of them are native to eastern North America. Two widely planted shrub bush-clovers are Japanese and bicolor lespedezas *(L. thunbergii, L. bicolor)*. Prairie bush-clover *(L. leptostachya)*, white-flowered, has been designated a threatened species. Closely related genera include tick-trefoils *(q.v.)*, prairie-clovers *(Dalea)*, and lead-plants *(Amorpha)*. Other legumes are lupine, birdsfoot-trefoil, clovers, alfalfa, and vetches (all *q.v.*).

Lifestyle: Bush-clovers produce 2 kinds of bisexual flowers: showy, 5-petaled, (potentially) cross-pollinated *(chasmogamous)* blossoms conspicuously displayed on terminal branches; and much smaller, budlike, inconspicuous, unpetaled, self-pollinated *(cleistogamous)* flowers. The latter flowers usually appear later than the former, though individual plants occasionally produce only a single kind in a given year. Both kinds produce viable seeds, but the self-pollinated flowers apparently produce most. The insect-pollinated chasmogamous flowers can also self-pollinate, however, and visiting insects may facilitate this process. As lespedeza researcher Andre F. Clewell wrote, "The possibility of selfing is enhanced in that bees usually visit several flowers on one plant before visiting another plant"; also, unlike many flowers, bush-clovers have floral mechanisms that hardly hinder self-pollination. Clewell concluded that more lespedeza flowers are self-pollinated than cross-pollinated. This tendency reduces the likelihood of hybridization in many populations while maintaining species identity, even as it reduces the adaptive benefits of outcrossing. Asexual, or vegetative, reproduction—by the extension and fragmentation of woody, horizontal, subsurface stems *(rhizomes)*—also occurs. Researchers believe that connecting rhizomes may sometimes rot away, separating individual clonal plants.

Lespedeza seeds, with their thick, impervious seed coats, may remain viable for a half century or longer. "The scarcity of seedlings in natural populations," wrote Clewell, "suggests that few seeds germinate the year after their formation and that seeds may remain dormant for many years pending . . . natural scarification [scarring or cracking of the outer seed coat]." Such aids to germination include frost-cracking of the seed and fire. Controlled-burn programs have demonstrated that many native lespedezas are fire-adapted species, often sprouting vigorously after fire passage. Game managers and agricultural technicians alike have used burn programs to encourage lespedeza growth for wildlife food patches and livestock forage growth.

Perennial bush-clovers have extensive root systems; taproots often extend 5 to 8 feet deep—much deeper than the plants' aboveground height—with many branching laterals in the topsoil. The annual lespedezas, by contrast, have shallow taproots.

Associates: Lespedezas, beloved of livestock farmers for forage (especially in the southeastern states) and of game managers for wildlife food plantings, also commonly appear in prairies and old fields and along roadsides. Most bush-clovers favor open land, sandy soil, and disturbed habitats, though trailing and violet bush-clovers can tolerate the light shade of open woods. Native perennial lespedezas are generally associated with tall-grass prairie and bluestem grass *(q.v.)* range. Round-headed bush-clover, among others, also grows amid other *Lespedeza* species, leading in some instances to hybrid populations. Clewell found that "almost all populations of about 50 or more plants may be expected to consist of two to five, or sometimes as high as seven, species which usually bloom concurrently." Native perennial lespedezas are considered *decreasers* on midwestern cattle range, naturally decreasing their presence in competition with other plants; in other words, they occupy early plant-successional habitats. Fire is an important, sometimes essential, environmental ingredient for the maintenance of such habitats.

Like most legumes, bush-clovers have root nodules with nitrogen-fixing bacteria *(Bradyrhizobium),* which convert atmospheric nitrogen into ammonia for protein production (see Alfalfa). Thus lespedezas increase soil fertility wherever they grow.

Bacterial and fungous diseases affect southeastern crop lespedezas (Korean, Japanese, and sericea) more frequently than the native plants. A fairly common fungus is the rust *Uromyces lespedezae-procumbentis,* which produces conspicuous black dots on leaflet undersides. The bacterial wilt *Xanthomonas lespedezae* causes stunting and foliage loss.

Lespedezas are frequent victims of dodder *(Cuscuta),* a yellow-stemmed, stringy, parasitic plant that tangles and twines around host-plant stems, tapping into them by means of stem-penetrating *haustoria* (rootlike structures by which parasite plants attach to host plants).

Insect foliage feeders include American grasshoppers *(Schistocerca americana);* and armyworm moth caterpillars *(Pseudaletia unipuncta),* dark green with white striping, often feeding en masse. Lespedeza webworms *(Pococera scortealis),* pyralid moth caterpillars, sometimes irrupt in large numbers, building webs and defoliating the plant. These and other leaf and stem feeders are more prevalent in the South than the North. Japanese beetles *(Popillia japonica),* the copper-and-green scourge of so many plants, also defoliate bush-clovers. An unknown seed beetle (Bruchidae) bores into the seedpods *(legumes),* devouring the seeds.

Butterfly caterpillars also feed on the plant. The eastern tailed blue *(Everes comyntas)*, a downy, dark green caterpillar, feeds in flowerheads and on leaves. Silver-spotted skipper caterpillars *(Epargyreus clarus)*, yellowish with orange-red eyespots, create nests in leaflets of the plant. The northern cloudy wing *(Thorybes pylades)*, a green and striped skipper, does likewise. Moth caterpillars on bush-clovers, in addition to those mentioned, include the bella or rattlebox moth *(Utetheisa bella)*, a spiny-haired arctiid species. Common ptichodis caterpillars *(Ptichodis herbarum)* are noctuids; black-spotted prominents *(Dasylophia anguina)* often erect their rear ends. Larvae of *Triclonella pergandeela*, a cosmopterigid moth, create mines in lespedeza leaflets. Other leaf miners include a tiny tineid moth caterpillar, *Parectopa lespedezaefoliella;* and a buprestid beetle larva, *Pachyschelus purpureus.*

Pollination of chasmogamous flowers is effected mainly by bees, less frequently by butterflies and other insects. Insects can also cause self-pollination in these flowers just by

slight agitation of the anthers (see Lifestyle). Clewell found that the "constancy of any one insect to a particular species of *Lespedeza* is pronounced." Because "bees are much more competent than taxonomists in identifying lespedezas," outcrossing between species is limited, thus maintaining genetic integrity and identity.

Shrub lespedezas have become popular as wildlife plantings mainly on the basis of their use as winter food for northern bobwhites, which consume the seeds. Seed feeding from bush-clovers by wild turkeys, ruffed grouse, mourning doves, and songbirds occurs but is relatively slight. White-throated sparrows and dark-eyed juncos are the primary finch feeders. Greater prairie-chickens consume leaflets of Korean bush-clover. Deer mice cache bush-clover seeds, and white-tailed deer relish the foliage. Sericea provides nesting and roosting cover for cottontail rabbits and northern bobwhites, but scant food.

Lore: This genus could have been labeled *Cespedes.* The name *Lespedeza* is apparently a misnomer. French botanist in America, André Michaux, intended to pay tribute to the 1784–90 Spanish governor of East Florida, one Manuel de Cespedes, by naming bush-clover after him. But somehow the name, probably through a copying error, came out as *Lespedeza,* thus saving the world from another memorial to a politician.

Bush-clover's brown seedheads, often produced by self-pollination, may feed several sparrows and gamebirds but probably have fewer wildlife users than other clovers.

Lespedezas, which thrive in open and disturbed sites, probably occur much more abundantly now than in presettlement times. Clewell believed that the probable original centers of distribution were the deciduous forest-prairie and coastal savanna borders of the East and Midwest.

Moxa, a variation on acupuncture practiced by Plains tribes, used small pieces of *L. capitata* (and probably *L. leptostachya*) dried stems. Moistened and stuck to the skin, they were ignited on the other end and allowed to burn down to the skin, supposedly relieving (replacing?) pains of neuralgia and rheumatism. Other tribes boiled the leaves to make a tea for unknown benefits. Researchers are finding that lespedezas are apparently loaded with biologically active compounds, most of which await further investigation. Extracts of the plant demonstrate considerable activity against certain types of cancerous tumors, also apparently lower blood cholesterol and blood nitrogen levels. Shrub lespedezas also have value as honey producers.

Butter-and-eggs *(Linaria vulgaris)*. Figwort family. Recognize this 1- to 3-foot-tall alien perennial by its terminal spikes of 15 to 20 bright yellow, lobed and spurred flowers appearing in summer and fall. Petals are 5 but united; the pouch-shaped lower lip protrudes with 3 lobes plus an orange spot or palate and a drooping conical spur. Leaves are narrow, often densely crowded, appearing opposite because of crowding but actually mostly alternate.

Other names: Yellow toadflax, eggs-and-bacon, flaxweed, brideweed, wild snapdragon, common linaria.

Close relatives: About 100 *Linaria* species exist, mostly Eurasian (as is *L. vulgaris*) and South American. Annual or blue toadflax *(L. canadensis)* is a native American species. Common *Linaria* perennials established in eastern North America include dalmatian toadflax *(L. dalmatica)* and *L. spartea*. Family relatives include blue-eyed Marys *(Collinsia)* and beardtongues, common mullein, speedwells, and painted cups (all *q.v.*). Before flowering, butter-and-eggs is often mistaken for *Euphorbia esula,* one of the spurges *(q.v.)*.

Lifestyle: The yolk-colored palate, serving as a nectar guide in this insect-pollinated flower, covers the throat of the petals. Weight of a landing insect depresses the lower lip, admitting the insect over the palate and through a restricted opening into the long, narrow spur, wherein pools the sucrose-rich nectar. In pushing through this tight slot, the insect brushes against the pollen-loaded (male) stamens projecting overhead, receiving a load of dust on its back. Between the 2 stamens—a short and a long one—projects the (female) stigma. The visitation sequence for a bumblebee bumbling its way into the flower would be, first, an overhead caress by the sticky stigma, relieving the bumblebee fur of a few pollen grains deposited on it elsewhere; then a liberal pollen dusting from the long stamens; then, as the bee backs out of the plant, a second dusting from the fur-snagged short stamens. A single bumblebee can thus pollinate most flowers of a spike in a single visit to each, easily invading some 10 flowers per minute. Though flowers are self-incompatible, rare exceptions may occur in which seeds develop without cross-pollination.

Staggered flowering sequences on and among flower spikes reduce chances of seed failure. The mean lifespan of individual flowers is 3 or 4 days. Seed capsules begin opening in late summer, dropping seeds mainly near the parent plant. *Linaria* seeds are, however, slightly winged, perhaps adapting them for dispersal by high winds—observers have seen them being blown across snowy fields in winter. The seeds also can float. Some of them, however, remain in the erect capsules over winter. Although the plant produces prolific seed, relatively few seeds are viable (only 40 percent in one study), and many remain dormant for years.

Most reproduction in this plant occurs vegetatively; a single plant can rapidly produce a thriving colony of clones, often circular in form, by means of budding from both taproots and laterals and from root fragments. "The importance of the root system for persistence and local spread," wrote a 1995 Canadian research team, "is illustrated by subarctic populations that are unable to produce seeds but that increased in abundance from 'scarce' to 'frequent' between 1959 and 1989." Individual taproots, which may extend 3 feet down, may survive at least 4 years, probably longer. The combination of poor seed dispersal/germination and quick duplication once colonies are established often results in dense, thriving local populations.

Stems die back to the roots in the fall, but the small, blue-green shoots at the base of old stems remain visible through winter.

Associates: Butter-and-eggs occurs in a wide range of open habitats, mostly disturbed areas, throughout the continent. Most frequently it appears in gravelly and sandy soil, along roadsides, on railroad embankments, and in vacant lots, dry fields, and waste ground. As a garden escape, it thrives, like lilacs, around old homestead sites. Because it does not require a long growing season or high seed production in order to survive and reproduce, it adapts well to hostile environments, survives fire, grazing, and herbicides with aplomb. Today the plant has a virtually global distribution.

Its plant associates typically include those that occur in disturbed open habitats, usually other alien species such as timothy, spotted knapweed, common ragweed, common mullein, common evening-primrose, and chicory (all *q.v.*), among many others. Range managers have found that the only reliable competitors of butter-and-eggs are vigorously aggressive grasses.

Pollinators of butter-and-eggs are mainly the larger, long-tongued bees that can reach into the long-spurred nectar reservoir of the flower. These include several species of bumblebees *(Bombus, Psithyrus)* and halictid bees *(Halictus, Dialictus).* Bumblebees are the most effi-

cient pollinators; a flower must be visited at least twice by a halictid bee for all ovules to be fertilized. "If you hold a flower up to
the light," wrote naturalist Donald W. Stokes, "you can actually
see the level of the nectar" in the bottom of the spur. (It takes
about 11 hours for a drained spur to refill.) Bumblebees and
yellowjackets *(Vespula)* have also been observed cutting
holes in flower spurs from the outside, tapping the nectar and thus bypassing the pollination gateway. Other
flower visitors include syrphid or hover flies (Syrphidae) and black bugs *(Corimelaena pulicaria).*
    Species of the fungi *Alternaria* and *Cladiospo-
rium* attack the seeds.
    Some 100 arthropod species feed on butter-
and-eggs in its native Europe; a few of them have
been introduced to North America either by accident or for possible biological control of the
plant, mainly in the West, where the plant invades
tallgrass prairie range.
    The flowers host several insects that feed
and reside there, often damaging flower parts
and reducing their reproductive fitness. Two
seedpod weevils *(Gymnaetron antirrhini* and *G.
netum)* feed as adult insects on the anthers and
pollen; they deposit eggs in the flower ovaries;

*The long spurs of yellow butter-and-eggs flowers
hold ample nectar, reached most efficiently by
bumblebees.*

and their larvae consume both developing and mature seeds. These accidentally introduced European beetles are probably the plant's most important biological control agents.
Larvae of the sap beetle *Brachypterolus pulicarius,* sometimes called the toadflax flower-eat-
ing beetle, also feed in the tips of flowering shoots and inside developing seeds, in some
cases reducing seed production by 90 percent or more; the shiny black adult beetles feed
on buds and young stems. (Since butter-and-eggs reproduces almost incidentally by seed,
however, these biocontrol organisms are not exactly front-line defense.) Another flower
feeder is a caterpillar called the toadflax pug *(Eupithecia linariata),* an inchworm moth.
    Foliage feeders include the common buckeye *(Junonia coenia),* a gray, yellow-spotted
butterfly that migrates southward in fall and northward in spring, frequenting flowers and
mud puddles. The toadflax brocade *(Calophasia lunula),* a yellow-mottled noctuid moth
caterpillar introduced as a biological control in 1962, also feeds on the leaves and flowers,
sometimes defoliating small patches of the plant. Twice-stabbed stink bugs *(Cosmopepla*

bimaculata) and treehoppers *(Campylenchia latipes)* also feed.

Stem feeders include the weevil *Mecinus janthinus,* whose larvae mine and bore into the stems; adult weevils feed on shoots of the plant.

Root feeders include 2 cosmopterigid moth caterpillars, *Eteobalea serratella* and *E. intermediella,* also European natives; they stunt the plant by feeding throughout the summer, spend winter in the roots as hibernating larvae.

Cattle generally avoid feeding on the plant; various sources have reported it as moderately or mildly toxic. Alkaloids in the foliage probably make the plant distasteful to livestock.

Lore: Butter-and-eggs displays an occasional flower abnormality called *peloria* (meaning "monster"). The deformed flower—usually the end flower on a spike—consists of multiple spurs, usually 1 per petal, presenting a regular but unrecognizable shape. Other floral anomalies also occur.

Native to the steppes of Eurasia, butter-and-eggs probably arrived in North America with New England colonists, brought as a garden ornamental sometime before 1672. Additional introductions, probably in crop seeds and baled hay, hastened its spread across the continent. Botanist John Bartram, writing in 1758, called "the stinking yellow *Linaria* the most hurtful plant to our pastures that can grow in our northern climate." "It is a troublesome weed," wrote Thoreau, parenthesizing that "flowers must not be too profuse nor obtrusive; else they acquire the reputation of weeds." Not until the 1930s did butter-and-eggs become well established in western rangeland, where by 1950 it had become a seriously invasive grain and pasture weed. Since about 1960, it has somewhat declined in abundance and distribution, probably because of the insect biocontrol species.

American natives had no acquaintance with this plant, but pioneer homeopaths widely prescribed it as an astringent, laxative, and diuretic; infusions treated dropsy and liver ailments, while external poultices and ointments made from the plant soothed hemorrhoids and skin sores. Other historical uses have included insecticide—boiled in milk, the flowers are said to produce an excellent fly poison. They also produce a yellow dye.

The intricate root system can be a useful soil stabilizer against erosion, as on sand berms and gravel slopes, and the plant may also help reclaim strip-mined lands and soils polluted by heavy metal sludge.

Obviously the name butter-and-eggs is visually derived, but the name most familiar to farmers and range managers—yellow toadflax—apparently originated from the supposed resemblance of the flower shape to little toads or to the wide mouth of a toad (a less credible old source claimed that the plant provided shelter to toads, hence the name—undoubtedly this has occurred). The *flax* came from the superficial resemblance of the early-summer plant to a flax *(Linum),* an unrelated genus of similar wasteland habitat. Indeed, the great Swedish namer Linnaeus assigned the name *Linaria* to toadflaxes because of this perceived likeness.

Buttercup, Common *(Ranunculus acris).* Buttercup family. Buttercups display yellow, wet-shiny, 5- to 7-parted flowers and deeply cut palmate leaves resembling those of celery. This alien perennial species, the most common, stands 2 or 3 feet tall, with overlapping wedge-shaped petals, hairy stems, and an erect, branching form.

Other names: Tall buttercup, meadow buttercup, blister-plant, tall crowfoot, kingcups, goldcups, butter-flower.

Close relatives: About 250 *Ranunculus* species reside worldwide. More than 30 species, both native and alien, occupy wetland, woodland, and meadow habitats in eastern North America. Among other buttercups of open habitats are bulbous buttercups *(R. bulbosus),* creeping buttercups *(R. repens),* and early or thick-root buttercups *(R. fascicularis).* Family relatives include anemones *(Anemone),* hepaticas *(Hepatica),* clematises *(Clematis),* marsh-marigolds *(Caltha),* and columbines *(Aquilegia).*

Lifestyle: Relatively few yellow wildflowers appear in April or May—most yellows are summer flowers—but marsh-marigolds and buttercups are conspicuous exceptions. This species continues flowering into September, then dies back to a basal rosette of leaves, which remains green over winter and from which the flower stalk rises in spring. Buttercup stems rise from thick, fibrous roots.

For the novice botanist, buttercups are among the easiest flowers for identifying male and female parts, since the flower demonstrates the prototypical dish-shaped form, with sexual organs plainly evident. The (male) stamens surround the domed, central (female) pistils, a simple arrangement that becomes variable and complex in more highly evolved plants. Buttercup flowers are *protogynous*—that is, the green pistils mature first, thus reducing chances of self-pollination; later, the stamens bearing the anthers expand in a fringed circle around the declining pistil. At the inner base of each shiny petal exists a tiny flap, the nectary, holding the flower's liquid invitation and reward to pollinating insects. Each flower lasts for about a week, opening only in daytime—or not at all, if the weather is overcast or rainy.

Notice the small, hooked seedcases, called *achenes;* some observers have thought they resemble tiny frogs in shape *(Ranunculus,* the Latin genus name, means "a little frog"). Seeds may germinate in either spring or fall. The plant reproduces mainly by erecting stems from short, budding *rhizomes* (subsurface stems) that rarely produce clonal colonies.

Associates: Common buttercups have adapted to many disturbed-soil and agricultural habitats in North America: pastures, hayfields, streambanks, roadsides, among others. The plant favors moist meadows, usually does not persist among cultivated crops. In England, its abundance in pastures and meadows is taken as an indicator of the ecological health of the field; its frequency increases with overgrazing (since cattle generally avoid it) and hay cropping. Its worst effects are upon livestock, as detailed below.

Most grazers avoid common buttercup's finely cut and lobed leaves because of their acute toxicity.

At least 60 species of insects are known to frequent buttercup flowers—mainly bees *(Ceratina* carpenter bees, halictid bees [*Halictus, Agapostemon,* and *Dialictus*]), syrphid flies, wasps, and beetles. Many of these pollinate the flower as they collect pollen or nectar; others, such as the blister beetle *Meloe impressus,* elongate and bluish black, feed upon the flower or, in the case of some predaceous beetles, capture other insects there. The flower also attracts numerous butterfly feeders—swallowtails, spring azures *(Celastrina ladon),* coppers, and pearl crescents *(Phyciodes tharos),* among others.

Buttercups are not important wildlife food plants. A variety of birds and mammals consume the foliage and seeds, but in relatively small amounts. Ruffed grouse chicks, however, may feed extensively on the leaves soon after hatching. Other seed and foliage eaters include ring-necked pheasants, wild turkeys, and cottontail rabbits. Winter seed foragers include snow buntings, eastern chipmunks, and voles. Cattle usually avoid the plant—its acrid juices can blister their mouths—though they can also develop something like an addiction to it, consuming it until it kills them. Wild animal grazers apparently do not suffer similar effects. Once the plant is dry (as in hay forage), the toxins vanish and it becomes harmless.

Lore: In a childhood game, the reflected glow of buttercup petals under a chin supposedly identified a lover of butter—or today we might say a person with a future cholesterol problem. From chin to mouth, however, is not a wise move.

Similar warnings apply to most plants in the buttercup family. The acrid toxin is ranunculin, also called protoanemonin, a volatile yellow glycoside that causes acute oral irritation and gastrointestinal distress if eaten. On skin contact in allergic individuals, the substance can cause rashes and blisters.

Buttercups represent one of the most ancient flowering plant groups that survive from the early Cenozoic era. Although this species originated in northern Eurasia and remains one of England's most common wildflowers, its presence in North America probably dates from the earliest colonial settlements. It may have been first brought and planted as a medicinal herb, a caustic "deep-heat rub" once widely applied for treatment of arthritis and rheumatism. American natives, though probably not familiar with this species, used native buttercups for similar ailments. Illinois tribes pulverized the roots and used them in a solution to treat cuts and wounds, and the Montagnais inhaled the odor of crushed leaves for headache. According to an old herbal, a decoction of buttercup splashed on the ground will make earthworms rise for a fisherman's plucking.

Butterfly-weed *(Asclepias tuberosa).* Milkweed family. Its bright orange flowers, hairy stems, and alternate, lance-shaped leaves (unlike the opposite leaf arrangement of most milkweeds) help identify butterfly-weed. A native perennial, it stands 1 to 2 feet tall.

Other names: Pleurisy-root, orange-root, orange milkweed, chigger flower, Canada-root, Indian-nosy, coralweed.

Close relatives: Common milkweed *(q.v.),* all other milkweeds.

Lifestyle: Our only "milkless milkweed" has watery sap, not the milky juice characteristic of most *Asclepias* species. It is also the showiest milkweed, its orange glow impossible to miss in a field where it grows. That color, however, varies somewhat depending on geography. In some locales, the flowers are clear yellow rather than orange; in others, they are bicolored. Leaf shape also varies; a study often cited by students of evolution detected a geographic progression of gradual changes in leaf shape for this plant in eastern North America. These manifest changes are believed to be subtle adaptations for drought conditions.

Floral and reproductive biology of this plant closely resembles that of common milkweed *(q.v.),* though it lacks the cloying fragrance of its relative. Looking closely, one can see that petals of the small florets are sharply reflexed (bent back); the erect, petal-like hoods are actually appendages of the (male) stamens and secrete nectar. The 4- to 5-inch-long, hairy, spindle-shaped seedpods ripen to maturity by late September. This plant reproduces both by seed and by root sprouts.

Butterfly-weed has a long, fibrous taproot, giving the plant drought resistance. Several clonal stems rising from the root crown often form a small patch or colony, flowering from May into July, sometimes later. Butterfly-weed may not flower for its first few years, however, and it may take 4 years to reach full size. Once established, though, individual plants may survive as long as adjacent plants do not shade them out.

Associates: Butterfly-weed favors dry, sandy soil and full sunlight; it can also tolerate light shade. A *xerophyte* (that is, a plant adapted to dry conditions), it will not survive where soil is too moist. The plant resides throughout most of the continent in temperate areas.

Pollination in this plant, as in other milkweeds, involves an insect's ensnarement by yoked pairs of pollen masses, or *pollinia,* in a floret, then pulling them loose and depositing

Butterfly-weed, the brightest milkweed, is aptly named from its chief pollinators which are attracted to its orange flowers and copious nectar.

them in the floret of another plant (see Milkweed, Common). The floret's device is a kind of slot adaptation into which long legs—specifically, the legs of butterflies, many species of which are attracted to the colorful blooms and ample nectar, thus aptly naming this milkweed—become snagged. Butterfly pollinators include several large swallowtails—black *(Papilio polyxenes)*, tiger *(P. glaucus)*, spicebush *(P. troilus)*, and pipevine *(Battus philenor)*; monarch butterflies *(Danaus plexippus)*; checkered whites *(Pieris protodice)* and European cabbage butterflies *(P. rapae)*; little sulphurs *(Eurema lisa)*; painted ladies *(Vanessa cardui)*; and many others, including hairstreaks, fritillaries, and skippers. Bees—digger bees *(Anthophora* and others), honeybees *(Apis mellifera)*, bumblebees *(Bombus)*, halictids *(Halictus* and others), and leafcutting bees *(Megachile* and others)—also pollinate the plant. Other pollinia carriers include thick-headed flies (Conopidae) and sphecid and vespid wasps *(Ammophila, Sphex, Polistes major)*.

Often trailing the pollinators come nectar thieves. "Lacking the quantity of sticky milky juice which protects [common milkweeds] from crawling pilferers," wrote botanist Neltje Blanchan, "the butterfly-weed suffers outrageous robberies from black ants." Other nectar-feeding visitors include ladybird beetles (Coccinellidae).

Most insect associates of common milkweed also frequent other milkweeds, including butterfly-weed. Very frequent on the latter is the small milkweed bug *(Lygaeus kalmii)*, a

red-and-black seed feeder; these and large milkweed bugs *(Oncopeltus fasciatus)* also pollinate the plant. Monarch butterfly caterpillars also feed and pupate on this plant, even
though they favor common milkweed.

Watch for ruby-throated hummingbirds feeding on the nectar. Butterfly-weed's
orange-red flowers strongly attract these tiny birds.

Mammal foliage feeders on butterfly-weed are rare, though it is occasionally grazed by
deer. Livestock generally avoid it.

Lore: Like all milkweeds, butterfly-weed is loaded with cardiac glycosides, making it
extremely toxic to mammals as well as to many insects. Whereas boiling water renders
other milkweeds harmless and edible, butterfly-weed is best left alone even by the hungri-
est devotee of cooked greens.

Yet many native tribes as well as pioneer doctors found the taproot medicinally useful. Teas and infusions treated pulmonary conditions such as pleurisy, bronchitis, and
asthma. Externally, the pulverized root formed poultices for all sorts of skin and arthritic
ailments, plus cuts and bruises.

The generic name *Asclepias* derives from Aesculapius, a Greek physician, later deified
as the god of healing.

Catalpas *(Catalpa* species). Trumpet-Creeper family. Two species, native to the southern United States but widely planted and escaped in the North, are northern catalpa *(C.
speciosa)* and southern catalpa *(C. bignonioides).* Both trees look much alike, have large,
heart-shaped leaves that grow opposite or in whorls of three; large, showy white flowers
appearing in late spring or early summer; and long, thin, podlike seed capsules that hang
on the trees through winter. Northern catalpa is a larger, hardier tree than southern
catalpa, with longer-pointed, odorless leaves and a notched lower petal on the flower.
Southern catalpa displays smaller flowers with unnotched petals, and the leaves have a
foul odor when crushed.

Other names: Hardy catalpa *(C. speciosa);* common catalpa *(C. bignonioides).* Both
trees are called simply catalpa, also catawba, candle-tree, cigar tree, and Indian bean.

Close relatives: Some 11 *Catalpa* species exist, most in the West Indies and eastern
Asia. Chinese catalpa *(C. ovata),* a shrub or small tree planted as an ornamental in North
America, also occasionally escapes. Family members include trumpet-creeper *(Campsis
radicans),* princess-tree or empress-tree *(Paulownia tomentosa),* and cross-vine *(Bignonia
capreolata).*

Lifestyle: Information in this section refers mainly to northern catalpa, though much
of it applies equally to both species.

Catalpas are somewhat hyperbolic trees, attractive yet unrefined, almost coarse, with little subtlety in their appearance. Their broad, rounded crowns; big, flaplike leaves; frilly, rococo-gaudy flower clusters; and rattling seedpods in winter make these trees conspicuous in any season.

Slow to leaf out in spring, catalpas also drop their leaves early in the fall, often with the first frost. Leaves resemble larger versions of lilac and basswood leaves. Nectar abounds, not only in the bell-shaped, insect-pollinated flowers, but also in a small gland at the base of each leaf where the primary veins meet the leaf stem. Leaf scars on winter twigs are large, almost circular in shape.

Catalpa flowers, white but mottled with yellow and purple, are bisexual, up to 2 inches long, and occur in pyramidal clusters *(panicles)* of several to many individual flowers. Individual candelabralike panicles, 6 to 12 inches tall, remain in flower 5 or 6 days; the entire tree flowers for only 8 to 12 days. As *obligate outcrossers,* catalpa flowers cannot self-pollinate.

About 3 seed capsules per panicle start to develop, the rest aborting even though pollinated. About 3 to 5 weeks later, a large proportion of the juvenile seed capsules also abort from the tree. Degree of this thinning depends to some extent on the amount of *herbivory* (leaf consumption) by catalpa sphinx caterpillars (see Associates); the more foliage consumed, the greater the fruit drop. Typically, the end result is that each panicle produces about 1 mature seed capsule. The stringbean-like capsule, 10 to 20 inches long, contains more than 100 papery, flakelike, inch-long seeds, their wings bordered with hairy fringes (northern catalpa) or tufts (southern catalpa) at both ends—seeds plainly adapted for wind distribution, which occurs mainly in winter and early spring when the dry pods split open.

Catalpas grow quickly, attaining typical heights of 40 to 60 feet. They are relatively short-lived, however, seldom surviving longer than 40 or 50 years.

Associates: The original range of both catalpa species overlapped in the central Mississippi basin. Northern catalpa grew from the Ohio River valley and southern Illinois to

Catalpa becomes a tree-size bouquet of white candelabras in summer, but most of its fertilized seed capsules abort before maturing.

Arkansas and Missouri. Southern catalpa's range encompassed most of the southeastern states, from South Carolina into Mississippi. Open floodplains and river bottomlands are the chief habitats for both species, though both have widely adapted to upland sites.

Catalpas host several fungus types. These include leaf spot and powdery mildew *(Microsphaera, Phyllactinia)* species, but most commonly a sac fungus *(Verticillium albo-atrum)* that infects the sapwood and inner bark of the tree. Verticillium wilt causes branch die-off, may kill the tree. Trunk rots include the velvet shank mushroom *(Flammulina velutipes)* and the pore fungi *Polyporus versicolor* and *P. catalpae.*

Insect pollinators of the spectacular flowers are mainly bumblebees *(Bombus)* and large carpenter bees *(Xylocopa virginica)* dur-

A catalpa tree in winter dangles abundant seedpods, which split open as the season advances.

ing daytime; and 15 or so moth species, some nocturnal. Common moth pollinators include the Virginia ctenucha *(Ctenucha virginica),* an arctiid moth; the saw-wing *(Euchlaena serrata),* itames *(Itame),* common lytrosis *(Lytrosis unitaria),* large lace-border *(Scopula limboundata),* yellow slant-line *(Tetracis crocallata),* and crocus geometer *(Xanthotype sospeta),* all inchworm or geometer moths; the eastern tent caterpillar moth *(Malacosoma americanum);* looper moths *(Plusia);* and the hermit sphinx *(Sphinx eremitus).* Honeybees *(Apis mellifera),* though they forage the flowers for nectar, are too small to pollinate catalpa effectively, rarely touch the flower's sex organs.

Feeders on the extrafloral (leaf) nectaries are mainly ants; a 1982 study of Michigan catalpas found several common species (2 carpenter ant *[Camponotus]* species, *Cremato-gaster cerasi,* 2 *Formica* species, and *Prenolepis imparis*). Ladybird beetles *(Coccinella)* also feed on the nectar. Ants and the ladybirds also attack catalpa sphinx caterpillars (see below), the trees' foremost foliage eater. Andrew G. Stephenson's 1982 catalpa research indicated that leaf nectar secretion provides mutual benefit to both the tree and these predaceous insects, a relationship known as *mutualism.* "The insects," he wrote, "receive high-quality nourishment and are brought within close contact of high-protein food [the caterpillars], while the plants receive sufficient protection to increase the number of fruits and seeds they produce." Also, the degree of herbivory by these caterpillars can determine the amount of seed production.

The aforementioned ants and a few butterflies, such as the hobomok skipper *(Poanes hobomok)*, also seek nectar in the large flowers. Because they, like honeybees, are too small to effect pollination, all are classed as *nectar thieves.* Catalpa flowers have evolved a chemical defense against such thievery: Ants are observed to become disoriented after ingesting the nectar, walking erratically, even falling from the tree; and small butterflies fall comatose from the flowers. Catalpa nectar apparently contains a distasteful or toxic substance that does not, however, deter or affect the flower's larger bee and moth pollinators.

Northern catalpa has what Stephenson labeled "two simultaneous pollination syndromes," varying day and night. Sugar concentration is higher in the daytime flower nectar—a concentration typical of bumblebee-pollinated flowers—whereas nighttime nectar is lower in sugars, as favored by moth pollinators.

Various insect sap suckers include the Comstock mealybug *(Pseudococcus comstocki)*, also called catalpa mealybug, a Japanese import that also feeds on many other trees and shrubs, its eggs wintering in bark crevices. Found in large, cottony masses at twig forks or leaf bases, these waxy-coated relatives of scale insects suck sap much like aphids. Copious honeydew secretions from these insects and consequent growth of black sooty mold *(Meliola camelliae)* on the sticky honeydew are often indicators of mealybug feeding.

Whitish to orange catalpa midge larvae *(Itonida catalpae)* feed on leaf undersides, leaving circular dead spots on the leaves, even causing defoliation at times. Their feeding on terminal buds can stunt and dwarf the trees. Later in the season, the maggots also infest developing seed capsules, destroying the seeds. The adult flies, which lay eggs on the emerging leaves in late May and June, are tiny and yellowish.

Foremost and best-known catalpa feeder is the catalpa sphinx *(Ceratomia catalpae)*, also called catalpa or catawba worm, a 3-inch-long moth caterpillar with a black, rear-projecting horn and green markings. Irruptions of these ravenous caterpillars, which occur at staggered yearly intervals because of heavy parasitism upon them, may defoliate entire trees. The brownish adult sphinx moths emerge in early spring from pupae in the soil beneath the trees where they have overwintered, then lay eggs in white masses on catalpa leaf undersides. The hatched caterpillars feed at first in groups, then separately, munching along the leaf margins mainly at night. Two broods per year may be produced, with caterpillars present into September. The trees adjust and compensate to some extent by aborting fruits and attracting caterpillar predators.

The fact that catalpa trees can survive these periodic depredations owes to the presence of parasitic wasps that lay eggs on the caterpillars, quickly depleting their populations and thus the immediate recurrence of irruptions. Some 15 species of parasitic wasps prey on *Ceratomia.* A common one is *Apanteles congregatus,* a small braconid wasp that inserts its eggs inside the young caterpillars; the wasp larvae literally eat the caterpillar alive.

Catalpas provide occasional nest sites for American robins and a few other birds that have become adapted to suburban landscapes. Many birds also relish catalpa sphinx caterpillars. The only semiregular feeders on catalpa seeds are probably evening grosbeaks.

Lore: Creek natives of Georgia and Alabama named this tree *kutuhlpa,* meaning "head with wings," describing either the flower lobes or seeds; the English name *catalpa* stems directly from that word.

Scarce indeed were plants native to North America that found absolutely no usage, either as medicine or food, among one or more native tribes; catalpas were no exception. Bark teas served as an antiseptic wash, also as a laxative, sedative, and snakebite antidote. The leaves made poultices for wounds and bruises. Seed teas treated respiratory ailments—the seed capsules have sedative and cardioactive properties.

Foremost modern use of catalpa lies in its durable wood, once widely sought for fence rails and posts. Farmers in Ohio and other northern states once planted groves of northern catalpa for harvest as fence wood. So fast do they grow that the trees could be cut for such purposes in only 6 years. During the "catalpa boom" of the early 1900s, thousands of midwestern farmers raised plantations of catalpa, intending to market the wood for railroad ties, telegraph poles, and fence posts. Their high hopes for financial reward did not pan out, and most of the plantations finally lay abandoned or destroyed.

Wandering English naturalist Mark Catesby regarded southern catalpa as a tree of "uncommon beauty." He took credit in the middle 1700s for bringing it to the Carolinas, where it had not grown previously, also introduced it to England.

Today catalpa trees are mainly valued for their showy flowers as ornamental yard trees. Fishermen have always valued catalpa as a "fish-bait tree," collecting catalpa worms, sometimes turning them inside out with a match or twig before placing them on the fishhook.

Weather is hard on this tree. The stout, brittle twigs break easily in wind and frost.

Catnip *(Nepeta cataria).* Mint family. Recognize this alien perennial herb by its softly furry, gray-green aspect and by its opposite, toothed, arrowhead-shaped leaves with whitish undersides; its crowded terminal spike of white or pale violet flowers with pink or purple spots; and the strong aroma of its crushed flowers and leaves. The plant stands 6 inches to 2 feet tall.

Other names: Catmint, catnep, catrup.

Close relatives: Some 150 *Nepeta* species exist, all of them Eurasian, as is catnip itself. Other family relatives include wild bergamot *(q.v.),* self-heal *(q.v.),* dragon-heads *(Dracocephalum),* mints *(Mentha),* skullcaps *(Scutellaria),* and many others.

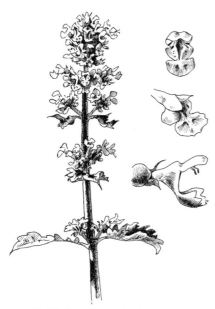

Catnip's elevated terminal spike and broad-lipped flowers (at right) plainly adapt this plant for insect pollination.

Lifestyle: Most mints have square-sided stems, and all have opposite leaves. Otherwise they appear in 2 flowering forms: with flowers growing in the angles of leaves or side branches; or with flowers in terminal spikes. Catnip exemplifies the latter group. The plant's odor and taste resemble that of no other mint—neither unpleasant nor often relished as a taste treat, but strong and thoroughly distinctive. Aromatic oils plus nepetalactone, a monoterpene, account for this odor and taste. (Unlike many mint species, catnip deposits the terpene and its odor on one's fingers.)

New leaves in early spring may show purple-tinged undersides. The bisexual, insect-pollinated flower is tubular with a 3-lobed lower lip. Flowers occur from July through October, even into early winter if mild. Fruits are nutlets, 4 to a pod. The summer's growth dies back to the fibrous taproot in late fall.

Associates: A common resident of weed patches and vacant lots throughout North America, catnip also appears along roadsides and railroads, in old fields and thickets. It is a *calciphile,* favoring lime-rich soils.

Foliage feeders are relatively few. Look for an inchworm moth caterpillar, the false crocus geometer *(Xanthotype urticaria).* The adult moths appear bright yellow with brownish spots. The small beet webworm *(Hymenia fascialis),* a pyralid moth, feeds on beet leaves as a caterpillar, but the adult moths may often be seen on catnip flowers, especially in the Southeast. A soldier beetle, *Trypherus latipennis,* also frequents the flowers.

American goldfinches and common redpolls relish catnip seeds, but few other birds or mammals have been observed eating them. Catnip is obviously not an important food plant in North America.

Lore: This plant's name derives from its well-known spectacular effect on cat behaviors (called "the catnip response"), which nobody yet fully understands. Many researchers believe, however, that nepetalactone mimics feline sexual scents. This aphrodisiac odor affects about 80 percent of all house cats and other felines, including lions, tigers, leopards, and lynxes. Many cats exhibit slightly loopy behaviors in reaction to it, nuzzling, chewing, rolling in it, losing all semblance of cat dignity, apparently becoming virtually intoxicated if not hallucinating. The catnip response seldom exceeds a period of 15 minutes or so, after which a cat seems to "mellow out" and get sleepy. Research suggests that cats with a friendly disposition react most overtly to the plant; young kittens, however, are not affected. "I never weed all the catnip from my yard," wrote botanist Edward G. Voss, "so that the premises will appear hospitable to visitors that purr." (Aside from luring cats with this "recreational drug," of course, cat attractants in one's yard may not favor wild bird visitors.)

Catnip tea, brewed from the leaves, is a traditional folk remedy for colds, fevers, diarrhea, and a variety of ailments. It induces sleep (nepetalactone is a mild sedative) and promotes sweating. The plant also exhibits herbicidal and insect-repellent properties. Recent research has established that the catnip terpene proves many times as effective as deet—the chemical in most insect repellents—for ridding mosquitoes and cockroaches.

To Thoreau, the aroma of catnip leaves in early spring "advances me ever to the autumn and beyond it. How full of reminiscence is any fragrance!"

Catnip is raised commercially in a few places, mainly for herbal teas and for making cat toys.

Cedar, Eastern Red *(Juniperus virginiana)*. Cypress family. This densely foliaged native evergreen tree displays 2 different kinds of leaves, depending on its age: Young trees have sharp-pointed, needlelike leaves, whereas older trees show flattened, overlapping, scalelike leaves similar to those of the related northern white cedar or arbor vitae. Loose, dry, shreddy strips of fibrous bark clothe the irregular, unround trunk.

Other names: Juniper, red juniper, baton rouge, pencil cedar, savin.

Close relatives: As tree manuals always point out, red cedar is not related to true cedars *(Cedrus)*, which are native to the Middle East. Red cedar is, in contrast, a true juniper. Two other *Juniperus* species—of some 60 worldwide in north temperate climates—are common in eastern North America: common, ground, or pasture juniper *(J. communis)*, and creeping juniper *(J. horizontalis)*. Both are low, spreading, shrubby species. Eastern red cedar's western counterpart is the Rocky Mountain juniper *(J. scopulorum)*. Other family members include Atlantic white cedar *(Chamaecyparis thyoides)* and northern white cedar *(Thuja occidentalis; see The Book of Swamp and Bog)*.

Lifestyle: A spire-shaped, columnar, or pyramidal evergreen tree (forms are diverse) standing by itself in a field, or widely spaced with others in a savanna habitat, is probably this species. Slow growing and long-lived (200 to 300 years) in open habitats, it is usually shade-intolerant; most do not long survive being overtopped by successional forest growth. Old-field stands invaded by hardwood shrubs and trees typically last about 60 years.

Some red cedars begin producing cones at about age ten; most begin at about 25 years. Unlike northern white cedar, which bears both male and female cones on the same tree, red cedar is *dioecious*—that is, it bears the cones of each sex on separate trees. The tiny, scalelike pollen cones, maturing in winter and shedding pollen in March or earlier, are easily overlooked. The female (seed) cones, also appearing in early spring, receive wind pollination in May and June and ripen the following autumn. Seed cones appear blue and berrylike with a whitish bloom, contain 1 to 4 small brown seeds (usually only 1). These juniper "berries," though highly resinous, are also sweetish and relished by many birds (see Associates). Most female trees produce cones every year, abundantly every 2 or 3 years. Many unopened cones remain on trees over winter; most are dropped or dispersed by March.

Seed germination usually occurs in early spring of the second year after seed production, since the hard seed coats require a period of cold stratification to break dormancy. The seeds remain viable for only a year or so; one study found only 5 percent of them able to germinate after 14 months. Like most conifers, red cedar cannot reproduce by stump sprouting or suckering from the roots.

Red cedar foliage, appearing almost blackish green at times, remains on the tree for 5 or 6 years before replacement, gradually browning as it ages. Trees in northern areas also tend to develop a brownish or purplish tint in winter. Unlike its shallow-rooted, easily tipped-over white cedar cousin, red cedar firmly anchors itself by a deep, fibrous root system. This tree is rarely windthrown.

Associates: Eastern red cedar, highly adaptable to a variety of climatic and soil conditions, grows in almost any open or semiopen land habitat in eastern America, residing from southern Canada to the Gulf and extending westward into the Great Plains. The tree favors rocky limestone areas, old fields, hillsides, and dunes. It also frequents areas of thin soil commonly called *glades,* where red cedars dominate a mixture of other plant species. Cedar glades, common in parts of the Ozarks, southern Illinois, and southern Wisconsin, are defined as savanna-type areas midway between forest and prairie biomes. Red cedar also appears in mixed forest growth. Elsewhere, red cedar typically forms savannas, ultimately achieves pure stands on abandoned farmland or dry upland sites. It is often one of the first woody invaders of old fields and cleared areas. One New England study discovered that in rocky fields where both red cedar and common juniper grow, boulders and American robins are key elements to these plants' mutual presence: The robins perch and defecate on the rocks; their droppings, containing *Juniperus* seeds, eventually wash into frost cracks in the rocks. These protective *microhabitats* collect and supply ample moisture to germinating seeds. To common juniper seed, which also requires extensive periods of cold stratification, this stone-side microhabitat affords the lengthy protection vital to survival. The more adaptable red cedar seed, however, needs only a single cold period, can germinate quicker than common juniper, either in the rock cracks or on the ground between rocks. The absence of common juniper in these areas often indicates the existence of few rocks.

Occasionally stands of red cedar are observed to survive for years beneath, and shaded by, deciduous trees, sometimes even outlast them. The red cedars may in these cases outcompete the hardwoods for water and soil nutrients or may produce toxic *(allelopathic)* substances that discourage competitive tree growth—nobody yet knows.

Red cedar hosts numerous fungi, at least 50 species. Probably the foremost killer and maimer of the tree is annosum root rot fungus *(Heterobasidion annosum)*. Often introduced into the tree by means of a cut or wound, this fungus produces a stringy white rot, consuming and decaying the root system, often causing the tree to tip over. The fruiting bodies *(conks)* are large, flat, brown pore fungi that form on the trunk at ground level. Another wood-rot fungus infecting red cedar is cubical rot, also called red fomes rot or rose conk *(Fomitopsis cajanderi)*, forming dark, woody brackets and crumbly brown cubes of wood decay in the top of the tree. This fungus plus the bracket (pore) fungus *Daedalea juniperina* and the juniper pocket-rot fungus *Pyrofomes demidoffii* are heart-rot fungi, consuming the tree from within but producing conks as reproductive structures on the outside.

Foliage fungi also appear conspicuously on red cedar. Several cedar rusts *(Gymnosporangium)* infect red cedar as an alternate host in completing their life cycles. Most common and widespread is cedar-apple rust *(G. juniperi-virginianae)*, which appears as corky, reddish brown galls ("cedar apples") from grape- to walnut-size on red cedar twigs. During rainy weather in spring, the galls sprout bright orange, spaghettilike spore-horns *(telia)*, elongating to 2 inches, that release teliospores to the air currents. By late May or June, the telia dry and drop off the galls, which shrivel and turn black; they produce no more telia but often remain attached to the tree. Teliospores that settle on moist leaves of apple *(q.v.)* germinate quickly between temperatures of 56 and 61 degrees F. Yellow rust spots *(pycnia)* appear

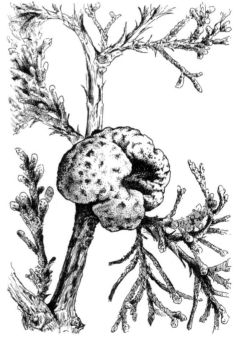

"Cedar apples," the reddish galls commonly seen on red cedar, release spores that infect apple trees with a Gymnosporangium *rust.*

on the apple leaves, increasing in size and producing pycniospores in a sticky secretion that attracts insects, which carry the spores between rust spots. The fertilized spores produce fruiting bodies *(aecia)* on leaf undersides and on fruit; the mature aeciospores, released to the winds in midsummer, produce new galls on red cedar twigs immediately or remain dormant there until the following spring.

Similar rusts for which red cedar provides an alternate host include cedar-hawthorn rust *(G. globosum)*, which produces smaller but more persistent galls (3 to 5 years), also infecting hawthorn *(q.v.)* and other fruit trees; and cedar-quince rust *(G. clavipes)*, producing swollen, elongated perennial galls on red cedar branches. These rusts do little harm to red cedar, but apple orchardists despise them because they reduce the yield and quality of fruit.

Another common fungus, forming cankers on diseased stems and eventually killing affected stems and branches in summer, is juniper blight *(Phomopsis juniperovora)*. It has no alternate host. Kabatina twig blight *(Kabatina juniperi)*, appearing in late winter or early spring, affects the previous year's shoot tips, causing foliage discolorations similar to symptoms of the spruce spider mite.

This mite *(Oligonychus ununguis)*, a common though almost invisible feeder in red cedar foliage, sucks plant juices, causing the foliage to turn gray and brown. Webbing between needles and grayish foliage may indicate their presence. A sheet of white paper held under a shaken branch will reveal whether spider mites are present—any tiny dots that move are mites.

Insect foliage feeders on red cedar are also common. Webbing, debris, and browning foliage indicate presence of the juniper webworm *(Dichomeris marginella)*, a brownish gelechiid moth caterpillar that forms colonial webs and pupates during summer in its webbing. Then the adult insects mate and lay eggs. The young larvae first feed as leaf miners, then construct a web on twig tips, passing the winter there, and resume feeding in spring. The evergreen bagworm moth *(Thyridopteryx ephemeraeformis)*, though it feeds on many ornamental plants, is a particular pest of red cedar. The young caterpillars construct portable cases of leaf and twig fragments webbed with silk. Cases may reach 2 inches long when the larvae become mature in August. They fasten their pendant bags securely to twigs, pupate there, and emerge as adults in September and October. The wingless female remains within the bag, to which the black-winged males come to mate, then lays 500 or more eggs in the bag. Young caterpillars emerge to build their own cases in June. Mites and bagworm moths may defoliate entire trees on occasion.

Caterpillars of the curve-lined angle *(Semiothisa continuata)*, an inchworm or geometrid moth, also feed on red cedar leaves. A dark green, slug-shaped caterpillar may be an olive or juniper hairstreak butterfly *(Callophrys gryneus)*, which produces broods in April and July.

A wax moth caterpillar *(Coleotechnites juniperella)*, a gelechiid, and a leaf roller caterpillar *(Choristoneura houstonana)* are also fairly common on red cedar foliage.

Sap-sucking insects include the juniper scale *(Carulaspis juniperi)* and the Fletcher
scale *(Parthenolecanium fletcheri);* dense masses of these tiny scale insects (Homoptera)
may crowd on twigs, causing foliage to brown and die. Female insects overwinter on the
tree, in May laying eggs that hatch in June. Uhler's stink bug *(Chlorochroa uhleri)*, common
on *Juniperus*, is bright green with yellow margins.

A bark and twig fauna also exists. The eastern juniper bark beetle *(Phloeosinus denta-
tus)* often attacks red cedars infected with annosum root rot, killing weakened trees. *P.
canadensis*, another species, also feeds on the tree. Larvae of these beetles feed and engrave
the wood beneath the bark. Wood-boring beetles also include the black-horned juniper
borer *(Callidium texanum);* the cedartree borer *(Semanotus ligneus);* the cypress and cedar
borer *(Oeme rigida);* and the pales weevil *(Hylobius pales)*, which also feeds on roots and
bark of saplings. Borers typically invade dead or dying red cedars, girdling them beneath
the bark. The juniper midge *(Contarinia juniperina)*, a gall gnat larva, bores into twigs at the
base of needles, killing the twig above the entrance hole. Weevil root feeders, including the
arborvitae weevil *(Phyllobius intrusus)* and strawberry root weevil *(Otiorhynchus ovatus)*,
also feed on the leaves.

Larvae of a fruit fly, *Rhagoletis juniperina*, consume the fruit pulp of the berrylike
cones, though not the seeds.

In contrast to most conifer leaf litter, which forms a highly acidic soil, red cedar
foliage's calcium content produces neutral or slightly alkaline soils beneath the trees, making such sites attractive habitats for earthworms, as many fishermen know.

Red cedar ranks as an important wildlife food plant because of its fruits. Some 90
species of birds have been recorded as periodic feeders at red cedar. The tree is largely dis-
seminated by *frugivorous* (fruit-eating) birds, including tree swallows, northern mockingbirds, European starlings, cedar waxwings, yellow-rumped warblers, eastern bluebirds,
purple finches (in contrast to all the others, purple finches depulp the fruits before eating,
consuming the seeds only), evening and pine grosbeaks. Less frequent consumers include
ruffed grouse, northern flickers, yellow-bellied sapsuckers, American crows, gray catbirds,
brown thrashers, hermit thrushes, northern cardinals, and fox sparrows. Especially important consumers and dispersers are American robins, many of which sustain, even glut,
themselves on red cedar fruits during their fall migration. (Sometimes the highly alcoholic
fruits, fermenting on the tree, produce drunken, staggering robins.) Most seed dispersal by
birds occurs between November and March; research has established that red cedar seeds
in bird droppings germinate 1 to 3 times more successfully than uneaten seeds. Most birds
pass the seeds within a half hour after ingestion, and a given tree's "seed shadow"—the

pattern of seed dispersal away from the tree—has been found to reflect bird movements, often along nearby fence lines or other perch sites. Most bird-dispersed seed of red cedar ends up less than 66 feet from the parent tree—but plenty of exceptions to the norm exist. A 1987 study indicated that red cedar dispersal into pastureland resulted primarily from starlings feeding on the fruits, the birds excreting the seeds in the short-grass habitats where they often forage. Thoreau, an assiduous explorer of scat along with so many other things, recorded that crow droppings around fishermen's ice holes at Walden Pond bore abundant red cedar seeds, the nearest of the trees being a mile distant.

Other red cedar fruit eaters include opossums, chipmunks, white-footed mice, meadow voles, foxes, skunks, and coyotes. In some areas, the fruits become an important winter food of red squirrels.

Terpenes, resins, and volatile oils make red cedar foliage unpalatable to most browsers. Although hunger-stressed white-tailed deer occasionally eat it, deer and cattle seldom touch it when other browse is available. Cottontail rabbits and mice sometimes browse on the seedlings.

Dense red cedar foliage provides escape, roosting, and nesting cover for a variety of birds. Cedar glades become frequent winter habitats for American robins, especially. Robins also nest in the tree, as do northern mockingbirds, chipping sparrows, and song sparrows. I have repeatedly found blue jay and loggerhead shrike nests in red cedar. Many small finches, including yellow-rumped warblers, dark-eyed juncos, and several sparrows, favor the tree for roosting cover. Eastern screech-owls also refuge commonly in this tree, and ring-necked pheasants often shelter in Great Plains red cedar windbreaks.

Lore: Eastern red cedar has long been cultivated (since 1664) as a versatile ornamental in landscaping and gardens, and many cultivars and varieties of both this and other juniper species have been developed for such purposes. "Although the best forms of red cedar are magnificent," wrote one landscapist, "the worst can be the rattiest and ugliest of trees in existence." The lack of species uniformity has somewhat hindered this tree's com-

A deer-browsed tree indicates scarce food resources, since red cedar is not a favored forage for deer.

mercial venues. Red cedar's practical uses extend to shelterbelt, windbreak, and living snow-fence plantings in parts of the Great Plains; its fibrous roots and adaptability to temperature extremes and poor soils— including mining spoils of coal, lead, zinc, and gravel—make it useful for erosion control, land conservation, and possibly mine-waste reclamation.

Red cedar fruits rank high in crude fat, fiber, and carbohydrates, moderately high in calcium. Their use in flavoring gin goes back to the 1650s. According to one account, "Dr. Franciscus de la Boie—nicknamed Dr. Sylvius—was searching for a means to get a good dose of juniper into his patients with kidney problems." He mixed grain alcohol with oil of juniper, and the potion "soon found a following among even the perfectly healthy." His name for his new medicine—*genievre*, after the French word for juniper—became gin. Thus red cedar, still used in gin making,

The density of red cedar foliage provides preferred nesting cover for several bird species.

became a main ingredient of this liquor from the outset. The berries—and other botanicals—are placed in tubes above the gin vats, their oils vaporizing into the alcohol. (Today, however, physicians consider juniper products—including gin—highly irritating to diseased kidneys.)

Juniper berries were used for food flavorings and spice in Egypt 5,000 years ago. Today they also find restrained use by chefs for food flavoring. However, "the possibility of overwhelming a dish and ending up with something that tastes and smells like eau de turpentine looms large," wrote food writer Molly O'Neill. The oils in red cedar foliage are toxic in more than slight quantity, and their usage in herbal medicines should be cautious. One discovery in the chemical cornucopia of red cedar is the antitumor compound called podophyllotoxin, also contained in may-apple, a woodland herb (see *The Book of Forest and Thicket*).

Yet red cedar has a long history of uses in native American and folk medicine. Just about every ailment to which human flesh is heir has, at some time, been treated (if not remedied) by teas, concoctions, rubs, or fumes of red cedar fruit, foliage, or bark. Venereal warts, asthma, bad dreams, worms, cold sores, and neck cramps are only a few of the conditions addressed by *Juniperus*. Probably every native tribe used some part of the tree in some way. The Chippewa used strips of the bark in matting and the reddish inner bark as a source of red dye.

Not a highly valued timber tree in most locales, red cedar has been used for fence posts (requiring 20- to 30-year-old trees) and sawlogs (40 to 60 years old) for furniture, woodenware, pencils, and interior paneling. Timber markets, especially in Asia, have expanded for this species in recent years, and American red cedar logs are now exported to Japan and Korea. The wood is durable, fine textured, aromatic, and easily worked. Its reputed moth-repellent capacity makes it a desirable material for cedar chests and closet or cupboard liners. (To renew the fragrance of old, oil-hardened cedar, one need only sandpaper the surface.) Historic uses include staves for French wine barrels and rail fences. Value of the wood for pencils once soared so high that red cedar rail fences were dismantled and sold by the pound (incense cedar, *Libocedrus decurrens,* an African species, has largely replaced red cedar as pencil wood). Red cedar remains an important source of cedarwood oil, an ingredient of many fragrant compounds used in soaps, liniments, insecticides, polishes, perfumes, and cosmetics.

Red cedar was introduced into Europe in the 1600s, and many of its modern landscape cultivars were developed there (many of which have never been introduced to their ancestral land). French-Canadian Acadians, deported from Nova Scotia by the British in 1755 to Louisiana (where they became known as Cajuns), found a familiar tree there and named their capital city for it—thus Baton Rouge ("red stick"), or red cedar. In Canada, the explorer Champlain used red cedar *(cypres rouges)* to make tall crosses attached with French insignia, which he placed on high points to claim land areas for France. Explorer Peter Kalm, in 1749, claimed that "the best canoes, consisting of a single piece of wood, are made of red cedar; for they last far longer than any other and are very light."

Native to every state east of the 100th meridian, eastern red cedar has extended its range into the Great Plains by regeneration from red cedar plantations. The tree readily hybridizes with its western counterpart, *J. scopulorum* (as well as with other juniper species), where their ranges overlap. Some studies suggest, in fact, that the entire western portion of the eastern red cedar population is hybrid in origin. Recent germ plasm studies also indicate that eastern red cedar may have derived originally from the western juniper complex.

Red cedar's foremost enemy is fire. Unlike many conifers, *Juniperus* is not adapted to periodic flame, and it cannot become established or persist on frequently burned sites. Adult trees may survive relatively cool ground burns, but seedlings and young trees need at least 20 years of fire freedom to mature. Many of the tree's typical habitats, however— such as sparsely vegetated rock, dune, and wetland areas—are not often threatened by fire.

Chickweed, Common *(Stellaria media)*. Pink family. Its 5 tiny, white petals, so deeply cleft that they appear as 10 atop the threadlike trailing stem or branching from leaf axils, and its paired oval leaves identify this low, inconspicuous, alien annual. Stems and lower leaf petioles show a fringe of hairs on one side. Chickweeds tend to spread out in extensive succulent mats.

Other names: Starweed, starwort, star chickweed, chicken-weed, white birdseye, winterweed, stitchwort, chickwhirtles, skirt buttons.

Close relatives: More than 100 *Stellaria* species exist, most in north temperate and arctic regions of the globe. Some 12 species reside in eastern North America; the narrow-leaved species are called stitchworts. Mouse-ear chickweeds *(Cerastium)* have shallower-notched petals, and some have hairy "mouse fur" leaves. Other family relatives include sandworts *(Arenaria)*, spurreys *(Spergula)*, sand-spurreys *(Spergularia)*, campions *(Silene)*, soapwort *(q.v.)*, and pinks *(Dianthus)*.

Lifestyle: Probably no other plant occupant of this book flowers for so long a duration through the year. Reproductively, chickweed is the mourning dove and house sparrow of the plant kingdom, may bloom and be seen from earliest spring to latest fall and even later. Yet the tiny flowers are not *easily* seen except during the plant's 2 main growth flushes: before tree leaves emerge in early spring, and after they fall in late autumn. Thus chickweed inversely reflects the deciduous seasonality of the year in its early and late ignitions on the ground.

Starlike bisexual chickweed flowers open anew each day, survive for only a day or so. They attract insects with copious, sometimes visible drops of nectar. The pollen-shedding anthers typically mature at the same time as the female stigmas, a timing confluence called *homogamy.* Chickweed does not depend exclusively on insects for pollination, however; during the colder seasons, when few insects are abroad, the flowers can and do self-pollinate. *Cleistogamy,* self-fertilization in unopened flowers, also occurs. The wind-dispersed seeds spill from cylindrical capsules (usually 9 or 10 seeds per capsule) that fracture at maturity. A typical plant produces more than 200 capsules, and seeds can remain viable in the soil for 40 years or longer, requiring sunlight to germinate. In milder climates, chickweeds often germinate in the fall and remain dormant over winter—though a warm spell in winter may bring on

Common chickweed displays its tiny flowers during most months of the year in the Northeast, yet is easily overlooked without close inspection.

rapid flowering. Thoreau once found frost-bitten chickweed blossoms in early February, concluding that "apparently it never rests." Lifespan of a spring or summer chickweed is about 5 to 7 weeks. The plant also reproduces by rooting at the *nodes* (joints) of the creeping stems. Chickweed roots are shallow and fibrous.

Chickweed is said to exemplify the phenomenon known as the "sleep of plants," in which the leaves fold over the new, about-to-open flower buds each night (I have not observed this), thus protecting them.

Associates: This plant's lengthy flowering season, ability to self-pollinate, extensive seed viability, and concurrent vegetative reproduction enable it to survive as one of the world's most successful weeds. Chickweed is also one of the world's most common plants, its green carpets appearing wherever humans settle in the Northern Hemisphere. It favors lawns, cultivated fields and gardens, disturbed soil of today, yesterday, or the day before. Preferring cool temperatures and moist ground, it can tolerate cold but not drought. Common microhabitats include partial shade near buildings and beneath row crops, in gullies and track marks. High-nitrogen soils, such as in barnyards and around chicken coops, are common chickweed sites. The plant can compete with crop seedlings, smothering out strawberry, barley, and potato plants, among others.

Common fungal parasites include a leaf spot, *Septoria stellariae;* and a rust, *Puccinia arenariae.* Aphids sometimes carry these fungi from plant to plant.

Chickweed is also an alternate host of fir broom rust *(Melampsorella caryophyllacerarum).* Aeciospores from balsam fir needles infect chickweed leaves in summer, producing basidiospores the following spring; these infect balsam needles, stimulating the formation of twiggy growths called yellow witches' brooms.

Chickweed harbors some dozen plant viruses, which in some cases parasitize the plant and may also be transmitted by aphids to crop plants. One virus vector is a tiny root nematode or roundworm *(Trichodorus)* that often overwinters on a newly germinated plant. The soybean cyst nematode *(Heterodera glycines)* also parasitizes chickweed roots.

Pollinators include many sorts of bees, flies, and small insects such as thrips (Thysanoptera), although this plant scarcely depends upon insects for reproduction.

Common sap-sucking insects include the shallot aphid *(Myzus ascalonicus)* and the green peach aphid *(M. persicae).*

Small, dark brown, seed-eating ground beetles *(Amara aenea),* carabids, are often seen near chickweeds. Ants also transport the seeds to their nests.

Moth caterpillars that feed on chickweed include the drab brown wave *(Lobocleta ossularia),* the chickweed geometer *(Haematopis grataria),* the simple wave *(Scopula junctaria),* the red twin-spot *(Xanthorhoe ferrugata),* and the sharp-angled carpet moth *(Euphyia unangulata);* all are inchworm or "looper" caterpillars (Geometridae). A dark green caterpillar with yellow and black stripes along the sides may be a dainty sulphur butterfly *(Nathalis iole);* the adult butterflies are small, yellow winged with brown markings.

Many if not most seed-eating birds relish chickweed seeds—birds are probably this plant's foremost dispersers—and some gamebirds and songbirds devour the tender leaves of new sprouts as well. Bird consumers include northern bobwhites, mourning doves, eastern towhees, American goldfinches, and chipping, savannah, American tree, white-crowned, and white-throated sparrows. Chickweed is a well-known favorite graze of barnyard chickens, hence the plant's name; and seeds and greens of the plant were long fed to caged birds. Cottontail rabbits also graze on the plant. Livestock, including pigs, cows, sheep, and horses, will eat it, but goats are said to reject it. The plant can accumulate nitrates to toxic levels, potentially causing digestive disorders in mammal foragers.

Lore: Chickweed tea, a mild diuretic and age-old soothing treatment for coughs, also served as a wash for itches and skin irritations, and the leaves were used for poultices. "In a word," wrote 17th-century English herbalist John Gerard, "it comforteth, digesteth, defendeth and suppurateth very notably" (what more could one ask of an herb?). Chickweed water was also said to "curb obesity."

Green leaves and stems, sources of vitamin C, iron, and phosphorus, can be added to salads, can also be boiled and served as spinachlike greens.

Chickweeds, natives of Eurasia but now global residents, vary in feature and appearance, reflecting their versatile adaptations to numerous habitats and climates. Plants differ in size, growth habit, length and shape of petals, number of stamens, and number and size of seeds. One researcher classified 32 varieties of this species based on such characters.

Chickweed is said to be the commonest weed of Europe.

Chicory *(Cichorium intybus).* Aster family. Blue, stalkless flowers with squared-off, fringed rays along a rigid, almost leafless stem characterize this summer alien perennial. Basal leaves appear dandelionlike. Chicory typically grows 2 or 3 feet tall.

Other names: Succory, blue or ragged sailor, bunk, blue daisy, coffee-weed, wild endive, forage chicory.

Close relatives: Some 9 *Cichorium* species exist, all European and Mediterranean region natives—among them, endive *(C. endiva),* a popular salad green. Aster family relatives include common dandelion, showy goat's-beard, asters (all *q.v.*), and many others.

Lifestyle: Chicory's blue, radiating flowerheads on straggly stems are familiar sights along summer roadsides. The flowerheads, an inch or more across, occur in loose clusters on the upper stem, but only a single flowerhead in a cluster blooms at a time. Some guidebooks state that chicory flowerheads typically open in early morning and close by noon,

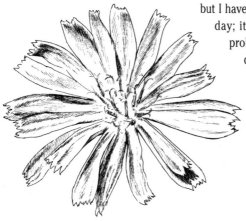

Chicory's blue, fringed ray flowers provide one of summer's most familiar field and roadside scenes.

but I have seen chicory flowering at all hours of the day; it seems more accurate to say that they probably flower most vigorously early in the day, gradually close and "lose face" as the afternoon advances. Occasional plants may bear white or pink flowerheads.

Unlike many of its aster relatives, which display both disk and ray flowers, chicory has only flat ray, or *ligulate,* florets on each flowerhead, usually some 12 to 20 of them. Each straplike, insect-pollinated floret is bisexual, bearing 5 stamens and an ovary at its base (the florets can, in the absence of insects, self-fertilize). The single-seeded fruits are angular, fringed *achenes.* Reproduction occurs solely by seed. Chicory blooms from July to the first frost.

Chicory produces long, thick, and fleshy taproots, typically extending 6 inches down or more. These plants have a milky, bitter sap, similar to dandelions (the substance taraxacine is common to both). After frost, the stems die back to a basal rosette of leaves much resembling those of dandelions. The rosette may overwinter, lowly and unnoticed, above the crown of its root or may itself die back to the crown, which sprouts new rosette leaves in the spring.

Associates: Chicory favors open, disturbed-soil habitats—roadsides, old fields, vacant lots—but seldom thrives in cultivated fields (except where it exists as a crop itself). It also favors limestone over acid soils. Chicory plants often emerge from cracks in pavement and asphalt. A 1992 study found that chicory germinated much more successfully on dry, rocky roadsides than in adjacent ditches with deep, fertile soil; the microhabitat of crevices formed by rock-soil interfaces sheltered the seedlings and supplied moisture for germinating chicory, whereas the plant litter on smoother, more fertile surfaces prevented such lodgment. I often find chicory growing as a foremost road-edge associate of foxtail-grasses *(Setaria)* and common ragweed *(q.v.).*

Soft rot diseases caused by bacteria—mainly *Erwinia* and *Pseudomonas* genera—sometimes infect chicory, causing leaf and crown decay. Chicory is one of many hosts for the virus disease called aster yellows, carried mainly by the aster leafhopper, a sap-sucking insect (see Asters).

A foremost agricultural associate of chicory is the sugar beet *(Beta vulgaris);* often planted and rotated with sugar beet crops, chicory reduces soil infestations of nematodes (roundworms) that attack the beets. The same machinery and culture methods are used for both crops.

Aphids such as *Dactynotus cirsii* suck chicory juices, sometimes causing distorted leaf growth. Shot-hole perforations in leaves indicate the presence of flea beetles (Chrysomelidae), insects noted for their enlarged rear legs and jumping ability.

Adult common buckeye butterflies *(Junonia coenia),* brown with large eyespots on the wings, often visit chicory flowers, as do syrphid flies *(Toxomerus marginatus).* Also look for lizard beetles *(Acropteroxys gracilis),* long, slender insects whose larvae feed in chicory stems. Slugs are common mollusk feeders on chicory seedlings.

Chicory's foremost pollinators are bees—mainly honeybees *(Apis mellifera),* leafcutting bees (Megachilidae), and ground-nesting bees (Andrenidae, Halictidae).

Chicory's foremost seed consumer is probably the American goldfinch. Chicory rosettes provide a nourishing and palatable livestock forage; the plant has long been cultivated for forage purposes in many areas of the globe but only recently in North America. Deer and other wildlife grazers mainly consume leaves and rosettes, since chicory's rigid flower stems are less digestible.

Lore: Chicory has a long history of human usages. Ancient Egyptians and Romans knew the plant well, and Europeans have cultivated it for at least a millenium. It continues to be grown as a vegetable and salad crop, especially in France, Belgium, and the Netherlands. The white subsurface leaflets are the tastiest parts of the plant.

Four groups of agricultural chicory exist: the loose-leaf chicories, used for salad greens; the heading chicories, forced varieties also used in salads; the root chicories, cultivated for food and chemicals; and the forage chicories, raised as livestock feed. Salad chicories are known in Europe as "Italian dandelion" potherbs, and French or Belgian endive (also called Witloof chicory) is force-grown for its root as a salad delicacy. In North America, recent interest has focused on growing chicory as a root crop. In addition to its uses as a noncaffeine coffee additive or substitute, chicory root contains large amounts of a fructose carbohydrate called inulin, used as a sweetener in food products. Not fully digestible itself, inulin reduces caloric content of foods while increasing bulk and is medically beneficial as a prebiotic (encouraging beneficial bacterial growth, retarding various pathogenic bacteria) in the colon. Chicory root extracts may prove useful in treating heart irregularities as well. The ground-up root is also utilized in the food industry as a seasoning and flavor enhancer, and some commercial dog foods contain chicory.

Chicory, along with several other plants, has evoked recent interest as a possible agent in *phytomining*—that is, the retrieval by plants of metallic substances or pollutants from soil. Gold, changed to soluble form by use of sodium thiocyanate, can be root-absorbed by chicory, though whether in sufficient quantity for economic benefit remains questionable. Recently chicory has also been used in fructan research; fructan polymers, containing fructose sugars, form carbohydrate reserves in plants and play important roles in plant metabolism, useful in biochemical studies.

Native to the eastern Mediterranean region of Europe, chicory was first introduced to America in 1785 by Massachusetts governor James Bowdoin, who liked it in his salads. It remained an import, however, both before and after the 1890s, when a few American farmers began cultivating it for salad greens and coffee.

The name blue sailor derives from a European legend about a woman left at the roadside by a sailor; she waited there faithfully for the lout until the gods tired of her (or "took pity on her," as the story goes) and changed her into a chicory plant, a transformation that apparently enraptured her (she was blue anyway, they probably reasoned). The word *chicory* may have originated in the Arabic name for the plant—*chicourey*—reflecting the influence of Arabian physicians in medieval Europe. "With only minor modifications," as weed botanist Pamela Jones wrote, "the word *chicory* has traveled through the millennia and been absorbed into virtually every European language."

Cinquefoils (*Potentilla* species). Rose family. Some of our most familiar summer yellow wildflowers, cinquefoils suggest wild strawberry in the disk or saucer shape of their 5-petaled flowers. Most cinquefoil species also show distinctive 5-parted leaves splayed like fingers (palmately compound).

The most common *Potentilla* species include common cinquefoil *(P. simplex)*, a low, sprawling, native perennial with arching stems and a single flower to a stalk; sulphur or rough-fruited cinquefoil *(P. recta)*, an alien perennial standing 1 or 2 feet erect with hairy stems and foliage and large (up to an inch across), notched, pale yellow flowers in flat terminal clusters; and rough cinquefoil *(P. norvegica)*, sometimes an annual, sometimes a biennial or short-lived perennial, native to both Old and New Worlds, standing 1 to 3 feet tall, and exhibiting 3 instead of 5 leaflets.

Other names: Five-finger, five-leaf, old-field five-finger or cinquefoil, creeping cinquefoil *(P. simplex)*; sulfur cinquefoil, sulphur five-finger, upright cinquefoil *(P. recta)*; strawberry-weed *(P. norvegica)*.

Close relatives: Some 200 *Potentilla* species reside in the Northern Hemisphere worldwide, almost 25 in eastern North America. Several alien cinquefoils have become common weeds of lawns and roadsides. Closest kin to common cinquefoil is probably dwarf cinquefoil *(P. canadensis)*, a more delicate plant with densely hairy stems. Other cinquefoils include both herb and shrub species, most in dry land habitats but several in wetlands (see *The Book of Swamp and Bog*). Closely allied plants include wild strawberry *(q.v.)*, Indian strawberry *(Duchesnea indica)*, avens *(Geum)*, and all other rose family plants.

Lifestyle: The broad petals and disk flower form seen in most cinquefoils also appear in unrelated plants such as marsh-marigold and other buttercups, frostweeds, and others, as well as in closely related plants like strawberry. The shallow bowl or dish prototype of these plants has evolved independently as an efficient host of nonspecialized insect pollinators. Cinquefoil can, however, also self-fertilize in the absence of insects. Some sources say this happens at night when the flowers close and the (male) anthers touch the (female) stigma.

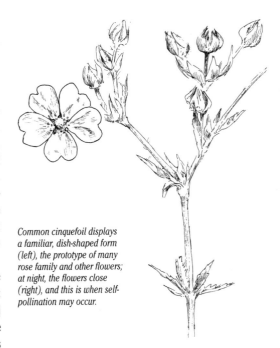

Common cinquefoil displays a familiar, dish-shaped form (left), the prototype of many rose family and other flowers; at night, the flowers close (right), and this is when self-pollination may occur.

One botanist described the cinquefoil pollination procedure thus: "The flowers secrete honey [nectar] on a ringlike ridge surrounding the base of the [male] stamens. Insects alighting on the petals dust themselves with the pollen but do not touch the stigmas, as the honey ring extends beyond. If they alight in the middle of the next flower, they dust the pollen against the stigma and cross-pollinate it." Another observer, biologist Bernd Heinrich, stated that bees seek only pollen from cinquefoils, and that these pollen collectors (since individual bees often specialize in visiting only a single plant species during the flowering season) "vibrated the flowers, shaking loose the pollen" without attempting the futile efforts (for their own mouthparts) of collecting nectar. Individual flowers usually last only for a day, strewing their petals on the ground in the afternoon, with new flower buds opening the next morning. The seeds, encased in *achenes*, develop loose inside the dried, goblet-shaped urn of the former flowerhead.

Common cinquefoil rises from a short subsurface stem *(rhizome)*, producing trailing stolons or runners up to 4 feet long that may also root at widely spaced nodes or joints. This plant also reproduces by "leapfrogging"—that is, by producing a terminal tuber and new plant where the bowed stem arches to the ground. Like the other perennial cinquefoils, *P. simplex* produces a basal rosette of leaves in the fall; it remains green beneath the snow, and from it rises a new flowering stem in spring.

Sulphur cinquefoil usually exhibits 5 leaflets, occasionally 7. It has a woody taproot with short, branching roots, but no rhizomes. This species displays a characteristic mode of regeneration from the root crown: New shoots encircle the root crown as the latter gradually rots away (over a period of 6 to 8 years); the eventual result is a circular stand of erect clones surrounding a central gap, in which grasses and other plants usually sprout. Otherwise this cinquefoil reproduces only by seed, which average some 60 per flower; a single plant may produce some 1,600 seeds. Many remain viable for 4 years or more in the soil. Cinquefoil plants as old as 20 years are not uncommon, the aging based on total diameter of a clonal colony. These plants often produce a continuous cover over large areas of roadside and in old-field patches.

Rough cinquefoil, the most adaptive of all 3 cinquefoils in its life history sequencing, also reproduces only from seed. It produces smaller but many more flowers per stem (about 100) than the others. Whether this plant develops as an annual, biennial, or short-lived perennial seems to depend upon its habitat and locale. In cultivated ground, it usually rises as an annual; in poor or waste ground, it is often a biennial; and in cold climates, it often becomes a perennial. This species typically flowers and produces seed later in summer than the others. Seedheads average about 100 seeds per flower, a single plant about 13,000.

Associates: It "weaves its embroidery over the stony and barren roadside," wrote one botanist. Common cinquefoil favors open sun, typically inhabits dry, sandy ground—fields, roadsides, open woods—throughout the East, Midwest, and South. Sulphur cinquefoil favors dry or wasteland sites from southern Canada throughout North America, also in Eurasia, north Africa, and Asia. Rough cinquefoil adapts to both moist and dry soils and has a more northern distribution, occurring from northern Canada into Mexico; it is also, like the preceding species, circumboreal. Separate, apparently indigenous populations and forms of rough cinquefoil occur in both Eurasia and North America; probably both forms now reside here.

Numerous fungi parasitize *Potentilla* plants. They include leaf spots *(Septoria),* leaf blights *(Marssonina potentillae, Ramularia arvensis),* black stem *(Mycosphaerella),* downy mildew *(Peronospora),* rusts *(Phragmidium ivesiae, Pucciniastrum),* and several others, some of which also afflict strawberry and other rose family plants. Sulphur cinquefoil provides an alternate host for the hop mildew *(Sphaerotheca humuli);* and rough cinquefoil sometimes hosts *Rhizoctonia solani,* a destructive rot and foliage blight on peas and alfalfa, among other plants.

Strawberry aphids *(Chaetosiphon fragaefolii)* winter in the egg stage on cinquefoils, moving to strawberry plants when they hatch.

Cinquefoil pollination is accomplished by a variety of flies, bees, and beetles, none exclusive to *Potentilla.* Notice that most bees seen on these flowers are laden with pollen.

Dorcas copper butterflies *(Lycaena dorcas),* displaying fawn brown, purplish-tinted wings, have been observed laying eggs on cinquefoils. Other coppers also visit the plants.

Bright yellow flowers such as cinquefoils do not look yellow to the compound eyes of pollinating insects but reflect ultraviolet "bee purple," invisible to human eyes, whereas the flowers we perceive as purple often look greenish to them. The scientific lesson here is that there is no absolute yellow—or any other color. The way one perceives the plants of field and roadside—indeed, one might say the visible world generally—depends greatly upon the kinds of radiant energy one's eyes have evolved to detect.

An occasional bud and stem feeder is the strawberry weevil (see Strawberry, Wild). Look for round galls on the leaf axils; these are caused by larvae of a cynipid wasp, *Gonaspis potentillae.* Two other cynipid wasp species, *Diastrophus niger* and *D. minimus,* also create stem galls.

Cinquefoil's characteristic 5-parted leaf gives the plant its name; it also symbolized curative powers to herbalists.

Cinquefoil seeds bear oily appendages called *elaiosomes* that are attractive to ants, which collect and store the seeds, aiding the plant's dispersal in the process.

Cinquefoils do not rank as important food plants for birds and mammals. The plants, owing to a high tannin content, are also unpalatable to livestock. Ruffed grouse and American woodcock are known to consume seeds and foliage; cottontail rabbits munch on the leaves; and voles sometimes collect and store rhizomes of common cinquefoil.

Lore: Sulphur cinquefoil is a potent aggressor, especially in many western states. Overgrazing, which reduces grass competition, favors its establishment, and it has become a major weed invader of the northern Rockies.

Cinquefoil is Middle English for "five-leaf"; *Potentilla* means "little powerful one," presumably referring to the plants' abundant tannins, making them potently astringent. Common cinquefoil found frequent usage among native tribes; the pounded rhizomes made medicinal tea, which was used to treat diarrhea, to poultice sores and stop bleeding, and as a skin wash. Use it "as a gargle for loose teeth and spungy gums," recommended aging botanist Manasseh Cutler in 1785. Certain modern antiwrinkle cosmetic preparations contain *Potentilla,* as did love potions and witches' brews and banes in medieval Europe. Roots or rhizomes of Eurasian cinquefoils "have been employed medicinally since the time of Hippocrates and Dioscorides," according to one source. The 5-fingered-leaf, because of its resemblance to the human hand, betokened healing to many of our forebears who believed in the doctrine of signatures (see Blue-weed).

Young shoots and leaves of cinquefoil are edible as salad greens.

Clovers (*Trifolium* species). Pea family. Round flowerheads and trifoliate leaves (divided into 3 leaflets) identify clovers. Most stand only a few inches tall. The 2 most common species are white clover *(T. repens)*, having white or pinkish flowers, the leaves on separate stalks, with rounded leaflets that show pale, angular markings (chevrons); and red clover *(T. pratense)*, often taller (up to a foot or more), with purple-red flowers and oval leaflets both on the same stalk, also with chevron markings. Both are alien perennials.

Other names: Dutch clover, honeysuckle clover, white trefoil, shamrock *(T. repens)*; purple, meadow, honeysuckle, or peavine clover, cowgrass *(T. pratense)*.

Close relatives: Some 17 *Trifolium* species—of about 250 worldwide—reside in eastern North America; most are Eurasian natives. They include alsike clover *(T. hybridum)*, zigzag clover *(T. medium)*, rabbit-foot clover *(T. arvense)*, and several hop-clovers. Other close kin include sweet clovers, bush-clovers, alfalfa, vetches, and tick-trefoils (all *q.v.*), among many others.

Lifestyle: Just about any meadow or grassland displays abundant-flowering white and red clovers in spring and summer, a sight that extends far into fall. Clovers are bucolic flowers, havens of busy bees, forming the turf of pastoral odes. That turf, of course, was mainly European, since clovers did not reside in North America before white settlement introduced them. As emigrants, clovers serve to remind us that plant imports are not invariably harmful additions to our native ecology.

Flowers of both white and red clovers are insect-pollinated, incapable of self-fertilization. Like most legumes, clovers also have nitrogen-fixing root nodules (see Alfalfa). At night, clover leaflets often close, the middle leaflet bending over the 2 folded side leaflets, probably a heat-conserving movement.

White clover, a somewhat prostrate plant, has creeping stems *(stolons)*—up to 12 per plant—that may extend 15 inches long or longer over the ground surface. These stems often sink roots at their joints, or nodes, where they touch soil, producing new plants. White clover thus usually occurs in clonal colonies. Size of the leaflets and of the plant itself varies widely with habitat and climate conditions. The plant develops a taproot that may go a foot or more deep, but this root usually dies off before or during the plant's second year.

White clover remains a perennial by virtue of its secondary root system—that is, because of its stolons and its foremost bud development into stolons rather than flowers. Independent plants result when the connecting stolons die off and decay. Detachment from the parent plant does not change an individual plant's clonal origins, however, and most patches of white clover—even though populated by separate plants—probably consist of single clones. The same or different clones may be identified by the specific patterns of white chevrons on the leaflets; these markings, genetic in origin, result from the presence of air spaces in the leaf palisade or photosynthetic tissue. Given habitat stability, clones may sur-

vive for 2 decades—in some cases, much longer, even though few
parts of an individual plant survive longer than a year. Leaves
can survive about 40 days in summer, longer in winter; flowers typically survive 3 to 4 weeks, sometimes longer.

Each white clover flowerhead consists of about
100 florets; flowering proceeds from base to apex of
the flowerhead. Each floret is a bisexual flower
that depends upon insect pollination, rarely pol-
linates itself. The (female) style and stigma project beyond the 10 (male) anthers. When an
insect alights, seeking nectar from the deep floret tube, it trips open the floret, brushes past
the stigma, and in so doing deposits pollen from
a previously visited floret or plant. On its way in
and out, it also collects new pollen on its body
for transportation to another floret. Entomolo-
gist George E. Bohart described the clover pollinating mechanism as "of the piston type," in
contrast to the floral devices of alfalfa and some other legumes. "Pressure against the standard and wing petals," he wrote, "operates a lever which forces the stigma and anthers
upward and out of the enclosed keel petals. When the pressure is released, the sexual parts
revert to their former position."

Specific shapes of the whitish chevron markings, seen most prominently on white clover leaflets, may identify individual clones of the plant.

After fertilization, the floret withers, turns brown, and droops, gradually transforming
the flowerhead to a crumpled mass. Seeds mature from 3 weeks to a month after fertilization. Most mature seeds are immediately viable, but about 25 percent or more have hard
seed coats, requiring time or abrasion to become permeable to moisture and thus germination. These hard seeds may pass intact through the digestive tracts of birds and mammals,
aiding distribution of the plant.

In subtropical areas, the perennial white clover of temperate regions becomes a winter annual—that is, it germinates from seed in the fall and overwinters as a shoot, completing its life cycle the following summer.

The floral biology of red clover is much the same as for white clover. Form of the
plant is somewhat different: Red clover usually stands larger, more erect; its leaflets and
flowerheads also appear larger and more elongated; its stems are thick and somewhat
hairy; and its leaf undersides are velvety, whereas the entire white clover plant is smooth.
Also, red clover flowerheads surmount leafy stems rather than leafless ones; and vegetative reproduction via creeping stolons only occasionally occurs. Usually this plant, in contrast to white clover, occurs solitarily or in small, single-plant groups.

Red clover florets, which may number from 50 to more than 200 per head, open over about a week's time, proceeding from base to top in sequence. This plant's pollination, it is said, has been more extensively studied than that of any other plant, not only in North America but also in Europe. Two ovules occupy each ovary, but usually only one of them develops into a seed. Red clover seed growers do not like to see fields that look like flower gardens, for widespread color in the field means that pollination is not occurring. Rusty brown and wilted florets, on the other hand, indicate successful pollination. Some cultivated red clover varieties are winter annuals or biennials, producing only a leafy rosette the first year, but most red clovers are short-lived perennials.

Associates: Both clovers adapt to a variety of soils and climates. They favor mild to cool, humid climates, abundant rainfall, and soils in the 6 to 7 pH range. White clover thrives from the Arctic Circle to the subtropics, limited only by excessive cold, drought, and equatorial heat and plant competition. It may be somewhat better adapted to cold climates than red clover; its tendency to sink roots at frequent nodes along the stolons makes it less vulnerable to winter injury. Its short-lived taproot and fibrous root system make it more vulnerable to drought, however. Red clover's range is approximately the same. It appears somewhat more shade-tolerant than white clover but requires a larger soil phosphorus component.

One may often find both clovers growing wild in the same field or fencerow. Grasses tend to dominate clovers wherever soil nitrogen is high; at lower nitrogen levels, clovers, being able to convert atmospheric nitrogen for their own use, increase. Nitrogen fertilizer may, in fact, retard development of nitrogen-fixing nodules—indeed, the best way to eliminate clovers from a field is to add nitrogen fertilizer. Many grass species associate with clovers in fields and lawns; a frequent one is ryegrass *(Lolium perenne)*.

The closest associates of clovers—indeed of most legumes—are the nitrogen-fixing bacteria *(Rhizobium trifolii)* that occur in root nodules (see Alfalfa). In addition to these bacteria are several species of *mycorrhizal fungi* (including *Glomus* and *Gigaspora*), vital to nutrient absorption by clover roots.

Lesser or small broom-rape *(Orobanche minor)*, a blue-flowered root parasite on *Trifolium* clovers, is a common associate. Research has shown that it invades clover roots through the nodules created by *Rhizobium* bacteria. Another common parasite, which twines and attaches to clover stems by means of numerous suckers *(haustoria)*, is clover dodder *(Cuscuta epithymum)*.

Both clover species host a long list of viral, bacterial, and fungal parasites. Such disease organisms, however, tend to infect crop clovers planted for forage or seed more often than volunteer plants and clones. Root rot fungi *(Fusarium, Rhizoctonia, Colletotrichum,* among others) attack clover roots and stolons. Leaf and stem spots *(Cercospora),* blotches, and rusts *(Cymadothea, Uromyces)* are all common fungi that may cause leaf loss. Crown rot *(Sclerotina trifoliorum)* and northern anthracnose (caused by the fungus *Kabatiella caulivora)* especially attack red clover.

Numerous insects find clover a foremost food plant. Most can be found on both white and red clovers. Leaf feeders include spider mites *(Tetranychus)*, which spin light webbing on leaf undersides; clover leaf weevils *(Hypera punctata);* and alfalfa weevils *(H. postica)*. Reddish, pinhead-size, spiderlike creatures called clover mites *(Bryobia praetiosa)* feed on clover roots and foliage. In the fall, like ladybird beetles and box elder bugs, they may amass in huge numbers inside houses or other shelters, seeking protected places to hibernate.

Sap-sucking insects include nymphs of meadow spittlebugs *(Philaenus spumarius)*, which leave frothy masses on stems and leafstalks (they also stunt clover growth and cause a bunching of terminal leaves); yellow clover aphids *(Therioaphis trifolii);* pea aphids *(Acyrthosiphon pisum);* clover leafhoppers *(Aceratagallia sanguinolenta);* potato leafhoppers *(Empoasca fabae)*, which cause stunting and browning of leaves; and pale legume bugs *(Lygus elisus)* and western tarnished plant bugs *(L. hesperus)*, which cause wilt.

A long list exists of moth caterpillar feeders on clover foliage. Common ones include the toothed somberwing *(Euclidia cuspidea)*, clover and forage loopers *(Caenurgina crassiuscula, C. erechtea)*, green cloverworm *(Hypena scabra)*, and black-banded owlet *(Phalaenostola larentioides);* all of these are noctuid moths. Other moth caterpillars include the black-spotted prominent *(Dasylophia anguina)*, the confused eusarca *(Eusarca confusaria)*, numerous wave moths *(Idaea* and others), and the chickweed geometer *(Haematopis grataria);* all except the first, a notodontid, are inchworm or geometer caterpillars. The clover head caterpillar, larva of a tortricid moth *(Grapholita interstinctana)*, feeds mainly in the developing flowerheads and bottom leaves of red clover.

Butterfly caterpillars also frequent clovers. Look for the following: the gray hairstreak *(Strymon melinus)*, reddish brown with a very small head; the silvery blue *(Glaucopsyche lygdamus)*, green and slug-shaped, much attended by ants; the alfalfa butterfly or orange sulphur *(Colias eurytheme)*, a striped green caterpillar; the common or clouded sulphur *(C. philodice)*, similar in appearance; the southern dog face *(C. cesonia)*, green and covered with small black tubercles; the cloudless sulphur *(Phoebis sennae)*, yellowish green; the sleepy orange *(Eurema nicippe)*, green and downy; the little yellow *(E. lisa)*, similar in appearance; and the northern cloudy wing *(Thorybes pylades)*, a skipper, green with wartlets. A butterfly field guide will help one identify the many clover-feeding species.

Insects that feed in clover flowerheads include flower thrips *(Frankliniella tritici);* larvae of the clover seed midge *(Dasineura leguminicola)*, which consumes flower parts, thus preventing seed formation; the clover seed weevil *(Tychius picirostris)* and red clover seed weevil *(T. stephensi);* and lesser clover leaf and clover head weevils *(Hypera nigrirostris, H. meles)*, which can prevent flowering. *Hypera* weevils usually undergo a summer diapause, a period of semidormancy as the host plants age. The weevils revive to lay eggs on the clovers in fall, some in spring. A wasp larva destructive to developing seed is the clover seed chalcid *(Bruchophagus gibbus)*.

Clover roots also support a fauna, including many species of nematodes (roundworms), some of which induce galls on the roots. At least one of them *(Tylenchorhyncus agri)* actually stimulates red clover root growth by feeding on epidermal cells in the region of root elongation.

Acrolophus popeanella, a tineid moth caterpillar, forms silken tunnels amidst red clover roots. Beetle larvae of the clover root curculio *(Sitona hispidulus)* also feed on roots, seriously damaging the plant. Another beetle pest of red clover is the clover root borer *(Hylastinus obscurus),* whose larvae mine tunnels in the roots, weakening them and often killing the plant. Clover stem borers *(Languria mozardi)* forage as beetle larvae in the stems of clovers and other legumes.

The main pollinators of both white and red clovers are honeybees *(Apis mellifera)* and bumblebees *(Bombus).* Bumblebees are the major pollinators of red clover; these long-tongued bees and red clover flowers seem "made for each other," in the words of one researcher. Queen bumblebees pollinate about 4 times as many clover florets per minute as do honeybees, which visit red clover primarily for pollen collection. Where red clover is being raised as a seed crop, however, the presence of other nectar-producing plants nearby—especially white clover, sweet clovers, and alsike clover—competes for bumblebee attention and may result in inadequate red clover pollination. About 2 to 3 honeybee colonies (hives) per acre are considered necessary for adequate white clover pollination. Solitary mason or leafcutting bees *(Osmia)* also visit clovers; common on beard-tongues *(q.v.), Osmia* may aid clover pollination where beard-tongues are also planted. Other, less frequently pollinating bees include solitary digger bees *(Tetralonia, Melissodes).*

Butterflies also frequent clover flowerheads for nectar. Especially prevalent on red clover, in my observation, are skippers (Hesperiidae). These small, skittering fliers sometimes swarm over the red blossoms in abundance. Large sphinx moths also visit clover flowers; hummingbird clearwings *(Hemaris thysbe)* and white-lined sphinxes *(Hyles lineata)* are often seen on red clover.

Grazing livestock and wildlife alike relish clovers as forage. These plants are often dispersed as seeds in cow and horse manure. Leaves of both white and red clovers provide choice foods for Canada geese, American widgeons, northern bobwhites, ruffed and sharp-tailed grouse, wild turkeys, prairie-chickens, sandhill cranes, and American coots. Snowshoe hares, cottontail rabbits, striped skunks, woodchucks, ground squirrels, lemmings, voles, and white-tailed deer also consume clover foliage. Horned larks, among other birds, eat the seeds.

Lore: White clover has probably become the most important pasture legume of temperate regions. Planted with grass mixtures in unfertilized pasture, the clover provides nitrogenous compounds from its nodules to grass roots, producing highly nutritious forage. White clover, though seldom raised by itself as a hay crop, may be harvested in a mixed clover-grass crop for hay and silage. More than 70 commercial cultivars of white clover exist. The main cultivated form in North America is ladino, which grows faster and 2 to 4 times larger than "wild" white clover. All varieties hybridize, so the genetic picture of white clover is a melange of variable features within a frame of broad botanical characteristics. Among plant breeders, white clover is known as the *Drosophila* (a genus of fruit or pomace flies, used extensively in genetic and evolutionary experimentation) of plant ecology for its complex, almost endless genetic variations.

White clover is not totally manna for livestock, however. Animals fed large amounts of white clover become subject to bloat, which can cause reproductive problems associated with increased estrogenic activity—the dominant estrogen is coumestrol—or even death. Providing balanced forage diets can easily control such risks in most cases. In any case, cattle tend to discontinue grazing pastures in which white clover exceeds 20 to 40 percent of the herbage dry matter. Most American white clover seed production occurs in Louisiana and in irrigated areas of the West; ladino seed comes mainly from California. In addition to forage, white clover is planted for erosion control on road banks, for soil improvement, and as a nitrogen-enriching cover crop in orchards.

Red clover, probably the most widely grown of all clovers, is raised as a hay or seed crop, as a pasture legume for soil renovation and forage, and in small-grain mixtures with oats, barley, or winter wheat. Deeper rooted and more shade-tolerant than white clover, it also tolerates moderately acid soils but requires abundant soil phosphorus and potassium. Many local and regional strains of red clover, largely sited according to latitude, exist throughout North America and Europe. Cultivated red clovers fall into 1 of 3 distinct types: early flowering, also called medium red clover, predominant in North America; late flowering, or mammoth red clover, requiring longer photoperiods or daylengths (16 to 18 hours); and wild red clovers, predominant, along with many intermediate forms, in Europe. Although highly nutritious, red clover can—like its white clover relative—produce bloat and estrogenic disorders in cattle that graze extensively upon it. Agronomists recommend a large proportion of grass mixture in clover pasture forage.

Both clovers, though aliens, are hardly recent immigrants. They apparently originated in Eurasia, were introduced about 1650 to England (white clover has become Britain's most abundant legume), from which colonists carried them to the New World. American natives reportedly called white clover "white man's foot grass" because—along with other plants such as bluegrasses *(q.v.)* and plantains *(q.v.)*—it seemed to spring up wherever the colonists trod. Both clovers had become well established in America by 1750.

Both also have a long folk-medicine tradition. Dried red clover flowers were once the chief ingredient of antiasthma cigarettes, and red clover floral tea is said to possess anticancer as well as sedative and other properties too numerous to mention. (Red clover was a prominent ingredient of the controversial Hoxsey herbal cancer treatments; one source suggests a reprise of the medieval doctrine of signatures belief to account for such a use of red clover—that is, the rounded flowerheads, seen as resembling tumors, thereby prescribe themselves for medicinal usage on such growths.)

As is true of just about any common plant, the list of maladies for which clovers have been prescribed, with miraculous cures claimed, is lengthy. Both clovers' estrogenic effects are well documented, however, making them subjects of modern cancer research.

Images of white clover include the shamrock (St. Patrick's symbol of the Trinity), widely adopted as a symbol of Irish land and culture (the "real" shamrock is probably another alien clover species, *T. dubium,* the little or least hop-clover); and the four-leaf (actually four-leaflet) clover, a fairly common genetic anomaly that bears a lengthy Celtic and Welsh lore as an omen and charm of good luck. Most lawns of any size produce a certain percentage of four-leaf plant eccentrics; a small industry even preserves and incorporates them into jewelry, cards, and other gifty gewgaws.

As humanly edible herbs, clovers do not rank as choice. Yet they are high in protein and vitamins, can be eaten as salad or cooked greens and in flowerhead teas. Flowerheads and leaves are much more easily digested after boiling. Also, care should be exercised, since red clover infected with a fungus called black patch *(Rhizoctonia leguminicola),* often showing no visible symptoms, may contain the toxic alkaloid slaframine. This substance, known to farmers as the "slobber factor," causes excessive salivation in grazing animals. During the Irish potato famines, dried white clover flowers and seedheads were ground into flour for making bread.

Clovers' main food value to humans comes in the form of clover honeys, often a blend of honeys from various legumes. Most of our so-called clover honeys come, in fact, from alfalfa *(q.v.).*

The word *clover* probably derives from the Latin *clava,* meaning "club." Hercules wielded a club with a clover-leaf shape, according to legend. "It is because of this connection," wrote naturalist Donald W. Stokes, "that the clover leaf on a deck of cards is called a club."

Red clover is the state flower—one of the few alien plants thus chosen—of Vermont.

Coneflowers; Black-eyed Susan (*Rudbeckia, Echinacea* species). Aster family. Recognize native coneflowers by their large flowerheads surmounting single stems. The dark, somewhat cone-shaped center of disk florets is surrounded by yellow rays in *Rudbeckia*, by purple to white rays in *Echinacea* species. Two commonly seen coneflowers are black-eyed Susan (*R. hirta*), with chocolate-colored center and bristly stem and leaves; and purple coneflower (*E. purpurea*), showing reflexed (swept-back), reddish purple ray flowers.

Other names: Black-eyed daisy, brown-Betty, brown-eyed Susan, bulls-eye, yellow daisy (*R. hirta*); black Sampson, comb-flower, Indian-head, purple daisy, snakeroot (*E. purpurea*).

Close relatives: Some 16 *Rudbeckia* species exist in North America, about half of them eastern residents. They include the eastern or orange coneflower (*R. fulgida*), the three-lobed or thin-leaved coneflower (*R. triloba*), sweet coneflower (*R. subtomentosa*), and cut-leaf or green-headed coneflower (*R. laciniata*).

Only 5 *Echinacea* species exist, all in North America; the prairie or pale coneflower (*E. pallida*), a paler flower that is mainly a western species, has been introduced in the East. Close family members include sunflowers (*q.v.*), Ratibida coneflowers, sneezeweeds (*Helenium*), and tickseeds (*Coreopsis*), among many others.

Lifestyle: Alien weeds are not the only plant pests that infest native croplands. Sometimes it is a native plant that invades agricultural fields. Such is the case with black-eyed Susans, the commonest coneflowers of all, which sometimes gain colorful pesthood status in summer fields.

Black-eyed Susan stands about 2 feet tall, with flowerheads about 2 inches across. As in many radially symmetrical flowers of the aster or composite tribe, 2 sorts of florets inhabit the flowerhead: the central disk florets, blooming inward from the outside rim in successive circles of pollinating florets, a progression easily seen by close inspection; and the 10 to 20 long, petal-like ray florets radiating from the central disk. Only the disk florets have bisexual parts; the ray florets in this species are reproductively neutral, lacking stamens and pistil, and tend to curl backward as they age, thrusting the central disk outward. The insect-pollinated disk florets develop into 4-angled seedcases called *achenes,* and reproduction occurs mainly by seed. In most places, black-eyed Susans are biennials—that is, they sprout a leafy rosette that overwinters the first year; then they flower, produce seed, and die in their second year. Some cultivars, however, can flower a third year, making them short-lived perennials. This plant's complex genetics manifest in several intergrading varieties, some of which (such as the so-called gloriosa daisy) have become popular garden ornamentals. Black-eyed Susan has a spreading, fibrous root system and tough, minutely grooved stems that resist breakage.

Purple coneflower has much the same biological characteristics as black-eyed Susan, except that it usually stands a foot or so taller. It also has a larger flower (2 to 3 or more

inches wide) with a very chaffy, almost spiny, cone-shaped central disk (a thicket for pollinating insects). The flowers are also partially self-compatible (that is, they can self-pollinate). The 15 to 20 drooping rays, neutral or with sterile pistils, are notched and often pale
gray at their tips. Purple coneflower is a native perennial.

Associates: Both *Rudbeckia* and *Echinacea* originated in the western prairie regions.
Forest clearing and settlement encouraged their invasion eastward—especially the black-
eyed Susan variety *(R. h. pulcherrima)* that thrives in disturbed habitats. Both coneflowers
are sun-loving, shade-intolerant species. They like space at their bases and also at the tops
of their stalks, hate hemming in. Vigorous grass growth usually outcompetes them. Black-
eyed Susan thrives in dry, sandy habitats. Although it is quite drought-tolerant, it also grows
in wetland fens and sedge meadows. Purple coneflower requires moister sites than the dry
habitats that *R. hirta* tolerates.

Several fungi commonly parasitize these plants. Leaf spot fungi include *Phyllosticta,*
Septoria, and *Cercospora* species. Both coneflowers are subject to the phytoplasmic parasite called aster yellows, vectored by aster or six-spotted leafhoppers (see Asters). Downy
and powdery mildews *(Plasmopora, Erysiphe)* are common on black-eyed Susans, as are
rusts *(Puccinia, Uromyces),* stem rots *(Sclerotium rolfsii),* and wilt *(Verticillium dahliae).* On
purple coneflower, the fungi *Botrytis cinerea* and *Rhizopus* produce a gray mold on foliage
and flowers. The bacteria *Pseudomonas cichorii* and *Xanthomonas campestris* also cause
leaf and flower spotting on purple coneflower.

Two-spotted spider mites *(Tetranychus urticae)* feed on leaf undersides, sometimes
forming webs.

Aphids, tiny sap-sucking insects, frequent both plants. Among common species on
purple coneflowers are the crescent-marked lily aphid *(Neomyzus circumflexus),* yellow and
black; the brown ambrosia aphid *(Dactynotus ambrosiae),* blood red in color; the melon or
cotton aphid *(Aphis gossypii),* greenish; and the green peach aphid *(Myzus persicae),* green
or pinkish. Most of these aphids parasitize many other plants as well.

Also common is the garden fleahopper *(Halticus bractatus),* a jumping insect that punctures leaves and stems. Other insects that eat holes in leaves are the four-lined plant bug
(Poecilocapsus lineatus), yellow and black striped; and the aforementioned aster leafhopper.

Beetle foliage feeders include the Fuller rose beetle *(Asynonychus godmanni),* a brown
weevil that forages on the leaves at night; and (especially on purple coneflower) the Japanese
beetle *(Popillia japonica),* copper and green, a ubiquitous, destructive feeder on many plants.

Wilting plants may indicate feeding of the stalk borer *(Papaipema nebris),* a noctuid
moth caterpillar. The blackberry looper moth *(Chlorochlamys chloroleucaria),* an inchworm
caterpillar, sometimes feeds on the ray florets of purple coneflowers. A gray, striped caterpillar often seen in S-shaped postures on the leaves may be a sawfly *(Macrophya intermedia).*

Pollinating insects are numerous. Pollen-collecting bees of various species land in the central disk "thickets," and long-tongued bumblebees *(Bombus)* and butterflies seek nectar in the tubular, brown disk florets. Two brush-footed butterflies commonly seen on black-eyed Susan are the pearl crescent *(Phyciodes tharos)*, brownish with crescent markings on hindwings; and the great spangled fritillary *(Speyeria cybele)*, large with silver spots on undersides of hindwings. Native solitary bees are the chief pollinators of purple coneflower in prairie areas. A number of other insects—wasps, flies, beetles—also frequent the flowers of both species.

Great spangled fritillary butterflies may often be seen on purple coneflowers, whose "pincushion" central disk is easiest worked by the larger bees and butterflies.

Neither black-eyed Susan nor purple coneflower provides much food for birds and mammals, though I have watched American goldfinches taking seed from both plants. Probably white-tailed deer and cottontail rabbits graze to some extent on the new shoots.

Lore: Although it is a New World native, black-eyed Susan received its scientific name in 1753 from a type specimen given to the Swedish father of taxonomy, Linnaeus. He honored 2 professors at the University of Uppsala named Olaf Rudbeck, father and son, by naming the foreign plant after them; the specific name *hirta* means "rough hairy" in Latin. His original type specimen resides today in a museum at Bognor Regis, England.

English poet John Gray wrote a love ballad titled "Sweet William's Farewell to Black-ey'd Susan" in 1720; the flower name probably followed from the poem rather than vice versa. No part of Susan is palatable to humans, even if nontoxic (except that some persons show allergic sensitivity to the bristly stems). American natives used root teas of *Rudbeckia* as a bitter drink to eliminate intestinal worms and as a skin wash for sores and earaches. Black-eyed Susan is Maryland's state flower.

The purple coneflower name *Echinacea* comes from the Greek term meaning "hedgehog" or "sea urchin" (the bristly "cone" of the coneflower), the same root as for "echinoderm," a creature belonging to the phylum of spiny marine invertebrates. This flower has had much more usage than Susan as an herbal remedy. According to some sources, purple coneflower was the most widely used medicinal plant by Plains tribes, who applied the root tea to a variety of internal and external ailments, also used it in sweat lodge rites. The Lakota Sioux, among others, still harvest purple coneflower roots for medicinal uses. Modern research has confirmed the validity of many traditional uses, also finding that extracts of purple coneflower stimulate the immune system. As salves or tincture treatments for wounds, sores, and insect and spider bites, so popular and profitable has *Echinacea* become in the herbal industry that the plant faces depletion in some areas, and plant poachers have been evicted from nature preserves where it grows. *Echinacea* pharmacological products also find wide usage in Europe, where the plant is alien.

Daisy, Ox-eye *(Chrysanthemum leucanthemum).* Aster family. The familiar summer field daisy with white radiating ray florets and a depressed, yellow hub of disk florets is an alien perennial. It stands 1 to 3 feet tall.

Other names: Marguerite, field daisy, big daisy, whiteweed, white daisy, bull's-eye daisy, Dutch-morgan, herb-Margaret, maudlin daisy, moon daisy, moonflower—and on into the night.

Close relatives: Some 100 *Chrysanthemum* species exist; most are Old World natives. The half dozen eastern North American residents are introductions or garden escapes; they include feverfew *(C. parthenium)* and costmary *(C. balsamita).* Garden chrysanthemums are mainly hybrid varieties of 2 Asian species *(C. vestitum, C. indicum).* Aster family relatives include ragweeds *(q.v.),* chamomiles *(Anthemis),* common yarrow *(q.v.),* and wormwoods *(q.v.),* among many others. The English daisy *(Bellis perennis),* extolled by Shakespeare and other English poets, is a related aster family flower that looks like a smaller version of ox-eye daisy.

Lifestyle: Hardly a pasture or roadside lacks daisies in summer. They beautify poor land, vacant lots, and waste places, yet they can be aggressive pests of agriculture. Entire fields once whitened the landscape with what was termed "the snows of June," acres of daisies that sometimes took over crop fields and gardens alike. Today daisies survive in nowhere near their former abundance, as much of eastern North America reverts to woodland or sprouts urban subdivisions. It is still a love-hate relationship, however, the bucolic meadow flower of poetry (one 19th-century poet saw daisies as "a smile of God") competing with the colorful weed that rampages in areas of the American rural landscape.

Ox-eye daisy bears a solitary flowerhead up to 2 inches across. This flowerhead, like that of most composites, is an aggregate bouquet consisting of many individual florets. Fertile bisexual florets occur only in the central disk, crowded with hundreds of the tiny tubular structures. In each floret, "as the [female] pistil within the ring of [male] stamens develops and rises," wrote botanist Neltje Blanchan, "two little hair brushes on its tip sweep the pollen from their anthers. . . . Now the pollen is elevated to a point where any insect crawling over the floret must remove it." After the anthers stop producing pollen, the closed central pistil opens and spreads its sticky surfaces, receiving pollen brought from other daisies (a type of sexual sequencing called *protandry*). The 20 to 30 radiating, petal-like ray florets are female but sterile, apparently having evolved as attention-fetchers for pollinating insects.

Ox-eye daisy reproduces mainly by prolific seeding; a single healthy plant may produce up to 26,000 (more typically, 1,300 to 4,000) seeds. Wind disperses most of its seeds near the parent plant, though animals may disperse some. The seeds remain viable for years; in one study, more than 80 percent germinated after 6 years, 1 percent after 40 years. Most seedlings emerge in the fall, though germination may occur continuously throughout the growing season. An individual daisy plant may consist of one to many rosettes on the soil surface, each of which produces a single flower stem and which together may form a dense mat of rosettes. Most ox-eyes begin flowering in their second year (that is, their first summer after germination), continue flowering in subsequent years. Ox-eye also reproduces by budding from shallow, branched *rhizomes* (subsurface horizontal stems). The plant has a small taproot and a shallow, fibrous root system.

Associates: Ox-eye daisy has become a global citizen, grows abundantly in some 40 countries worldwide, occupying temperate regions (up to 70 degrees N latitude in Europe). It resides in every state of the United States.

Ox-eye daisies frequent the company of other open-country (mostly alien) plants, including plantains, common St. John's-wort, hawkweeds, common evening-primrose, Canada thistle (all *q.v.*), and black-eyed Susan (see Coneflowers). In pastures, growing mainly in small or large patches rather than solitarily, daisies often outcompete grasses because cattle tend to avoid them. These plants grow just about anywhere that is open and not too moist. They occupy a wide range of soils, especially those low in acidity and nutrients.

A variety of fungous parasites and nematodes (roundworms) attack garden and commercially raised chrysanthemums, but relatively few mildews, rusts, leaf spots, and blights parasitize wild-growing daisies. The aster yellows phytoplasma (see Asters) sometimes affects ox-eye daisies. Another occasional plant parasite on the roots is the wildflower called painted cup *(q.v.)*.

The plant's bitter pyrethrum content apparently limits the number of insect foragers that can feed on it. Foliage and stem feeders include several moth caterpillars, including the rigid sunflower borer *(Papaipema rigida)*, a noctuid. The blackberry looper *(Chlorochlamys chloroleucaria)*, an inchworm moth, feeds on the white ray florets. Daisy plant bugs *(Orthocephalus mutabilus)* puncture leaves and flower buds, as do chrysanthemum lace bugs *(Corythucha marmorata)*, brownish and banded lacy-winged insects. Nymphs of meadow spittlebugs *(Philaenus spumarius)* tap the young flower stalks, creating frothy "tents" over their bodies and sometimes deforming the stems. The chrysanthemum leaf miner *(Chromatomyia syngenesiae)*, a fly larva (also called the Marguerite fly), mines irregular tunnels in the leaves.

Colorful red-blue checkered beetles (Trichodes nutalli) *frequent ox-eye daisy flowerheads, feeding on pollen and smaller insects.*

A large variety of insects—bees, butterflies, beetles, flies, and wasps—pollinate ox-eye daisies. "Almost every insect on wings alights on them sooner or later," wrote Blanchan. A common colorful resident of daisy flowerheads is the red-blue or Nuttall's checkered beetle *(Trichodes nutalli),* blue-black with red crossbands. It preys on thrips, also eats pollen. The redbud bruchid *(Gibbobruchus mimus),* a seed beetle, also inhabits the flower as an adult insect. Other flower visitors and residents include alfalfa plant bugs (see Alfalfa), black bugs *(Cormelaena pulicaria),* two-spotted grass bugs *(Stenotus binotatus),* European skippers *(Adopoea lineola),* and tumbling flower beetles *(Mordellistena).*

Though cattle are reluctant foragers on daisies, horses, sheep, and goats have no such compunctions and graze the plant readily. (Naturalist John Burroughs claimed that ox-eye "makes a fair quality hay if cut before it gets ripe.") Probably white-tailed deer and cottontail rabbits graze it to some extent, but virtually no sources list ox-eye daisy as a wildlife food of any importance.

Lore: Neither as human food nor medicament does ox-eye daisy glow on the menu, though both uses are occasional. The young leaves can make an "interesting" addition to salads, according to one herbal source; and Europeans brewed teas from the plant for treating asthma and whooping cough and, in poultices and lotions, for wounds and skin irritations. A nightly daisy wash is said to aid the complexion. Ox-eye's polyacetylenes and thiophenes are insecticidal (though not to the extent of the related oriental pyrethrum daisies). English farmers mixed the dried plant with straw bedding as insect repellent for livestock and hung it inside their houses as flea repellents. Many hikers and anglers know that crushing and rubbing daisy flowerheads into the clothing provides good natural protection from blackflies, mosquitoes, and deer flies (most commercial repellents repel the chance of seeing wildlife, since the aromas, carrying far downwind, smell unlike any natural odor). Odor of the plant is variously described as resembling sage and valerian. Some people react allergically to the plant sap on the skin.

In religious iconography, ox-eye daisy became associated with Artemis, Greek goddess of women, owing to its medicinal usage for menstrual complaints. Christians transferred the association to St. Mary Magdalen—the plant thence became known as the maudelyn or maudlin daisy. It was also dedicated to St. John.

Ox-eyes have also entered the culture via daisy chains and "he/she loves me, loves me not" options by means of one-by-one ray-flower destruction (the outcome is always uncertain owing to the irregular number of ray flowers on any given flowerhead).

Ox-eye daisy's dispersal all over the world from its Eurasian origins chiefly occurred via seed contaminants in rye, timothy, and other forage grasses and legumes. One daisy source in America, it is claimed, was the German fodder imported to feed the horses of British troops during the Revolution. Another account claims that John Winthrop, Jr., son of the first Massachusetts Bay Colony governor (a collateral ancestor of this book's author), brought the first ox-eye seeds from London for his Boston flower garden. Centuries after escaping to our fields and roadsides, however, ox-eye continues to be planted as a popular garden ornamental. Today it is said to infest some 13 crops worldwide as a serious pest or competitor. Barley, oats, sunflowers, and wheat are among its victims. Scots farmers named daisy crop invaders "gools" and appointed "gool-riders" to check that every landholder rigorously removed all daisies from wheat fields.

Yet ox-eyes appear to be among those alien plants that—for various possible reasons—have lost some vigor and potency during their long acclimation to New World ecologies. Although they can still summon ample hostility from livestock and crop farmers, the plants seem, in many areas, less aggressive than they once were. This phenomenon follows the typical pattern of invading plant and animal species, the gradual process of naturalization by which ecological balance tends to reassert.

A daisy epiphany once occurred in Philadelphia. This flower, it is said, inspired the career of North America's foremost pioneer botanist, John Bartram (1699–1777)—and indirectly, that of his prolific botanist-naturalist son William Bartram (1739–1823). While plowing his fields one day (at the site of Bartram's Gardens in Philadelphia), the sight of a daisy stopped the uneducated Quaker farmer in his tracks. The vision prompted Bartram's subsequent lifework of exploring, collecting, and naming much of North America's plant bounty. It seems ironic that a colorful alien "weed," rather than a charming native wildflower, birthed Bartram's devotion to American flora. Until 1941, the ox-eye served as North Carolina's state flower (it was replaced by native flowering dogwood).

The word *daisy* originated from "day's eye," referring to the English daisy, which opens only in daylight. The ox-eye is also a night's eye, accounting for the appellation "moon daisy" or "moonflower."

Chrysanthemum leucanthemum. Try it aloud, advises one naturalist; "though at first blush it seems bulky and overly burdened with syllables, the name is one of the most mellifluous that botanists have devised." The scientific name derives from the Greek chrisos ("golden") and anthos ("flower"); *leucanthemum* means "white flower."

Dandelion, Common *(Taraxacum officinale).* Aster family. Familiar in spring on lawns and roadsides everywhere, its bright yellow flowerheads adorn single hollow stems containing milky sap; its jagged-lobed basal leaves also identify this alien perennial. When it is "gone to seed," the fluffy white, globular seed clusters become distinctive.

Other names: Blowball, lion's tooth, fortune-teller, puffball, Swedish mums, many others.

Close relatives: Other eastern North American dandelions—of some 60 *Taraxacum* species worldwide—include red-seeded dandelion *(T. laevigatum),* northern dandelion *(T. ceratophorum),* and marsh-dandelion *(T. palustre).* Close kin among aster family plants include hawkweeds *(q.v.),* goat's-beards *(q.v.),* hawk's beards *(Crepis),* dwarf dandelions *(Krigia),* fall-dandelions *(Leontodon autumnalis),* and chicory *(q.v.).*

Lifestyle: Some 150 to 200 individual bisexual florets constitute the aggregate flowerhead of a dandelion. Instead of holding both ray florets and disk florets, or all disk florets, as do many aster family flowers, dandelion heads consist entirely of overlapping ray florets—a more crowded, compact version of the chicory flowerhead. Each floret displays an evolutionary fusion of 5 once-distinct petals, now seen only in the 5 tiny teeth that tip each floret and in the longitudinal lines separating them. Each floret has its own male and female organs, the (female) style surmounting the (male) stamens. Stamens are unnecessary, however, for the plant to produce seed; much, if not most, dandelion seed reproduction occurs asexually *(apomixis),* without pollen fertilization or any genetic involvement of male cells. But insect pollination (each floret produces abundant nectar in its tubular base) and self-pollination, plus vegetative reproduction via sprouting of new plants from roots and root fragments, also occur—so this plant has all reproductive fronts covered, surely an important reason for its wide abundance and distribution.

Flowerheads display only during daylight, opening about 9 A.M., closing in the afternoon. They also close during wet or cloudy weather. The closing helps protect the flower parts "at times when insects will not actively visit them," as naturalist Donald W. Stokes wrote, "and the pollen and nectar from dew and rain." Strong ultraviolet reflectance, especially of the outer part of the flowerhead, makes it visible to pollinators from afar and, close-up, provides a highly conspicuous "welcome mat" to insects. Each flowerhead lasts only a day or so, then seals tight for about 2 days in a so-called "swine's snout," named for its shape. Reflexed (bent-back) green bracts beneath the flowerhead form outer wrappings, bending upward to enclose the flowerhead at night and sealing it closed during seed set. The stem lengthens during this sealed-off period, elevating the developing seedhead into the wind currents. Then the head reopens, presenting a feathery, symmetrical seedhead, a globe of 1-seeded *achenes,* each equipped with tiny barbs and capped with a fragile "parachute" *(pappus)* that adapts it for wind distribution. Heat convection currents also lift seeds from the head. Each head produces about 200 achenes. In the spring, this seed globe "is interesting," noted Thoreau, "as the first of that class of fuzzy or downy seeds so common in the fall." Dandelions flower most profusely in early spring; another lesser growth flush occurs in autumn—at both times when day length lasts less than 12 hours.

Dandelion leaves never rise far off the ground, remain green year-round in a circular basal rosette atop the root crown. Each leaf, grooved lengthwise at midvein, channels the rain falling on it "straight to the center of the rosette and thus to the root," according to one botanist.

Dandelion's thick, fleshy taproot, often extending many branches, may plunge a foot, sometimes much more, into the soil. In some instances, this root system may form up to half the entire plant's biomass. Younger plants have longer taproots than older plants. Most dandelion plants survive for several years.

The bitter, milky juice seen in all parts of the plant is a latex, chiefly composed of sesquiterpenes, also called taraxacin.

The dandelion seedhead, final stage of a complex flowering sequence, disperses its achenes not only to the wind, but also to rising convection currents as the ground heats.

Associates: All but the wettest open, sunny areas and soils host dandelions. Where profuse, they may compete with lawn grasses by hogging soil nutrients in their vicinity, but many lawn keepers welcome a scatter of meadowlike color in an otherwise uniform green carpet (many others, of course, prefer solid uniformity, attacking dandelion forays with flashing trowels, scoops, herbicides, and fury). In their native Eurasian habitats, dandelions are indeed meadow residents, though they appear hardly as numerous as in our mowed and chemically dosed lawns and roadsides. This is mainly a plant of the temperate global Northern Hemisphere, extending to the Arctic. Tundra soils of the far North host few dandelions because of a lack of nitrogen—but where outhouses once stood in human coastal settlements, nitrogen exists and dandelions thrive.

Insect foliage feeders find dandelions tasty and nourishing. A leaf-mining fly larva *(Agromyza youngi)* creates winding mines in dandelion leaves, also in the leaf and flower stalks. Larvae of the dandelion gall wasp *(Phanacis taraxaci)*, a cynipid, create clusters of round galls on leaf midribs.

Among hairy moth caterpillars, look for the agreeable tiger moth *(Spilosoma congrua)* and the little virgin moth *(Grammia virguncula)*. Noctuid moth caterpillars include the ruddy quaker *(Protorthodes oviduca)*, the small brown quaker *(Pseudorthodes vecors)*, and other quakers; the two-spotted looper *(Autographa bimaculata);* and the miranda or rough-skinned cutworm moth *(Proxenus mindara)*. Common inchworm caterpillars (Geometridae) on dandelion include the confused eusarca *(Eusarca confusaria)* and many wave moth species. The tufted apple bud moth *(Platynota idaeusalis)*, a tortricid, plus many other moth caterpillars forage nonexclusively upon dandelion as well.

Onion thrips *(Thrips tabaci)* commonly feed in dandelion flowerheads.

One observer noted 100 different species of pollinating insects, mainly bees and flies, frequenting dandelion flowerheads; probably many more visit as well. Among the visitors are green lacewings *(Chrysopa)*, ladybird beetles (Coccinellidae), and the European cabbage butterfly *(Pieris rapae)*, probably our commonest white butterfly. Other butterfly visitors include the West Virginia white *(P. virginiensis)*, the olympia marble *(Euchloe olympia)*, and various thistle butterflies (see Thistle, Canada).

Minute seed weevils *(Ceutorhyncus)* are common larvae that often infest the closed, developing seedheads.

Livestock graze dandelions, though not as a preferred forage. White-tailed deer, woodchucks, and cottontail rabbits relish the plant, are probably the foremost wildlife consumers. Ruffed and sharp-tailed grouse, ring-necked pheasants, and northern bobwhites forage on both foliage and seeds. House sparrows, chipping sparrows, and American goldfinches consume dandelion seed, neatly clipping off the feathery plumes before they ingest. Indigo buntings, pine siskins, and other sparrows—field, song, white-crowned, white-throated—also find dandelion seed a choice food. In western mountainous areas, the northern pocket gopher derives about half its diet from stored dandelion roots.

Lore: "How emphatic it is!" noted Thoreau, "a sun itself in the grass." Yet it takes more than French hyperbole for most of us to see *dent de lion*—a lion's tooth—in the jagged leaves of dandelion; thence came the name from ages past, according to conventional botanical wisdom. Since dandelions are hardly prevalent where lions roam, the name looks like a case of imagination running as rampant as the plant itself. (Examples abound in biology, of course, of studiously misnamed organisms.) *Taraxacum,* the genus name, is a Persian word meaning "bitter herb"; *officinale* means "medicinal."

The plant has much to recommend it as a nutritious food for humans. As salad or cooked greens (collected from unsprayed areas), the leaves contain high amounts of vitamins A and C, potassium, iron, and calcium. The ground and roasted roots, their bitterness baked out, make an agreeable coffee additive or substitute; farmers raise dandelion commercially for this purpose in Russia and the Rio Grande valley in Texas. Dandelion wine comes from the fermented flowers; from the flowers also comes dandelion honey, yellow and strong-tasting.

As with any ubiquitous plant, dandelions have a long history of medicinal uses, both internal and external. Traditionally the root tea was served as a diuretic for kidney and bladder ailments (hence the folk names "pissabed" and "peedabed"), also as a liver treatment, tonic, and laxative. The milky latex—which can cause contact dermatitis in allergic individuals—has been applied on pimples and warts.

Probably the first North American dandelions came over with the Pilgrims in 1620, not as accidental hitchhikers but as medicinal herbs, which spread from gardens like yellow wildfire wherever forests fell and meadows grew. Dandelion's original locus was probably the Mediterranean area. Ritual dances and rites made use of dandelion rings and chains in Europe. Shakespeare called the flowers "golden lads" and likened the plumed seeds to the brushes of chimney sweepers. ("Golden lads and girls all must, As chimney sweepers, come to dust." *Cymbeline.*)

Dandelions demonstrate evolution in action on suburban lawns. Over several seasons of mowing, the only dandelions that can flower are short-stemmed plants that duck the blade. Mowing thus becomes a selective factor, and in time most of the yard's surviving dandelion flowers hug the ground.

Dock, Curly *(Rumex crispus).* Smartweed family. Recognize this tall (up to 4 feet), alien perennial by its greenish terminal flower clusters on ascending branches and its long leaves with wavy, crumpled margins.

Other names: Curled dock, bitter dock, yellow dock, sour dock, sorrel.

Close relatives: Some 200 *Rumex* species exist worldwide. About 18 of them reside in eastern North America. Species similar to *R. crispus* (but lacking the distinctive wavy-edged leaves) include yard or long-leaved dock *(R. longifolius)* and bitter or broad-leaved dock *(R. obtusifolius),* the latter often hybridizing with curly dock. Other relatives include rhubarb *(Rheum rhabarbicum)* and sheep sorrel, knotweeds, and buckwheat (all *q.v.*). Common burdock *(q.v.)* is unrelated.

Lifestyle: Many plants in this book require close observation and paging through manuals and field guides for positive identification, but curly dock's distinctive leaves—resembling the lolling tongues of dogs—make this plant instantly recognizable. Another way to recognize docks, as well as many other plants of their family, is by the sheath *(ocrea)* circling just above the base of each leaf stem.

The valentine-shaped bracts (actually tepals) that back the bisexual flowers are stemmed, greenish, and veiny; they later provide wings for the dry fruits. Flowering is *acropetal;* that is, it proceeds upward from the base of the flower stalk, so that (in vertical progression) seeds, flowers, and flower buds may all occur on the same stalk, or *panicle.*

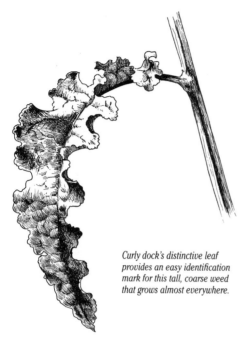

Curly dock's distinctive leaf provides an easy identification mark for this tall, coarse weed that grows almost everywhere.

The entire panicle (often multiple ones) may extend up to 2 feet long. Growth of the panicle ceases just before pollen production begins. Usually the flowers, producing no nectar, are unisexually sequenced *(protandrous)*, liberating pollen before the (female) stigmas mature. The wind-pollinated flowers are mainly cross-fertilized, but self-fertilization may also occur. Curly dock's dangling flower clusters, at first greenish yellow, turn reddish, then reddish brown. The flowers have no petals, but a prominent tubercle or wartlike swelling is prominent on each "valentine" bract. Each flower produces one reddish brown, triangular, 1-seeded fruit *(achene)*. The entire plant, in fact, turns reddish brown at seed time in summer and fall. Sources differ on how many seeds a single plant may produce; figures range from 160 to 4,000. Seed dispersal occurs mainly by wind and bird excreta. The tubercle on each achene also helps float the fruit in water.

Curly dock reproduces entirely by seed, which may germinate anytime during the growing season. Often, though, it germinates in late summer or fall, producing only a basal rosette of leaves that remains green over winter. Then the plant flowers for the first time the following spring. Curly dock exhibits, however, a high frequency of *germination polymorphism;* that is, seeds from separate plants in the same habitat—and often even seeds from the same plant—show variable sprouting capacities. Some germinate soon after maturing, while others may not sprout for weeks, months, even years. Deeply buried seeds of curly dock have been found viable for up to 80 years. This variability probably gives the plant greater adaptability for colonizing new areas in both space and time dimensions. Most individual plants survive at least 3 years, many longer.

The plant's thick, fleshy taproot, somewhat branched, anchors it firmly. Several stems may rise from a single root crown, though a single stem per root is typical. The root may extend 5 feet deep, though usually less. Roots have a radishlike taste and odor. Fragmented roots can sprout new plants.

Associates: Said to be one of the 5 most widely distributed plants in the world, curly dock resides in temperate South America, Eurasia, and Africa, also in North America up to

65 degrees N latitude in Alaska. Curly dock thrives in disturbed ground, moist or dry, often favoring sandy and rich loam soils but able to survive in all but the most acid soils. Typical sites include roadsides, irrigation ditches, pastures, fields, and vacant lots. The plant often invades gardens and croplands, in some areas has become a pest of alfalfa *(q.v.)*. Curly dock typically occurs in small patches, reflecting seed drop near the parent plants.

According to one elder botanist, "It is providential that docks grow near the stinging nettles because rubbing dock leaves on the sting relieves it instantly." (Far from instantly, in my own experience; sometimes BH [botanists' hyperbole] sprouts thicker than dock.)

A rust fungus that attacks only curly dock, *Uromyces rumicis,* has been introduced into some areas as a biological control agent of dock. A leaf-spot fungus, *Ramularia rubella,* also attacks the leaves.

Numerous insect foragers—thrips, aphids, and moth, beetle, and fly larvae—have been recorded on this plant in its native Old World habitats. Presumably a large variety of insects occur on curly dock in North America as well, though comparative research has lagged.

Aphis fabae, the bean aphid, black with cream-colored legs, sucks sap on stems and leaves, massing in large numbers; it deposits honeydew that often attracts black carpenter ants *(Camponotus pennsylvanicus).* The rosy apple aphid *(Dysaphis plantaginea),* rosy or purple in color covered with a powdery, grayish wax, moves to dock and plantains *(q.v.)* from apple trees in summer, feeding and reproducing there until fall. Rapid plant bugs *(Adelphocoris rapidus)* also feed on the plant. Dock sawfly caterpillars *(Ametastegia glabrata)* eat irregular holes in the leaves; in late summer and fall, they migrate to apple trees, burrowing into the fruits, where they pupate. They become apple pests only where docks grow in or around orchards.

Larvae of a leaf beetle, *Hippuriphila modeeri,* create blotch mines on *Rumex* leaves. Another chrysomelid beetle that feeds on dock is *Gastroidea cyanea.* One of the largest snout beetles in eastern North America, the rhubarb curculio *(Lixus concavus),* bores into dock stems as a larva, also feeding on the plant as an adult. It also feeds on rhubarb as an adult, so rhubarb growers often try to eliminate dock plants from the vicinity. Shothole perforations in the leaves indicate feeding of flea beetles, probably species of *Chaetocnema* and *Mantura.*

Caterpillars of the tufted apple bud moth *(Platynota idaeusalis),* a tortricid, also feed on dock plants that grow in the orchard vicinity. Another stem feeder—a common pest that feeds on many other plants as well—is the stalk borer caterpillar *(Papaipema nebris),* a noctuid moth. Adult moths emerge in late summer and early fall. The cross-lined wave *(Calothysanis amaturaria),* an inchworm moth caterpillar, also feeds on the plant.

Butterfly caterpillar feeders on curly dock include the bronze copper *(Lycaena hyllus),* yellowish green and slug-shaped; the related purplish copper *(L. helloides),* greener with whitish spines; and the American copper *(L. phlaeas),* also slug-shaped, reddish or green in color.

Although curly dock flowers rely on wind rather than insects for pollination, bumble-bees *(Bombus)* collect pollen from them, probably pollinating some of the flowers in passing.

Bird and mammal feeding on curly dock is not well documented in America. The plant may well be an important food resource for finches and sparrows, especially. The seeds are a favorite food of bullfinches and caged canaries in England (a seed diet that is said to increase plumage quality in these birds). Ring-necked pheasants consume the leaves, and ducks, geese, and other waterbirds probably forage on the plant where it appears in wetland areas. Probably seed and foliage consumers are generally the same for most *Rumex* species (see Sorrel, Sheep).

Regarding curly dock's usage as mammal forage, few plants have inspired such directly contradictory information. According to one source, cottontail rabbits favor the leaves over those of carrots or lettuce—"a good reason for leaving a few dock plants near one's garden," advised one herbalist. Other authoritative sources claim that curly dock is "rabbit resistant," that rabbits as well as livestock avoid it. In Europe, at least, the plant is said to be relished by deer. (The best way to circumvent botanical and herbalist misinformation is to trust one's own observations.)

Lore: Aside from the nettle cure aforementioned, curly dock has a long history of medicinal usage. Homeopaths and herbalists prescribe the dried root tea for rheumatism, liver problems (stimulation of bile production), and sore throat, among other ailments. It "may cause or relieve diarrhea, depending on dose," states one source. Externally, root teas were applied as a wash for skin sores, ringworm, and "spongy gums." Active ingredients include rumicin, anthraquinone glycosides, and tannins. Rich in protein, zinc, and vitamin A, curly dock leaves taste too bitter to eat without boiling for a duration. Fresh young leaves, however—mildly bitter and lemonlike in flavor—can add interest to salad greens. Curly dock is one of the few alien plants that native Americans quickly adopted into their own medicine troves. Iroquois nations as well as Ojibwa, Cheyenne, and Malecite tribes used it for both internal and poultice treatments.

Experiments in 1973 established that curly dock is *allelopathic* (chemically toxic to other plant growth via root exudates) to certain crop and garden plants. These include redroot (see Amaranths), grain sorghum, field corn, and radish. Curly dock also resists certain common herbicides.

Swedish botanist-explorer Peter Kalm described this plant in 1749 as a resident in New Jersey; Linnaeus named it for science a few years later, in 1753. *Rumex* is the Latin name for docks; *dock* itself derives from the Old English *docce,* which may mean "a dark-colored plant."

Evening-primrose, Common *(Oenothera biennis)*. Evening-primrose family. Standing 1 to 5 feet tall, this native biennial or short-lived perennial has conspicuous, 4-petaled, lemon yellow flowers up to 2 inches across surmounting its stem. The large, X-shaped stigma projecting from the flower center; the reflexed (bent-back) sepals beneath the flower; the coarse, reddish, almost woody stem; and the alternate, lance-shaped leaves also identify it.

Other names: Yellow evening-primrose, tree-primrose, night-primrose, fever-plant, night willow-herb, evening star, scabish.

Close relatives: All of the 80 *Oenothera* species are New World natives. Those that reside in eastern North America include the small-flowered evening-primrose *(O. parviflora)*, garden evening-primrose *(O. glazioviana)*, white evening-primrose *(O. speciosa)*, and several species of sundrops *(O. tetragona, O. fruticosa, et al.)*. Other family members include water-primroses *(Ludwigia)*, fireweed *(q.v.)* and other willow-herbs *(Epilobium)*, gauras *(Gaura)*, and enchanter's nightshades *(Circaea)*. The true primroses *(Primula)* are members of the unrelated primrose family.

Lifestyle: Botanists believe that common evening-primrose is of hybrid origin, most likely a cross between gray common evening-primrose *(O. villosa)* and large-flower evening-primrose *(O. grandiflora)*. Because most of the flowers are *cleistogamous* (self-pollinated while still in the bud), most evening-primrose populations are highly inbred and tend to remain genetically stable over many generations. Complex variations in physical features exist, however, among populations. And since insect pollination and outcrossing with other primroses—as well as hybridization with other *Oenothera* species—do occur, variations arise almost despite, it seems, the plant's own self-reproductive strategies. Anthers of the 8 (male) stamens in each flower often fail to produce pollen, or they produce sterile pollen, so visits by insects from pollen-productive flowers are necessary if outcrossing is to occur. Yet insects transfer at least 35 percent of the stringy pollen on large plants—where it exists at all—to flowers on the same plant, again resulting in self-fertilization. The insect pollination that does occur is primarily by night-flying moths, since the flowers open widest late in the day, on dark overcast days, or at dusk (hence the plant's name), tending to wilt the following morning. Again, however, individual plants show much variability; many flowers remain at least partially open for a day or two. Flowering occurs over a period of several weeks, mainly in July and August. Various observers have described this flower's sudden, spectacular opening, not at all a gradual process.

The seeds occur in long, woody, cylindrical capsules—"each one a graceful vase with four flaring tips," as one naturalist wrote. Each plant produces an average of about 140 capsules, each containing about 180 seeds, though sometimes many more. During winter, those capsules not raided by seed-eating birds split their seams, releasing the seeds. Seeds germinate in spring, summer, or fall; the seedling usually overwinters as a leafy rosette, 5 or 6 inches across, atop the *caudex* (root crown). After producing flowers and seeds the following year, the entire plant dies. Evening-primrose is, however, *semelparous*—that is, it may survive more than a year in the rosette stage before conditions allow it to produce a flowering stem; once it does so, however, its life cycle is ended. Size of the rosette apparently determines whether a plant will flower. A rosette less than 5 or 6 inches across will probably delay flowering. Buried seeds may remain viable for up to 80 years, but seeds must lie no deeper than $1/4$ inch or so in the soil in order to germinate. Most seeds fall within 3 feet or so of the plant; others are dispersed by wind, birds, or human agency such as mud on tires or farm implements. Evening-primrose reproduces entirely by seed.

A pinkish, carrotlike taproot, often branching, anchors the plant.

Associates: Evening-primrose favors light sandy or gravel soils. It commonly grows along roadsides and in almost any disturbed dry ground, though rarely on beaches or dunes. Native to temperate North America, it probably occurs much more abundantly now than in presettlement times because of agriculture and forest clearing. Introduced to Europe as a garden plant from Virginia in 1614, it now thrives there as well as in temperate regions of Asia, Africa, and South America.

Evening-primrose hosts several fungi, among them powdery mildews *(Erysiphe)*, downy mildews *(Peronospora)*, rusts *(Puccinia, Uromyces)*, and a few others. The leaf-spot fungus *Septoria oenotherae* often precedes infection by a common blight fungus, *Botrytis cinerea.*

Insect foragers are fairly numerous. Leaf feeders include sap-sucking aphids, mainly *Aphis oenotherae* and *Macrosiphum gaurae;* crinkled and twisted leaves indicate their presence. Cotton fleahoppers *(Pseudatomoscelis seriatus)*, spotted, silvery insects, also suck sap, as do meadow spittlebugs *(Philaenus spumarius)*, the feeding nymphs identified by the froth they create.

Sphinx moth caterpillar feeders, with a conspicuous horn rising from the abdominal tip, include the banded sphinx *(Eumorpha fasciata)*, the proud sphinx *(Proserpinas gaurae)*, and the white-lined sphinx *(Hyles lineata)*. The pearly wood-nymph *(Eudryas unio)*, which as an adult moth at rest resembles bird droppings, is a noctuid caterpillar. Other moth caterpillars include the double-banded carpet moth *(Spargania magnoliata)*, an inchworm; the grape leaffolder moth *(Desmia funeralis)*, a pyralid species; and *Conchylis oenotherana*, a cochylid, which webs small leaves together at stem tips.

Flea beetles *(Psylloides, Altica)* make shotholelike perforations in the leaves, sometimes defoliating entire plants.

Flower parasites include the western flower thrips *(Frankliniella occidentalis)*, yellow or brown but barely visible, common on many plants. Inside the unopened flower buds lurk primrose moth caterpillars *(Schinia florida);* they also forage on opened flowers and seed capsules at night. The adult moths, unmistakable with bright pink forewings tipped with yellow, sometimes hide during daytime inside partially closed evening-primrose flowers, often pollinating them. *Acanthoscelidius* weevil larvae also feed solitarily inside the bud, and the adult beetles feed on flower buds and in leaf axils.

Another weevil, *Tyloderma foveolata,* lays eggs in stems, where the larvae feed on the pith. Crack open lengthwise a dry evening-primrose stalk during winter, and chances are you will find a chambered lineup of wormlike insect larvae. Downy woodpeckers often tear apart the stalks to feast on this provender. They seem to know just which stalks contain the larvae.

Several species of momphid moth caterpillars *(Mompha)* feed on various parts of evening-primrose. *M. stellata* devours floral tissues in the bud; *M. eloisella* bores into stems; and *M. circumscriptella* feeds in the seed capsules, as does *M. brevivitella.*

The plant sometimes attracts large numbers of Japanese beetles *(Popillia japonica),* copper-and-green foliage eaters, which often shred the leaves to skeletons. Some gardeners suggest that evening-primrose plants may protect a yard from these insects by attracting the beetles like collection traps, there to be whisked into a container of alcohol.

Flower visitors include bumblebees *(Bombus)* and butterflies—monarchs, fritillaries, and sulphurs, among others.

Livestock and other mammal herbivores (deer, rabbits) find evening-primrose palatable; in the West, the plant is a choice food of mule deer and pronghorns. In the East and Midwest, however, the plant cannot be ranked as a major food source for birds and mammals. I have watched ruby-throated hummingbirds forage on the nectar and American goldfinches—probably this plant's foremost seed consumers—perch for lengthy periods on the seed stalks, raiding the capsules, leaving them ragged and torn. Goldfinches also tear open the flower bases, presumably for nectar.

Lore: Like cattails *(Typha)* and a few other plants, every part of evening-primrose is edible, if not tasty, to humans—peppery but palatable is the common verdict. The taproots, astringent but rich in potassium and magnesium, can be served as a boiled vegetable, and new leaves and flowers can be added to salads, or the leaves can be prepared as cooked greens. Seeds have been used as a poppy-seed substitute. The plant has been raised for food

Torn seed capsules on evening-primrose indicate food forays by American goldfinches; downy woodpeckers tap into the dead stalks for larval weevils.

in Europe and is still commercially grown for its seed oil. Evening-primrose oil (EPO) is a primary source of gamma-linolenic acid and tryptophan, both used in various medications, dietary fatty acid supplements, and cosmetics. Anti-inflammatory and analgesic, EPO is mainly used to treat eczema and menstrual pain. Native tribes used root teas for bowel disorders and for poultices on bruises and sore muscles.

The genus name *Oenothera* apparently stems from a Greek word meaning "ass-catcher"; at least that's one of the meanings posed—others include "donkey-chase" and "wine-imbibing," all with puzzling connections to the plant.

For unconventional gardeners, evening-primrose—though not exclusively night flowering—can become chief resident of a night garden. Night gardens, raised more for scent than color, attract some of the rarer sphinx moths that usually remain unseen and inactive during daylight.

Everlasting, Pearly *(Anaphalis margaritacea).* Aster family. Recognize this native perennial, which stands 1 to 3 feet tall, by its gray-green, somewhat downy foliage; its narrow, linear leaves; and its white, globular flowerheads in flat-topped clusters, the flowers with dry, overlapping, scalelike bracts. The flowers bloom in summer and fall.

Other names: Cudweed, cottonweed, silverleaf, silver button, immortelle, life everlasting.

Close relatives: Some 25 other *Anaphalis* species exist in north temperate climates, mainly in eastern Asia. Pearly everlasting is the only eastern North American *Anaphalis*. Near relatives include cudweeds *(Gnaphalium)*, field pussytoes *(q.v.)*, edelweisses *(Leontopodium)*, and all other aster family plants.

Lifestyle: Its silvery foliage and papery, scaly flowerheads sometimes give this plant the appearance of an artificial bloom—"a truly elysian flower," Thoreau called it, "suggesting a widowed virginity." Although its appearance may not suggest so much to most of us, it has a biological feature rare in both composites (aster family plants) and wildflowers generally: The yellow flowers in the densely packed central disk are mainly unisexual, with male and female flowers appearing on separate plants. Male plants are always exclusively so, but female flowerheads often show a central pit in which a few bisexual florets exist. One must look closely to detect which sex one is viewing: Pistillate (female) florets have a divided style or stalk, whereas staminate (male) stalks are undivided. Female florets have been likened to miniature lotuses or water-lilies in appearance, male florets to white nests with a central yellow clutch of eggs spilling out. The surrounding scaly, overlapping bracts—"a shell-like mass," as one observer called it—are not ray florets but highly modified leaves.

Each short branch near the stem top bears 4 to 8 flowerheads, the clusters forming a flat-topped array. These "dry bouquets" are, however, nectar producing and insect-pollinated, the female florets producing 1-seeded *achenes.* Reproduction occurs mainly by seed, but the plant also extends underground stems *(rhizomes)* anchored by roots, producing cloned patches that are likewise unisexual. Even rhizome fragments can reproduce the plant.

The amount of white *tomentum* or *trichome* (matted hairlike growth) appears thickest on stems and underleaf surfaces, variable on upper leaf surfaces.

Associates: Pearly everlasting favors open sun or light shade. Dry, sandy fields, dunes, rocky shores, open woods and thickets, and roadsides are common habitats. It often emerges on recently logged land or following fire. Thoreau noted its frequent association with sweet fern *(Comptonia peregrina).*

Insect foliage feeders are not numerous on this plant, owing to its protective downy "gloss." Nymphs of the meadow spittlebug *(Philaenus spumarius),* identified by the froth masses they

Downy, dry-looking pearly everlasting has white, papery flowers and bears sexes separately on individual plants (dioecious).

exude, often attack upper leaf surfaces that are relatively free of tomentum; the plant's defensive coat seems to prevent spittlebug feeding on stem and underleaves. The tomentum also discourages ant climbers and nectar raiders.

Tomentum does not deter at least 2 spring butterfly caterpillars, probably pearly everlasting's most spectacular foragers: the American or painted lady *(Vanessa virginiensis),* and the painted lady or beauty *(V. cardui).* The first is velvety black with yellow crossbands, the second yellowish green with black markings, a widespread migrant as an adult butterfly. Both, known as thistle butterflies, construct simple compact nest shelters of plant fragments, leaves, and silken webbing on the plant, sometimes enclosing flowerheads in the web. Two broods per year are typical.

The everlasting bud moth caterpillar *(Eumicremma minima),* a noctuid, forages on the flower buds.

Pollinating insects include flies, bees, butterflies, and moths, none specific to this plant.

Pearly everlasting seems unimportant as a food source for bird and mammal wildlife. Livestock and deer rarely graze it, probably owing to its cottony "fabric," and its seed is not widely foraged by birds.

Lore: Pearly everlasting is a plant seemingly made for dried ornaments and bouquets. Its winter appearance doesn't change much—even while still alive and flowering, it looks already dried and preserved. Some observers have found its aspect funereal, "the most uncheering of winter bouquets," wrote one naturalist. It is "stiff, dry, soulless," like a wreath "made from the lifeless hair of some dear departed." The plant's name "everlasting" refers to this long-lived dust-catching proclivity. "Pearly," of course, refers to the white chaffy bracts. Some botanists postulate that the generic name *Anaphalis* may be an anagram of a closely related genus *Gnaphalium* (cudweeds). The species name *margaritacea* derives from the Latin word for "pearl."

This plant has never provided food for humans, but it has a long tradition of medicinal usage among numerous native tribes. Peoples as diverse as Cherokee, Montagnais, Mohegan, Cheyenne, Chippewa, Menomini, Potawatomi, and Mohawk—plus early European settlers and pioneers—brewed tea from the plant for colds, coughs, diarrhea, and other ailments, also using it as a sedative. Its astringent properties also made it useful for poultices on skin ailments and contusions. Flowerheads were apparently widely used as a smoking tobacco substitute, and herbalists also recommended the dried flowers "as a quieting filling for the pillows of consumptives." Some tribes attributed strong mystical power to this plant; it was used in rites for purification, for protection from witches and evil spirits, and in sorcery.

Botanist Edward G. Voss identified pearly everlasting as "one of the few native American species that has become established as a weed of waste ground in Europe." Also native in northeastern Asia, the plant is one of those that successfully migrated to North America before Pleistocene glaciation stabilized the continental flora.

Fireweed *(Epilobium angustifolium).* Evening-primrose family. Recognize this native perennial wildflower by its elongated spike of magenta-pink or rose-purple flowers, each with 4 roundish, lobed petals; its long, vertically erect seedpods; its narrow, willowlike, alternate leaves; and its 3- to 7-foot height.

Other names: Great or spiked willow-herb, rosebay, blooming Sally, wickup.

Close relatives: Some 12 *Epilobium* (willow-herb) species reside in eastern North America (see *The Book of Swamp and Bog*). The genus, consisting of about 200 species, occupies temperate and arctic regions worldwide. Other family members include water-primroses *(Ludwigia),* common evening-primrose *(q.v.),* gauras *(Gaura),* and enchanter's nightshades *(Circaea).* Pilewort *(Erechtites hieracifoli)* is an unrelated aster family plant also called fireweed.

Lifestyle: Seldom observed except in large cloning colonies (though I have occasionally seen individual plants standing alone), fireweed blooms spectacularly in summer, cannot be missed if present. It is often tall (typically 3 to 5 feet), and its spires can (and often do) reclothe a black, fire-barren landscape with acres of rose-pink color.

This plant is a *geophyte*—that is, it reproduces mainly by subsurface stems *(rhizomes)* creeping horizontally in the top 2 inches of soil cover. Its 4-petaled flowers—15 to 50 on a spike—splay at right angles from the tip of the long ovary. Flowering is *acropetal,* begins at the bottom and proceeds up the spike. Three-inch-long, gracefully curved seedpods stand erect behind the flower progression. (Old-time weather forecasters say that frost is due when fireweed flowers arrive atop the spike.)

The insect-pollinated flowers, measuring about an inch across, contain a small, green, nectar-secreting disk and are *protandrous*—that is, the 8 purplish, pollen-producing anthers mature and decline a day or so before the (female) pistil matures, thus promoting cross-pollination. Another aspect that promotes cross-pollination is the behavior of pollinating insects: Typically they visit the lower, more mature flowers (that is, those in their female phase) first, working spirally upward along the flower spike to the upper, male-phase flowers. Then they move to the bottom of another spike, depositing pollen on new female-phase flowers. Thus the pollen reaching a receptive stigma has usually originated from either a different plant or a different flower on the same plant. Fireweed is also self-compatible, however, and can self-fertilize. Since most fireweed patches consist of cloned shoots of genetically identical plants, the practical distinctions between cross- and self-pollination become rather obscure.

Fireweed flowers produce abundant nectar. Biologist Bernd Heinrich calculated that an average fireweed flower contains enough sugars (some 7 calories) to support the maximum metabolic rate of a bumblebee *(Bombus)* for about 14 minutes. (Heinrich performed many of his insect thermoregulation studies, detailed in his book *Bumblebee Economics* [1979], on fireweed.)

The seedpods, which split open lengthwise in late summer, release masses of seeds (300 to 500 per pod) attached to

Green, plant-feeding katydids sometimes land in the tall tops of fireweed, whose spectacular flowers and tubular seedpods instantly identify it.

feathery down, giving the plant "a wild and disheveled appearance," as one observer wrote. A single plant may produce up to 80,000 seeds—though about half that number is typical—through a season. The silky plumes can carry seeds far on wind currents; wind becomes the only efficient distributor for a plant that must establish itself on bare mineral soil. Air humidity is an important aspect of this distribution—an increase in humidity causes the seed plumes to decline in lifting efficiency, thus increasing the chances for the seed to drop in areas with adequate moisture for germination. A 1987 study demonstrated that 20 to 50 percent of fireweed seed plumes cruise on air currents at altitudes higher than 300 feet, and that they may travel for hundreds of kilometers. The plant's continuous production of seeds over a season means that dispersal occurs during most of the summer and fall. Seeds can germinate almost immediately and up to 2 years following deposition.

A spring fire may result in a profusion of fireweed growth as soon as 3 months afterward, testifying to fireweed's ample seed bank in many wilderness areas. The sprouting seeds typically form radial rosettes that last over winter, producing their first flowering stalks the next spring. Fireweed's fibrous roots may extend 5 inches or so into the ground, often less.

White-flowered plants of this species are not uncommon.

Associates: Broadly tolerant of diverse climates and soils, fireweed resides from latitudes 25 to 70 degrees N worldwide. It can also tolerate light shade and low, damp ground (often on riverbanks or lakeshores). Frequently a dominant pioneering species, fireweed often appears as one of the first plants to rise in profusion following fire or other site disturbance. Favored habitats include open ground bearing little plant competition; like aspen trees, one of its frequent associates, it germinates best on bare ground. In addition to burns, it also favors such disturbed sites as forest clear-cuts, river sandbars, gravel pits, roadsides, and old fields. It frequents mountainous areas in its southern range, often colonizing avalanche scars, and it clothes tundra in the North. Yet, depending on the ecosystem, fireweed also appears in smaller colonies and much thinner abundance, such as in dunes and woodland clearings. Its adaptability makes fireweed "one of the most completely circumpolar of all plants," wrote one botanist.

Fireweed's flush of abundance following fire may rapidly diminish after only a year or two of postburn plant growth. Yet its plant associations are many if, in many instances, relatively brief. Typical postburn successors of fireweed include blueberries, bracken fern *(q.v.),* and raspberry/blackberry species, all much longer-lived.

Fungal parasites of fireweed include some dozen or so leaf spots and rusts. A needle rust of balsam fir *(Pucciniastrum epilobii)* uses fireweed as an alternate host to complete its life cycle. This rust can also become perennial in fireweed, overwintering in the roots and surviving in the absence of conifers.

Several sap-sucking aphid species favor fireweed. A 1978 study established that the 4 North American species most frequently found on the plant exhibit *resource partitioning*— that is, each species utilizes different parts of the same plant or becomes abundant at different times of the season. Thus *Aphis varians* feeds at tips of the unopened flower buds, whereas *Macrosiphum valerianae* forages on the lower parts of the buds; *A. helianthi* feeds on the developing seedpods, and *A. salicariae* clusters on leaf undersides. (Winter host of the last 2 aphids is red-osier dogweed *[Cornus sericea]*; that of *M. valerianae* is western rose *[Rosa woodsii]*; alternate host plants are also frequent fireweed associates.)

Nymphs of the boreal spittlebug *(Aphrophora gelida)*, also sap feeders, inhabit frothy masses of their own making on plant stems of fireweed and other plants.

Insect leaf foragers include several moth caterpillars. The white-lined sphinx *(Hyles lineata)* and the galium sphinx, also called fireweed hornworm *(H. gallii)*, are large, variably colored caterpillars (usually greenish with spots and with a projecting rear horn) that devour leaves. The latter species, native to Eurasia, is especially troublesome in Alaska, where "populations can build up to outbreak conditions and really 'hammer' fireweed for a season or two," reported one entomologist. The adult insects, hovering at the flowers, resemble hummingbirds in behavior, are sometimes called hummingbird moths.

Black army cutworms, the larval stage of the Finland dart moth *(Actebia fennica)*, a noctuid species, feed at night on the foliage of many plants, including coniferous seedlings. Irruptive, the fat, black caterpillars can defoliate fireweeds. The adult egg-laying moths are attracted to recently burned areas.

Two forester moths, also noctuids—Langton's forester *(Alypia langtoni)* and MacCulloch's forester *(Androloma maccullochii)*—also feed on fireweed and other willow-herbs; the caterpillars are bluish and banded.

Pollinating insects are mainly bumblebees *(Bombus)*; some 8 species, including *B. vagans, B. terricola,* and *B. perplexus,* have been observed on fireweed flowers, also the bumblebee *Pyrobombus ternarius*. Pollinating flies include species of syrphids or hover flies (Syrphidae), male horse and deer flies (Tabanidae), and male black flies (Simuliidae). Red admiral butterflies *(Vanessa atalanta)* seem to have a fondness for fireweed nectar; blues (Polyommatinae), hairstreaks (Theclinae), and tiger swallowtails *(Papilio)* are also relatively common butterfly visitors.

Probably the only bird feeders of any frequency are several hummingbird species (mainly ruby-throated hummingbirds in the East), which forage the flowers for nectar. Chipmunks consume the seeds, and fireweed foliage is a preferred food for several deer species, including elk, moose, woodland caribou, and white-tailed and mule deer. Mountain goats, muskrats, and snowshoe hares also consume the plant, and cattle find it highly palatable.

Lore: Fireweed's young shoots (especially the stem pith) and tender leaves make edible fresh or cooked greens, and the dried older leaves make a decent tea. All were used by native peoples; some tribes established fireweed clans in their social systems. They made poultices of the peeled roots for burns and skin sores, drinking leaf and root teas for abdominal ailments and using the tea as a mouthwash for sore gums. They also smoked the leaves as a tobacco substitute and used tough, fibrous peelings from outer stems in making twine for fishnets and other needs.

Fireweed contains high amounts of beta carotene and vitamin C, and leaf extracts are anti-inflammatory on the skin. Fireweed's main contribution to the human palate is its rich honey; the plant makes "excellent bee pasture," according to one Canadian source. Beekeepers once followed logging camps and burns to plant their hives for fireweed harvest, leaving them for 5 to 7 years—in some places, they still do.

Fireweed invades and clothes the most devastated sites. It is sometimes planted, with variable success, for revegetation of strip-mined lands and on sites of crude oil spills in the Arctic. It was one of the first plant colonizers in the heavy ash deposits of Mount St. Helens, Washington, following that volcano's 1980 eruption. In London, following raids by German bombers in 1940–41, fields of color, mostly fireweed, blazed in the bomb rubble. "You see it everywhere," reported correspondent Lewis Gannett, "great meadows of it in Lambeth . . . waves of it about St. Paul's," even growing high on fragmented buildings.

Epilobium, a Greek term for "flower upon a pod," quite accurately describes the fireweed bloom. The plant is the official wildflower of Canada's Yukon Territory.

Fleabanes *(Erigeron* species). Aster family. These native annuals, biennials, and perennials display numerous small, daisylike flowers that strongly resemble asters *(q.v.)* in appearance. Unlike asters, however, fleabanes begin flowering in spring, and the ray flowers radiating from their central disks are much more numerous (40 to 150) than in most (though not all) asters. Flowerheads are flat, about 1/2 inch across, delicate in appearance. Fleabanes stand 1 to 4 feet tall.

The most common species are Philadelphia or common fleabane *(E. philadelphicus),* a biennial or short-lived perennial with wide-rayed, pinkish or magenta flowers and stem-clasping leaves; rough or daisy fleabane *(E. strigosus),* annual or sometimes biennial with narrow-rayed, white, sometimes pinkish flowers and mostly untoothed leaves; and annual or (also) daisy fleabane *(E. annuus),* also narrow rayed and white flowered, hairy, and with many toothed leaves.

Other names: Daisy, tall daisy, horseweed, sweet scabious; Philadelphia daisy, skevish *(E. philadelphicus);* whitetop *(E. strigosus).*

Close relatives: Some 200 *Erigeron* species exist in north temperate regions world-wide; about 9 reside in eastern North America. Robin's plantain *(E. pulchellus)* is a common woodland species. Close aster family kin include asters *(q.v.)*, horseweeds *(Conyza)*, English daisy *(Bellis perennis)*, and marsh-fleabanes *(Pluchea)*. The common fleabane of Europe *(Inula dysenterica)* is also an aster family plant related to elecampine *(I. helenium)*.

Lifestyle: Floral biology of fleabanes is much the same as for asters *(q.v.)*. About 100 tubular florets make up the central disk, and varying numbers of petal-like ray florets (100 to 150 in Philadelphia fleabane, 40 to 70 in the other two) radiate from it. In Philadelphia fleabane, which typically flowers about a month earlier than the others, both ray and disk florets are sexually functional, but the rays are pistillate (female) only, whereas the disk florets are perfect (bisexual), and the plant is insect-pollinated.

The reproductive situation is different in *E. strigosus* and *E. annuus.* Both are entirely asexual, reproducing without a fusion of sexual gametes (thus even self-fertilization does not occur), a system called *apomixis* or *apogamy.* The flowers nonetheless produce large amounts of pollen, which is sterile. Since all progeny are clonal, apomictic reproduction has long been viewed as disadvantageous to a plant's capacities for evolutionary change and adaptation, thus to its long-term survival success. Experiments with fleabanes, however, have demonstrated that a wide variety of adaptations exist in these clonal populations—so wide that a literal plant succession, not of different species but of differentially adapted *biotypes* among separate *Erigeron* clones, may sequentially appear in a single field habitat. As Neil T. Kenny, one of the 1996 researchers, wrote: "In an asexual population, selection operates solely through the differential survival and reproduction of clonal lineages, and not by selection acting independently on genes."

Fleabanes reproduce only by seed; an annual fleabane plant may produce some 10,000 to 50,000 one-seeded *achenes,* all of them genetically identical. The plants are shallow rooted. Those that germinate in late sum-

Asterlike daisy fleabane, common almost every-where in summer, flowers earlier than most asters, also has many more ray flowers.

mer or fall may last over winter as low sprouts, then flower in the following year. Most flea-banes, however, germinate in spring from seeds of the previous year. The flowers close at night, as if to shelter their supply of impotent pollen.

Associates: Fleabanes primarily colonize open, disturbed sites; they commonly appear in overgrazed pastures, are regarded as indicator species of mismanaged range. Weedy gardens and roadsides are also typical habitats. These plants adapt well to dry con-ditions and to various soils throughout most of North America. Annual fleabane, however, seems more prevalent in cultivated (that is, more disturbed) land than rough fleabane; and Philadelphia fleabane adapts to somewhat moister habitats—swamps, ditches, beaches, riverbanks—as well as to field and roadside areas.

Relatively few insects feed on fleabanes. Larvae of a flat-faced long-horned beetle, *Hippopsis lemniscata,* feed in the stems. Caterpillars of the lynx flower moth *(Schinia lynx),* a noctuid, feed on both flowers and seeds; look for the brown-patterned adult moths laying eggs on the plant in spring and summer. A geometrid (inchworm) caterpillar seen on the ray florets of fleabanes and many other aster family flowers is the confused eusarca *(Eusarca confusaria).* A downy, striped caterpillar may be that of the checkered white but-terfly *(Pontia protodice),* also called southern cabbageworm.

Nectar and pollen seekers include a variety of butterflies—sulphurs, crescents, painted lady, admirals, blues, coppers, skippers—as well as flies and thread-waisted wasps *(Podalonia).*

Crab spiders *(Misumena),* predators of insect visitors, also inhabit the flowerheads.

American goldfinches relish the seeds of fleabane; other ground finches and sparrows likely feed on it too. Cattle and probably deer graze the young plants, but fleabanes are not considered an important food resource for mammals and birds.

Lore: A bane of existence for our Old World ancestors was the near-constant pres-ence of biting mites and insects—chiggers, fleas, gnats and other flies, and bedbugs, among others. This plant's name derives from its supposed repellent powers against fleas, a claim much overstated if not totally false. If fleas plague you, reach for something other than flea-bane; it won't relieve your problem. The "bane claim" is supported only by those experts who have not actually used them dried, powdered, or "sprinkled in kennels, from which, however, they have been known to drive away dogs," according to one botanist. Neverthe-less, the ugly and descriptively inaccurate name stuck, as so often occurs in biological nomenclature, ill serving these lovely and delicate asters. *Erigeron* stems from a Greek compound meaning "early old man," supposedly a reference to fleabane's spring-blooming habit and the hoary appearance of some species.

These are not plants that provide tasty nibbles of any sort, but their astringent prop-erties led to medicinal usages among many native tribes. Ailments as diverse as diarrhea, kidney stones, diabetes, internal bleeding, fevers, bronchitis, and tumors—plus many more—were treated by drinking the bitter tea. The distilled oil treated external wounds and sores as well. Northern tribes, which called these plants *cocash* or *squaw weed,* found them especially useful for menstrual ailments and during childbirth. Some allergic individuals may develop contact dermatitis from handling fleabane.

The American fleabanes of this account have gone to Europe, usually as garden plants, adding to the roadside weed flora there—and reminding us that alien plant traffic travels both ways.

Goat's-beards (*Tragopogon* species). Aster family. Recognize these alien biennials by their grasslike leaves; their summer-blooming, yellow, dandelionlike flowerheads atop 1- to 3-foot-tall stems; their big, fluffy, puffball seedheads; and their milky sap. Two species are most common in eastern North America: showy or yellow goat's-beard *(T. pratensis),* with curled leaf tips and slightly enlarged flower stalks *(pedicels);* and fistulous or western goat's-beard *(T. dubius),* with straight leaf tips and thick, inflated pedicels.

Other names: Meadow goat's-beard, meadow salsify, noonflower, star-of-Jerusalem, Johnny-go-to-bed-at-noon.

Close relatives: Some 50 *Tragopogon* species occur, mainly in Eurasia and North Africa; no native North American species exist. Salsify or oyster-plant *(T. porrifolius),* resembling goat's-beards, has purplish flowers. More than 100 related aster family genera exist in North America, many of them represented in this book. Among the nearest goat's-beard kin are fall-dandelion *(Leontodon autumnalis),* cat's-ears *(Hypochoeris),* and ox-tongues *(Picris).* An unrelated plant called goat's beard *(Aruncus dioicus),* of the rose family, grows in woodlands.

Lifestyle: Goat's-beard follows the sun, opening toward the sun in the morning and closing by midday on bright days (often closing later on cloudy days). All the florets in a goat's-beard flowerhead are ray florets, and all are bisexual and insect-pollinated. They occur, however, in 2 distinct belts, inner and outer. As in many aster family flowers, a progression of development occurs on the flowerhead, with the outer ones opening and maturing first; the

Flowering in goat's-beards is centripetal, proceeding inward toward the center from the outer florets.

Goat's-beards' seedhead, resembling a glorified dandelion seedhead, consists of a quill-like stalk and a feathery pappus attached to each seed.

unopened inner florets resemble the central disk florets on daisylike flowers. Each plant may produce several flowering stems—6 is about average.

The plant's fluffy seed ball—like a dandelion's seed globe on a larger scale—is a grand example of radial symmetry. Each plant produces 100 to 850 one-seeded achenes, each crowned with a bristle (somewhat resembling radiating porcupine quills) and a feathery umbrellalike *pappus,* an adaptation for wind dispersal. The seeds are of 2 types *(morphs),* with the peripheral or outer-belt florets producing heavier, darker seeds than the central florets. These outer seeds also float on wind with a terminal velocity about 1.3 times greater than the central seeds, which have smaller pappi. Both morphs, however, germinate at equal frequency. Studies have demonstrated that in comparison with other wind-dispersed seeds such as common dandelion *(q.v.), Tragopogon* seeds are relatively slow-moving, creating much air-drag. Probably few of these seeds disperse much beyond a quarter mile, most of them not that far. The plants reproduce entirely by seed, but seeds are short-lived. One study found that less than 3 percent of buried seeds remained viable after 13 months; thus a large, persistent seed bank for these plants does not exist. The surfaces of *T. dubius* achenes contain fluorescent compounds, perhaps protective against fungous parasites.

Upon germination in spring or fall, goat's-beard produces an erect rosette of grasslike leaves, enabling the plant to emerge through ground litter. It rapidly develops an extensive root system with a fleshy taproot. Goat's-beards are usually labeled binennials because of their typical 2-year life cycle, but "they are better described as *monocarpic perennials,*" as other botanists suggest; that is, the rosette may produce flowering stems during the current growing season or—depending on local habitat, temperatures, and plant competition—may survive for several years without flowering; once it flowers and produces seed, however, the plant dies. Ideal habitat conditions encourage faster life cycles, whereas more competitive sites may lead to prolonged vegetative (rosette) phases, hence longer occupancy in successional stages of plant growth. "The extended life-span," wrote one researcher, "could be the key strategy for the success of [goat's-beard] in nature." The plants may also produce a bud bank of new growth from rosette crowns, thus offsetting years of low seed production.

Goat's-beards hybridize readily wherever 2 or more species grow together.

Associates: Adaptable to a broad range of cover types throughout temperate North America, goat's-beards can establish themselves in bare soil, amid grasses and old-field vegetation, and in heavy ground litter. Such adaptability permits them to thrive across a range of early plant successional stages, though they favor open, unshaded areas. Occasionally goat's-beards may form dense colonies, excluding less competitive species, but typically they occur in scattered, thinly dispersed stands. In certain areas, especially in the West, *T. pratensis* associates with perennial grasses such as needle-grasses *(Stipa)*. On the western rangelands, goat's-beards have become serious competitors of the native blue-bunch wheatgrass *(Elytrigia spicata)*. *T. dubius* often appears as a minor member of weedy old-field plant communities.

Goat's-beards host the rust fungus *Puccinia hysterium,* a potential biological control agent where the plants become cropland pests.

While a variety of insects are known to feed on the florets and seeds of goat's-beards, detailed research is lacking. Thrips (Thysanoptera) and larvae of fruit flies (Tephritidae) have been observed feeding in the florets.

Goat's-beard seedheads are choice food sources for American goldfinches. In the West, *T. dubius* is a major seed-food source for blue grouse. Probably other birds and small mammals consume the seeds as well. Most species of deer, squirrels, and rabbits graze the plants, especially the young rosettes; deer also consume the flowering stalks, and livestock relish the young plants. Mice and American goldfinches may collect the seedhead down for nesting. Root feeders include plains pocket gophers.

Lore: Fairly recent (19th-century) plant immigrants from northern Europe, goat's-beards are absent from some of the older American plant and wildflower manuals. The plants were apparently unknown to Thoreau. Probably early settlers in the West brought them as food plants for their gardens, but they rapidly escaped cultivation, spreading east-ward—*T. dubius* became established in eastern Canada only in the 1970s. Certain native tribes adopted the plants for food and medicine (chewing the milky stems was said to cure indigestion), but the plants have never been widely used by humans in North America.

In Europe, however, they were widely cultivated, especially during the 16th century, mainly for their fleshy, parsniplike roots. These are most palatable before and after the plant flowers in spring and fall, and they are still grown, in some places, for food—usually boiled and eaten, or roasted and ground into coffee. Unlike the foliage of most aster family plants, the leaves of goat's-beard—especially the new rosettes—are also palatable to humans and can be eaten as raw or cooked greens.

Tragopogon—the name literally means "goat beard," referring to the fuzzy pappus tufts on the seedhead—has proven a useful genus of plants for genetic and evolutionary researchers. The great Swedish taxonomist Linnaeus crossed *T. pratensis* and *T. porrifolius* in 1759, thus producing the first plant species hybrid created for scientific purposes. Hybridization in this genus has been studied extensively since then, especially as it relates to species with multiple chromosome sets.

Goldenrods *(Solidago* species). Aster family. Probably the most common flowers of summer and early fall, these native perennials adorn fields, open woods, and roadsides almost everywhere. Their bright yellow flower clusters surmounting straight, leafy stems, and their alternate, mostly linear leaves identify them. Among the most commonly seen species are early goldenrod *(S. juncea),* late or smooth goldenrod *(S. gigantea),* and common or Canada goldenrod *(S. canadensis).*

Other names: Yellow-weeds, yellow-tops, flowers-of-gold.

Close relatives: Almost 100 *Solidago* species exist, mainly in North America; about half of these reside east of the Mississippi. Regional goldenrods and goldenrods of specialized habitats include New England goldenrod *(S. cutleri),* northern bog-goldenrod *(S. uliginosa),* seaside-goldenrod *(S. sempervirens),* rough-leaved goldenrod *(S. patula),* forest-goldenrod *(S. arguta),* and Great Lakes goldenrod *(S. houghtonii),* among others. The flat-topped goldenrods *(Euthamia)* are sometimes included in the *Solidago* genus. Asters *(q.v.)* are closely related.

Lifestyle: Yellow flowers predominate in summer, and of all the yellow flowers, the goldenrods are the most showy and abundant. The species vary in form of the flowering clusters—some are bushy and plumed, some gracefully spread or pyramidal and nodding like elms, some clublike, some wandlike; a few are flat-topped and zigzag stemmed. All 3 species considered here have dense, plumelike flowers and bloom from July through September (though late goldenrod typically begins flowering in August, extending into October). Common goldenrod's flower branches often appear somewhat arched and recurved (bent back). Early goldenrod has untoothed upper leaves; all leaves of the other two are toothed. Other minor differences also exist.

Look closely and you will see that a tiny, apparently individual flower of a goldenrod cluster actually consists of aggregate flowers arranged in the typical daisylike form—that is, with central disk florets and with spreading but irregular ray florets, the main source of goldenrod's yellow appearance. Both sorts of florets are relatively few in number—a pocket magnifier reveals them clearly. Common goldenrod has 2 to 7 disk florets, 6 to 12 ray florets; early and late goldenrod florets range from 8 to 15 and 3 to 7 disk florets, respectively, and 7 to 12 and 10 to 15 ray florets. Disk florets are all bisexual, having both stamens and pistils, whereas ray florets are pistillate (female) only. Most goldenrods are self-incompatible—that is, they require outcrossing via insect pollination from another cloning goldenrod, cannot self-fertilize. Goldenrod pollen is heavy, sticky, stringy. Both ray and disk florets produce 1-seeded *achenes,* wind-dispersed by means of the attached fuzzy tuft called the *pappus* atop the achenes.

Each flowering stem typically produces more than 10,000 achenes. Thoreau described the fluffy seedheads in early November as "richly and exuberantly downy. . . . So fine that when we jar the plant and set free a thousand, it is with great difficulty that we detect them in the air. . . . They cover our clothes like dust. No wonder that they spread over all fields and far into the woods." Seeds of the previous year germinate in June or July, but those shoots usually do not produce flowering stems until the next year.

Reproduction also occurs by cloning. In any field of goldenrods, you are not seeing large numbers of individual plants but of individual stems *(ramets)* from considerably fewer numbers of clonal groups. Cloning stems rise from the nodes, or joints, on *rhizomes* (underground stems), which spread horizontally outward from the parent plant. The rhizomes with their sprouts form a circular grouping, or *clone,* that tends to expand in diameter each year. Clones that extend 10 feet across are not uncommon. Very old clones may completely die off in their central areas, become replaced by other plant species, and thus form a surrounding "fairy ring" of goldenrods like a circular ripple on a pond. On Iowa virgin prairie, goldenrod fairy rings more than 30 feet in diameter have been reported. Probably a single clone can survive for many decades, given a stable habitat.

Rhizomes, extending mainly in late fall after seed production, lie dormant over winter. In the spring, a new shoot rises from the apex or tip of each rhizome, producing a rosette of scale leaves, then a rapidly rising, upright stem. Each shoot may produce 2 to 6 daughter rhizomes, and each rhizome can potentially produce a single shoot from its tip in the following spring. Ramets do not grow from the same rhizome nodes in successive years but always from the tips of new rhizomes; these underground connections may persist for 5 or 6 years. Flowering stems typically rise *only* from rhizomes, not as seed sprouts. The plant roots are shallow and fibrous.

Associates: Early, late, and common goldenrods—the 3 species mentioned—are probably the most widely distributed of all goldenrods. All reside in fairly dry, open areas—old fields, roadsides, disturbed soils. They are shade-intolerant, though many survive in light shade, but they show wide tolerance for various soil and fertility conditions. They range throughout North America from the Northwest Territories south to the Gulf. Easily controlled by tilling, goldenrods are not usually crop pests, though they can invade run-down pastures, perennial gardens, and forest nurseries. Farmers regard them as *increasers* on grazing lands—that is, they tend to increase in abundance with overgrazing. Once established on abandoned farmland, they become successful plant competitors, often the dominant herb species, sometimes persisting as such for several decades. This situation may owe considerably to the plant's chemical allelopathy (see Lore). Goldenrods also thrive, however, on native tallgrass prairie, coexisting with more than 300 species of prairie forbs and grasses. Some evidence indicates that critical population sizes of certain goldenrod species exist, below which the plants do not produce abundant seed crops. In Japan, invasive goldenrods from North America (mainly *S. canadensis*) seriously compete with the native susuki or silver grass beloved of haiku poets.

Most goldenrod roots are associated with mycorrhizal fungi (frequently *Endogone* species), which enable the plant to take up nutrients.

Fungal parasites include several found on many other plants as well, most notably powdery mildew *(Erysiphe cichoracearum)* and a root rot *(Phymatotrichum omnivorum)*. Goldenrods and asters are alternate hosts of needle blister rust *(Coleosporium solidaginis)*, which mainly affects red pine trees (see *The Book of Forest and Thicket*).

Higher-plant parasites include at least 2 species of dodder *(Cuscuta)*, a wiry, yellowish vine that taps into goldenrod and other plant stems as it twines around them. Buttonbush-dodder *(C. cephalanthi)* and hazel dodder *(C. coryli)* are documented on goldenrods. One-flowered cancer-root *(Orobanche uniflora)*, a lavender-flowered, pale-stalked broom-rape, parasitizes the roots of damp-habitat goldenrods.

Relatively few North American plants host the abundance and variety of insect species that frequent almost every part of goldenrods; these plants are virtual insect magnets and showplaces.

Foliage feeders include several plant bug species: the shiny black *Slaterocoris atritibialis*, plus *Lopidea media,* orange with black stripes, and *Polymerus venaticus,* all of which feed on young leaves early in the season. *Lygus vanduzeii* and *Coquillettia mimetica,* the latter an ant mimic and predator on other insects, are also goldenrod plant bugs.

Beetle foliage feeders include 3 species of goldenrod beetles: *Trirhabda canadensis, T. borealis,* and *T. virgata.* One study concluded that *Trirhabda* beetles were the most abundant goldenrod herbivores in eastern North America. The larvae hatch just as the stems emerge in May, feeding on leaves near the plant tip and occasionally causing widespread goldenrod defoliation. After the larvae pupate in soil beneath the plants, the adult beetles emerge in July, also feed on the leaves, then lay eggs in ground litter beneath the plant; the eggs, protected by secretions of the female insect, overwinter. These larvae and oval-shaped adult beetles are sometimes attacked by nymphs of the predatory stink bug *Perillus circumcinctus.* (Another common predatory stink bug is the spined soldier bug *[Podisus maculiventris],* brownish with side-projecting spines, which attacks leaf beetles in both its nymphal and adult stages.)

Most other beetle foliage feeders on goldenrod are likewise chrysomelids (leaf beetles). Some 7 or so species, including *Exema canadensis, Ophraelia conferta,* and *Paria tho-*

racica, are fairly common, but one study of sweep samples reported 20 chrysomelid beetle species taken from a single goldenrod stand; some were goldenrod specialists like *Trirhabda*, while most were generalist or incidental feeders.

Leaf-mining larvae include those of the leaf beetle *Microrhopala vittata* and leaf miner flies *(Ophiomyia, Phytomyza)*. The fly larvae *Agromyza coronata* and *A. posticata* create blotch mines in goldenrod leaves. Chrysanthemum lace bugs *(Corythucha marmorata)* tap the mesophyll inner layer of leaves.

Flower residents (excluding pollinator visitors), even more numerous, include not only nectar and pollen feeders, but also consumers of flower parts and developing seeds, plus a number of predatory spiders and insects that lurk and ambush insect visitors amid the florets. A 1984 study by Owen D. V. Sholes identified 5 *guilds* (individual groups of species that share a resource in a biotic community) of insects and spiders that feed in goldenrod heads: chewing herbivores, sucking herbivores, pollen and nectar feeders, parasitoids (insects that are parasitic only as larvae), and predators.

Chewing herbivores include oblong-winged katydids *(Amblycorypha oblongifolia)*, large, green, grasshopperlike insects. The adult leaf beetle *Diabrotica longicornis*, found on goldenrods and known as the northern corn rootworm, is a major pest on corn roots and foliage; these green beetles show 2 indented marks atop the *pronotum*, the narrowed area just behind the head. The black blister beetle *(Epicauta pennsylvanica)* consumes pollen and stigmas, especially in disk florets, sometimes destroying almost all of the mature florets; these beetles exude blood containing cantharidin when disturbed, can raise blisters on one's skin. Casebearer moth caterpillars *(Coleophora duplicis)*, goldenrod's major seedeaters, feed in the developing seeds and floral parts; identify them by their portable cases of plant fragments held together by larval silk. Other moth caterpillars of this feeding guild include several noctuid species: the asteroid *(Cucullia asteroides)*, the brown-hooded owlet *(C. convexipennis)*, and the goldenrod flower moth *(Schinia nundina)*. Other noctuids include the lost sallow *(Eupsilia devia)*, the five-lined sallow *(Catabena lineolata)*, the pink-barred lithacodia *(Lithacodia carneola)*, and the green leuconycta *(Leuconycta diphteroides)*. The false crocus geometer *(Xanthotype urticaria)* and the confused eusarca *(Eusarca confusaria)* are inchworm moths. *Dichomeris* species and *Trichotaphe flavocostella*, small gelechiid caterpillars, also feed in the flowers.

The sap-sucking guild—the largest guild of flower feeders based on insect abundance—includes flower thrips *(Frankliniella tritici)*; the flat, oval nymphs of psyllids *(Aphalara vaeziei)*; a leafhopper *(Neokolla hieroglyphica)*; and the tarnished plant bug *(Lygus lineolaris)*, brown to pale green in color. A treehopper *(Publilia concava)* exudes excess sap as it feeds, attracting *Formica* ants. These ants protect the treehoppers from predators, also attack the aforementioned *Trirhabda* goldenrod beetles, which usually damage the plants to a greater extent than the treehoppers. At least 9 species of aphids—most of them *Uroleucon* species—feed in goldenrod flowers; often dominant is *U. erigeronensis.* Aphid feeding, resulting in honeydew secretion, also attracts ants, which also feed on the flower nectar.

Resident nectar and pollen consumers include *Olibrus* shining mold beetles, shiny black and ladybirdlike in size and form, often prevalent. This beetle often damages florets by chewing through the basal parts and "thieving" nectar instead of entering from above. Adult parasitoid wasps also feed on nectar and pollen, as do many pollinating insects classified as visitors that move from plant to plant (mentioned hereafter).

Insect parasitoids on goldenrod, mainly tiny, shiny black platygasterid wasps, include *Leptacis, Platygaster, Inostemma, Synopeas,* and *Metaclisis* genera. As larvae, they parasitize immature gall gnats (*Rhopalomyia* and others), laying their eggs in or on the gnat eggs or larvae. The adult wasps can often be seen between the florets, feeding and searching for host gnats. Other parasitoid wasps include ichneumons (Ichneumonidae), elophids (Eulophidae), Pteromalids (Pteromalidae), and other chalcids.

Predators, which prey on flower insect visitors and residents alike, are also numerous on goldenrod. The dominant ambush predator is often the jumping spider *Metaphidippus galathea,* brownish with white bands. It stalks prey, mainly *Olibrus* beetles, aphids, and small wasps. Other spiders common on these flowers include cobweb weavers *(Theridion differens),* small and brownish, always hanging upside down in an irregular web; and several crab spiders *(Misumena vatia, Misumenops, Misumenoides),* waiting in crablike posture and camouflaged color, often assuming the yellow flower hue. The life cycle of *Misumena* generally coincides with the flowering schedules of its 2 favored hunting habitats, common milkweed *(q.v.)* and goldenrod: Adult spiders ambush their prey (often bumblebees) on flowers of the earlier-blooming milkweed but build their nest sacs within 3 feet or so of a not-yet-flowering goldenrod; as the milkweeds languish and the goldenrods burst forth, the spiderlings hatch and find the goldenrod blooms, which become their chief hunting habitat.

Ambush bugs *(Phymata erosa, P. americana),* greenish yellow or brownish and very common, attack insects as large as bumblebees; as do wheel bugs *(Arilus cristatus).* The insidious flower bug *(Orius insidiosus),* an oval and flattened anthocorid bug with white markings, also preys on larger insects. Recent studies on ambush bugs have revealed unique communication systems between the wandering males and the waiting females, using leaves and stems as conduits for inaudible vibrations created by the males. These insects, like the crab spiders, tend to turn yellower with length of stay on the flowers. Aphid predators include larval and adult ladybird beetles (Coccinellidae); larval green lacewings (Chrysopidae), also called aphid lions; *Aphidoletes* gall gnat larvae; and *Oecanthus* tree crickets.

Pollinating insects on goldenrod are relatively unspecialized, collecting and transferring pollen on and from many parts of their bodies as they forage through the florets. Most are nectar or pollen eaters. Probably the foremost pollinators are honeybees *(Apis mellifera)*, followed by bumblebees *(Bombus)*—*B. vagans, B. fraternus,* and *B. griseocollis,* among scores of species. Pollinating insects also include small carpenter bees *(Ceratina),* large carpenter bees *(Xylocopa),* halictid bees *(Halictus),* and plasterer bees *(Colletes).* Goldenrod's "individual florets generally contain minute quantities of food reward," wrote biologist Bernd Heinrich, "but since the florets are massed, the perching foragers, such as bumblebees, may achieve a relatively high . . . energy intake by extracting [nectar] from large numbers of florets in a short time."

Wasps do not collect and transfer much pollen, but they frequently visit the flowers for nectar and sometimes attack and carry off spiders. Most are paper wasps *(Polistes),* but others include chalcid wasps *(Perilampus),* large, thick-bodied, and blue-black; scoliid wasps *(Scolia),* often large and hairy; potter wasps (Eumeninae); sphecid wasps, such as cricket and spider hunters *(Chlorion)* and bee-wolf wasps *(Philanthus),* plus several others; eastern yellowjackets *(Vespula maculifrons)* and baldfaced hornets *(Dolichovespula maculata),* both of which become increasingly sugar-hungry in late summer and fall; and several thread-waisted wasps (subfamily Sphecinae).

Other common pollinators include soldier beetles *(Chauliognathus pennsylvanicus),* also called Pennsylvania leather-wings, yellow and black, often seen in mating pairs; *Ellychnia* lightning bugs (actually lampyrid beetles); and locust borers *(Megacyllene robiniae),* large, velvety black, and gold banded with a yellow W across their backs—the adults feed on nectar and pollen, whereas the larvae bore into black locust sapwood. Nectar feeders/pollinators also include flies, especially syrphids such as *Toxomerus marginatus,* beelike and hovering; tachinid flies (Tachinidae), many also beelike; and blow flies (Calliphoridae), often metallic bluish or green.

Butterfly visitors to goldenrod include some of the most spectacular. Look for the clouded or common sulphur *(Colias philodice);* the American copper *(Lycaena phlaeas);* the monarch *(Danaus plexippus);* the giant swallowtail or orangedog *(Papilio cresphontes);* the gray hairstreak or cotton square borer *(Strymon melinus);* the northern checkerspot *(Chlosyne palla);* and several skippers *(Polites).*

Some adult moths also visit the flowers. Watch for the black-and-yellow lichen moth *(Lycomorpha pholus),* an arctiid; wasplike moths such as the Virginia ctenucha *(Ctenucha virginica),* also an arctiid; and the ailanthus webworm, an ermine moth (see Ailanthus). The goldenrod stowaway *(Cirrhophanus triangulifer),* a bright yellow noctuid moth, perches well camouflaged on the flowers.

Stem feeders are mainly sap-sucking, stem-boring, or gall-making insects. The aforementioned *Uroleucon* aphids—some red, some green—mass on stems as well as flowers and the new spring rosettes. Other sap suckers include the meadow spittlebug *(Philaenus spumarius)*, nymph stage of homopteran froghoppers; these spittlebugs, identified by the frothy masses they create and in which they feed, are probably goldenrod's most damaging insect pest, reducing leaf and root mass by their parasitic feeding on the plant's xylem tissue. The boreal spittlebug *(Aphrophora gelida)* is another widespread species on goldenrod, as is the two-striped planthopper *(Acanalonia bivittata)*, a greenish insect with net-veined wings held vertically. Other stem borers include the *Epiblema* tortricid moth caterpillar and the smartweed borer *(Ostrinia obumbratalis)*, a pyralid moth caterpillar. A crane fly larva *(Tipula)* also bores into goldenrod stems.

The most conspicuous insect associations with goldenrods are those involving stem galls, created by a stem-feeding larva and reacting plant tissues. The 3 most common galls, readily identifiable by shape, result from the activities of 2 fly larvae and a moth caterpillar.

Most conspicuous is the goldenrod ball gall, a spherical bulge in the stem caused by the tephritid or fruit fly *Eurosta solidaginis,* called the goldenrod gall fly, also called "one of North America's most abundant but least-noticed insects." Research focused on this house-fly-size insect has discovered an entire microecology operating around the ball gall. The adult fly lays a single egg in the leaf bud of the stem apex just before the goldenrod leaves open. When the larva hatches, it bores into tissue at the base of the bud and begins to

Goldenrod ball galls, created by feeding of the gall fly larva (Eurosta solidaginis), *are sometimes present on almost every stem of a goldenrod stand.*

feed, and here the gall forms; from egg deposition to beginning gall formation spans about 3 weeks. The stem continues growing upward from the swelling tissue. Just how this larva induces the chemical reaction that produces a gall remains one of nature's elusive secrets—perhaps the larval saliva mimics plant growth hormones. In late summer and fall, the gall-enclosed larva bores outward, leaving a thin layer of epidermal tissue capping its exit tunnel. Instead of exiting, however, the larva enters a dormant period *(winter diapause)*, during which it can tolerate actual freezing of body tissues. Then it pupates in the now-dead gall and stem. "The pupal stage lasts about 2 weeks," wrote researcher Doug Collicutt, "then the adult fly emerges and crawls out to the end of the previously excavated exit tunnel. Here it anchors itself and pumps body fluids into a special portion of its head. This swelling 'balloon' bursts the outer 'skin' of the gall and the fly pulls itself out." The gall, typically about an inch in diameter, ends up located midway up the full-grown stem. Double-galled stems are not infrequent—the later galls appear higher on the stem and significantly smaller. *Eurosta* appears highly selective in choosing goldenrod species; in the mid-Atlantic states, the original and exclusive host is tall goldenrod (sometimes classified as a separate species, *S. altissima,* or as a variety of *S. canadensis*); but from New England to the Great Plains, the insects have also adapted to late goldenrod *(S. gigantea).* This host shift indicates that the insect has evolved into 2 races based on host preference. A 10-day difference in spring emergence dates of the 2 races prevents their interbreeding. Thus the evolution of a new gall fly species may be occurring under our noses in the goldenrod clones—a process called *sympatric speciation* (that is, evolution of a species via behavioral or genetic instead of geographic isolation).

Eurosta flies also host several parasitoids and *inquilines,* organisms that live in an abode, such as a nest or gall, produced by others. Most important is the chalcid wasp *Eurytoma gigantea,* much smaller than the gall fly but with a sharp ovipositor. It injects an egg into the still-green gall; the resulting wasp larva consumes the fly larva therein, then feeds on the inner gall tissue (though unlike the fly, it cannot stimulate further gall growth). Success of the wasp parasitism largely depends on size of the gall. Large galls with thick, corky walls prevent the wasp's relatively short ovipositor from reaching the central chamber, sparing the fly. Smaller galls, including those that develop high on the stem later in the season, become especially vulnerable to the wasp. By late July, however, most gall tissue has hardened, and the wasps cannot penetrate it.

Another chalcid wasp parasitoid is *Eurytoma obtusiventris*—an all-female *(parthenogenetic)* species that oviposits into the fly egg inside the stem even before it hatches and produces a gall. This tiny wasp larva bides its time inside the fly larva until late summer; then, when the latter is full grown, the wasp larva commences to devour its host. Recent studies have shown that this wasp favors the 2 host goldenrod species aforementioned, has not adopted quickly to *S. gigantea,* thus sparing more of the gall fly larvae.

The other parasitoid of *Eurosta* flies is the tumbling flower beetle *Mordellistena convicta,* a black, humpbacked insect that lays its eggs on the outside of the gall; the larvae then bore into the gall and feed on the fly larva.

Bird and mammal predators on *Eurosta* complete the ecological web based on this insect (see below).

The second major stem gall on goldenrod appears tapered, elliptical, or spindle-shaped. The gall maker is the caterpillar of the goldenrod gall moth *(Gnorimoschema gallaesolidaginis),* a gelechiid. It emerges from the gall in August as a grayish brown adult moth and hibernates over winter. In the spring, it lays eggs on goldenrod stems and dried leaves

Another common goldenrod gall, a bushy mass that halts further stem growth, is caused by a fly larva, the goldenrod gall gnat (Rhopalomyia solidaginis).

near the stem base. The eggs overwinter; then the larva, hatching in spring, bores into the apical bud, tunneling downward several inches in the stem, creating a gall where it stops to feed. In midsummer, it burrows an exit channel but, like the *Eurosta* fly, leaves a thin layer capping the exit. Then the larva pupates, and the adult moth emerges in late summer. Parasitic wasps that attack these caterpillars include *Copdisoma gelechiae,* an encyrtid; *Eurytoma bolteri,* a chalcid; *Calliephialtes notandus,* an ichneumon; and *Tetrastichus paracholus,* an eupholid.

The third common gall is not a stem swelling but a densely bushy rosette at the apex of the stem, causing stem growth to cease and all subsequent growth to arise on side branches. The gall maker is the larval goldenrod gall gnat *(Rhopalomyia solidaginis),* a cecidomyiid fly. It attacks buds on most goldenrod species, transforming them into bunchy masses of deformed leaflets by preventing node elongation. This larva is parasitized by a chalcid torymid wasp *(Torymus).*

A stem gall near the flowerhead, narrower than that created by the goldenrod gall moth, is the work of another gall moth caterpillar, *Epiblema scudderiana,* a tortricid. This gall frequently "makes the plant above it split out into more bushy appearance," wrote one researcher, "so you can often find the galls by looking at the appearance of the plant." This caterpillar's parasites have not been precisely identified. In the fall, the caterpillar moves down from the gall into a silk-lined, hollowed-out chamber in the stem, where it overwinters. High concentrations of glycerol in its tissues keep this caterpillar from freezing.

Another rosette gall that frequently arrests side-branch growth is created by larvae of *Procecidochares polita,* another tephritid fly. Several other gall gnats also produce small galls on stems and foliage. *P. atra* creates a stem gall similar to that of the *Rhopalomyia* gall gnat.

Goldenrod stem galls have definite effects on growth of the plants. One study found that both ball and elliptical galls resulted in significant reductions of floral biomass, also decreased the number of achenes and new rhizomes produced. Another study, however, indicated that galls act as passive energy "sinks," rather than as aggressive consumers of plant resources.

Goldenrod rhizomes also host insects. *Eurosta comma*, another fruit or tephritid fly, creates galls on rhizomes, and the tortricid moth caterpillar *Eucosma dorsisignatana* bores into them.

The total number of insects that feed on goldenrod—excluding the predators that consume the plant feeders—varies with the particular research. A 1996 study found at least 103 species that fed extensively on *S. altissima;* a 1948 study collected 241 insect species on *S. canadensis* in a single year; whereas a 1994 study on 4 goldenrod species in Florida collected 122 insect herbivores. A substantial minority of these totals are specialists on goldenrods and asters *(q.v.)*. Yet "many of the diterpenes and polyacetylenes that have been isolated from *Solidago* species are toxic to specialist herbivores," one research team reported. Thus presumably the plants defend themselves from many herbivores that are less adapted than the specialists to goldenrod chemistry.

Backyard Biology

Our work with goldenrod gall flies showed that natural selection usually favors larvae that produce big galls. Readers can check this for themselves. Sometime between February and April, collect 100 or more goldenrod galls (by wintertime, the green galls have faded to pale brown). Measure the diameter of each gall, either with calipers before opening it or with a ruler after splitting the gall down the middle. Use pruning shears to cut partway through the gall, then twist to break it open; don't cut all the way through or you will chop the larva in half and will never know if it survived. It is easiest to cut in the same direction as the stem—from pole to pole, rather than around the equator.

Once the gall is open, identify its contents. Full-grown gall fly larvae have an oval shape and are about a quarter of an inch long and almost an eighth of an inch wide. Score galls with a *Eurosta* larva as "survived." Galls that contain other kinds of insect larvae (for example, the one-eighth-inch-long, teardrop-shaped larva of a *Eurytoma gigantea* wasp; the small, white, cylindrical larva of a *Mordellistena* beetle; or the brown pupal case of an *E. obtusiventris* wasp) should be scored as "dead." Galls with woodpecker or chickadee holes also obviously count as dead. Calculate the average size of the survived and the dead galls. Can you tell which size galls natural selection favored in your area this year?

Arthur E. Weis and Warren G. Abrahamson, *Natural History.* With permission from *Natural History,* September 1998. Copyright the American Museum of Natural History 1998

Bird and mammal usage of goldenrods is relatively low in proportion to the plants' abundance. Foliage feeders include ruffed, sharp-tailed, and spruce grouse; greater prairie-chickens; beavers; cottontail rabbits; and white-tailed deer. Goldenrods provide fair to poor forage for cattle, sheep, and horses in early spring and summer. Among seedeaters are dark-eyed juncos, pine siskins, American goldfinches, and American tree sparrows. Voles and pine mice also eat goldenrod seedheads and foliage.

Bird predators on *Eurasta* gall fly larvae are mainly downy woodpeckers and black-capped chickadees. They typically tap into goldenrod galls during fall and winter months after the galls are fully developed. Both birds focus their attention on large rather than small galls; the large galls most often contain living, unparasitized larvae, whereas the smaller galls are often stunted in size because of wasp-parasitized or dead larvae inside. In cases where "both *Eurytoma gigantea* wasps and downy woodpeckers are common," reported one ecologist, "the two competing selection pressures produce a net selection for intermediate (medium) sized galls." (Individual clone genetics may also determine gall size.) Recognize bird predation by their distinctive drill holes: Downy woodpeckers find the larva's emergence tunnel beneath its epidermal cap by tapping, then drill a neat, coni-cal hole and extract the larva; chickadees are messier excavators, pulling off shredded bits and pieces to get inside. Some evidence indicates that when the birds find a parasitic *Eury-toma* wasp larva inside, they abandon the attack, perhaps because the wasp is distasteful.

Another forager on goldenrod gall fly larvae is the eastern gray squirrel, which com-pletely severs galls from the stem, gnaws into them like nuts.

Lore: "Why so many asters and goldenrods now?" Thoreau queried himself one late August. "The sun has shone on the earth," he answered himself, "and the goldenrod is his fruit. The stars, too, have shone on it, and the asters are their fruit."

Their astringent oils gave goldenrods wide usage for native tribal medications that served a roster of curative purposes. The flower tea was said to quell fevers and ease sore throats; externally, the infusions treated boils and burns.

The only goldenrod palatable to humans is a relatively uncommon species called sweet or licorice goldenrod *(S. odora)*, which makes an anise-flavored tea. Goldenrod honey, however, is a widely relished gourmet treat. And pioneer families as well as Indians often boiled the flowers, making clear and durable yellow dyes for fabrics.

Inventor Thomas Edison seriously pursued the idea of creating an ersatz rubber from goldenrod sap, his last major research project (1927–29). Through breeding and cultiva-tion, he produced a goldenrod almost 12 feet tall that yielded up to 12 percent rubber (about 12 gallons of latex per 100 pounds of goldenrod). The tires on the Model T given to him by Henry Ford were made from goldenrod rubber. Samples of the highly durable mate-rial can still be seen in Edison's New Jersey laboratory at West Orange. Edison turned his research over to the federal government in 1929, and goldenrod experiments ended before the development of synthetic rubber during WWII.

Goldenrods' bitter diterpenoid compounds probably account for the plants' *allelopathic* effects (that is, chemical inhibition) on many plant species, preventing or, in most cases, reducing seed germination and thus plant competition in the goldenrod vicinity. *Solidago* has also been shown to inhibit the growth of maple seedlings. Tree farmers know that while goldenrods may be the beekeeper's friend, they do not help matters in the plant nursery. Yet these plants' fibrous root systems also help prevent soil erosion, usefully stabilize disturbed ground.

Goldenrods have achieved an undeserved reputation as "pollen plants," anathema to hay fever and allergy sufferers. The blame is misplaced, for goldenrod pollen is heavy and sticky, does not readily disperse into the air. The sneeze culprit is usually common ragweed *(q.v.)*, which also frequents old fields and roadsides, shedding vast amounts of windblown pollen at about the same time that goldenrods flower.

Most goldenrods are native to North America, though a few species reside in Central and South America. Eurasia has only a single native species *(S. virgaurea* in some 30 varieties), but *S. canadensis* and a few other American goldenrods have become popular garden flowers in Europe, where horticulturists have developed many hybrid forms for ornamental planting. The shortest American goldenrod is probably New England goldenrod *(S. cutleri),* 6 to 12 inches tall and a mountain resident; the largest are common, late, rough-stemmed, and stiff goldenrods *(S. canadensis, S. gigantea, S. rugosa, S. rigida),* 4 to 6 feet tall.

The name *goldenrod* derives obviously from the color and forms of the plant, especially those with wandlike flower stalks. *Solidago* comes from a Latin word meaning "to make whole," referring to the plant's once-valued medicinal properties.

Despite some of its negative traits, "if we were to choose a national flower," wrote one naturalist, "the leading contender would probably be the goldenrod." Famed author-gardener Katharine S. White made such a proposal, but only Kentucky and Nebraska have made *Solidago* their state flower.

Hawkweeds *(Hieracium* species). Aster family. Resembling yellow or orange dandelions but with much different leaves, most hawkweeds are coarse, bristly perennials—some native, some alien—that often grow colonially on poor ground. The most commonly seen ones, all aliens, have hairy stems and basal rosettes of tongue-shaped hairy or woolly leaves.

They include mouse-ear hawkweed *(H. pilosella),* a short (4 inches to a foot high) lawn and field weed with a solitary yellow flowerhead and cordlike runners *(stolons)* forming mats over the ground; orange hawkweed *(H. aurantiacum),* 1 to 2 feet high, having 5 to

30 red-orange flowerheads; yellow hawkweed or king-devil *(H. piloselloides)* and meadow hawkweed *(H. caespitosum),* both with several yellow flowerheads clustered atop the stem. Most native hawkweeds, by contrast, have leaves ascending the stem rather than clustering in basal rosettes.

Other names: Devil's-paintbrush, orange-red king-devil, lungwort, tawny hawkweed *(H. aurantiacum);* glaucous king-devil, king-devil hawkweed *(H. piloselloides);* field hawkweed, yellow king-devil *(H. caespitosum).*

Close relatives: Some 18 *Hieracium* species, about half of which are Eurasian natives, reside in eastern North America; worldwide, according to the Gleason and Cronquist *Manual* (see Bibliography), exist "perhaps hundreds of species, mostly in temperate (or mountainous tropical) regions." Closely allied plants include common dandelion, chicory, goat's-beards (all *q.v.*), hawk's beards *(Crepis),* and all other aster family plants.

Lifestyle: Mouse-ear hawkweed, flowering in May, often blooms the earliest of this mainly summer- and fall-flowering genus. Orange hawkweed is easily identified, but the many alien yellow hawkweeds often hybridize and are highly variable. "Hundreds of variants have been dignified with scientific names (as well as unprintable, unscientific ones)," wrote botanist Edward G. Voss.

Hawkweed florets, yellow or orange atop the crowded aggregate flowerhead (up to an inch across), are all *ligulate* (that is, petal-like or strap-shaped with square, fringed tips) and have bisexual flower parts. In mouse-ear and probably most other hawkweeds, the individual florets are *protandrous,* sequentially unisexual, with male pollen-producing parts maturing before female parts. All stages of sexual development may simultaneously occur on a flowerhead with, however, the younger florets located toward the center. Yet all of the usual sexual processes in most plants essentially amount to vestigial systems in hawkweeds, for their reproduction is asexual; the flowers of most North American hawkweeds are *apomictic* (that is, the seeds develop without pollination). The offspring are thus clones, genetically identical to the parent plant, and large colonies of such clones are typical in hawkweeds.

Most reproduction in these plants, however, occurs vegetatively. Nonseedling clones originate from creeping *stolons* (horizontal aboveground stems) in mouse-ear and orange hawkweeds; the latter hawkweed also extends elongate *rhizomes* (horizontal underground stems). Only plants in flower produce stolons, which spread like tentacles, some 4 to 12 in number, across the ground surface. Stolons (hawkweeds' main means of reproduction) elongate throughout summer, reaching up to a foot long, developing new rosettes and roots at their tips. These rosettes survive over winter; each may or may not produce several to 30 flowering stems the following summer. If the plants do flower, both stems and rosettes die in the fall; if not, the rosettes sometimes survive for a year or longer, usually producing more stems. The connecting stolons themselves often decay after a year or so, severing the original ties but not genetic identity to the parent plant. Vigorous stolon growth rapidly expands the colony, forming dense, matlike patches of hawkweed rosettes that often choke out all other plants. Some hawkweed species also produce clones from budding rhizomes and roots as well. Flowering occurs mainly near the outside edges of a colony; density of plants in the center inhibits the growth of flowering stems. *H. piloselloides* has no stolons and very short rhizomes.

Hawkweed roots are shallow and fibrous, and the plants have a milky latex sap. Each ridged, 1-seeded achene—12 to 50 on each flowerhead—has a hairy crown, or *pappus,* that aids in wind distribution. Most ripe seeds, however, fall within the hawkweed colony. Seedlings that develop outside a colony have low survival rates, though a colony can only originate from 1 or more seedling hawkweeds. Seeds can germinate immediately, may remain viable in the soil for up to 7 years.

Associates: Hawkweeds grow almost anywhere on moist or dry ground, favoring open or lightly shaded areas. In June, I frequently note how the shape of a dense hawkweed colony follows the edge of a tree or shrub shadow. Such "shadow colonies"—though often somewhat indistinct, for shadows move as the day advances—can sometimes be quite sharply marked. Whether this sun-shadow preference reflects a possible soil moisture gradient or simply a favoritism for light shade remains unknown. Orange hawkweed's native range is alpine slopes and meadows. If the plant were less adaptable to almost any open or disturbed land habitat, "we would regard its beauty with enthusiasm," wrote Voss. "However, it is too aggressive in dry fields and waste places for most people's tastes."

Alien hawkweeds can be fierce plant competitors; their basal rosette leaves overlap and form dense mats that exclude grasses and other open-field plants. *Allelopathy* (chemical inhibition of seed germination) probably also occurs to an unknown extent. Some studies indicate

Shadow colonies of orange hawkweed sometimes outline the pattern of tree shade—a sort of shadow footprint populated by flowers.

that mouse-ear hawkweed may inhibit the growth of several clover species. Ox-eye daisies *(q.v.)*, which thrive in similar habitats, are frequently noted hawkweed associates. Other frequent plant associates include sulphur cinquefoil (see Cinquefoils), spotted knapweed, Queen Anne's lace, common dandelion (all *q.v.*), and gray goldenrod *(Solidago nemoralis).*

Eurasian fungous and insect associates of these hawkweed species are much more numerous in the plants' native lands than in North America (as is true of most alien plants). Some of these Old World feeders and parasites have likewise been imported to America for possible biological control attempts on hawkweeds; others are currently being researched for such potential purposes.

Two fungal pathogens that attack hawkweeds are *Puccinia hieracii,* a rust that appears on the leaves in May; and *Entyloma hieracii,* a spot or blister smut causing blackish round or oval spots in the leaves.

The hairiness of these plants probably discourages many insect foliage and stem-climbing nectar feeders. Hawkweed roots, rhizomes, and stolons, however, seem highly vulnerable to certain larval insects. Larvae of the Asiatic garden beetle *(Maladera castanea),* for example, may cluster in populations of up to 100 per square foot in orange hawkweed roots. Biological control studies on hawkweeds mainly focus on root and stolon feeders (since the garden beetle is so destructive to a wide variety of plants, it is not a suitable candidate). Native European invertebrates that invade hawkweeds include nematodes (roundworms), mites, true bugs, a dozen moth caterpillars, and gall wasps. A long-legged, pale yellow insect often seen on orange hawkweed is the common stilt bug *(Neides muticus).*

Most hawkweed flowers don't need pollinators, but insects in abundance still fly to them. Orange hawkweeds, especially, are good sites to watch for various butterfly nectar

Spectacular eastern tiger swallowtail butterflies (Papilio glaucus) *often land on orange hawkweeds despite thin nectar rewards.*

feeders. These include pearl crescents *(Phyciodes tharos)*, orange-brown with darker patches; eastern tiger swallowtails *(Papilio glaucus)*; clouded and orange sulphurs *(Colias philodice, C. eurytheme)*; Milbert's tortoise shell *(Nymphalis milberti)*; painted lady *(Vanessa cardui)*; the monarch *(Danaus plexippus)*; and several skipper species (Hesperiidae). Numerous other insect flower foragers include bumblebees *(Bombus)* and other bees (mainly *Andrena* and *Halictus* species). Syrphid flies (Syrphidae) and several sphinx moth species *(Hemaris)* also visit hawkweeds. Despite hawkweeds' attraction to insects, the nectar rewards are small. "To get even the tiniest droplet visible to the human eye," wrote researcher Bernd Heinrich, "the whole inflorescence with its dozens of tiny florets must be squeezed at the base, and even then one is rarely rewarded with the sight of nectar. . . . It barely matches the energy the bee expends in collecting it." Yet insects need only small amounts to keep going, and the flowers' magnetic brilliance testifies to its reliable if not lavish rewards.

Livestock generally shuns hawkweeds—which increases their plant-competitive advantage—but ruffed grouse and wild turkeys consume the seeds and young leaves, and American goldfinches, probably the foremost seed foragers on aster family plants, also feed on the plant. Cottontail rabbits, white-tailed deer, and elk also graze on hawkweeds, though they are not a favorite forage. In England, researchers noted that rabbit grazing of mouse-ear hawkweed resulted in the formation of longer, more numerous stolons.

Lore: Austrian monk Gregor Mendel, who formulated the laws of heredity from his observation of pea plants, later tried to expand his investigations to hawkweeds—and failed to duplicate his pea-plant results because of hawkweed's then-unknown characteristic of reproducing asexually. The failure may have discouraged his further pursuit of heredity studies, which ended 15 years before his death.

In terms of floral economy, it is difficult to see how hawkweeds benefit by putting out so much apparently "wasted" energy. They don't need to attract insects in order to reproduce, yet they gaudily do; and vigorous colonies, which reproduce only at their outer edges, where stolons can spread out, maintain a large, living, unproductive biomass in their centers. Yet hawkweeds continue to thrive, often densely.

Hawkweeds' recent rapid invasion of northwestern rangelands has alarmed agricultural researchers, who now seek means of biological control, focusing on the most vulnerable parts of the plants, their stolons. Mouse-ear hawkweed is becoming a serious pasture pest in New Zealand, displacing native and forage species.

No part of these plants is palatable to humans; yet the name *hawkweed*, it is said, derives from the folklore that eating the plant will sharpen eyesight to hawklike keenness. The Greek word for *hawk* is "hierax," whence emerged *Hieracium.* The Roman scholar Pliny—first of a long line of wrong botanical experts—reported that hawks themselves ate the plants to aid their vision. Exactly how the idea of keen vision came to be associated with these plants remains an enigma perhaps based on a long-ago not-so-keen observation. (In science, though truth will out, it is error hallowed by tradition that seems to provide the most durable labels.)

English gardeners, who planted orange hawkweed for its color, named it Grim the Collier, after William Haughton's play of that name, for the downy, rusty coating of the bracts beneath the flowerhead—"as it were the dust of coles," as English botanist John Gerard observed in 1633. The species came to North America in 1875 as a garden ornamental. When orange hawkweed first appeared in Maine, folks there called it burmah-weed, associating its arrival with the return of a local missionary from Burma. It had spread westward to Michigan by the 1890s. The yellow-flowered *H. caespitosum* had arrived in America earlier (1828).

European herbalists once used astringent preparations of the plant as treatments for asthma and lung diseases, as well as kidney stones and "griping pains in the bowels." Mouse-ear, the least bitter of its tribe, still finds use as a homeopathic remedy for whooping cough and hemorrhages, among other ailments.

Hawthorns (*Crataegus* species). Rose family. Recognize these thorny native shrubs and small trees by their spiny, thicket-forming branches and their applelike flowers and fruits. Probably more than 100 species, identified as such, exist in North and South America. Estimates vary as to the number of species in eastern North America, from about 25 to 40. Specialists disagree on how many hawthorn species actually exist throughout North America; taxonomic "splitters" say more than a thousand, "lumpers" claim less than a hundred. Many Eurasian species also exist.

The Morton Arboretum located near Chicago identifies 4 basic types of common hawthorns:

1. The downy hawthorns; first to bloom in May; lower branches tend to droop; large, broad, yellow-green leaves; short, stout, relatively few thorns; sweet-flavored scarlet fruit, earliest to ripen; an example is *C. mollis,* downy hawthorn.

2. The cockspur hawthorns; latest to bloom in May or June; rigid, zigzag branches forming a broad, round-topped head; narrow, glossy, dark green, leathery leaves; long, slender thorns slightly curved; dull red fruits that hang on until spring; an example is *C. crusgalli,* cockspur-thorn.

3. The thicket hawthorns; shrublike, with dense, upward branching; small triangular leaves; pinkish flower centers; an example is *C. coccinea,* scarlet hawthorn.

4. The doffed hawthorns; flat-topped trees with horizontal branching; late blooming; deeply veined leaves; fruit dull red or yellow with large pale dots; an example is *C. punctata,* dotted hawthorn.

Nonspecialists, however, may most productively observe this group as a genus rather than labor to identify separate species of uncertain validity.

Close relatives: *Crataegus* taxonomy is so complicated as to "drive most botanists to distraction," as botanist Edward G. Voss wrote. "Hybridization, polyploidy, and apomixis presumably account for much of the complexity, asexual populations breeding true and acting as species but better thought of as individuals."

Popular ornamental hawthorns include the Washington-thorn *(C. phaenopyrum)*, the mayhaw *(C. aestivalis)*, and 2 alien hawthorns: single-seed hawthorn *(C. monogyna)* and English hawthorn *(C. laevigata)*. Hawthorns somewhat resemble crab apples *(Pyrus)* in general form, but thorns of crab apples, unlike those of hawthorns, often bear buds or leaves, and they occur on older wood rather than on twigs, as in hawthorns. The medlar *(Mespilus germanica)* is a closely related Asian shrub.

Rose family kin includes multiflora rose *(q.v.)*, cherries *(Prunus)*, apple *(q.v.)*, mountain-ashes *(Sorbus)*, shadbushes *(Amelanchier)*, and many others.

Other names: Thorn, thornapple, haw, May bush.

Lifestyle: The most conspicuous variations in hawthorns occur in leaf shape and appearance of fruit. Leaves are jaggedly toothed but may also be lobed and variably shaped even on the same plant, depending on whether they appear on vegetative or floral branches. Hawthorns, deciduous, become dormant and lose their leaves in the fall.

The flowers, appearing with or after the leaves in spring, are spectacular white or pinkish, apple-blossomlike, bisexual, and insect-pollinated. They're not very fragrant; indeed, some are malodorous. They present a large repertoire of reproductive strategies. Within a given (so-called) species may exist both sexual (including self-fertile) and asexual *(apomictic)* populations, apparently based on differences in multiple chromosome number within cells. Cockspur-thorn, for example, produces large amounts of single-parent seed by both selfing and apomixis. Any given stand or thicket of *Crataegus* is likely to consist of seeded clones from a single parent tree. Yet "every now and then," as botanist Monique Reed wrote, "they may have a sexual generation to mix things up a little more." Relatively few other plants share these options of producing seed both sexually and asexually, a situation that indicates hawthorns' current state of evolutionary flux. Another conspicuous variation in North American hawthorns is the differential number of stamens (male pollen-producing structures) in individual plants, varying from 10 or fewer to about 20; Eurasian hawthorns do not display such disparities. Many hawthorns do not begin flowering until they are 5 to 10 years old, and abundant flowering may occur only every other year.

Hawthorn fruits, like apples, are *pomes* containing 1 to 5 nutlets, each with (usually) only a single seed. Ripe fruits (thornapples) may vary in color from yellow to red to black; their fat content is low (1 to 2 percent by weight). Seeds require a period of cold stratification in order to germinate—some may lie dormant for as long as 2 years because of their hard seed coats. New shoots originate almost entirely from seeds, rarely from roots of established trees. Seedlings develop a strong taproot, and shallower horizontal roots also spread as the tree matures. Hawthorns are shade-intolerant, needing full sunlight and generous space for their spreading crowns (which sometimes exceed the tree's height) and root systems.

The long, spiny thorns so characteristic of *Crataegus* are actually abortive branches. They develop from short shoots that sprout leaves; the shoots then lose their leaves and become *sclerified* (hardened) woody extensions. The trees readily accept grafts, and apple and pear scions can be raised on hawthorn stock.

Associates: Hawthorns stand solitary in fields or form dense thickets in open woods and overgrown pastures. They usually compete for space only with one another—hawthorn thickets often consist of even-aged trees *(cohorts)*. Such thickets typically form savannas similar to those of red cedar *(q.v.)*, with which hawthorns frequently share a common rust fungus (see below). Both trees often occur together in overgrown pastures and old fields. Also, different hawthorn species often grow together and hybridize (although flowering times may differ

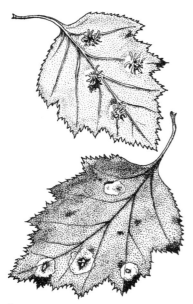

somewhat, much overlap occurs). A typical hawthorn community might include cockspur-thorn together with pear-hawthorn *(C. calpodendron)* and dotted hawthorn. Habitats for most species appear similar; some may favor drier or wetter ground, but many adapt to either condition. "One of the peculiarities of the Chicago region," wrote one regional botanist, "is the manner in which the hawthorns, their seeds distributed largely by birds, will march across abandoned fields and take possession. Undisturbed by ax or fire, in twenty years there will be an almost impenetrable thicket from 10 to 20 feet in height."

A number of fungi frequently invade hawthorn leaves. Yellow or orange spots on upper leaf surfaces may signal cedar-hawthorn rust *(Gymnosporangium globosum)*. During late summer, the spores produced by the hairlike growths on leaf undersurfaces are carried by wind and

Gymnosporangium rust, common on hawthorn leaves, also produces galls on red cedar. The leaf undersurface (top) sprouts hairlike spore producers; the leaf upper surface (bottom) shows yellow-orange spots of the rust in its early stages.

may produce galls on the fungus's alternate host, red cedar. The 2 trees must usually be located within a mile of each other for this fungus to exist.

Hawthorn leaf blight *(Fabraea maculata)* produces angular, reddish brown spots on upper leaf surfaces, each containing a black, pimplelike fruiting body. Spots may enlarge to kill the entire leaf; in severe cases, this blight may defoliate much of the tree.

Farmers dislike hawthorns not only because they invade pastures and require bull-dozers to eradicate once they become established, but also because they often host fungal and insect parasites of fruit crops. Many if not most of the common insect pests on hawthorn also reside on apple *(q.v.)* and pear trees. Overgrown pastures that contain hawthorns mixed with orchard trees provide ideal habitats for this interchangeable fauna.

Insect feeders on hawthorn foliage are numerous. Curled or crinkled leaves usually indicate aphid feeding; the apple aphid *(Aphis pomi)* and hawthorn aphid *(Eriosoma crataegi)* are common species. Stippled and speckled leaves indicate hawthorn lace bugs *(Corythucha cydoniae)*, dark, gauzy-winged insects; their spiny nymphs may also be present. The gall gnat *Cecidomyia bedeguar* produces a tufted, roundish gall on leaf midribs. Another gnat, *Trishormomyia crataegifolia,* makes a cockscomb gall on the leaves.

The hawthorn mealybug *(Phenacoccus dearnessi),* a scale insect, often masses in fluffy, popcornlike clusters on branches. These masses are females, which lay wax-covered egg clusters at the base of buds. The nymphs suck plant sap from the leaves, producing heavy honeydew secretions (which, in turn, become a medium for the growth of black sooty mold fungi); then the nymphs migrate to trunk and branches to hibernate over winter. These insects also attract ladybird beetles (Coccinellidae), major predators of the mealybugs.

Moth caterpillars that feed principally on hawthorn include the hummingbird or common clearwing *(Hemaris thysbe),* a sphinx moth. The large, reddish brown adult, with transparent wing windows, is a daytime flier. The eastern tent caterpillar *(Malacosoma americanum),* an irruptive, sometimes hugely populous species, creates large webs in forks of the trees. Larvae of several underwing species, including hawthorn underwing *(Catocala crataegi),* wonderful underwing *(C. mira),* and woody underwing *(C. grynea)*—plus several other *Catocala* species (plump caterpillars tapering at both ends)—are also common. Wormy fruits may indicate infestation by codling moth caterpillars *(Cydia pomonella),* also called apple worms, one of the most serious pests in apple orchards. Another fruit feeder is the apple maggot (see Apple), a tephritid fly larva.

Bees, flies, and beetles pollinate the flowers.

Larvae of the weevil *Anthonomus nebulosus* feed on the anthers of the flowers while still in bud.

Predatory insects that attack other insects also abound on hawthorns. *Deraeocoris* plant bugs, feeding mainly on aphids, are common, as are thread-legged bugs *(Acholla multispinosa),* resembling small walking-stick insects.

Hawthorn fruits, perhaps owing to their low food-energy value, are not consumed by wildlife to the extent that one might think. Though some 36 species of birds and a lesser number of mammals are known to eat them, only a few species consume them to any extensive degree. These include ruffed and sharp-tailed grouse, ring-necked pheasants, wild turkeys, northern bobwhites, cedar waxwings, American robins, purple finches, pine grosbeaks, and fox sparrows. Birds occasionally become intoxicated on fermented hawthorn fruits when feeding during a warm, wet fall. In winter, when many preferred fruits become unavailable, the fruits are more appreciated. Squirrels, raccoons, opossums, gray foxes, cottontail rabbits, and white-tailed deer also consume the fruits.

A hawthorn savanna, often an overgrown pasture, provides excellent shelter habitat (as do smaller hawthorn islands) for bird and mammal wildlife, providing semiopen yet effective cover for concealment and nesting. Among the most common nesters in hawthorn trees are mourning doves, black-billed and yellow-billed cuckoos, willow flycatchers, gray catbirds, brown thrashers, yellow warblers, yellow-breasted chats, and northern cardinals. Also look for nests of loggerhead shrikes; any insects, amphibians, or small birds or mammals impaled on a thorn are signs of shrike presence. Unlike hawks, these birds have no grasping talons, must lodge their prey on a thorn or barbed wire or wedge it into a tree crotch to feed upon it. The impaled prey may also serve as territorial markers.

Lore: If you've sampled many thornapples, you know they vary widely in both taste and texture. Some are dry, mealy, or bland; others taste succulent, sweet, "just right." Most make a good apple jelly—they contain plenty of pectin. Steeping the fruit also makes a decent tea. And hawthorn flowers provide a fine honey.

Native Americans squeezed the raw, ripe fruits, then dried and stored them as small fruitcakes for winter cooking. Women drank a decoction of the root for menstrual pain, and the thorns were used as awls. During the last century, researchers found extracts of the fruit beneficial for treatment of certain heart and rheumatic disorders.

The immensely tough wood has no commercial value, since the trees are so small, though wood craftsmen value it for making tool handles or other small items. Many ornamental hawthorns, showing immense variations in showy flowers, attractive fruits, and colorful foliage, have been developed for planting in yards, parks, and gardens.

Haw is an old English word for "hedge," and hawthorns at one time formed the living fences that divided the fields, not only in Britain but other parts of Europe as well.

Hawthorn is the state flower of Missouri.

Horsetail, Common (*Equisetum arvense*). Horsetail family. Recognize this spore-bearing plant by its coarse, hollow, jointed stems of 2 types: unbranched, brownish, 4 to 10 inches tall, topped by a spore cone, appearing in early spring and soon withering; and branched, green, non-spore-bearing stems 8 to 12 inches tall, the ascending branches in whorls of 20 or so, each branch 4 to 6 inches long, appearing in May and lasting until frost. Both stems rise annually from buds on perennial creeping *rhizomes* (subsurface stems). Most *Equisetum* species differ from this one by producing only one kind of stem; in most horsetail species, all stems are fertile and spore bearing.

Other names: Field horsetail, horse pipes, mare's tail, snake grass, scouring rush, bottlebrush, jointed rush, shave brush.

Close relatives: Horsetails are more closely related to ferns than to seed-bearing plants. About 15 *Equisetum* species exist worldwide, some 10 of them in eastern North America. Most horsetails inhabit temperate climates and moist or wet ground, among them dwarf horsetail *(E. scirpoides),* common horsetail *(E. hyemale),* and meadow-horsetail *(E. pratense).* No family or generic relatives exist. Along with mosses and ferns, horsetails are labeled *cryptogams,* plants that lack true flowers and seeds. They are probably most closely allied to the calamites, ancient, long extinct, treelike plants of the Carboniferous period, known only as fossils.

Lifestyle: Horsetail biology is similar to that of bracken fern *(q.v.)* in its alternation of *sporophyte* (spore-producing) and *gametophyte* (gamete- or sex cell–producing) generations. The horsetails we see growing are all sporophytes; horsetail gametophytes, or *prothalli,* are tiny, barely visible, lobed or branched unisexual structures that germinate from spores. Gametophytes produce swimming sperm from male *antheridia* that fertilize eggs in the female *archegonia;* the resulting sporophyte plant sprouts from the fertilized female prothallus.

The brownish or sometimes pale pinkish stems surmounted by *strobili* (spore cones, often described as "armored catkins") emerge first; they quickly mature, shed their spores, and die. Naturalist Anna B. Comstock described the spore cone as "made up of rows of tiny discs which are set like miniature toadstools around the central stalk." Each frontal disk bears ridged rows *(sporangiophores)* of spore sacs behind it, with the topmost discs emptying their contents first.

Then the green, branched, sterile stem appears. Tough, grooved, and wiry, it lasts until fall or winter, when it too dies back. The perennial rhizome, however, survives and keeps growing, sometimes for many years.

Unlike the stems, rhizomes are not hollow; they produce small, attached, starch-filled tubers. Spreading horizontally, the brown-felted rhizomes also branch vertically downward for a foot or so, establishing successively lower horizontal levels as deep as 6 feet or even farther. Most rhizomes, however, lie within the top 10 inches or so of soil. They branch and grow

quickly, dying out behind the aerial stems, can reach a length of 300 feet or more. Aerial stems rise from buds on nodes and internodal tubers along the rhizomes, appearing on the surface as separate plants. The nodes also produce fibrous roots that last for only a single growing season. Buds for the next year's spore stems develop on the rhizomes in summer; those for the vegetative shoots develop in the fall. Rhizomes and tuber fragments may also produce new plants, the main reason why horsetails, once established, are not easily eradicated.

Most horsetail reproduction occurs in this vegetative manner rather than by spores. Each developing spore on the strobilus bears 4 long, stringy appendages called *elaters,* which are *hygroscopic*—that is, they expand and contract with changes in humidity. The elaters wrap the spores tightly until the latter mature; then they uncoil like watch-springs, tossing spores to the wind. Once landed, the twisting elaters, remaining attached, also help dig the spore into the soil, tangling the spores together in clumps, thus increasing chances that fertilization of adjacent developing prothalli will occur. Spores are quite short-lived; their germination can only occur in optimum conditions—that is, where the ground is suitably moist, since the male gametes must swim to reach the female prothalli.

The common horsetail produces its strobilus or spore cone atop a brownish or pale stem, followed by growth of a green, sterile stem.

Epidermal cells of *Equisetum,* giving the plant its coarse, gritty feel, are loaded with silica deposits, mineral compounds most familiar to us in quartz or sand form. The silica deposits *(spicules)* look blocky, jagged under a microscope. Silica content may range from 1 up to 12 percent of the dried plant ("a virtual Fort Knox of silica," as one botanist wrote).

The inconspicuous scalelike leaves on the stems ring the joints.

Associates: Common horsetail, almost cosmopolitan worldwide between latitudes 39 and 83 degrees N, grows less commonly outside that range. Like all horsetails, *E. arvense* favors wet, poorly drained ground. But unlike most other horsetail species, it also thrives on some of the barest, driest, most sterile surfaces created by industrial culture—railroad embankments, roadside fill, cracks in asphalt pavement, also on dunes, rocky slopes, and in crop fields. Common horsetails often occur in pure cloning stands, but they also associate with willow-alder communities in wetlands, appear as one of the foremost early colonizers on floodplains. This horsetail was probably one of the earliest plants to colonize in the wake of continental glaciation. The plant regenerates quickly after fire passage, owing to its deeply buried rhizomes. It favors semishaded conditions; shaded stems usually grow taller than those in full sunlight.

Horsetail alkaloids are apparently toxic *(allelopathic)* to the germination and seedling vigor of surrounding plants, especially grasses.

Fungous parasites on horsetails include the root-rots *Fusarium* and *Phoma. Gloeosporium equiseti* causes stem spots.

Dodder, a parasitic vine, twines on horsetail stems, tapping into the tissue by means of suckers *(haustoria).* A common species on horsetail is button-bush-dodder *(Cuscuta cephalanthi).*

A typical railroad-bank habitat for common horsetail clones, which often thrive where few other plants can.

Relatively few insects feed on horsetails. *Macrosteles borealis,* a leafhopper, is one that does. Beetle feeders include the bronze-colored *Hippuriphila modeeri,* called the horsetail flea beetle; and a weevil or snout beetle, *Grypus equiseti.* Twenty of some 35 *Dolerus* sawfly species are larval feeders on horsetails. Adult ichneumon wasps—*Perilissus, Tryphon,* and *Hadrodactylus* species—parasitize these sawfly larvae. Potato stem borers *(Hydraecia micacea),* also called rosy rustic moths, sometimes feed as noctuid caterpillars in *Equisetum* rhizome tubers.

Bird and mammal feeders include blue and snow geese and tundra swans, which consume the rhizome tubers. Muskrats also excavate and eat the tubers, and black and grizzly bears are known to consume the young stems in spring and early summer. Cattle usually avoid the plant, but moose graze readily upon it.

Lore: "Squeaky noiseweed"—an apt name for the plant, as anyone who has walked through a stand of glassy-stemmed horsetail knows—was dubbed as such by the Potawatomi, who valued horsetail tea as curative for kidney and bladder disorders. (Strain it well for such purposes, advises one herbalist, else the fine hairs "will act like a pot scrubber on your stomach.") Young shoots were also eaten, cooked or raw. Other tribes used various preparations of the plant for ailments ranging from constipation to putrid wounds. Homeopathic practitioners use the plant as a diuretic, to stop blood loss, and to "remineralize" the system with silica and potassium.

Human intake of horsetail as food or medicine should be cautious. Sources differ considerably on this plant's toxic effects. It can, in excessive amounts, poison and kill horses, especially if they ingest it dried and mixed in hay. Yet directly contradictory accounts also exist; certain native tribes claimed that it made "excellent horse feed." Equisetine or thiaminase disrupts vitamin B1 metabolism, the probable source of its toxicity, over a period of days or weeks. This substance occurs mainly in the spores and strobili.

Tribal and pioneer usage of the plants as pot scrubbers and wood and metal polishers—whence derives the name "scouring rush"—is well known. Natives and settlers also produced a yellow dye from the plant, using it for clothing and decoration, as in coloring porcupine quills and beadwork. "When my horsetail needs thinning," wrote one gardener unaverse to these plants, "I make a new supply of pot scrubber 'butterflies' by taking handfuls of five-inch pieces and binding them in the middle with rubber bands."

Horsetails absorb not only silica into their tissues, but several other compounds plus heavy metals as well, especially selenium, gold, and mercury. The plant can accumulate up to 4.5 ounces of gold per ton of fresh stalks, but its value is primarily as an indicator rather than a commercial source of riches. A 1992 study concluded that commercial silica extraction from these plants, though offering some potential, was not currently feasible. Horsetail's frequent appearance in mine tailings and ore waste has also been noted. It may yet prove valuable in *phytoremediation,* the use of plants for removal of toxic contaminants from the soil, also as a biological monitor and indicator of copper, zinc, cadmium, and lead pollution.

The name *Equisetum* derives from the Latin *equus,* "horse," and *seta,* "bristle" or "hair." To see resemblances to an actual mare's tail in the branching of these plants requires stout imagination.

Botanists consider horsetails the most primitive of all the fern families. Horsetails once thrived as the dominant vegetation on earth; hollow, jointed horsetails reached tree heights of 50 to 100 feet in immense Carboniferous forests of 250 million years ago. These forests now exist only as coal seams, and the gases of their former plant tissues gain final release in our coal-fueled power plants. Their ancient spores remain in beds of cannel coal and the dense black coal known as jet. The horsetail is a "great-grandparent of plantdom," as one naturalist called it. Today the largest horsetail is *E. giganteum,* giant horsetail, growing in Cuba and South America; with only an inch-thick stem, its height can exceed 30 feet.

Knapweed, Spotted *(Centaurea maculosa).* Aster family. Spotted knapweed's thistlelike flowerheads—pink or white but most often purplish—also resemble those of blazing stars *(q.v.).* Its rough, wiry stem, branching above the middle, and deeply cut leaves also help identify this alien perennial, biennial, or short-lived perennial as a knapweed. This species shows fringed black tips on the bracts below the flowerhead, hence its name. It stands up to 3 or 4 feet tall.

Other names: Star-thistle.

Close relatives: Some 500 *Centaurea* species, mostly Old World natives, exist. Eleven of these aliens reside in northeastern North America. Probably spotted knapweed is the most abundant of these, but tumble or diffuse knapweed *(C. diffusa),* mainly white flowered, is also well established. American knapweed or basket-flower *(C. americana)* is a native annual species of the Ozarks. Cornflower or bachelor's button *(C. cyanus)* is a bright blue garden escape. Closely related aster family plants include Canada thistle *(q.v.),* white lettuces *(Prenanthes),* lettuces *(Lactuca),* sow-thistles *(Sonchus),* and hawkweeds *(q.v.).*

Lifestyle: Summer fields and roadsides are largely taken over by these thistlelike tufts on wiry, gray-green stems, increasingly widespread both East and West. Naturalists and farmers alike loathe them for their aggressiveness, but of course—like all plants—they go mainly where invited by land disturbance and other prepared habitats.

Some 25 to 35 tubular flowers exist in each inch-wide flowerhead, about 16 of which develop, on average, for each plant. The flowers, I have noted, often bear a subtle honey-like fragrance (though the nectar is said to be bitter). Unlike many aster family flowers, knapweed has no outer ray florets, only disk florets. The stiff, spine-fringed bracts beneath each flowerhead provide a vaselike enclosure. Although the bisexual flowers are insect-pol-linated, they are also sexually self-compatible. The single-seeded *achenes* bear a short tuft *(pappus)* of bristles at one end; dispersal usually occurs in August, 2 or 3 weeks after the achenes mature. Movement of the stem by wind or jostling causes the achenes to shoot forth up to a yard distant from the seedhead; they also attach to feathers or fur (or trousers or socks) that may brush against the plant. In September, when most knapweed stems are dead, I note that some of the plants still flower but at a lower level—instead of thigh-high, these late-flowering stems rise only shin-high or lower.

Spotted knapweed reproduces mainly by seed, which germinates in the fall (less than 6 percent) or spring (20 to 40 percent); germination in 2 seasons increases chances of seedling survival. Although experts claim that *vivipary* (seed ger-mination while still on the seedhead) does not occur in this species, I have witnessed that it does; one early October after a spell of warm, rainy weather, I could see minute green leaves sprouting vigorously from knapweed seed-heads. Seeds in the soil may remain viable for 5 or more years.

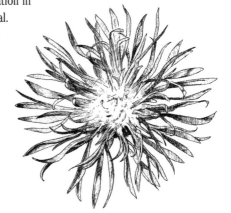

Seedlings form a stout taproot, a root crown, and in the fall, a leafy basal rosette that lasts over winter and produces 1 to 6 (sometimes more) flowering stems in spring. The "biennial" designation for this plant applies only to a fall-ger-minated rosette that produces a flowering stem

Spotted knapweed's flowerhead, faintly fragrant, consists entirely of tubular disk florets surrounded by spiny bracts; it is pollinated mainly by honeybees (Apis mellifera).

the next year, then dies (probably a minority of knapweed plants). Most knapweed plants spread lateral shoots an inch or so from the root crown, producing another rosette at their tips; these become mature plants in the following year. The root crown of a single plant may survive up to 9 years, though 5 years or less is probably a plant's typical lifespan (the plants can be aged by their root rings, similar to tree rings). Spotted knapweed populations thus enlarge mainly by means of peripheral expansion, via seed and lateral shoots, of existing stands.

Knapweed roots also exude a natural herbicide (cnicin), found mainly in the leaves and shoots, which inhibits the germination of nearby plants—an effect called *allelopathy.* Allelopathy plays a minor part, however, in accounting for knapweed's competitive success.

Associates: Disturbed ground—whether by cow, plow, fire, axe, or bulldozer—invites spotted knapweed to come stay awhile. Occasionally knapweed also invades ground undisturbed by grazing or human activity. It thrives in open land and sandy or gravelly soil, is quite shade-intolerant, ranges worldwide in temperate regions up to about latitude 55 degrees N. Spotted knapweed favors moister, more northern and mountainous environments than most other knapweed species. Its native range is the grassland steppes of southeastern Europe and western Asia. Invasion of this plant usually results in a loss of plant diversity, as it competes aggressively with grasses and with other forbs.

Just how it competes has been the subject of recent investigation. As with most plants, knapweed roots maintain a *symbiotic association* (that is, an intimate coexistence) with mycorrhizal fungi, which aid the absorption of nutrients by the plant. Researchers have found that where spotted knapweed has invaded native bunchgrass or fescue *(Festuca),* knapweed's mycorrhizae have indirectly enhanced its competitive vigor; the fescue thrived much more abundantly in the experimental absence of mycorrhizae in knapweed roots. A similar coaction that bears on knapweed competitiveness may also involve insects (as detailed later in this section), so that herbivory (animal eating of plants) in combination with mycorrhizal action may actually stimulate knapweed growth.

Much agricultural research has gone into hunting for possible agents of knapweed *biocontrol*—that is, means of reducing or eliminating the plant by the use of other plant or animal species. Many species that consume or parasitize knapweed (most of them, like spotted knapweed itself, are non-native organisms) have become candidates at some time for this superhero role. To date, these efforts have shown only random success at best.

Among fungi, the stem rot and wilt ascomycete (sac fungus) *Sclerotinia sclerotiorum* attacks the root crown, also damages numerous crop plants. *Microsphaeropsis centaureae* of the group called fungi imperfecti causes leaf wilt and death. Several *Puccinia* species of club fungi also attack the plant.

Pseudomonas syringae bacteria form circular leaf spots on many plants; in knapweeds, they sometimes cause stem dieback.

Clover mites *(Bryobia praetiosa)* and carmine spider mites *(Tetranychus cinnabarinus)* sometimes infest knapweeds, as do *Eriophyes centaureae* mites, which create small wartlike galls. Differential grasshoppers *(Melanoplus differentialis)*, a spur-throated species, also feed on the plant.

Among heteropterans (true bugs), feeders and predators include the large big-eyed bug *(Geocoris bullatus)*, yellow and black with large compound eyes, which often attacks other insects around knapweed's plant base; the four-lined plant bug *(Poecilocapsus lineatus)*; a seed bug, *Nysius thymi*; *Ortholomus scolopax*, another seed bug; and the shield-backed bug *Homaemus bijugis*. I have also seen nymphs of meadow spittlebugs *(Philaenus spumarius)*, homopterans, abundant in their frothy masses on the shoots in spring.

Several leafhoppers (Cicadellidae)—elongate, tapering insects—suck the sap of knapweeds. They include the clover leafhopper *(Aceratagallia sanguinolenta)*, the intermountain potato leafhopper *(Empoasca filamenta)*, plus *Chlorotettix unicolor*, *Gyponana hasta*, *Xerophloea viridis*, and the aster leafhopper (see Asters). *Phenacoccus* mealybugs also feed on the sap.

Several weevil or snout beetle species have been introduced from Eurasia to war on knapweed in North America as they do in their native areas. The blunt and lesser flower-head weevils *(Larinus obtusus, L. minutus)*, imported from Greece, lay eggs in the flowerheads; the larvae feed there, reducing seed production of the plant. The root-boring weevil *Cyphocleonus achates*, first released in the United States in 1987, feeds on knapweed's central rosette leaves as a mottled brown-gray adult insect, lays eggs atop the root crown. The larvae burrow into the taproot, feeding and overwintering there, stunting and weakening the plant.

Another seed feeder introduced for biocontrol is the knapweed seedhead moth *(Metzneria paucipunctella)*, a Swiss gelechiid that feeds on flower receptacle tissues as a caterpillar and winters in the seedhead, emerging as an adult moth the following summer. This moth does not tolerate cold weather well, will probably not survive in the North. The sulphur knapweed moth *(Agapeta zoegana)*, a cochylid species from Yugoslavia, small and bright yellow with brown wing bands, rests vertically on knapweed stems or beneath the leaves, resembling a dead leaf. Females lay eggs on stem and leaves; the caterpillars move into the root crown, often killing rosette shoots, feeding and overwintering in the taproot. Caterpillars of the six-plume moth *(Alucita hexadactyla)*, a many-plumed alucitid species, feed on knapweed flowerheads in its native Europe, probably also globally. The native cabbage looper moth *(Trichoplusia ni)*, a noctuid caterpillar that looks greenish and inchworm-like, also feeds on knapweed; the adult moths are 2-toned brown, with darker forewings.

Caterpillars of the painted lady butterfly *(Vanessa cardui)*, spiny and yellowish green, build silken nests on the plant; they feed on other aster family plants as well.

Two seedhead gall fly larvae *(Urophora affinis, U. quadrifasciata)*, now well established on spotted knapweed, attack the flowerheads. The adult flies lay eggs between the bracts of flower buds before they open in late spring. Larvae cause the flowerhead to produce 1 or more spindle-shaped galls in which they feed and remain over winter, emerging as adult flies the next spring. The latter species produces 2 generations per year. These flies have reduced seed production by 50 to 95 percent in experimental knapweed populations. Recent research, however, has revealed that deer mice relish these fly larvae and may devour some knapweed seeds while foraging on the galls. The seeds, surviving passage through the mouse's digestive system, may be carried and germinate elsewhere. "Seeds may travel even farther," wrote biologists Dean E. Pearson and Yvette K. Ortega, "if an owl catches the mouse and then . . . regurgitates the seeds along with undigested bones." Demonstrating how readily introduced biocontrol species themselves become part of complex ecological webs, this unexpected seed-dispersal pathway, ironically, began with the fly larvae introduced to curtail knapweed's spread.

Some 14 Eurasian insect and fungous species have been released as potential knapweed biocontrol agents since 1970. Recent studies on the effects of knapweed biological control seem to indicate that *Agapeta* moths and perhaps other insects feeding on the plant may increase allelopathic secretions from the roots or induce compensatory growth, perhaps both—thus actually increasing rather than diminishing knapweed's competitive success. Perhaps "the biocontrols we are releasing all over the place," stated researcher Ragan M. Callaway in 1999, "are having no effect, or worse, they might be giving knapweed more of a competitive advantage." As Callaway suggested, "We need to know a lot more about how communities actually work before we release many more non-native species into our environment."

I have heard it claimed by some botanist friends that "no bee will touch this plant." Minimal observation reveals that not only honeybees *(Apis mellifera)*, but also bumblebees *(Bombus)* and several butterflies—great spangled fritillaries *(Speyeria cybele)*, Compton tortoiseshells *(Nymphalis vau-album)*, red-spotted purples *(Limenitis arthemis)*, common buckeyes *(Junonia coenia)*, painted ladies *(Vanessa cardui)*, and common checkered skippers *(Pyrgus communis)*, among others—often frequent spotted knapweed. Honeybees, insects as alien as the plant, are probably knapweed's chief pollinators. Knapweed achenes are *myrmecochorous*—that is, adapted to dispersal by ants. Attracted to the hooked base of the seed, where an oil-bearing spot *(elaiosome)* of tissue exists, ants carry away the achenes for food, new knapweed stands probably germinating from their burrows.

Knapweed stems and spiny bracts on the flowerheads make spotted knapweed an undesirable forage, and cattle mostly avoid it. The rosette leaves are nutritious but cling so flatly to the ground that cattle can't graze them. The plant has been reported toxic to horses, causing "chewing disease" (equine encephalomalacia). White-tailed deer graze both rosettes and seedheads, but the upper part of the plant consists mainly of fiber with little nutrients. North Africans are said to feed knapweed to their camels. Birds and rodents apparently utilize spotted knapweed rarely, though knapweed species common in the West—especially yellow and Maltese star-thistles *(C. solstitialis, C. melitensis)*—provide seed food for a variety of birds and mice.

Lore: In addition to clothing the land with color, knapweeds afford notable opportunity not only for honeybees, but also for humans in researching the ecology and distribution of invasive plants. Probably many North American plants were likewise invasive before they became "native" in ages past. With knapweeds, purple loosestrife, garlic mustard, and a few others, we see invasion happening before our eyes, and we can study the process as it occurs.

According to one report, spotted knapweed has spread across North America at a phenomenal rate since its accidental introduction in the late 1890s, probably in imported alfalfa seed. The plant has reached greatest abundance and weed pest status in the states of Idaho, Montana, Oregon, and Washington.

The name *knapweed* is said to derive from the German word *knobbe,* meaning "bump" or "button." As "bachelor's buttons," the flowerheads decorated the clothing of eligible young women, according to folklore. The *Centaurea* connection—with the Greek centaur, the mythological beast with man's head and arms and horse's body and legs—remains uncertain but probably stems from Charon the centaur, who taught Achilles healing herbal knowledge for his warriors before the siege of Troy.

No part of knapweed is palatable to humans, although yellow star-thistle produces a tasty honey. Even herbalists and homeopathic practitioners (who often seem to value the bitter as best) have scant use for it. Use as a wound salve, treatments for sore throat and bleeding gums, and a diuretic are infrequently mentioned in old herbal accounts.

Knotweeds; Smartweeds *(Polygonum* species). Smartweed family. Recognize *Polygonum* by the swollen, papery sheath *(ocrea)* covering each joint of the stems. Botanists define knotweeds as *Polygonum* species that bear small, greenish flowers in the leaf angles on the stem, whereas smartweeds have spikelike clusters of pink or white flowers. Other biologists define knotweeds as upland *Polygonum* species, smartweeds as lowland or wetland plants (see Smartweeds in *The Book of Swamp and Bog*).

Three common species residing on drier ground are prostrate knotweed *(P. aviculare),* small and matlike, sprawling in sidewalk cracks and disturbed ground, with tiny, greenish, pink-tipped flowers in leaf axils; erect knotweed *(P. erectum),* much like the latter except standing mostly erect from a few inches to 3 feet tall; and lady's thumb *(P. persi-*

Black smudge marks on the leaves identify lady's thumb, a common knotweed resident of high foot-traffic areas.

caria), with fringed sheaths on the reddish joints, pink flower spikes, reddish stems, and blackish, triangular smudge marks, like a finger-print, on the top surface of leaves (a few other *Polygonum* species also bear these leaf mark-ings). Lady's thumb is an alien, erect knotweed is native, and prostrate knotweed is ubiquitous worldwide. All 3 species are annuals.

Other names: Common knotweed, knotgrass, doorgrass, bindweed, stoneweed, wiregrass, wire-weed, many others *(P. aviculare)*; redleg, redweed, red-shanks, heart's-ease, black-heart, willow-weed, common persicary, goose grass, heartspot, heartweed, spotted knotweed *(P. persicaria)*.

Close relatives: Some 200 *Polygonum* species range world-wide, mostly in temperate climates. Almost 40, many favoring marshes and wet ground, exist in eastern North America. Family kin includes curly dock, buckwheat, sheep sorrel (all *q.v.*), and rhubarb *(Rheum rhabarbicum)*.

Lifestyle: *Polygonum* plants display so many variants that botanists puzzle whether certain of them are indeed true species, as labeled, or mere forms and vari-eties of other species. Almost every plant manual treats them differently—in itself a signif-icant indicator of plants undergoing rapid evolutionary changes. Botanists likewise remain uncertain as to what extent many of these plants are natives or aliens introduced from Europe and Asia. *Polygonum* species probably hybridize extensively, but the frequency and identification of possible hybrids remain major headaches for plant taxonomists. Even within the identified species, variations appear common and puzzling.

The flowers, emerging in summer and often lasting into fall, are bisexual and insect-pollinated. Lacking petals, they show colored sepals in lady's thumb, greenish or tinged sepals in the two others. *Polygonum* stamens and pistils—the sex organs—are *homogamous* (maturing at the same time), and self-pollination often occurs. The flowers produce little pollen and nectar, yet seem to attract numerous foragers.

Polygonum fruits are 1-seeded *achenes*, typically 200 to 800 per plant in lady's thumb. They fall from the plant, often producing dense colonies the next spring; birds and mam-mals (see Associates) also disperse them.

The small taproot, which may extend from 1 to 8 inches downward, produces many fibrous side branches.

Associates: *Polygonum* species can grow in almost any spot of disturbed soil. The 3 common species mentioned thrive especially in what English ecologists call "trodden" (and what syllable-loving American botanists call *anthropophilic*) habitats—the trampled, compacted soil of footpaths, driveways, trails, barnyards, routes of frequent passage by people and other animals. Thoreau noted the typical frequency of prostrate knotweed's occurrence "where the earth is trodden, bordering on paths," and he was "not aware that it prevails in any other places." What were the original habitats of these plants? Where did they originally grow? One botanist labeled lady's thumb an "archaeophyte," a plant invariably associated with human disturbance of the ground; perhaps it originally occurred most frequently on pond margins. Other plants that share trodden habitats include path rush *(q.v.)*, plantains *(q.v.)*, goose or yard grass *(Eleusine indica)*, as well as other *Polygonum* species.

Erect and prostrate knotweeds will often be found growing in close association, the latter flowering and reaching maturity before the later-emerging erect knotweed. One older text on weeds pointed out that prostrate knotweed is "very frequently the first plant to spring up where a heap of stable manure has stood"—a hostile habitat for most plants, owing to the high temperature that kills most seeds.

Powdery mildew fungi (species uncertain) often coat these plants with a grayish or whitish dustlike covering. Smartweed-dodder *(Cuscuta polygonorum)*, a parasitic climbing vine, also attacks them, winding in yellow coils and tapping into the *Polygonum* stems.

A foremost associate of prostrate knotweed, especially, is the mechanical lawn mower. Mowing reduces grass competition and does not touch the low *Polygonum,* giving it advantage for spread and seed production. *Polygonum* does not typically compete with field crops.

Numerous insects—mainly moth and butterfly caterpillars—feed on *Polygonum* leaves and stems. Among noctuid moths are the purple-lined sallow *(Pyrrhia exprimens);* the smartweed caterpillar, also known as the smeared dagger moth *(Acronicta oblinita);* the black-dotted and pink-barred lithacodias *(Lithacodia synochitis, L. carneola).* The chickweed geometer *(Haematopis grataria),* the cross-lined wave *(Calothysanis amaturaria),* the red twin-spot *(Xanthorhoe ferrugata),* the gem *(Orthonama obstipata),* and the bent-line carpet *(O. centrostrigaria)* are all inchworms. *Nomophila nearctica* is a pyralid. And the bidens borer *(Epiblema otiosana),* a tortricid caterpillar, bores into the stems. The smartweed borer *(Ostrinia obumbratalis),* a pyralid moth caterpillar related to the European corn borer *(O. nubilalis),* also bores into *Polygonum* stems (mainly lady's thumb and Pennsylvania smartweed, *P. pensylvanicum),* causing wilting of stem tips.

Butterfly caterpillars often include some of the lesser fritillaries *(Boloria),* spiny larvae whose main food plants are violets; the gray hairstreak or cotton square borer *(Strymon melinus),* a green, sluglike caterpillar; the bronze copper *(Lycaena hyllus)* and purplish copper *(L. helloides),* green and spiny; and the pipevine swallowtail *(Battus philenor),* a large, purplish brown caterpillar with fleshy tentacles—the adult butterfly lays single orange eggs on knotweed leaves.

Aster leafhoppers favor knotweeds, along with many other plants, and sometimes are vectors of the crop-destructive aster yellows disease (see Asters).

Pollinating insects mainly include the smaller bees, such as andrenids (Andrenidae), and flies (syrphids, muscids, tachinids).

Harvester ants *(Pogonomyrmex)* store *Polygonum* seeds in their burrows, along with those of many other plants. *Polygonum* provides a rich seed supply for ground-feeding birds. These include ring-necked pheasants, sharp-tailed grouse, greater prairie-chickens, American woodcocks, mourning doves, horned larks, and many songbirds: northern cardinals, rose-breasted grosbeaks, common redpolls, eastern towhees, dark-eyed juncos, and many sparrows (savannah, song, grasshopper, Henslow's, vesper, American tree, chipping, white-throated, fox, and swamp). Others include snow buntings, house finches, house sparrows, bobolinks, eastern meadowlarks, red-winged blackbirds, and brown-headed cowbirds. Mammal seedeaters include least chipmunks, ground squirrels, and white-footed mice. White-tailed deer and probably rabbits also consume the plants.

Lore: The beauties of *Polygonum* are subtle and easily overlooked. As with so many relatively harmless weeds, "familiarity alone breeds contempt," as naturalist Neltje Blanchan wrote. Their low hues and tinges present an appearance (as well as a taxonomy) full of ambiguity, good medicine for the either-or mind-set of the obsessively orderly among us.

As actual medicine, *Polygonum* is strong stuff; even native healers used it sparingly. These plants provided astringents for external poultices and for internal bleeding plus menstrual and urinary disorders. Rutin, a glycoside ingredient found also in tobacco and buckwheat leaves, strengthens blood capillaries, acting as a coagulant to prevent or stop bleeding. Juice from stems and leaves can cause skin irritation in allergic individuals.

The leaves have a peppery taste ranging from mild and pleasing to acrid and inedible, depending on species. Young leaves and shoots of lady's thumb make an acceptable salad green. Southwestern natives, according to one source, parched the seeds of prostrate knotweed and ground them for a pinole meal. *P. persicaria* was also used for producing a durable yellow dye for woolens and other cloths.

The name *smartweed* comes from the plants' tongue-burning taste, the name *knotweed* from their swollen stem joints.

Lamb's Quarters *(Chenopodium album)*. Goosefoot family. One of the commonest weeds of roadside and garden from May to October, lamb's quarters stands 1 to 3 feet tall. Small, greenish, dense flower clusters develop on short stems rising from the leaf axils and atop the main stem. A native annual, it has broadly toothed leaves with powdery white undersides. Stems are ridged, sometimes purple striped.

Other names: Pigweed, fat-hen, white goosefoot, wild spinach.

Close relatives: Almost 20 of the 100 or so *Chenopodium* species that exist worldwide reside in eastern North America. Some of these, such as Jerusalem-oak *(C. botrys),* are aliens—but many, including Mexican tea or wormseed *(C. ambrosioides)* and strawberry-blite *(C. capitatum),* are New World natives, as is quinoa *(C. quinoa),* a food staple of Andean Indians. Lamb's quarters bears close resemblances to the unrelated amaranths *(q.v.),* but its nearest generic relatives include oraches *(Atriplex),* glassworts *(Salicoruia),* sea-blites *(Suaeda), Salsola* (katune, Russian thistle, saltwort), beets *(Beta),* and spinach *(Spinacia oleracea),* among others.

Lifestyle: The bisexual flowers, occurring in dense, green clusters resembling tiny broccolis, lack petals. They are wind-pollinated and *protogynous* (female parts maturing before male pollen matures), thus abetting cross-pollination; self-pollination also occurs as the flowers age.

Lamb's quarters reproduces exclusively by seed. Fruits are tiny, bladderlike, 1-seeded structures called *utricles,* and a typical plant may produce almost 75,000 of them. Seed dispersal is probably effected mainly by birds. Seeds germinate early in the season but also throughout, sometimes in *cohorts* (even-aged seedling groups). Seeds may remain viable up to 40 years, though one study found only 23 percent seed survival from 20-year-old buried seeds. The plant produces a short, branching taproot that dies in the fall.

Associates: Lamb's quarters occurs between latitudes 70 degrees N and 50 degrees S except in desert areas. It thrives in both acid and alkaline soils but favors limy soils and cultivated habitats. As with most annuals, this plant favors disturbed open habitats—gravel pits, construction sites, roadsides, weedy fields. Being a reliable indicator of rich soil, it also frequents compost heaps and manure piles, accounting for 2 of its less pleasant names: mixenweed and muckweed. Like many knotweeds of the preceding account, this is an *anthropophilic* plant—that is, it associates with humans, their sites and traffic routes. Nobody knows where the plant would (or originally did) appear without its dominant associate. Certainly its 34 subspecies, varieties, and forms in North America (according to one classification) indicate the ongoing evolution of adaptations in this species. Since lamb's quarters is often a strong crop competitor, humans have become weed-killing competitors of the plant as well. Studies also indicate that lamb's quarters exhibits strong intraspecific competition within its own populations, another characteristic often seen in annuals.

Fungous parasites on lamb's quarters are numerous. Many also attack related plants, such as spinach and beets. They include a spinach rust *(Albugo bliti);* the leaf spots *Alternaria amaranthii, Cercospora beticola,* and *C. dubia;* black root *(Aphenomyces cochlioides),* a damping-off disease of seedlings; downy mildews *(Peronospora);* the foliage blight and crown rot *Rhizoctonia solani;* the stem rot *Sclerotinia sclerotiorum,* causing wilt; and the rust *Uromyces peckianus.*

The stem nematode *Ditylenchus dipsaci,* a roundworm, infests *Chenopodium. Pratylenchus pratensis,* the meadow nematode, feeds in the roots, as do *Meloidogyne* nematode species.

Insect sap suckers and foliage feeders also forage abundantly on lamb's quarters. Among the tiniest are the garden springtail *(Bourletiella hortensis),* found on seedlings, and several species of thrips (Thysanoptera). Leaf or plant bugs include *Melanotrichus flavosparsus* and the tarnished plant bug *(Lygus lineolaris).* The ash gray leaf bug *Piesma cinerea,* flattened and grayish yellow, also frequents the plant. Lamb's quarters also hosts the aster leafhopper (see Aster), which transmits aster yellows, a disease that affects many crop plants.

Aphid sap suckers include the bean aphid *(Aphis fabae),* one of the commonest aphids, plus corn root aphids *(A. maidiradicis),* erigiron root aphids *(A. middletonii),* spirea aphids *(A. spiraecola),* green peach aphids *(Myzus persicae), Macrosiphum* species, and others.

Moth and other caterpillars that feed on lamb's quarters include the eight-spot *(Amyna octo),* a noctuid; the clover cutworm *(Discestra trifolii),* a green noctuid caterpillar that feeds on leaf undersides, gradually working up the plant; and the plume moth caterpillar *Emmelina monodactyla.* An olive green downy caterpillar may be the common sootywing *(Pholisora catullus),* a skipper.

An anthomyiid fly larva, the spinach leaf miner *(Pegomya hyoscyami),* creates reddish, winding tunnels and blotch mines in the leaves.

Harvester ants *(Pogonomyrmex)* store seeds of lamb's quarters deep in their mounds for winter food.

Greenish flower clusters of lamb's quarters, a common garden and cropland invader, produce seeds relished by many bird species.

Seeds of lamb's quarters provide choice nutritious, late-season food for many bird species. Almost all ground birds seem to relish them. In addition to finches, sparrows, and buntings, sharp-tailed grouse, ring-necked pheasants, wild turkeys, northern bobwhites, mourning doves, and horned larks consume the seed. Studies indicate that *Chenopodium* seed passage through birds increases germination of the plant by a considerable percentage. Least chipmunks and ground squirrels also consume the seeds, and white-tailed deer graze the plant, though it is toxic in large amounts to sheep and swine (and possibly other grazers) owing to a high oxalic acid content.

Lore: Lamb's quarters, by statistics and consensus, is one of the world's most abundant and noxious weeds. It competes with some 40 crops, is especially invasive in tomato, potato, sugar beet, soybean, and corn fields in Europe and North America. The plant accumulates high levels of nitrates and pesticides in addition to its oxalic acid content. Yet it also ranks high in vitamins A and C, calcium, potassium, and phosphorus, plus other vitamins and trace minerals.

Harvested from a nonpolluted soil source, the young leaves and shoots make an edible, nutritious cooked green. The flowers are also edible, as are the seeds for cereal or flour (giving "a pumpernickel complexion to biscuits and breads," wrote one culinary artist). Harvested *Chenopodium* seeds helped relieve a Russian famine in 1891, and they were also used in crafting the granular-surfaced leather called shagreen.

Native Americans used this plant for food, as treatment for scurvy and digestive upsets, and in burn poultices. Homeopathic healers also used lamb's quarters for treating vitilago skin pigmentation. The plant contains ascaridole, an anthelminthic oil that can be extracted from the leaves, useful for treatment of intestinal worms.

It was once a popular botanical gospel that all noxious or abundant weeds in North America arrived from far shores to corrupt our native flora. A 1964 archaeological investigation of a Michigan Indian village site, however, established the common presence of *C. album* seeds dating from the years 800 to 1320. Sites in Ohio and Ontario indicate usage of the plant many centuries prior—so if indeed the plant first appeared as an introduced species, it probably came with prehistoric migrations from Asia.

Plant names always indicate perspectives and viewpoints of the namers; thus plants with several or many names, as *C. album,* suggest a roster of varying experiences. *Chenopodium,* from Greek words meaning "goosefoot," refers to the supposed shape of the leaves in some species (another sign, some would say, that plant people make wretched bird-watchers). The name *lamb's quarters* probably refers to the woolly leaf coating; *pigweed* refers to the plant's use as hog fodder (despite its toxicity in large quantities).

Lupine *(Lupinus perennis).* Pea family. A spike of spectacular blue, pealike flowers and radiating basal leaves of 7 to 9 segments identify this 1- to 2-foot-tall native perennial of spring and summer.

Other names: Wild lupine, blue lupine, sundial-lupine, wild pea.

Close relatives: Some 200 lupine species, mostly North American natives, exist. These include white lupine *(L. albus),* silvery lupine *(A. argenteus),* garden lupine *(L. polyphyllus),* yellow bush lupine *(L. arboreus),* and bluebonnet lupine *(L. caudalus),* the state flower of Texas. Family relatives include wild indigos *(Baptisia),* rattleboxes *(Crotalaria),* wisterias *(Wisteria),* locusts *(Robinia),* and peanut *(Arachis hypogaea),* as well as birdsfoot-trefoil, clovers, sweet clovers, alfalfa, vetches, tick-trefoils, and bush-clovers (all *q.v.*).

Lifestyle: "It paints a whole hillside with its blue," waxed Thoreau, likening a lupine meadow to "the Elysian Fields." Yet he also noted that lupine's color seemed to disappear with distance—"a third of a mile distant I do not detect their color on the hillside." The reason for this has to do with the fade-away property of blue, a color produced not by pigments, but by optical angles and reflections of light.

Lupine's bisexual flowers (usually blue but occasionally pink or white) are 2 lipped, the upper one double-toothed, the lower one unlobed. As with most pea family flowers, sex organs and nectar lie concealed inside the bottom keel petal. The pollen-bearing stamens thrust forward in a pistonlike action, likened to a grease gun, when an insect alights and depresses the side wing petals, thus depositing pollen on the nectar-seeking forager. Nectar is actually sparse or lacking in most lupines; the flowers attract insects by color, fragrance, and pollen. Flowers often self-fertilize, though cross-pollination apparently produces more seed.

The pods *(legumes)* contain an average of 4 to 9 seeds. As the pods dry, they suddenly twist and pop open, tossing the seeds several feet. The hard-coated seeds require a period of stratification or freezing in the soil before moisture can penetrate and break their dormancy. Seeds remain viable for at least 3 years.

Lupines also form colonies by reproducing vegetatively from buds on subsurface stems *(rhizomes).* Over several years, clonal groups may become so densely established that individual plants cannot easily be distinguished. A long taproot enables the plant to reach soil moisture in its often dry habitats.

Like most legumes, lupines improve soil fertility by hosting bacteria that convert atmospheric nitrogen into a form usable by plants (see Alfalfa). Sites of this activity are nodules that form on the roots.

"Its leaf was made to be covered with dewdrops," wrote Thoreau. Lupine leaflets, with their wedge shapes and grooved midribs, are said to channel dew and rainwater into the root crown, thus aiding the plant's irrigation in its dry habitats. The leaflets are also said to track the sun throughout the day, accounting for one of its names, sundial plant.

Associates: Lupine thrives in dry, sandy, nitrogen-poor soils that contain, however, sufficient phosphorus. It favors open land and lightly shaded clearings, frequently associates with oaks and pines in savanna habitats. These are fire-maintained complexes, today increasingly rare as fire control, plant succession, and habitat loss continue to alter these unique areas. Heavy shade and competition from such plants as hawkweeds *(q.v.)*, Pennsylvania sedge, spotted knapweed *(q.v.)*, lamb's quarters *(q.v.)*, and common ragweed *(q.v.)* tend to suppress lupine growth. Lupine populations today exist mainly as isolated, discontinuous stands in patchy though sometimes extensive clearings.

Lupines host many fungi; common species include powdery mildew *(Erysiphe polygoni)* and the leaf rusts *Puccinia andropogonis* and *Uromyces* species. *Microsphaera* powdery mildew and the downy mildews *Peronospora* and *Phytophthora* also grow on lupines. The gray mold *Botrytis cinerea,* a fuzzy growth, causes flower and leaf blight. Leaf-spot fungi include *Alternaria, Diplodia, Septoria,* and others. *Sclerotium* and *Fusarium* rots produce cottony masses around the soil line, wilting and killing the plant.

The aforementioned nitrogen-fixing bacteria are *Rhizobium lupini,* which inhabit the root nodules. These form one of lupine's most important associations; without them, the plants tend to languish.

Insect foliage feeders on lupine, though numerous in kind, are seldom abundant in number. Some may be specially adapted to the alkaloid chemistry of lupines and perhaps other legumes.

The lupine aphid *(Macrosiphum albifrons),* large, green, and covered with a powdery wax, sucks sap from lupine tips; its sticky honeydew may attract fungi and ants. It occurs most abundantly on western lupines. The seven-spotted lady beetle *(Coccinella septempunctata),* often seen on lupine, attacks and feeds on these aphids. Another sap sucker, the four-lined plant bug *(Poecilocapsus lineatus),* yellow and black striped, causes funguslike sunken spots on leaves. Blister beetles (Meloidae) can sometimes defoliate lupine.

Moth caterpillars that feed on lupine include the bella or rattlebox moth *(Utetheisa bella);* the placentia tiger moth *(Grammia placentia);* and the phyllira tiger moth *(G. phyllira).* All are arctiids, mostly hairy caterpillars. The toothed somberwing *(Euclidia cuspidea)* is a noctuid. The tiny gelechiid moth caterpillar *Anacampsis lupinella* folds leaves on the plant.

Some butterfly caterpillars on lupine feed on foliage; others forage on buds and flowers. The frosted elfin *(Incisalia irus),* yellowish green and slug-shaped, bores into flowers and pods. Melissa blue caterpillars *(Lycaeides melissa),* pea green and short-haired, feed mainly on the leaves but seldom eat completely through a leaf; they are much attended by ants, a good way of finding them. The alfalfa or orange sulphur caterpillar (see Alfalfa) also feeds on lupines, as does the common or clouded sulphur (see Clovers). The wild indigo dusky wing *(Erynnis baptisiae),* a skipper, feeds on leaves and makes a rolled-leaf nest; the smooth-surfaced caterpil-

Lupine, bluest of blue summer flowers, is the food plant of at least 8 butterfly caterpillars, including the eastern tailed blue (Everes comyntus), *seen here in its adult, egg-laying phase.*

lars show a necklike constriction behind the head. A spiny, yellowish green, striped caterpillar may be the painted lady *(Vanessa cardui),* which creates a compact silken nest on the plant and may defoliate it. I have watched another flower and bud feeder, the eastern tailed blue *(Everes comyntus),* frequently alight on the plant as adult butterflies. Pipevine swallowtail butterflies *(Battus philenor)* also visit the flowers.

Best known of the butterfly species that depend on lupine is a subspecies of the Melissa blue, called the Karner blue *(L. m. samuelis).* The Karner blue has received much attention and study because it feeds exclusively on *Lupinus perennis*—and also because, despite areas of local abundance, the Karner blue has been listed, since 1992, as a federally endangered species owing to the decline of lupine habitat. The butterfly deposits eggs twice yearly on lupine leaves, in late May and late July—greenish, turban-shaped, singly laid. Another indicator of Karner blue presence is the distinctive feeding patterns seen on the leaves. The green-striped, velvety-haired caterpillars eat away all but the upper epidermal layer, leaving translucent "windows" in the leaflet. The second brood of caterpillars may hatch out in late summer or may overwinter as eggs, hatching in May and leaving their window signatures on the new leaves. Masses of adult Karners sometimes roost together on or near lupines during rainstorms and at night.

The Karner blue represents an entire ecological complex, attracting a roster of insect predators and ant associates. Among its larval predators are the spined soldier bug *(Podisus maculiventris),* northern paper wasps *(Polistes fuscatus),* certain ants *(Formica),* and the aforementioned seven-spotted lady beetle. Caterpillar parasites include a tachinid fly *(Aplomya theclarum),* a braconid wasp *(Apanteles),* and the ichneumon wasps *Neotypus nobilitator* and *Paranoia geniculate.* Karner caterpillars secrete a nectarlike substance avidly collected by ants, and the ants probably provide protection from Karner insect predators and parasites. Ant associates include *Camponotus, Crematogaster, Formica, Lasius,* and *Myrmica* species, among others; one study identified 9 ant species attending 2 small colonies of the caterpillars.

Chief pollinators of this lupine are bumblebees *(Bombus),* heavy enough to trigger the pollinating "grease gun." Honeybees *(Apis mellifera)* also pollinate the plants, though the nectar rewards are slim.

Sweetclover root borers *(Walshia miscecolorella),* cosmopterigid moths, bore into lupine stems and roots.

Soybean cyst nematodes *(Heterodera glycines),* tiny roundworm parasites that prey on the roots of many legumes and other plants, also attack lupines.

Most records of bird and mammal feeding apply to western species of the lupine, known to be consumed by gamebirds, rodents, and mule deer. In the East, bird data relating to lupines are scant, though woodchucks and white-tailed deer graze the plant. Deer, where numerous, may indeed devastate entire lupine populations. Livestock that graze on commercially raised lupine stubble may develop a disease called lupinosis from a mycotoxin. Swine appear more susceptible to lupine toxicity than other animals.

Lore: Ironically in view of the lupinosis hazard mentioned, some of this lupine's many relatives (including white, yellow, and blue lupines, *L. albus, L. luteus, L. angustifolius*) have been cultivated in the Old World as livestock feed for thousands of years. The seed, though high in protein, also contains toxic alkaloids, which may be removed by soaking or, in recent years, by genetic tinkering. The Latin poet Virgil noted lupines as commonplace crops, and Roman youngsters used the seeds for play money. Spanish explorers in the Andes found lupine crops "as we have in Spain." Lupine cultivation probably began in Egypt. Today these large-seeded, low-alkaloid species mentioned continue to be raised as forage and grain legumes in Russia, Poland, Germany, and Australia, as well as in the American Midwest.

In North America, botanists believe that *L. perennis* arrived in the East from the West during the hypsithermal interval (ca. 7000 to 600 B.C.), a postglacial arid period. One North American lupine *(L. arcticus)* produced what are reputedly the oldest known viable seeds: An ancient burrow of a collared lemming in frozen silt, discovered along a Yukon creek in 1954, contained a trove of the seeds that were dated at least 10,000 years old; in 1967, some of them were germinated in a laboratory, and one of the plants even flowered.

Seeds of most legumes, many of which produce agricultural crops all over the world, are edible and relished by humans. Lupine, however, is another story. The alkaloid toxicity of the various species—and of individual plants within species—seems to vary greatly enough that the pealike seeds should not be eaten. Native Americans used the plants sparingly for medicine.

Lupinus is Latin for "wolfish." The plant is said to be so called from the peasants' belief that lupine's barren habitats were the result of the plant's "wolfing" of nutrients from the soil ("this is scurrilous," Thoreau remarked). Rather, the opposite is true: Lupine root nodules help increase soil fertility.

Lupines bear an indirect connection to the renowned novelist Vladimir Nabokov, also an accomplished lepidopterist. Nabokov reclassified the blue butterfly group, naming the Karner blue after the locality—a tiny whistle-stop called Karner near Albany, New York— where the first described specimen was found. Later Nabokov became convinced that he had erred, and that the Karner blue deserved full species rather than subspecies status—a question not yet resolved.

Milkweed, Common *(Asclepias syriaca).* Milkweed family. This familiar summer native perennial stands 3 to 5 feet tall, has large, oblong, opposite leaves with downy undersides. Flower clusters—reddish or purplish and highly fragrant—droop from the upper leaf axils; the large, gray-green, twinned seedpods are also distinctive. Packed with seeds on feathery plumes, the pods split open in fall, releasing the aerial sailors to the winds and the countryside. All parts of the plant contain a milky latex.

Other names: Silkweed, wild cotton, cotton weed.

Close relatives: Some 150 milkweed species exist, mainly in the Western Hemisphere. Of these, about 22 reside in eastern North America—among them, butterfly-weed *(q.v.),* swamp-milkweed *(A. incarnata),* purple milkweed *(A. purpurascens),* and white milkweed *(A. variegata).* Related family members include silk-vine *(Periploca gracca),* swallow-worts *(Vincetoxicum),* and angle-pods *(Matelea).* The dogbanes *(Apocynum),* in a separate family that some botanists classify as inclusive of milkweeds, are also closely related.

Lifestyle: In some areas of the Northeast, common milkweed may be the most abundant summer wildflower. Wherever it grows, its features make it one of the most conspicuous plants of any season—even in winter, when its empty, twisted seedpods dangle from the dead stems. In summer, common milkweed, somewhat coarse appearing, has big felted leaves set in right-angled tiers down the stem, probably an adaptation for maximal sunlight exposure. Its sweet-smelling flowers, so attractive to insects, yet sometimes dangerous to them, and—in fall—its warty pods crammed with spilling, silk-plumed seeds also make this plant distinctive.

Individual flowers in the ball-like floral cluster droop from long stalks *(pedicels).* Anatomy of the milkweed flower is quite complex. Each flower shows a 5-parted crown resembling petals (the actual petals are bent back along the pedicel), and each of these petal-like parts is a *hood,* cupping a nectary. Milkweed nectar is copious; few North American flowers produce such an abundant supply, secreted mainly in the evening and through the night. Aside from its function as a food lure, it also provides an optimal germination medium for incoming pollen.

Circling the base of the interior floral structure are 5 V-shaped slits, each containing a *pollinium,* a set of 2 saddlebag-shaped pollen sacs connected together by strands called *translators.* Each flower produces 5 pairs or sets of pollinia. The insect's feet or mouthparts, slipping into the slits, entangle in the translators. A snagged insect jerks free of the trap and in so doing carries away the pollinia dangling from its feet. Insects may collect up to a dozen tangles of pollinia in the course of feeding in milkweed. When the insect lands on another milkweed flower, the pollinia twist, rotating their sacs and slipping into the stigmatic slit, sometimes breaking off and fertilizing the stigmatic chambers. The intricate mechanism doesn't always work to perfection, and insects sometimes become permanently wedged as the fissures trap their feet or the pollinia entangle them, and they die hanging from the flowers; I have seen skippers, among other lepidoterans, thus trapped. A 1989 study revealed that about 5 percent of milkweed flowers visited by honeybees, one of their chief pollinators, entangle them fatally.

Common milkweed requires cross-pollination, rarely self-fertilizes, thus is highly dependent upon insects. Flower clusters *(umbels)* open and mature upward on the plant, and all flowers in an umbel usually open within 2 or 3 days. Flowers may number relatively few (less than 10) in an umbel or more than 100. Each flower has a sexual lifespan of 4 or 5 days. Only 2 to 4 percent of the flowers eventually produce mature pods *(follicles).* This situation results from the fact that milkweed clones are often large; pollen deposited from a flower in the same clone, being genetically identical, will not fertilize the flower—or if it does, the young pods soon abort. Thus milkweed seeding success depends upon pollination from outside clones. One study recorded an average of 4 to 6 mature pods per milkweed stalk, the average pod containing 80 to 200 seeds that resemble overlapping fish scales packed in the pod. Thoreau meticulously detailed milkweed's seed arrangement within the pod. "Who could believe in prophecies of Daniel or of [William] Miller that the world would end this summer," he ruminated, "while one milkweed with faith matured its seeds?"

"In spite of their silk parachutes," wrote milkweed expert Douglass H. Morse, "most of the seeds do not get far." Wind carries only 1 or 2 percent of the seeds farther than a few acres from the plant. (Other plants may also play a role in milkweed distribution; I have observed milkweed plumes snagged and impaled on the seedheads of asters, spotted knapweed, and Queen Anne's lace, as well as on the bristly canes of red raspberry adjacent to the pod-spilling clones.) Small seeds with large plumes travel farthest, but small seeds often fail to germinate or survive. Seeds require about a year of afterripening before they germinate in moderate abundance. They can survive at least 3 years in the soil; stored under proper conditions, they may remain viable for 10 years or longer.

A seedling does not produce a flowering plant until its second or third year or more. Common milkweed propagates not only by seeds, but also by budding on lateral roots or at the subsurface stem base. Stems die back in the fall, but subsurface buds remain alive all winter, and many sprout in the spring, producing clonal colonies (though many buds also remain dormant). Thus new stems arise each year from buds on the previous year's roots. In one 4-year study, a seedling milkweed eventually produced 56 clonal stalks and 94 seedlings in an area of 9 square meters. Root extension occurs mainly in middle to late summer. The thick, fleshy rootstocks run horizontally, some as deep as 3 or 4 feet, and can extend 10 feet in a year. Parent roots survive 2 or more years.

Associates: Typically a plant of roadsides and other disturbed areas, and widely adaptable to both alkaline and acid soils, common milkweed has in recent years extended both its habitat and geographical ranges. Observers have noted its increasing shift into fertile land and cultivated fields. Common milkweed is *allelopathic* (chemically toxic) to grain sorghum, its root secretions inhibiting the latter's growth. It also competes successfully with Kentucky-bluegrass (see Bluegrasses) in old-field swale areas. Ordinarily, however, common milkweed does not successfully compete with crop plants; its spread into grain and grass fields may be related to herbicidal weed treatments, to which milkweed is resistant, in such fields. Until recently, common milkweed's geographical boundaries lay between 35 and 50 degrees N latitude and 60 and 103 degrees W longitude. Rapid southward expansion, however, has shifted; the plants now range far south of 35 N.

Like goldenrods *(q.v.)* and some other native plants, common milkweed centers a populous community ecology, "rich and varied enough to be of interest," as Douglass H. Morse wrote, yet "not so complex that the number of links between species becomes unmanageably large." Also, many of the invertebrate fauna associated with milkweed are largely exclusive to this plant alone—a fact that makes milkweed a favorite, neatly compact project for ecological researchers. Relatively few other noncrop plants have, in fact, received such lavish attention from field biologists.

Several fungous parasites infect common milkweed. The most common include fungi imperfecti such as *Cercospora clavata* and *C. asclepiadis,* causing leaf spots; *Uromyces asclepiadis,* a rust; and others.

Milkweed latex is essentially a defensive adaptation of the plant against herbivores. The leaf, in the words of researcher D. E. Dussourd, is "a ramifying network of latex canals pressurized with a lethal brew of toxic cardenolides in a quick-setting glue." Insect foliage feeders on milkweed have evolved special physiological adaptations enabling them to tolerate these cardiac glycosides (see Lore). The number of such insect species—which are themselves toxic to predators—is fairly large. Many are brightly colored in conspicuous patterns of red, orange, or yellow (called warning, or *aposematic,* coloration). A 1979 study found 11 insect species that fed exclusively on common milkweed.

The oleander aphid *(Aphis nerii),* yellow and black, clusters thickly on milkweed stems, sucking sap. *Ceresa* treehoppers also suck from the pith, as does the small milkweed bug *(Lygaeus kalmii),* also called milkweed stink bug.

Beetle feeders include the red milkweed beetle *(Tetraopes tetrophthalmus),* or eastern milkweed longhorn, bright red-orange with black spots; and the large red milkweed beetle *(T. femoratus),* similar but more western in distribution. Larvae of these beetles feed in stems and roots, the colorful adult beetles on the leaves. The milkweed leaf beetle *(Labidomera clivicollis),* blackish blue and orange-yellow, is also a leaf feeder, as are dogbane beetles *(Chrysochus auratus)* and blue milkweed beetles *(C. cobaltinus).*

Foliage feeders also include several moth and butterfly species. Among moth caterpillars are the unexpected cycnia *(Cycnia inopinatus),* the delicate cycnia or dogbane tiger moth *(C. tenera),* and the milkweed tussock moth *(Euchaetes egle);* all are hairy tiger moth caterpillars, rolling into a ball when disturbed. Milkweed's best-known and most conspicuous feeder is the spectacular caterpillar of the monarch butterfly *(Danaus plexippus),* striped with yellow, black, and white, and 2 inches long when full grown. This large migrant butterfly lays single eggs on milkweed leaf undersides; the caterpillar pupates in a shiny green, gold-speckled chrysalis suspended beneath a leaf. Monarch caterpillars not only ingest the toxic cardenolides in milkweed leaves, but carry these substances lifelong even as adult insects, making them poisonous, unpalatable prey to birds and mice. A devoured monarch makes a venturesome bird throw up (still, it would seem that many monarchs must be sacrificed in the process of providing a bird's first-time learning experience). So effective is this defense that mimicry of the adult monarch's pattern and coloration is seen in the unrelated, nontoxic viceroy butterfly *(Limenitis archippus),* which benefits by visual identification with the monarch. Yet even monarch caterpillars are not impervious to milkweed's own defenses. Recent studies find that milkweed latex

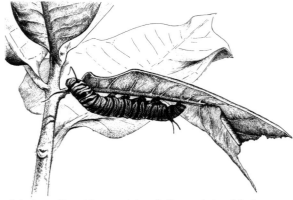

Striped caterpillars of the monarch butterfly (Danaus plexippus) *feed on chemically defensive common milkweed, though not without considerable mortality.*

often glues up the mandibles of young caterpillars, preventing them from eating. Milkweed plants with higher than usual cardenolide levels may also poison some of the young larvae. Monarch caterpillar survival rates on milkweed, researchers have discovered, are in fact relatively low (only 3 to 11 percent), and about 30 percent larval loss results from miring in the sticky latex. The caterpillars' first bite into a leaf is "the most dangerous thing they ever do in their life," wrote monarch researcher Stephen Malcolm; "it's like being hit by a tidal wave of glue." The caterpillars have, however, evolved some protective strategies that keep them from getting swamped on the leaf. A small circle "trenched" by a caterpillar in the leaf surface blocks the flow of latex to the enclosed surface area, which the caterpillar then devours. Larger caterpillars may cut through the midvein of a leaf, damming latex flow to the entire leaf beyond the trench. A further hazard to monarch caterpillars is that the tachinid flies *Lespesia archippivora* and *Parachytas,* among others, sometimes parasitize them. During migration, monarchs lose some of their cardenolide chemistry; in Mexico, some become vulnerable to predators that have not learned the toxic lesson.

The queen *(Danaus gilippus),* a reddish brown relative of the monarch, is also a milkweed feeder but is more southern in distribution.

Nectar feeders on milkweed are far more abundant than insect foliage feeders, but those large and strong enough to pollinate the plant and escape with pollinia include relatively few species: cabbage white or imported cabbageworm butterflies *(Pieris rapae),* fritillary butterflies *(Speyeria),* bumblebees *(Bombus terricola, B. vagans,* others), honeybees *(Apis mellifera),* and—at night—noctuid, arctiid, and geometrid moths. Noctuids include the variegated cutworm moth *(Peridroma saucia),* one of the commonest moths worldwide; the black cutworm or ipsilon dart moth *(Agrotis ipsilon);* the many-lined wainscot *(Leucania multilinea);* the ilia or beloved underwing, also called the wife *(Catocala ilia);* and the armyworm moth *(Pseudaletia unipunctata).* Yellow-collared scape moths *(Cisseps fulvicollis),* day-flying arctiids, appear bluish with yellow or orange collar marks and partly translucent wings; they feed on nectar, occasionally carrying the pollinia. Japanese beetles *(Popillea japonica),* scourges of garden plants, sometimes cluster thickly on milkweed flowers.

Butterflies, including the monarch, are relatively infrequent pollinators, though almost every nectar-sipping butterfly—swallowtails, admirals, fritillaries, and numerous others—shows up sooner or later at the lavish founts of milkweed. Soldier beetles *(Chauliognathus pennsylvanicus),* gold-yellow and black, commonly feed on milkweed pollen and nectar. Several wasps also carry pollinia to and from flowers. These include the paper wasp *Polistes variatus,* the eastern yellowjacket *(Vespula maculifrons),* the sphecid wasp *Prionyx atratus,* the great golden digger wasp *(Sphex ichneumoneus),* and the tiphiid wasp *Myzinum 5-cinctum.*

Foremost among insects that "steal" nectar from the flower without pollinating the plant are ants, including the turfgrass ant *(Lasius neoniger)* and the odorous house ant *(Tapinoma sessile)*. Others, such as the silky ant *(Formica fusca)*, consume aphid secretions. Many ants fall victim to the pollinia traps.

Butterflies, as this fritillary, feed frequently on common milkweed's ample nectar, sometimes becoming ensnared in the stringlike pollinia.

Several seed feeders also attack common milkweed, feeding as larvae within the developing pods. These include the small milkweed bug *(Lygaeus kalmii)*, with red and black markings; the large milkweed bug *(Oncopeltus fasciatus)*, red or orange and black; and the seed weevil *Rhyssomatus lineaticollis*. Adult seed weevils bore small holes into pods and stems, laying eggs there; latex-filled punctures often indicate the invaded pods.

Insects that feed on milkweed foliage, flowers, and seeds attract other insects that prey on them; these predators can sometimes be almost as numerous as the nectar feeders. Predators of the aforementioned oleander aphids include several lady beetle species *(Coccinella)*. Ambush bugs *(Phymata)*, dusky or three-spotted stink bugs *(Euschistus tristigmus)*, and spined assassin bugs *(Sinea diadema)* attack insect visitors, killing and devouring many. Mantids—especially the Chinese mantid *(Tenodera aridifolia)* and the European or praying mantid *(Mantis religiosa)*—prey especially on the aforementioned milkweed bugs, also on other insects, and are themselves avoided by other predators.

One common predator, not an insect, is the crab spider *Misumena vatia*, which lurks in the flowers and hunts from ambush. "Many crab spiders on milkweed," wrote researcher Morse, "grow rapidly by exploiting the heavy insect traffic. The most successful adult females increase their mass tenfold in as little as two weeks, attaining . . . the size of a queen bumblebee." Yet even the most successful spiders consume no more than 1 or 2 percent of the visiting insects. Pollinia-tangled prey account for only about 3 percent of their total prey; evidently they prefer doing the capturing themselves. Another study found that crab spider behaviors differ during day and night; contrary to their lurking use of camouflage by day, they often move to the extreme tops of flowers at night, ready to capture the first nocturnal moth that hovers close. Looking closely, you may see the silken drag lines of crab spiders on the flowers even when the spiders themselves remain hidden. Look too for crab spider egg sacs on the turned-under, silk-tied end of a milkweed leaf; usually the spider sits nearby guarding its eggs. A 1993 study found that crab spiders favor nesting locales near goldenrods *(q.v.)*, since many goldenrods come into flower just as milkweed flowers decline, thus providing new, busy hunting sites (on the goldenrods) for the hatched spiderlings. The crab spider egg sac is itself vulnerable to parasitic flies and ichneumon wasps. Also, crab-hunting wasps such as spider wasps (Pompilidae) and thread-waisted mud-daubers (Sphecidae) capture adult spiders, paralyzing them with a sting and carrying them to their own nests as food for wasp larvae.

Foliage and nectar feeders plus their predators may be observed in any clonal stand of common milkweed. Completing the milkweed faunal assemblage are the scavengers—the cleanup specialists—on the remains of predation and on the dead, flower-trapped insects. These consist mainly of ants and of spiderlike harvestmen or daddy longlegs *(Phalangium opilio)*. The harvestmen also feed on nectar feeders and capture small insects and crab spiders; thus they "figure at several levels in the food web," as Morse wrote.

Common milkweed is scantily used as a food plant by birds or mammals. I have noted that white-tailed deer occasionally graze it, especially during seasons of drought, when almost any succulent plant seems desirable. Usually the deer only sample it, leaving a mess of latex on the wounded leaves—as well as covering, no doubt, their snouts. Several bird species, however, use the plant materials—mainly the stout, stringy stem fibers—for nesting materials. These include Baltimore orioles and yellow warblers, retrieving fibers from last year's dead milkweed stems. Milkweed down begins flying at about the time that common goldfinches begin to nest, and these birds raid spilling milkweed pods as well as thistledown for their cushiony nests.

Lore: Common milkweed, according to one economic botanist, "can easily qualify as the greatest underachiever among plants." Its actual usage in human enterprise has apparently never matched its potential for same.

The plant's most conspicuous feature—the silky tufts that transport the seeds in late summer and fall—became the source of a brief industry during World War II. Researchers discovered that this down—or *floss,* as it is termed—had buoyant properties like those of kapok, a silky fiber from pods of the silk-cotton tree *(Ceiba pentandra),* cultivated in Java, that was used in life-preserver jackets ("Mae Wests"). When Japanese occupation of the East Indies cut off the kapok supply, the War Hemp Industries of the Commodity Credit Corporation created a Milkweed Floss Division to manage the production and use of milkweed. The chief processing plant opened in Emmet County, Michigan, called the most densely milkweed-infested county in the United States. From 1943 to war's end in 1945, thousands of tons of pods were harvested for floss, much of it by schoolchildren ("Pick a weed, save a life!" preached posters, offering the collectors 20 cents per bag). Eventually more than a million Mae Wests bulged with floss from 11 million kilograms of milkweed pods. Twenty-six ounces of the waxy, hollow threads packed inside a Mae West jacket could keep a 150-pound man afloat for 48 hours. After the war, when kapok—and later, synthetic fibers—became cheaper to use, the milkweed floss industry wafted away. Today, however, research and field studies on milkweed floss production continue in Kansas with a view toward renewing its use for insulative and absorptive materials. Although imported goosedown from China is the currently preferred insulative batting material, its high cost has brought back milkweed floss—a product of equal thermal values—as an added component in sleeping bags and arctic clothing.

Other economic uses for milkweed have never gotten far beyond proposal and study stages. These include the white latex for manufacturing natural rubber, liquid fuel, and hydrocarbons; the stem fiber (bast) for textile and paper making; and the seeds as a source of oil and meal. Clearly this plant offers raw materials of considerable potential value and utility. Also, of course, there is the lavishly produced nectar, transformed by bees into a light, mild-flavored honey. Beekeepers have often noted pileups of milkweed pollinia at hive entrances, where the foragers rid themselves of their tangled loads.

In view of the cardenolide chemistry of this plant, one would not expect milkweed to be humanly edible—yet, in sprout and bud form, and with several changes of boiling water, it is relished by many. Milkweed-root tea treated a large variety of native and frontier ailments, both external and internal. A root concoction was said to be an effective (if not shockingly toxic) contraceptive for women when mixed with jack-in-the-pulpit. People drank the tea for laxative, emetic, and diuretic purposes, also for asthma and rheumatism, and used the latex and floss as dressings for warts and wounds. Milkweed has never been cultivated as a drug plant, however.

Natives and pioneers alike used milkweed floss for pillow and mattress stuffing.

A recent milkweed/corn/monarch butterfly interaction in agricultural cropland of the Midwest has evoked alarm from conservationists. Pollen from corn that has been genetically modified with *Bacillus thuringiensis* (Bt) bacteria as an internal organic pesticide may settle on the milkweed food plants of the monarchs where milkweed grows adjacent to corn cropland. Preliminary research indicates that Bt hybrid pollen is moderately toxic to monarchs, affecting their growth and survival rates.

The great Swedish biological namer Linnaeus described common milkweed for science from an alien European specimen that he thought was native to the Orient, instead of North America, thus misnaming it *syriaca,* "of Syria."

Mullein, Common *(Verbascum thapsus).* Figwort family. This common alien biennial, one of the most conspicuous wildflower-weeds of summer, displays a clublike, sparsely flowered wand of bright yellow, 5-petaled blossoms. Its large, flannel-surfaced leaves, ridged and felted stem, and height of 2 to 6 feet are also distinctive.

Other names: Great mullein, Aaron's-rod, Jacob's-staff, blanket-leaf, candlewick, felt-wort, flannel-leaf, mullein-dock, shepherd's club, torchwort, lungwort, and some 40 others.

Close relatives: All 300 *Verbascum* species are Eurasian in origin. Other eastern North American mulleins include moth-mullein *(V. blattaria),* white mullein *(V. lychnitis),* and clasping mullein *(V. phlomoides).* Among familiar family relatives are beard-tongues, speed-wells, painted cup (all *q.v.*), turtleheads *(Chelone),* figworts *(Scrophularia),* snapdragons *(Antirrhinum),* foxgloves *(Digitalis),* eyebrights *(Euphrasia),* and louseworts *(Pedicularis).*

Lifestyle: Mullein's long, green flower spike looks blackish, rather greasy, as if wiped by a car underside. One never sees this spike blazing in full or even abundant flower; instead, the yellow blossoms emerge singly—2, 3, or 5 at once, low or high on a spike—often in a loose spiral pattern. This unevenness adds to the plant's coarse, somewhat ragged appearance. Beginning in late June and continuing into fall (depending upon spike height), flowering proceeds in successive spiral patterns from bottom to top of the spike. Each spiral, as the season advances, begins slightly higher on the spike, overlapping with former spirals, sometimes densely crowding together toward season's end. Individual flowers do not last long, typically open before dawn and close in the afternoon. Although bisexual in form, the flowers are sequentially unisexual, undergoing a practical "sex change" during their brief tenure; they are *protogynous,* the female part *(stigma)* maturing and bending away from the later-maturing male parts *(stamens, anthers),* thus hindering self-pollination. The pollination mechanism consists of 2 long and 3 short stamens, showing a tight coevolution with insect pollinators. "Three stamens furnish a visitor with food, two others clap pollen on him," as naturalist Neltje Blanchan wrote, while the sticky stigma catches a smear of pollen from the insect's traveling underside. If cross-pollination has not occurred by the end of the day, however, the flower closes and the stigma pushes against the anthers, effecting self-pollination *(autogamy).* This one-way-or-another, sexual backup system (which also occurs in many other plants) virtually guarantees an abundant crop of mullein seed capsules—some 200 or more, each containing 200 to 500 seeds, per plant. A single plant may produce 150,000 seeds or more.

The seeds have no dispersal mechanisms; most fall within 3 feet of the parent plant, creating an abundant seed bank in the soil. Seeds remain viable up to 100 years or more; even archaeological soil samples dating from 1300 have produced viable mullein seeds. Clearly this is a seed that remains long prepared to germinate whenever the right conditions offer (see Associates). Common mullein reproduces only by seed; no vegetative sprouting takes place, and the plant does not occur in self-sustaining populations. Its typical life cycle is biennial, with seeds germinating in early spring and forming a rosette of feltlike leaves that remains into autumn and overwinters as such. The next June, this rosette pad produces a single flower stalk (which may, however, branch into several "candelabra" stalks), and flowering continues up the stalk until the plant dies in its second fall season. Occasional plants in northern populations extend to a 3-year life cycle, becoming triennials.

Mullein's branching taproot, usually shallow, may in some instances descend a foot or so into the soil, enabling the plant to withstand drought conditions. The distinctive velvety, whitish, frost-green leaves, clasping the stem at their bases and decreasing in size as they ascend the stem, are "so arranged that the smaller leaves above drop the rain upon the larger ones below, which direct the water to the roots," as one botanist wrote—another drought adaptation. Viewed through a microscope, the soft flannel pile on leaves and stem "consists of a fretwork of little, white, sharp spikes," wrote naturalist Anna Botsford Comstock. The branched meshwork of leaf hairs, also "a feature of the leaf-atmosphere interface," as another researcher wrote, reduces water transpiration and heat loss from the plant, as well as protects it from herbivore munching.

Associates: Common mullein, residing throughout temperate Eurasia and North America, often appears as one of the pioneering plants after land disturbance, clear-cutting of forest, or abandonment of crop fields. Despite its presence almost everywhere and its prolific seed production, common mullein is a here today–gone tomorrow sort of plant, often not regenerating beyond a sole biennial life cycle on a site. After a rapid flush of growth, often in dense stands, it quickly dies out as other plants succeed it. "The typical pattern of the species," as one research team wrote, "is one of ephemeral adult populations and long-lived seed pods." Common mullein does not long withstand competition even by grasses. As a weak, nonaggressive contender with other plants, often leaving only dead stalks of the previous year to indicate its former presence, it typically colonizes abundantly during the second or third year after soil disruption or exposure, often becoming a dominant plant, then rapidly diminishes during subsequent years. It maintains stable populations only in worn-out soil or topsoil-sparse areas, such as old gravel pits, that cannot support other plant communities. Typically it depends upon repeated soil disturbance for survival, a requirement easily met throughout increasingly urbanized and developed areas of North America. It is shade-intolerant, thrives best in dry, sandy soils, though solitary mulleins frequently rise along roadsides and railroads, also decorating landfills and vacant lots with their yellow-dabbed flower spikes.

At least a half-dozen species of parasitic fungi inhabit common mullein leaves and stems, usually appearing as spots or discolored areas beneath the woolly surfaces. Two of the most common, which also occur in other plants, are powdery mildew *(Erysiphe cichoracearum*) and a root rot *(Phymatotrichum omnivorum)*. *Peronospora sordida*, a downy mildew, also parasitizes the leaves. Common mullein is a vector of fire blight *(Bacillus amylovorus)*, one of the most serious bacterial diseases of apple and pear trees.

The only insects that feed on the plant to any extent are sap suckers and seedeaters. Most such feeders are, like mullein, introduced species. Mullein thrips *(Haplothrips verbasci)*, tiny and black with a sharp-pointed tail, are extremely common on the plant in all seasons; I have often observed groups of them hibernating deep in the plushy leaf rosette during fall and winter. Lugen's stink bug *(Mormidea lugens)*, a small bronze or yellowish bug, and a small black-and-red stink bug, *Cosmopepla bimaculata*, feed on plant juices. A rarer stink bug found on mullein is *Pseudocnemodus canadensis*. The mullein leaf bug *(Campylomma verbasci)* migrates from apple foliage to mullein and other plants in midsummer, feeding on these alternate hosts until early fall, when it returns to lay overwintering eggs in the orchard; these plant bugs also feed on mites, aphids, insect larvae, and apple fruits.

The only avid consumers of mullein foliage that I have observed are short-horned grasshoppers (Acrididae), which leave large holes in the leaves.

Caterpillars of the mullein moth *(Cucullia verbasci)*, a noctuid native to Europe, have been imported as a possible biological control agent for mullein but are not widespread (in England they are called "mullein sharks" because of their voracious appetite for mullein). Ravenous seedeaters, also imported as a biological control some 70 years ago, are mullein seedpod weevils *(Gymnaetron tetrum)*; these beetle larvae mature in the seed capsules, may devour up to 50 percent of the seeds.

A wide variety of insects visit mullein's brilliant yellow flowers, but the foremost pollinators are bees, including bumblebees *(Bombus)* and honeybees *(Apis mellifera)*. Syrphid flies (Syrphidae), sometimes called hover flies, also pollinate the flowers. The soft pile of a mullein rosette often attracts hibernating insects (besides the aforementioned thrips) in fall and winter. Tarnished plant bugs *(Lygus lineolaris)*, yellowish brown pests of crops and ornamentals, are common winter residents that lie dormant beneath the leaves, as do black bugs *(Galgupha atra)*, scentless plant bugs *(Harmostes reflexulus)*, and ladybird beetles *(Hippdamia convergens, Coleomegilla maculata)*.

American goldfinches consume mullein seeds, and hummingbirds are said to use the leaf flannel for nest lining. Livestock and other grazing mammals avoid common mullein, as the woolly hairs of the plant can severely irritate mouth membranes.

Lore: Colonists brought common mullein to the New World sometime in the 17th century as a medicinal herb and garden ornamental. It rapidly spread wherever land was cleared and ground broken, grew commonly in the East by 1820 and the Midwest by 1840. Not regarded as a major weed pest because of its ephemeral, nonagressive habits, common mullein arouses most hostility from farmers because it hosts certain insect vectors (such

as the mullein leaf bug) of crop diseases. For the
gardener, however, a mulch of common mullein
leaves is said to repel slugs effectively, probably irritating their skin membranes.

Common mullein has a long history of
medicinal usage since the time of Hippocrates. This plant was probably the "phlomos"
that was widely prescribed as a treatment for various
ailments. "Many of the ailments that plague mankind from ear
aches to dysentery to toothaches," wrote naturalist Sarah Hopkins, "were thought to be alleviated by mullein medications" in
teas, decoctions, and infusions, plus poultices for warts and
slivers. Primarily used as a respiratory remedy for coughs, con-
gestion, and bronchial and lung disorders, mullein leaves were
smoked in pipes for such purposes. When dried, after the fuzz
disappears, the leaves, which contain soothing mucilage and
anti-inflammatory properties, make a bland, mildly sedative tea.
Mullein also contains coumarin and rotenone, powerful compounds with toxic effects. The latter is a well-known *piscicide*

*American goldfinches, proba-
bly common mullein's only regular bird feeder, often devour
seeds on the flowerhead.*

(fish killer); pioneers in Virginia (as well as ancient Greeks)
would throw the plant into water, then harvest the intoxicated fish brought to surface.
("Stingin' fish was one easy way of gittin' food at first, so feltwort seeds were brung 'long,"
as one Virginia resident spoke of this practice of his forefathers.)

Such an all-purpose remedy for ailments had its shamanistic virtues as well. Mullein
found use in incantations by and against witches, served as a botanical safeguard from
demons and dire magic. Ulysses waved its stalk in the horrific face of Circe, escaping her
wiles thereby. Who among us could recognize in this coarse roadside weed the "noble herb"
of Ulysses—could dream of the spiritual significance this plant carried for the ancients?

Mullein also had a host of nonmedicinal uses. The ancients reputedly used the dried
stalks dipped in tallow for funeral torches and the downy, rolled leaves for incendiary lamp
wicks. Although native American tribes had no historic association with the plant, many
adopted the pioneer habit of inserting the big, soft leaves inside footwear and clothing for
effective insulation. Colonists also used it as a homemade cosmetic called "Quaker rouge";
the rubefacient, flannel-like leaves raise a red blush (that is, contact dermatitis) on the
rubbed face (something to remember about mullein, advises one outdoor manual, "when
you're in the woods looking for toilet paper substitutes"). Roman and American women alike
used the bright yellow dye produced by boiling the flowers for coloring hair and clothing.

Sources differ on derivation of the name "mullein." Probably it stems from the Latin *mollis,* meaning "soft." Other sources attribute the old English word *muleyn,* meaning "woolen," from the Latin *malandrium,* that is, malanders or leprosy, for which mullein medication was reputedly prescribed.

Mustard, Garlic *(Alliaria petiolata).* Mustard family. Recognize this invasive Eurasian biennial by its triangular, sharply toothed alternate leaves, its white flower cluster surmounting the stem, and the strong garlic odor of crushed leaves.

Other names: Hedge-garlic, hedge-mustard, poor-man's-mustard, garlic-root, leek cress, European wild mustard.

Close relatives: Only 2 *Alliaria* species exist, both native Eurasians. Closely related mustards include yellow rocket *(q.v.),* dame's rocket *(Hesperis matronalis),* wallflowers *(Erysimum),* and hedge-mustards *(Sisymbrium);* about 40 other mustard genera (of several hundred worldwide) also reside in eastern North America.

Lifestyle: A mustard that smells and tastes like garlic! Some mustards adopt astonishing characters, and this species is one of them. Like all mustards, however, its flower is 4-petaled—and like most, its elongate seedpods *(siliques)* stand erect beneath the terminal flower cluster.

Garlic mustard's 2-year life cycle begins as a leafy rosette hugging the ground; it remains green beneath winter snow and provides the greenest greeting of late winter when the snow melts. The flowering stem rises 1 to 3 feet from the rosette in the spring of the plant's second year, with peak of flowering from mid-April to mid-May. Although insect-pollinated, the bisexual flowers are also completely self-compatible, do not require cross-pollination in order to produce seed. They open in *acropetal* (ascending) progression up the flower spike *(raceme);* most remain open 2 or 3 days, but sexual action typically occurs on the first day of flowering.

Each plant produces, on average, 4 to 16 siliques, each containing 10 to 20 black seeds. When the siliques split open in the fall, thousands of seeds are forcibly ejected; you can hear the seeds popping out if you walk through a patch at the right time. Seeds genetically identical to the sole parent plant can colonize large areas, producing essentially clonal stands. New seeds usually remain dormant 8 to 22 months in northern areas, requiring a period of cold stratification (freezing in the soil) to break dormancy—thus a seed is often at least a year old by the time it germinates. Seeds typically fall near the plant, are also dispersed by rodents, birds, and (especially) people, on clothing, footwear, and machinery.

This taprooted plant (an S-curve at the top of the root is distinctive) reproduces entirely by seed, dying at the end of its second season. Axillary buds on the root crown may, however, produce one or more additional stems, especially if the primary stem is cut or damaged.

The density of garlic mustard plants in any given site tends to fluctuate annually, reflecting their biennial habit. "These annual fluctuations are deceptive," according to one research report, as the plant "occurs with increasing frequency through time, on average doubling in four years and tripling in eight years." Often overlooked at low density, "it can be present for a number of years before appearing to 'explode' in favorable years." Garlic mustard seems to spread by an advance-retreat pattern (also called *jump dispersal*); small vanguard populations, jumping ahead of the plant's dense, ragged front, gradually coalesce to form a new front.

Associates: Garlic mustard favors moist, partially shaded soils of all kinds except highly acidic ones. It thrives on disturbed land. Open forest, forest edges, riverbanks, and shaded roadsides are its foremost North American habitats; it also adapts to drier, more open locales such as fields and railroad embankments. Seedlings, however, are vulnerable to drought; many die in this first-year stage of growth. In Europe, garlic mustard's main habitats are hedgerows and open woodlands, ranging south from about 68 degrees N latitude to the Mediterranean. North American populations range from southern Canada to Tennessee and Georgia, thriving most abundantly in New England and the Midwest.

Garlic mustard's erect siliques, or seedpods, each eject up to 20 seeds that cannot immediately germinate but may remain viable in the soil seed bank for years.

Garlic mustard's spread across the continent has been rapid; most weed manuals of only a few decades ago did not even list it. Studies have revealed that once it invades a site, it usually becomes a permanent part of the plant community—but unless soil disturbance becomes repeated or continuous, its population gradually declines to a level of low stability. "This strategy of increased presence and low but continuous abundance," wrote one researcher, "allows garlic mustard to rapidly expand when disturbance occurs."

Garlic mustard typically associates with a numerous variety of other plants, mainly woodland and edge species. Little disagreement exists that garlic mustard invasions can and do displace native vegetation, but individual situations show variation. Because garlic mustard frequently invades sites with lower species diversity than uninvaded sites, observers often assume that the mustard outcompetes the native ground flora. This does happen some-

First appearance of garlic mustard seedlings in an area often occurs at the base of a tree trunk, a microhabitat that may offer this aggressive plant an optimal nursery.

times, but one study showed that orange touch-me-not or jewelweed *(Impatiens capensis)* and boxelder *(Acer negundo)* shoots usually outcompeted the mustard. Another study, however, indicated that garlic mustard is *allelopathic* toward (that is, it chemically inhibits) soil mycorrhizae, the fungi that play so vital a function in nourishment uptake for most plants. Recent research suggests that allelopathy is the foremost means by which garlic mustard comes to dominate forest understory ecosystems. The plant also competes with native spring ephemeral plants by its early-season canopy, shading them out (also threatening some insect species that forage upon them). Easily observed is the frequent fact that garlic mustard first invades an open woodland at the bases of scattered tree trunks. Whether birds disperse the seeds in their droppings at such locales, or whether shelter and moisture conditions at such sites produce the most favorable microhabitats for germination, remains uncertain—perhaps both.

In its native Europe, garlic mustard hosts at least 7 fungi and several mosaic viruses. North American populations in the East host a destructive root rot *(Fusarium solani)*, a leaf blight *(Alternaria alliariae)*, a leaf spot *(Ramularia armoraciae)*, and a downy mildew *(Peronospora parasitica)*. Mosaic leaf patterns indicate infection by a strain of turnip mosaic virus (TuMV-Al), common also in Europe. This strain is not, however, transmissible to turnip or rutabaga crops.

Some 70 insect species feed on garlic mustard in Europe; at least 5 are exclusive to the plant. It is a preferred host for pierid butterflies (whites and sulphurs) there, but American pierids have thus far not adapted to the plant. Although mustard whites *(Pieris napi)* and West Virginia whites *(P. virginiensis)* are known to lay eggs on garlic mustard—a plant they apparently confuse chemically with native toothworts *(Dentaria)*, their mustard food plants—their caterpillars usually die before transforming to adults. Experiments indicate that some mustard whites may now be adapting to garlic mustard, but lepidopterists generally regard the plant as a population *sink* (that is, a habitat where death rate exceeds birth rate) for native butterflies. The imported cabbageworm or cabbage butterfly *(P. rapae)*, introduced from Europe about 1860, also feeds on the plant to an unknown extent.

Several species of aphids, leafhoppers, and flea beetles forage on the plant, though none to an extent that would aid biological control. Likewise, slugs and snails occasionally graze garlic mustard. Currently in Europe, the 5 insect species exclusive to garlic mustard—4 *Ceutorhynchus* weevils and a flea beetle, *Phyllotreta ochripes*—are being investigated for potential use as North American biocontrols. Yet biocontrols are double-edged swords; in the words of Ohio University biologist Brian McCarthy, "Do we import a non-native to control a non-native?"

Garlic mustard flowers "are adapted for pollination by short-tongued bees and flies," according to one research team. Pollinating and nectar-feeding insects include midges (Chironomidae) and syrphids or hover flies (*Eristalis* and other species). Halictid and andrenid bees *(Halictus, Andrena),* mainly ground nesters, also visit the flowers, as do some butterflies—notably the spring azure *(Celastrina ladon).*

Scant data exist regarding usage of garlic mustard seeds as food for birds and small mammals. Finches probably consume and disperse them to some extent. Sources differ on garlic mustard's use as forage by large mammals (deer, horses, cattle); some state that these animals rigorously avoid it, while others state that in some habitats, they eat "significant quantities"—cows consume enough to taint their milk at times. One study suggested that white-tailed deer may enhance spread of the plant by distributing seed on their hooves, by trampling and exposing bare soil, and by consuming competitor plant species. No current proof exists, however, that such an association is significant.

Garlic mustard's main associates, it must be said, are humans, for this plant depends mainly upon people for its dispersal (called *anthropogenic* distribution). Seeds ride on boots, clothing, tires, mowing machinery, and other items involved in human motion. The plant's liking for paths and trails testifies to this association, but seeds also travel widely by stream and flood, as ample shoreline populations show.

Lore: In its native Europe, garlic mustard lurks modestly in the hedgerows, is not a terribly aggressive plant. It first appeared in North America on Long Island in 1868, in Canada in 1879. Thoreau in New England never saw it. By the year 2000, garlic mustard had spread to 34 states (mainly the northern and central tiers) and 4 provinces. It now occurs globally—in North Africa, India, and New Zealand, among other places.

A substance called allicin gives the distinctive flavor to garlics and garlic mustard alike. Garlic mustard's odor and taste gradually dissipate during the plant's later growth stages in summer and fall. In Europe, the plant has long been used as a potherb, a salad green called "sauce alone," and a garlic substitute in cooking. Its vitamin A and C contents rank higher than in spinach and oranges, respectively, on a weight basis. As a homeopathic medicine, the leaves found use as a sweat inducer, for treating edema and dropsy, and as poultices for sores and boils. Colonists probably brought the first plants into areas other than North America for use as garden potherbs and herbal remedies, and the plants soon overran the garden walls, widely escaping.

Purple loosestrife in wetlands, spotted knapweed in dry fields, and garlic mustard in open woodlands, edges, and roadsides—these 3 foremost alien plant invaders, despite their homeopathic uses, probably raise the highest blood pressure of any plants among botanists and conservationists. Thoreau in his day led huckleberrying parties, but today many local natural history groups organize aggressive "pulling parties," eager to eradicate each alien stem and root of these plant invaders, putting violent impulses to environmental service. While such actions may retard or temporarily interrupt the alien plant progression—and, of course, reward well-meaning naturalists with the feeling that they are somehow "helping" nature—some ecologists view such activities as, essentially, the replacement of one disruption by another. Tearing up vegetation often disrupts established symbiotic and fungal mycorrhizal systems (although garlic mustard itself apparently has no such symbiosis, most of its plant neighbors do). Also, the uprooting of one alien species may result in the increase of another.

No question exists that garlic mustard can and does infest and dominate forest understory areas, invading native vegetation and reducing biodiversity. Yet this plant, plus the 2 other alien species mentioned, always thrive most abundantly in areas of human land disturbance—the places where people walk, dig, reside, or alter the landscape either by accident or design. Plants adapted to disturbance conditions usually arrive by human invitation, and altruistic pulling parties tend to increase rather than withdraw such welcomes. Sometimes such interventions, whether by chemical or physical means, encourage rather than hinder further disruptions "by keeping the population cycle from going to completion" as biologist Bernd Heinrich wrote, "since diseases, parasites and predators [are] not allowed to build up." Probably the best, most effective control method for garlic mustard is to prevent its initial establishment. Eradication efforts, where undertaken, should focus on the early rosettes and on those aforementioned vanguard islands of population. Garlic mustard's total eradication from areas where it is well established becomes extremely difficult, given the plant's prolific seed bank. Probably the most effective means of eradication from such areas, combined with the least amount of soil and habitat disturbance, is repeated mowing over a period of years.

As with all invasive and irruptive organisms, adjustment and adaptation usually occur, though not necessarily swiftly. In time, these organisms become integrated into native ecosystems, become "naturalized" citizens. Biologists have watched it happen repeatedly. Much of our so-called native flora apparently originated in a near continuous belt called the Arcto-Tertiary Geoflora across Eurasia and North America, dispersed via Miocene land bridges between the continents. Such arrivals may have caused great disruption to the native ecology of the time. It is some of these ancient naturalized immigrants, no doubt, that plants like garlic mustard threaten. Today the threat to biodiversity lies in the scale of human-assisted invasions.

The research opportunities offered by introduced and aggressive alien plants can reveal many close-up insights into the biology of population dispersal and distribution. Nobody, of course, should deliberately attempt to alter native habitats. But the welcome mats have long been spread, and once spread, they cannot easily be withdrawn. Instead, one can use the situation to some advantage; one can watch such invasions, note their speed and strategies, study them to increase our knowledge of particular biological events beyond the ordinary. Such studies may be a worthier, more rewarding task, in the final analysis, than ripping up roots from the substrate. Garlic mustard, however, is a plant—a force—that amply provides both such opportunities. The issue remains controversial.

Nettle, Stinging *(Urtica dioica).* Nettle family. Standing 2 to 4 feet tall, this common perennial can be seen along roadsides and in damp, fertile soil. Skin contact with this plant will immediately and painfully identify it. Otherwise recognize stinging nettle by its square-angled, densely hairy stems; its opposite, coarse-toothed, heart-shaped leaves; and its summer-to-fall, strung-out clusters of greenish flowers projecting from the leaf angles. *U. d. gracilis* is the native American subspecies, marked by stinging hairs only on leaf undersides and unisexual flowers on the same plant. *U. d. dioica,* the European native subspecies also widely established in North America, tends to sprawl and bears stinging hairs on both leaf surfaces plus unisexual flowers on different plants.

Other names: Tall nettle, big string nettle, common nettle, naughty man's plaything.

Close relatives: Some 25 *Urtica* species exist worldwide. *U. urens,* another alien nettle, also resides in North America. Other family members include the wood nettle *(Laportea canadensis);* false nettle or bog-hemp *(Boehemria cylindrica);* clearweed or richweed *(Pilea pumila);* and pellitory *(Parietaria pensylvanica).* Stinging nettle bears resemblances in form to certain unrelated plants, especially mints such as hemp-nettle *(Galeopsis tetrahit)* and white vervain *(Verbena urticifolia).*

Lifestyle: Most of us learn to identify stinging nettle the hard way—that is, by direct contact while walking through a colony of these coarse plants. Hands or bare arms or legs brushing against a leaf or stem produce immediate stinging pain and red welts, searing burns that seldom last long but can be intense for a few moments. The "stingers" consist of the glandular hairs *(trichomes)* that cover stems, leaf surfaces, and flowers. Bulblike tips of the hairs break off when touched, exposing sharp-pointed needles that readily inject the chemical irritants (substances that remain largely unanalyzed) from their soft basal sacs.

Stinging nettle's long, curling flower clusters are unisexual, both male and female flowers developing on the same plant (monoecious).

Observing without handling is sufficient to reveal an interesting plant. The stringy, radiating flower clusters *(panicles)* produce abundant pollen, which is mainly wind dispersed. Unisexual flowers are usually borne on the same plant, though variations occur. Male flowers usually develop earlier than female flowers. One way of detecting the difference between them is to note the relative lengths of the flower clusters; male flower clusters extend as long as or longer than their stalks, while female clusters are shorter than their stalks. Ripening (male) anthers turn explosive, catapulting pollen grains up to 2 centimeters into the air. The plant is also self-compatible and often self-pollinates, producing seeds in small *achenes.*

A typical colony or stand of nettles usually consists of a single genetic plant, cloning stems that rise from a dense rhizome system, which may extend for yards underground.

Associates: Stinging nettle favors open, sunny, nitrogen-rich sites, where it often forms part of a plant community that includes other rank weeds such as boneset, angelica, and jewelweeds, among others. Its greatest abundance occurs in lowland habitats, often in the vicinity of human gardens and dwellings. The native subspecies resides throughout much of North America, extending from latitude 53 degrees N (in the East) to Virginia, Missouri, and Louisiana.

Stinging nettle hosts various fungi. These include the blight *Didymella eupyrina;* leaf spots *(Leptosphaeria acuta, L. doliolum, Ramularia urticae, Septoria urticae);* a *Puccinia* rust; and a stem rot *(Sclerotinia sclerotiarum).*

Dodder *(Cuscuta),* a climbing plant parasite, occasionally victimizes stinging nettle.

A fairly large number of insects and invertebrates forage on the plant. One study concluded that "factors of body size and feeding behavior allow them to feed with little interference from nettle stings," and that the plant's chemistry has evolved primarily as a defense against mammal foraging. Some 28 insect species feed exclusively on the European nettle subspecies in England, with another score or so of nonexclusive users. Although such tight associations have not yet been identified for the American subspecies, they may well exist.

Stinging nettle is primary host for the hop cyst nematode *(Heterodera humuli)*, a threadworm that also infests forage crops. The land snail *Anguispira alternata* is also a nettle herbivore.

Loose webbing among the leaves may indicate the presence of two-spotted spider mites *(Tetranychus urticae)*, which feed on the leaf sap.

Calocoris norvegicus, the potato mirid, is a common plant bug feeder, green with long antennae; another plant bug resident is *Plagiognathus obscurus*. A burrower bug *(Sehiris cinctus)*, shiny black with white margins, can also be found on nettle.

Some of our most spectacular butterflies feed as caterpillars on stinging nettle. These include 3 anglewings: the question mark *(Polygonia interrogationis)*; the hop merchant or eastern comma *(P. comma)*; and the satyr comma *(P. satyrus)*. Anglewing caterpillars are brown and spiny, often cock their heads when not feeding. Milbert's tortoiseshell caterpillars *(Nymphalis milberti)*, also spiny and black with greenish yellow sides, feeds colonially on nettle. The red admiral *(Vanessa atalanta)* feeds quite exclusively on nettle family plants; spiny but variable in color, the caterpillar folds over a leaf, lining it with silk, where it rests and pupates.

A common noctuid moth caterpillar that feeds on nettle is the unspotted looper *(Allagrapha aerea)*.

Larvae of several leaf miner flies—*Melagromyza* and *Agromyza* species—make narrow, winding mines in the leaves.

Larvae of the potato stalk borer *(Trichobaris trinotata)*, a flower weevil, feed in the stem, as do larvae of lizard beetles *(Acropteroxys gracilis)*.

Vertebrate herbivores generally avoid nettles, but American goldfinches and probably other songbirds feed on the seeds to some extent. Indigo buntings are known to nest in nettle stands.

Lore: Despite its infamous ability to repel mammalian herbivores, stinging nettle is relished as a potherb by wild-food gourmets. Cooking "disarms" the plant from its stinging hairs; young shoots and tender top leaves are the parts most valued for greens. Nettle was used for centuries in Europe as a rennet for curdling milk. The leaves, rich in vitamins A and C as well as iron, also make a nourishing tea. Harmless also when dried, the plant has been cultivated in many places as a rich fodder for livestock.

Old World nettle usage mainly consisted of linen woven from the fibers, a craft extending back to the Bronze Age. As recently as World War I, Germany raised nettle for textile fiber ("nettle cloth"), from which tents and durable army uniforms were manufactured. The plants also provided fodder for German cavalry horses.

American natives found many medicinal uses for the native plant, especially in treating urinary disorders. Iroquois and Huron tribes also used the tough plant fibers as hemp for making thread, twines, and netting. As a tonic for a multitude of ailments, the leaf tea has long been a favorite of homeopathic healers. Researchers have found that it can aid blood coagulation and hemoglobin formation, and depresses the central nervous system. It may provide benefits for treating kidney and gall bladder diseases as well. Recent research indicates its effectiveness in treatment of certain prostate disorders; it also has possible aphrodisiac properties. On the downside, stinging nettle pollen commonly causes and aggravates hay fever allergies.

Treatment for nettle stings often grows close at hand—the crushed, juicy stems of jewelweed *(Impatiens)* rubbed on the affected area provide almost immediate relief. Leaves of dock (see Dock, Curly) are said to provide similar relief.

Olive, Autumn *(Elaeagnus umbellata).* Oleaster family. Recognize this shrubby alien tree by its alternate, wavy-edged leaves; its silvery, scaly leaf undersides; its reddish, berrylike fruits with whitish bloom; and occasional spines on the branches.

Other names: Cardinal olive, autumn elaeagnus, Japanese silverberry.

Close relatives: Most of the 45 *Elaeagnus* species are Eurasian natives, including the North American imports Russian olive or oleaster *(E. angustifolia)* and *E. multiflora.* Silverberry *(E. commutata)* is a native oleaster. The only close relatives are 2 native *Shepherdia* species: rabbit-berry or soapberry *(S. canadensis)* and buffalo-berry *(S. argentea).* All of these plants are unrelated to the olive *(Olea europaea),* an Old World evergreen of the olive family.

Lifestyle: Autumn olive's fragrant, trumpet-shaped, light yellow flowers consist of fused parts, including petals. They appear along the spurred twigs in May and June after the leaves have emerged. This tree is as *polygamous* as a plant can be; flowers may be bisexual; unisexual on the same tree; unisexual on separate trees; or show unisexual and bisexual floral combinations on the same tree. They produce abundant nectar and are insect-pollinated. Most trees begin flowering at age three to five.

The fruits, juicy *drupes,* appear silvery at first, then turn a speckled red in late summer and fall, often remaining on the tree through winter. Each drupe contains a single seed that requires a period of cold stratification or freezing to germinate, and the germination rate is usually high. A single tree may produce from 20,000 to 50,000 seeds per year. Autumn olive may also reproduce by sprouting from its root crown.

Autumn olive may attain a height of 20 feet, often somewhat spreading and sprawling. It has a long taproot, making the plant highly drought-tolerant. Like legumes, the roots of all oleaster family plants grow nodules that convert atmospheric nitrogen to ammonia, a form of nitrogen usable by plants. Instead of containing nitrogen-fixing bacteria as in legumes, however, oleaster nodules shelter actinomycetes (a group of organisms often positioned by microbiologists between fungi and bacteria), which perform the same function.

Leaves turn dull yellow in autumn or drop while still green. Some strains of the plant are highly vulnerable to cold, often showing winter dieback.

Associates: Autumn olive thrives in and invades many open or semiopen habitats, owing to a unique combination of characters: fast growth, a versatile sexual system, prolific fruiting, efficient seed dispersal and propagation, self-nourishment by nitrogen-fixing actinomycetes, and tolerance of acid soils, drought, pollutants, and heavy browsing. Autumn olive's native region is east Asia—China, Korea, and Japan—where the tree has noninvasively adapted to many habitats. Streambanks and mountain thickets are its native sites.

In North America, autumn olive resides mainly in the Northeast, though it has extended its range south to the Carolinas and west to Oklahoma. As of the year 2000, it inhabited 41 states and several Canadian provinces. Autumn olive is shade-intolerant and favors dry sites, though it can and does grow in semishade and semiwet conditions in a variety of soil types. It typically invades grasslands, pastures, open woods, and forest edges, spreading both from hedge or landscape plantings and by bird dispersal. It competes with and displaces native plant species, not only by shading them out, but also by changing (via its nitrogen-fixing capacity) the soil nitrogen balance of ecosystems, affecting plant survival and succession sometimes to the point of reducing biodiversity.

Autumn olive's most important associates are, of course, the aforementioned symbiotic actinomycetes *(Frankia)*, which enable the plant to thrive in often infertile ground. A 1993 study revealed that many birds' nests—even some of those that do not use soil as a building material—host *Frankia* actinomycetes, possibly indicating an adjunct role for birds in dispersing autumn olive.

In addition to its displacement of native vegetation, I have noted autumn olive's frequent appearance as a sheltering "nurse hedge" for other alien shrubs, particularly common buckthorn (*Rhamnus cathartica;* see *The Book of Forest and Thicket*). Plantings and bird dispersal also account for buckthorn presence; at any rate, the 2 shrubs often grow closely together in old autumn olive plantings.

A *Verticillium* wilt (probably *V. albo-atrum*) has decimated autumn olive trees in some areas. This vascular fungus, which affects many tree species, causes rapid wilting of foliage and branches in summer; sometimes the trees recover, often not. *Phomopsis* cankers, possibly originating in frost-cracked bark, also damage many autumn olives in the northern states. The cankers, reddish brown to black and girdling the branches, tend to form low on the tree at first, then progress upward.

In some areas, autumn olive becomes a winter alternate host for artichoke aphids *(Capitophorus elaeagni),* yellow and green colored; often they migrate from thistles. Olive scale *(Parlatoria oleae)*, purplish brown beneath its gray shell, is an introduced scale insect that becomes an irruptive pest on autumn olive and many other shrubs.

Japanese beetles *(Popillia japonica)*, scourge of many plants, relish autumn olive leaves.

Autumn olive's fragrance and abundant nectar attract numerous insect feeders and pollinators—butterflies, bees, wasps, and flies, among others.

About 30 bird species—most of them *frugivores* (fruit eaters)—consume the drupes of autumn olive, often transporting the seed elsewhere via their droppings. These include several thrushes—American robin, eastern bluebird, Swainson's and hermit thrushes—plus tree swallows, cedar waxwings, gray catbirds, northern mockingbirds, European starlings, and northern cardinals. Northern bobwhites, ruffed grouse, and ring-necked pheasants also feed on the fruits. A Kansas study found autumn olive second only to rose plants in frequency of usage by birds. Another study suggested, however, that autumn olive may crowd out native shrubs that mature their fruits simultaneously with the main fall passage of migratory birds—autumn olive fruits typically ripen earlier, in August and September—thus depriving transient birds of the diverse, nourishing menu of fruits and associated insects they rely upon. Some wildlife biologists believed even during autumn olive's glory days as a wildlife panacea that its value to birds and mammals was highly overrated. And some studies have shown that, given a choice between native plants such as hawthorns *(q.v.)* and autumn olive plantings, birds exhibit feeding and nesting preferences for the former.

Mammals that consume autumn olive fruits include raccoons, skunks, opossums, and black bears. White-tailed deer browse the foliage, as do sheep and goats. Cottontail rabbits and voles gnaw the bark in winter.

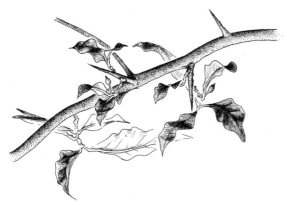

Not all autumn olive trees bear thorns, but many do, making this densely foliaged tree, once highly recommended by conservationists, even more thicket forming.

Lore: Introduced into the eastern and central United States in 1830 as a "quick fix" for denuded landscapes, autumn olive (specifically, a strain of the plant from the Himalayas) surged in popularity as a wildlife planting during the 1950s, becoming a favorite of game biologists and soil conservationists. Along with multiflora rose *(q.v.)*, it became useful for stabilizing road banks, strip-mine spoil, and other disturbed land; for screening highways, dumps, and sewage ponds; for hedging fields and creating windbreaks and highly visible boundary lines; and for providing wildlife food and cover. It worked for all of these purposes but soon began overlapping its bounds, invading and replacing native vegetation in many areas. Today the shrub has achieved pest status in some eastern states, is seen as a potential problem in others. Cutting and burning only encourages its resprouting, and birds spread its prolific seed far and wide. Autumn olive is here to stay. Most state conservation departments have finally seen the light and stopped preaching its benefits, no longer encourage planting.

Some states found autumn olive's reflective silvery coloration useful for planting as highway crash barriers. Beekeepers also value the tree for its abundant nectar production.

Autumn olive's nitrogen-fixing capacity has been put to use for improving soil fertility in stands of black walnut timber. Interspersed with the nut trees as a so-called "nurse crop," it also reduces low branching in the latter by shading, thus improving the tree form for lumber.

The drupes are humanly edible, range in taste from astringent to semisweet. In Japan, they are used for pickles and, when fermented, for brewing alcoholic beverages.

Painted Cup *(Castilleja coccinea)*. Figwort family. Green, 3-lobed bracts topping a short terminal spike dipped in scarlet paint is the visual impression of this 1- to 2-foot-tall native biennial. The undivided basal leaves form a rosette; upper leaves show deeply cleft linear segments. The unbranched stems are hairy.

Other names: Indian paintbrush, Indian pink, fire pink, prairie-fire, bloody-nose, wickawee, election posy.

Close relatives: About 150 *Castilleja* species exist, mainly in western North America. Two eastern residents besides *C. coccinea* are downy paintbrush *(C. sessiliflora)* and northeastern paintbrush *(C. septentrionalis)*. Hemiparasitic relatives (see Lifestyle) include eyebrights *(Euphrasia)*, louseworts *(Pedicularis)*, and cow-wheat *(Melampyrum lineare)*. Other figworts include common mullein, beard-tongues, butter-and-eggs, and speedwells (all *q.v.*).

Lifestyle: "It is all the more interesting," wrote Thoreau of this plant, "for being a painted leaf and not a petal, and its spidery leaves, pinnatifid [featherlike] with linear divisions, increase its strangeness."

Not only are the lobed terminal bracts red; scarlet too are the tips of the tubular *calyx* (the outer part of the flower, collectively the sepals). The inner flower (the 2-lipped *corolla*) is greenish yellow, hidden inside the bracts. These garish bracts (occasional plants display yellow instead of red bracts) attract numerous insect pollinators to the flower; yet the lack of a flower lip landing place for insects may indicate reliance on another pollinator (see Associates). Each shoot produces 5 to 20 flowers.

The resulting 2-chambered capsules hold up to 300 seeds apiece, shaken out of the capsules by wind. Some seeds may germinate immediately, producing a leafy rosette that survives winter under the snow and raises a flowering shoot in spring. Most seeds, however, germinate in spring, producing only rosettes the first year and a flowering stem the following spring.

Associates: Painted cups favor open, sandy areas and limestone soils, often shores and damp meadows.

Some 500 figwort species, including this one, are classified as *hemiparasites* (that is, partial parasites, not exclusively dependent on another plant host—they commit "petty larceny," in the words of one botanist). Although painted cups are green and perform photosynthesis like most plants, they also take water and mineral nutrients from the roots of adjacent plants. They tap into these root structures from their own roots by means of connecting structures *(haustoria)*, penetrating to the vascular channels of the host roots. No painted cup plant grows to maturity without tapping into a root host. This hemiparasite is blindly nonselective, its haustoria even attaching to pebbles, sand grains, and organic debris at times, as well as to almost any plant roots in the vicinity, herb or tree. Grass roots are common hosts, as are those of wild strawberry *(q.v.)*, ox-eye daisy *(q.v.)*, and tall lettuce *(Lactuca canadensis)*, all of which promote rapid growth of painted cups. Host suitability, however, apparently depends more upon the density of neighborhood root distribution than on host identity.

Painted cup's flower spike, its bracts smeared a bright red as if dipped in a paint can, attracts not only numerous bee species, but also ruby-throated hummingbirds.

At least 2 butterfly species consume painted cup foliage as caterpillars, though not exclusively: the common buckeye *(Junonia coenia)*, an olive-gray, spiny and spotted caterpillar; and the northern checkerspot *(Chlosyne palla)*, also spiny and sometimes feeding in groups.

Painted cup attracts many insects, especially bees: bumblebees *(Bombus)*, halictid bees *(Halictidae)*, leaf-cutter bees *(Megachile)*, and honeybees *(Apis mellifera)*. Bumblebees often perforate the corolla tubes for nectar instead of entering the flower from the top, and other bees also feed from these holes. Clearwing sphinx moths *(Hemaris)* also forage these plants for nectar.

Painted cup seems especially adapted for ruby-throated hummingbird pollination, not only in its tubular floral anatomy, but also in its early-May flowering (through July), which coincides with hummingbird arrival. The hummingbirds seek it for nectar; wild columbines (see *The Book of Forest and Thicket*), flowering at the same time, also attract these bird pollinators.

Painted cup provides scant food resources for bird and mammal wildlife.

Lore: Chippewa tribes used a weak tea steeped from *Castilleja* flowers for "diseases of women" and for rheumatic aches. It was said to be good for both "paralysis and a cold," according to one report. The Menomini used it as a love charm in food, "the scheme being to try to secrete some of the herb upon the person who is the object of the amour," wrote ethnobotanist Huron H. Smith. On dubious authority, the plants are also said to be potentially toxic.

Wyoming chose Indian paintbrush *(C. linariaefolia)* as its state flower in 1917, the only state to choose a parasitic plant for this honor.

Plantains *(Plantago* species). Plantain family. The 2 most familiar plantains, both perennial weeds of lawns and roadsides, are common plantain *(P. major)*, with broad basal leaves that show prominent trenched veins and grow in a rosette, and 1 or several flower spikes up to 10 inches long, tightly lined with inconspicuous greenish flowers; and English plantain *(P. lanceolata)*, with narrow, lance-shaped leaves and several flower stalks standing up to 2 feet tall, topped by an inch-long, thimblelike flowerhead often ringed at the base by projecting whitish anthers.

Other names: Broad-leaved or round-leaf plantain, dooryard plantain, rat's tail, white man's foot *(P. major);* narrow-leaved plantain, ribgrass, ribwort, buckhorn, lamb's tongue, jackstraw *(P. lanceolata).*

Close relatives: Almost 200 *Plantago* species exist worldwide, more than a dozen of them in eastern North America; some are native, some alien. They include leafy-stemmed plantain or psyllium *(P. psyllium),* American or Rugel's plantain *(P. rugeli),* king-root or heart-leaved plantain *(P. cordata),* and buckhorn or bracted plantain *(P. aristata).* Other family relatives include *Littorella* species. The tropical tree plantain *(Musa paradisiaca)* is an unrelated species of the banana family.

Lifestyle: Common and English plantains differ not only in appearance, but in biology as well.

Common plantain flowers, wind-pollinated and self-compatible, open progressively up the spike, each tiny, inconspicuous flower bisexual but *protogynous* (female parts maturing before male parts). Thus only the first-opened flowers—that is, those lowest on the spike—have the possibility of being cross-pollinated by another plantain; the higher flowers, as they sequentially open and develop, become almost exclusively self-pollinated.

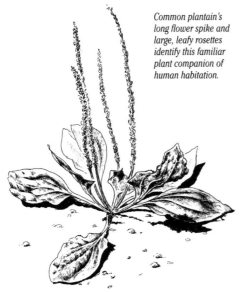

Common plantain's long flower spike and large, leafy rosettes identify this familiar plant companion of human habitation.

Common plantain seed capsules, containing 5 to 20 seeds each, turn brown before splitting open. Seed germination occurs throughout summer, but buried seeds may remain viable for 20 years or longer. Vegetative reproduction—that is, sprouting of single cloned shoots from a root crown—occurs infrequently, mainly in disturbed-soil sites. The *ramet* (cloned shoot) remains attached to the parent plant for 2 or 3 years, then separates and develops its own root system. Many if not most common plantains tend to aggregate in large or small clonal stands, either seed-borne or vegetative in origin. Common plantain's short, thick rootstock is anchored by a dense, fibrous network.

English plantain's reproductive scheme is somewhat more complex. Flowers may be pistillate (all female), staminate (all male), or bisexual—but all flowers are the same on an individual plant or clone. Unlike flowers of common plantain, English plantain flowers are both wind- and insect-pollinated and are largely self-incompatible, requiring cross-pollination. The capsules usually hold only 1 or 2 seeds. Seed production is relatively small, compared with most weeds; mean seed number per plant ranges from 130 upward, depending upon habitat conditions. The seed coat swells when wet, becoming sticky, a characteristic that may aid seed dispersal on dewy mornings or during rainy weather, causing them to cling to fur, clothing, even lawn mowers. Buried seeds may remain viable for several years, though most germinate or die within the first year. Vegetative reproduction also occurs, the ramets sprouting from root extensions, which usually decay, leaving separated clonal plants. Many survive only 1 or 2 years, but in stable habitats a plant may live for 12 years or longer. English plantain roots, fibrous with a short, erect underground stem *(caudex)*, often develop a vestigial taproot as well.

Both species die back to their ground-hugging leaf rosettes in winter, producing new flower stalks from the roots each year.

Associates: Although both plantains are Eurasian natives, they have long been thoroughly naturalized global residents; the designation "alien" applies to them in the same sense that all white and black Americans are alien residents. Common plantain, some botanists believe, may even be a native plant in parts of North America. It ranges from south of the tree line throughout the continent, favoring open, sunny sites, adaptive to almost all soils except the highly acidic. It often grows on and along dirt roads in woodland areas. "Paths are often demarcated by this plantain," wrote one weed botanist. English plantain, likewise wide ranging, favors drier sites, is more shade-tolerant, and frequents hard-packed soils. It is one of England's most abundant weeds. Both species are *anthropophilic* (associate with humans); they frequent roadsides, parking areas, driveways, and vacant lots, occurring almost everywhere in disturbed ground. Where one species grows, the other can often be found nearby. Other plants in the *Plantago* community often include clovers, timothy, bluegrasses, Queen Anne's lace, common dandelion (all *q.v.*), black medick *(Medicago lupulina)*, orchard-grass *(Dactylis glomerata)*, and others.

Various fungi attack plantain leaves and seeds—*Cladosporium* and *Phoma* species parasitize the seeds of English plantain—but none exclusively so.

Insects that forage on plantain include rosy apple aphids *(Dysaphis plantaginea)*, a destructive pest that moves from apple *(q.v.)* trees to English plantain, one of its alternate hosts, in early summer. Winged, brownish green adult aphids develop there, then fly back to apple trees in late summer or fall, laying eggs in bark crevices.

The flea beetle *Dibolia borealis*—an oval, jumping insect—feeds preferentially on common plantain; its larvae create long, winding mines in the leaves. The sap beetle *Glischrochilus quadrisignatus,* black with ball-ended antennae, feeds on English plantain. Other insects on the latter plantain include the alfalfa plant bug *(Adelphocoris lineolatus)* and a related *Plagiognathus* species.

Common plantain sometimes hosts aster yellows disease, transmitted by the aster leafhopper (see Asters). It also alternately hosts the pear psylla *(Cacopsylla pyricola)*, an aphidlike homopteran and pest in pear orchards.

Common buckeye butterfly caterpillars *(Junonia coenia)* feed on plantain leaves, as do several tiger moth caterpillars: the joyful, bog, and orange holomelinas *(Holomelina laeta, H. lamae, H. aurantiaca);* the isabella tiger moth or banded woollybear caterpillar *(Pyrrharctica isabella);* the pink-legged tiger moth *(Spilo-*

The 2 plantains bear differing flower stalks: Common plantain (left) has a long, tapering stalk, whereas English plantain (right) bears a thimble-shaped spike ringed by whitish anthers.

soma latipennis); the ruby tiger moth *(Phragmatobia fuliginosa);* the harnessed moth *(Apantesis phalerata);* and several others.

Plantain seed feeders include the seedpod weevil *Gymnaetron pascuorum.* Earthworms often ingest plantain seeds on the ground, passing them intact in their castings, which provide favorable microsites for their germination.

Several nematodes or roundworms *(Meloidogyne)* attack plantain roots. Snails and slugs rarely feed on plantains.

English plantain flowers receive insect visitors and are occasionally pollinated by them. The flowers produce no nectar but abundant pollen for collectors, which include syrphid flies *(Mesograpta, Toxomerus),* halictid bees (Halictidae), bumblebees *(Bombus),* and honeybees *(Apis mellifera);* most plantain pollen is, however, released by wind.

Leaf foragers include ruffed grouse, cottontail rabbits, and white-tailed deer. Woodchucks relish common plantain. Many birds—though few to any large extent—consume the seed capsules. Northern cardinals and grasshopper sparrows, plus ground squirrels and various mouse species, are among plantain seed feeders. In fodder quality, these plants do not rank as high as grasses, but sheep and cattle find English plantain palatable.

Lore: Plantains have versatile curative as well as culinary properties; nobody need go hungry or untreated for sores where plantains grow. These plants contain an abundance of beta carotene, calcium, potassium, and ascorbic acid. Cure-all claims for common plantain's beneficial medical uses include a leaf tea for coughs, diarrhea, dysentery, lung and stomach disorders, and the root tea as a mouthwash for toothache. Literary references to plantain's healing properties abound. John the Baptist, in the lore of saints, used it as a healing herb; Anglo-Saxon gardeners called it the "mother of herbs." Plantain is "in the command of Venus and cures the head by antipathy to Mars," according to 17th-century English herbalist-astrologist Nicholas Culpeper. Plantains also bear frequent mention in the works of Chaucer and Shakespeare. Their most frequent and demonstrably effective use as a modern herb remedy, however, is as a leaf poultice for insect bites and stings plus other skin irritations. The leaf's antimicrobial properties reduce inflammation, and its astringent chemistry relieves itching, swelling, and soreness.

Plantain seeds are also therapeutic. The gelatinous mucilage surrounding seeds can be readily separated, has been used as a substitute for linseed oil. Its widest usage is in laxative products for providing bulk and soluble fiber called psyllium, mainly derived from the plantain species *P. ovata* and leafy-stemmed plantain *(P. psyllium),* both Mediterranean natives. Most psyllium is imported from India to the United States, the product's foremost national consumer. The plants are also used as a homeopathic cancer remedy in Latin America, have recently been marketed as a stop-smoking aid, supposedly causing tobacco aversion. Thus their cure-all reputation continues.

Plantain leaves make a tasty cooked or salad green when collected very young. The Aztecs apparently raised the plant for food. Most North American natives were historically unfamiliar with plantain, but many tribes that encountered it during its spread along with pioneer settlement quickly recognized its medicinal properties and widely adopted it, especially in use as poultices for skin ailments, contusions, and snakebite.

Plantains have prominent associations with human feet. The word *plantago* derives from a Latin word meaning "sole" or "footlike," perhaps because of common plantain's foot-sole-shaped leaf or the plant's footpath habitat. One naturalist wrote of "the wanderlust of plantains." Supposedly common plantain followed the Roman legions wherever they set foot. Native Americans, observing the plant's spread, carried the analogy further by naming it "Englishman's foot" and "white man's footprint." Check it out: Almost anywhere your feet can carry you on dry land, they will meet a plantain. By colonizing and binding disturbed soil quickly, plantains also restrict erosion.

Plantains also carry less desirable traits, even ignoring their patchwork growth that some lawn owners deem unsightly. Probably their worst effects lie in the airborne pollen they shed in large amounts, contributing to many hay fever allergies.

Pokeweed *(Phytolacca americana).* Pokeweed family. Pokeweed's height (4 to 10 feet), its long white-flowered spikes often paired opposite the large leaves, its purple-black berry spikes supplanting the flowers, and its reddish stems and fruit stalks identify this common and distinctive native perennial.

Other names: Poke, pokeberry, American nightshade, American spinach, bear's-grape, Indian greens, inkberry, skoke, pigeonberry, many others.

Close relatives: Some 35 *Phytolacca* species exist, most in warm and tropical regions worldwide. *P. americana* is the only eastern North American species, though an Asian species, *P. acinosa,* has become established in the Midwest. Plants in the same family of 18 genera include blood-berry *(Rivina humilis).*

Lifestyle: The long, erect, cylindrical *racemes* (flower stalks) atop the plant carry a dense cluster of small white or greenish bisexual flowers (usually 50 or more) that lack petals but have 5 rounded sepals that look like petals. Racemes are 4 to 8 inches long, tapering toward the end, and flower through summer. The insect-pollinated flowers exhibit *protandry* (that is, the male parts mature and decline before the female parts, effecting a sort of sequential unisexualism). If pollinators fail to show up, however, the flowers can self-fertilize after a time. Almost all pokeweed flowers seem to set fruit; such high frequency of fruiting often indicates primarily self-fertilized species. Each flower produces a

The fruiting racemes of poke-weed ripen from the stalk base toward the tip. A maturing cluster of blue-black berries (left) contrasts with a still-green cluster; both can often be seen together on the same plant.

10-seeded, inky purple berry, the clusters resembling grapes as they heavily weigh the now-drooping racemes. Seeds, distributed mainly by birds (purple-stained bird droppings are not unusual sights in summer), can remain viable in the soil for 40 years or longer.

Pokeweed reproduces exclusively by seed. "I personally believe that it is a frustrated tree," wrote weedlorist Pamela Jones. The plant's thick, succulent, trunklike stalks springing from an old root may achieve a diameter of 4 inches, yet they all die back to the root in autumn. The taproot is itself imposing, fleshy and white, sometimes 6 inches across at the crown. Pokeweed roots produce *allelopathic* (growth-inhibiting) chemicals that deter germination of its own seeds, and possibly those of other potential competitor plants as well.

Associates: Pokeweed often suggests its close association with birds by the sites it frequents—along fencerows, beneath power lines, around shrubs, anywhere that fruit-eating birds perch. It "never invades cultivated fields," observed naturalist John Burroughs, "but hovers about the borders and looks over the fences like a painted Indian sachem." The plant also favors barnyards, roadsides, vacant lots, in open land or shade, usually in fairly rich, moist soil. Pokeweed "is bound to disturbed sites," wrote researcher Jonathan D. Sauer, "and nowhere does it seem to belong to a stable plant association." Sauer believed that its foremost habitat before pioneer land settlement was "open stream-bank woods," where shifting streams constantly created new open ground. Research has not yet established whether pokeweed's allelopathy works to delay its seed germination until the spring following its production, thereby increasing its survival chances. Despite any allelopathy that may exist, pokeweeds, as Thoreau noted, often group "in a community," islands of tall, treelike plants on hillsides and in fencerows. Pokeweed needs an average July temperature of at least 68 degrees F in order to thrive. From its origins in eastern North America—still its primary range—it has been introduced into Europe, Africa, and the Middle East.

Pokeweed is subject to some 15 mosaic and other plant viruses. A common leaf-spot fungus on pokeweed, producing leaf lesions, is *Phoma sorghina,* currently being evaluated as a potential biocontrol for the plant.

Two-spotted spider mites *(Tetranychus urticae)* frequently reside on pokeweed. For all of pokeweed's conspicuous presence in the landscape, relatively little research has gone into identifying insects associated with the plant. Probably its foremost foliage consumer, especially in the South, is the southern armyworm moth *(Spodoptera eridania)*, a noctuid caterpillar; pokeweed is one of its preferred hosts.

The eggplant flea beetle *(Epitrix fuscula)* riddles young foliage with holes; its larvae feed in the roots. Often they infest pokeweed until alternate crop hosts become available.

Pollinating insects consist mainly of flies and the short-tongued bees, such as *Halictus.*

Pokeweed provides at least 30 species of birds a major food resource. The berries, once staple fruits for the now-extinct passenger pigeon (hence one of pokeweed's aliases, pigeonberry), today supply an important food source for a pigeon relative, the mourning dove. But almost all *frugivorus* (fruit-eating) birds relish them as well: eastern bluebirds, American robins, thrushes (gray-cheeked, hermit, Swainson's, and the veery), northern mockingbirds, and cedar waxwings. Other bird consumers include northern bobwhites, woodpeckers (yellow-bellied sapsuckers, northern flickers, hairy and red-bellied wood-peckers), several flycatchers (great crested, eastern kingbirds, eastern phoebes), gray cat-birds, and finches (northern cardinals, rose-breasted grosbeaks, fox and white-throated sparrows), plus several others. Pokeweed berries provide an important transient food in late summer and fall for bird migrants as they stop to rest and feed en route. Birds that have consumed pokeberries leave obvious clues around their stained bills and vents.

Mammal pokeweed berry eaters include opossums, raccoons, black bears, gray and red squirrels, and white-footed mice.

Lore: Thoreau waxed eloquent over the beauties of pokeweed, regarding it as one of the most perfect floral emblems in nature. "Its stems are more beautiful than most flowers," he wrote, and even its "death is an ornament to nature."

Many plant manuals note pokeweed's unpleasant odor. My own observations indicate that writers have much exaggerated this characteristic—many plants smell worse, and pokeweed's odor is, if not fragrant, fairly innocuous.

Toxic chemistry does abound in this plant, however—foremost in the large rootstock and the seeds, also in the foliage and berries. Even the plant juice on one's skin can raise a rash and invade cellular tissue, causing chromosomal damage and mutations. One should always wear gloves when handling this plant. ("I love to press the berries between my fin-gers and see their rich purple wine staining my hand," wrote Thoreau, "it speaks to my blood"—perhaps in ways he couldn't dream.) Poisonous not only to humans, pokeweed is also toxic to horses, sheep, cattle, and pigs. Yet a roster of birds, as aforementioned (including poultry), and wild mammals seems impervious to the toxic compounds, which probably consist of oxalic acid, saponins, and an alkaloid (phytolaccin).

Despite the plant's toxicity, gourmands relish (after 2 boilings) pokeweed's young ten-der shoots and the leafy tips for asparaguslike greens. Delaware and Virginia native tribes, among others, collected the sprouts for food. "The flavor is delicate and delicious," wrote one sampler, author Marjorie Kinnan Rawlings, "with a faint taste of iron." Wild-food expert Euell Gibbons called it "a delicious vegetable," albeit needing salt and "quite a lot of butter, margarine or bacon drippings." Collectors, however, are advised to discard any shoots tinged red and never to harvest any piece of the root. Cooking destroys many toxins, and pokeweed's ripe berries, though sour tasting, have also been used for pies. Yet, as Pamela Jones remarked, "Why should I run even the slightest risk to my safety and health when there are so many other far safer weeds for my veggies and herbal teas?" For accidental pokeweed poisoning, Appalachian homeopaths recommended drinking lots of vinegar while eating a pound of lard (raising real questions, perhaps, as to which demise might be prefer-able). Introduced as cuisine into Europe in 1770, pokeweed sprouts were, for a time, culti-vated in France and northern Italy. Scam artists in France and Portugal added pokeberries to color low-grade wines, thereby increasing their market value; the juice, it is said, spoiled the wine taste, and laws soon required that pokeweeds be cut down wherever they grew.

Herbal and tribal healers have long valued pokeweed for a variety of curative pur-poses; it was taken internally as a berry tea and used externally as a root poultice for can-cers, arthritic pains, sprains, swellings, and skin ailments. As a witchcraft brew, shamans claimed, the violently purgative effects ejected bad spirits along with everything else. Phy-tolacca, an extract made from the dried roots and berries of pokeweed, found ample use by dairy farmers as a soothing ointment for cows' udders. Current researchers, advancing beyond homeopathy, are working with an antiviral protein (PAP) cloned from pokeweed leaves that offers hope as a possible inhibitor of HIV and herpes simplex viruses.

Pokeweed berry juice found frequent use as a fabric coloring agent. As a dye for woolens, however, the deep purple stain fades fairly rapidly, and no mordant has been found to fix the color. Native tribes used the dye for clothing and other items, as well as for horse and skin painting. The juice "makes a better red or purple ink than I have bought," wrote Thoreau. (In a journal entry of September 24, 1859, he wrote the word "poke" in the ink of the berry itself; by 1906, the word had faded to a light brown stain on the paper.) Pokeweed ink is still used in home crafts for decorating cards or letterheads.

Pokeweed even occupies a place in American political history. Supporters of James K. Polk's 1845 presidential campaign wore stem twigs of pokeweed (Polk = poke) as campaign insignia on their lapels.

The name *pokeweed* apparently derives from the Algonquin Indian name for the plant, *pokon,* from a word meaning "bloody," alluding to the plant's berry stain. The generic name *Phytolacca,* from the Greek, means "crimson plant."

Prickly Pear, Eastern *(Opuntia humifusa)*. Cactus family. This prostrate cactus, a native perennial, forms mats or colonies of flat, green, oval, leathery pads (jointed stems) up to 3 inches long, tufted with hairy bristles. In summer, buds rising from the pad margins produce showy yellow flowers, often with reddish centers.

Other names: Eastern cactus, Indian fig, devil's tongue, beaver-tail cactus.

Close relatives: Some 150 *Opuntia* cacti exist (some botanists identify almost 300), all occurring in the Western Hemisphere and most in semiarid regions and the tropics. Other *Opuntia* sometimes resident in eastern North America include the plains prickly pear *(O. macrorhiza)* and the little prickly pear *(O. fragilis)*. Two related eastern *Coryphantha* cacti also exist. About 1,000 cacti species all reside in the New World, though many have been introduced elsewhere.

Lifestyle: Always an exotic find when encountered in a sandy field or roadside, prickly pear seems out of place, a desert refugee, in our green Northeast. Yet the same adaptations that allow cacti to survive in dry areas allow them to exist in other places too, especially areas in the cold North. These adaptations are mainly water-conservative; they include the spines, which serve as heat-radiating points; the tough, rindlike skin of the pads, which protects the succulent, spongelike inner tissue; and the plant's process of dehydration in the fall, triggered by cold weather, concentrating its sap into an antifreezelike solution that withstands subzero temperatures. Shade-intolerant, prickly pear remains green and flabby, flat under the snow, during winter.

Specialized prickly pear anatomy includes small, cushionlike organs on the pad surface called *areoles,* containing the buds from which develop new stem growth, spines, flowers, and fruit. Spines, if any (this *Opuntia* species usually bears few), rise from the base of the areoles; also from the areoles arise *glochidia,* short, fuzzy, multibarbed bristles that provide this porcupine of plants its defense against munching herbivores.

Eastern prickly pear's gaudy yellow flower attracts various pollinating insects, but this plant reproduces mainly by root extension.

Prickly pear begins flowering in its second year. The sunburst of waxy yellow flowers opens in June along the marginal tips of the previous year's pad joints. Each flower measures up to 3 inches across, consists of 8 to 12 petals. As in most cacti, the flowers are *protandrous* (male parts maturing before female parts, thus deterring self-pollination), are probably self-sterile as well. Insect-pollinated, the bisexual blooms produce a spiny knob that ripens into a reddish or purple, somewhat pear-shaped fruit—actually a pulpy, sweet-flavored berry—containing numerous stonelike seeds. The fruits may remain on the plant over winter but are usually consumed by an animal before spring.

Most successful prickly pear reproduction, however, is a vegetative rather than a sexual procedure, especially in its northern range. Root growth can occur from any joint surface in contact with the ground, and the typical clumped and matted form of the plant indicates this mode of reproduction. Roots, a shallow meshwork, quickly absorb water and nutrients from even a quick rain shower.

Prickly pear flowers and fruits occur year-round in the plant's semiarid habitats of the Southwest.

Associates: Open sandy areas—fields, roadsides, dunes, shores—are this cactus's favored habitats. It resides from New England and the Midwest to Florida and Texas; a small population even exists in southern Ontario, where it hangs on as an endangered species. Prickly pear sometimes invades beach-grass *(q.v.)* populations in dune areas. In one southern Michigan area, it associates with eastern red cedar *(q.v.)* and yucca *(q.v.)* in field-savannas.

Insect feeders seem relatively few. A pyralid moth caterpillar *(Melitara prodenialis)* bores into the pads, as does the related *M. dentata,* called the blue cactus borer. Another pyralid, *Dicymolomia julianalis,* feeds likewise. Several other related moth borers (*Cactoblastis cactorum,* the cactus moth or tropical cactus borer; and *Ozamia lucidalis)* have invaded Florida from South America and the West Indies, posing threats to native prickly pears.

Southwestern prickly pear species host cochineal insects (Dactylopiidae), sucking red scale insects long used as the source of a crimson dye.

A common pollinating insect visitor to the flower is the spring rose beetle *(Strigoderma arboricola),* a greenish purple, iridescent scarab beetle related to the Japanese beetle. Bees, wasps, ants, and other beetles also visit, and some of them pollinate.

Many birds and mammals relish prickly pear fruits; especially in the Southwest, the source of most relevant data, prickly pear species are important bird and mammal food plants. In the East, cottontail rabbits, which devour the fruits, are probably the plant's most important seed dispersers. White-tailed deer and livestock also eat the pads and fruits without apparent injury from spines and areoles. Ground squirrels, mice, and voles also consume fruits and seeds, as does the ornate box turtle, a prairie species. Other fruit and seed consumers probably include northern bobwhites, wild turkeys, mourning doves, skunks, opossums, and raccoons, among others.

Lore: Almost every part of prickly pear makes a nutritious, tasty human food if properly prepared (with gloves; sticky tape or tweezers will remove the barbs from careless fingers). The peeled pads can be cooked like green beans, and the fleshy pulp of the fruit (bristles removed with a damp cloth), when chilled, makes an excellent sweet jelly ("tastes like pink lemonade," wrote one sampler). Even the seeds, ground when dried, can be used as flour or a thickener. Prickly pear is not so abundant in the East, however, that it can survive collection for food or other purposes.

Native Americans and homeopathic healers found many medicinal uses for the plant as well. They applied the pads as poultices for wounds and joint pains, drank a tea made from the pads for lung and kidney ailments.

Prickly pear fruits (specifically those of *O. ficus-indica*), cultivated and relished in Mexico, are called *tunas,* sold there in market stalls. Prickly pear fruits also enjoy popularity in Italy, where the plants were introduced in the 16th century. Today California cactus orchards produce some 3 million pounds of prickly pear cactus fruits per year, selling them mainly in Italian-American urban areas in the East.

Puccoons *(Lithospermum* species). Borage family. Recognize these yellow spring and summer wildflowers by their branching, somewhat flat-topped or curled-over flower clusters atop the stem. Each flower radiates 5 petals from a central tube that hides the sexual parts. Leaf shape and hairiness vary among species, but leaves in all species are alternate and untoothed.

Our most common species is probably hoary puccoon *(L. canescens),* with softly hairy leaves. Plains, hairy, or yellow puccoon *(L. caroliniense)* has roughly haired foliage, while narrow-leaved or fringed puccoon *(L. incisum)* has fringed petals and narrow, grasslike leaves. All 3 are native perennials and grow a foot or more tall.

Other names: Indian paint *(L. canescens);* plains-stoneseed *(L. incisum);* Carolina puccoon *(L. caroliniense).*

Close relatives: About 75 *Lithospermum* species exist worldwide, 7 of which reside in eastern North America. These include American gromwell *(L. latifolium)* and 2 alien Eurasian species: gromwell *(L. officinale)* and corn-gromwell *(L. arvense).* Family relatives include blue-weed *(q.v.),* forget-me-nots *(Myosotis),* comfreys *(Symphytum),* and borage *(Borago officinalis).*

Lifestyle: Puccoons hide their sexual organs inside the flower's central corolla tube, from the top of which the yellow petals flare outward. The flowers of hoary and plains

Puccoon's yellow flowers, their sexual parts hidden in a central corolla tube, display a complex system of pin and thrum morphs that probably hinders self-pollination.

puccoons are *dimorphic*—that is, 2 different forms or morphs, based on differing lengths of sexual parts, occur. For example, both hoary and plains puccoons are *heterostylous,* meaning that these differing lengths of (female) styles and (male) stamens appear on separate plants. One morph bears flowers with long styles and short stamens; the other has short styles and long stamens. Heterostyly reduces the likelihood of self-pollination because only the pollen of *pin* (long-styled) morphs is compatible with *thrum* (short-styled) morphs, and vice versa. Thus successful reproduction requires both morphs. These puccoons depend upon insects for pollination, but an imbalance exists in most populations of the 2 species mentioned, the thrum morphs outnumbering pin morphs—probably because thrum morph floral anatomy results in more pollen being received from, and collected by, insects (see Associates).

Narrow-leaved puccoon, by contrast, is not heterostylous; its stamens and styles are of equal length. Also, in addition to its showy visible flowers, it produces yellowish green *cleistogamous* (self-fertilized) flowers in the leaf axils that produce an abundance of single-parent (clonal) seeds. Cleistogamous-flowered plants also occur in *L. caroliniense* populations. Most researchers view cleistogamous flowers in puccoons as a complementary reproductive strategy, since cleistogamy frequently produces more seed than cross-pollination.

Puccoon seeds are ivory-white nutlets, 4 from each flower, but sometimes only a single nutlet matures. Seed distribution appears passive, with most seeds falling near parent plants. Puccoons reproduce exclusively by seed, but the stony seeds do not germinate quickly, can remain viable but dormant for many years in the soil.

Taproots of hoary and plains puccoons are short and thick; that of narrow-leaved puccoon is woody.

Associates: The 3 puccoon species mentioned frequent dry, sandy, unshaded ground. *L. caroliniense* frequents dunelands, whereas *L. canescens* more often resides in prairie remnants and openings; *L. incisum* favors disturbed ground as well as prairie patches. Hoary puccoon often associates with lupine *(q.v.)* and eastern red cedar *(q.v.),* is quite intolerant of grazing or soil disturbance. The 3 puccoons range spottily throughout eastern North America from southern Canada to the Gulf.

Sparse information exists on puccoon insect associates. Pollinators, mainly bumblebees *(Bombus)*, also include some smaller bees and butterflies. Look for small blue butterflies called spring azures *(Celastrina ladon)*, and Juvenal's duskywings *(Erynnis juvenalis)*, dark brown skippers, feeding on the flowers. According to one study, thrum morphs of the flower, owing to their longer, more extrusive anthers, deposit pollen on both face and proboscis of the insect; whereas pin morphs, with their shorter anthers, tend to deposit pollen only on the proboscis. The double likelihood of receiving pollen (at least according to theory) accounts for the fact that thrum morphs end up reproducing more abundantly than pin morphs.

White-tailed deer graze puccoons to some extent; livestock seldom do. Seedeaters probably include some birds, though information is lacking. Rodents—deer mice, voles, and wood rats ("pack rats")—are probably the main seed feeders.

Lore: Apart from the fascinating examples of heterostyly they exhibit (also seen in buckwheat *[q.v.]* and primroses *[Primula]*, among others), puccoons have received relatively scant attention from plant researchers. Even many wildflower manuals give them short shrift, for reasons that remain unclear. These attractive native wildflowers illumine many dry summer landscapes, especially in combination with the blue of lupine. Perhaps the name *puccoon* repels some "serious" observers? This word derives from the Algonquian word *poken,* for plants that yield red or yellow dyes, the same root word as for pokeweed *(q.v.).*

Native tribes used puccoons—the pulverized small, dried taproots—for dyes, producing various red shades for body and garment decoration. Facial painting (not just war paint) and hair dying functioned as important elements of many tribal rites, and the equally native puccoons supplied these colors of tribal identity. A leaf tea from *L. canescens,* used as a skin wash, treated persons suffering fevers and convulsions. Pioneer herbalists, noting the stonelike seeds (see doctrine of signatures in Blue-weed account), prescribed the plant as a remedy for kidney stones.

Purslane, Common *(Portulaca oleracea).* Purslane family. This cosmopolitan flat-sprawling, mat-forming annual with purplish red succulent stems has fleshy, paddle-shaped leaves that grow in rosettes at the ends of branches. Centering most rosettes are tiny, 5-petaled yellow flowers.

Other names: Pressley, purslance, pusley.

Close relatives: Some 100 *Portulaca* species occupy temperate and warm climates worldwide. Other eastern North American members include moss-rose *(P. grandiflora),* a popular garden native of Argentina. Family relatives include spring-beauties *(Claytonia)* and fame-flowers *(Talinum)*.

Lifestyle: The reddish mats of this ubiquitous weed accompany almost all human efforts to plant, till, and raise something worth eating. Purslane, itself, is worth eating (see Lore); like so many weeds, however, it may be invited but is not the guest one intended. Purslane's sprawling, fleshy stems produce up to 8 degrees of subbranching, a dense mass that often shows a radial form, which may extend up to 2 feet in diameter (but usually less). The small, spatulate leaves often crowd toward the branch tips. Purslane's thick epidermal layers and inner spongy tisues that store ample water indicate that the plant is a *xerophyte* (a plant with drought-survival adaptations).

Purslane seed cannot germinate until seasonal temperature exceeds 86 degrees F, and after rain; thus it usually emerges in late spring or early summer, continues to germinate through summer. The tiny flowers, mainly self-pollinated (though about 5 percent cross-pollination is effected by wind), appear 4 to 6 weeks after emergence of the plant, but they open only during the mornings of hot, sunny days. They last only a day and produce no nectar.

Round seed capsules, ripening some 2 weeks later, contain variable numbers of seeds, averaging 60 or 70, and open with a circular lid. Seeds generally fall near the parent plant and can germinate immediately, so several purslane generations per year are possible. The durable seeds can survive temperature extremes, remaining viable for 40 years or longer. This hardy little plant cannot, however, survive the cold. Most plants live for only about 3 months, then succumb to low temperatures in September.

Broken stem pieces of the plant—resulting from a hoe chop, perhaps—can produce adventitious roots (that is, roots growing from unusual or atypical locations) that regenerate entire plants. Uprooted plants can also ripen seed and can even reroot if in contact with the soil. Purslane knows how to live and linger, has a thick taproot plus numerous fibrous secondary roots.

Sprawling, succulent common purslane, a hot-weather plant, also a nutritious, edible weed, appears in gardens and disturbed soil almost everywhere.

Associates: This "hot-weather weed," as one gardener called it, resides in fields, gardens, gravel pits, and waste ground almost everywhere. Purslane's northern limit is about 60 degrees N latitude. It grows in both acid and limy soils but thrives best in soils with high nitrogen and phosphorus levels. Vegetable gardens and crop fields—among rows of corn, strawberries, tobacco, spring wheat—are its favored habitats. It often associates with other weed species, including quickweeds *(Galinsoga)*, barnyard-grass *(Echinochloa crus-galli)*, black bindweed *(Polygonum convolvulus)*, redroot (see Amaranths), spurrey *(Spergula arvensis)*, common ragweed (see Ragweeds), yellow and green foxtail-grasses *(Setaria glauca, S. viridis)*, and northern crab-grass *(Digitaria sanguinalis)*.

White rust *(Albugo portulacae)*, a common fungous parasite on purslane, produces white, blisterlike spots on leaves. Another common fungus is *Helminthosporium portulacae*.

Relatively few insects parasitize this plant. Caterpillarlike larvae of the purslane sawfly *(Schizocerella pilicornis)* mine the leaves, sometimes to an extent that defoliates the plant. Larvae of the portulaca leaf-mining weevil *(Hypurus bertrandi)* also channel in the leaves. An orange-red butterfly caterpillar, the variegated fritillary *(Euptoieta claudia)*, feeds on this among other plants, as does the white-lined sphinx moth caterpillar *(Hyles lineata)*, sometimes called the purslane sphinx.

Purslane is one of the weed hosts of the sugar beet cyst nematode *(Heterodera schachtii)*, a parasitic roundworm, one of the most destructive pests of beet crops. Soybean cyst nematodes *(H. glycines)* also feed in purslane roots.

A few birds and rodents consume the seeds. Mourning doves, horned larks, chipping and vesper sparrows, Lapland longspurs, and probably other finch ground feeders, as well as mice and voles, eat the seeds.

Livestock graze purslanes. Some sources report nitrate and oxalate poisoning from the plants, but others contradict these findings.

Lore: Essayist Charles Dudley Warner probably still speaks for most American gardeners in viewing purslane as "a fat, ground-clinging, spreading, greasy thing, and the most propagatious plant I know." Yet, for all the ardent spleen lavished on this plant for its tendency to carpet ground space in fields and gardens (even botanists dislike purslane for its tendency to drop leaves in herbarium collections), little evidence exists that it causes crop losses or competes successfully with other plants.

Also, purslane is one of the most nutritious of wild foods, perhaps one of humanity's earliest vegetables. No part of the plant is inedible raw, cooked, pickled, or mixed, as a salad green, potherb, or source of seed flour. Gardeners' dislike of this plant is not shared by farmers in southern Europe and Asia, who cultivate a strain of purslane for food.

This plant has a long history of human interaction. Persians and East Indians raised it more than 2,000 years ago, and popularity of the plant led to its spread throughout Europe.

"It cools the blood and causes appetite," summed up 16th-century English herbalist John Gerard. Not only did it reputedly repel evil spirits when strewn around one's bedstead, but its use as treatment for all sorts of ailments both internal and external has made it one of the world's most popular herbal medications. One source lists 75 symptoms, diseases, and sores for which purslane has been recommended—from ardor in Turkey and herpes in China to palpitations in Trinidad. Whatever the factual merits of such claims, the plant is rich in iron, calcium, phosphorus, and vitamins A and C. Recent agricultural research in California has established that as a *halophyte* (salt-tolerant plant), purslane can be raised as a vegetable and oil seed crop by irrigation from "water reuse systems" (that is, sulfate and saline drainage waters from industrial areas).

Purslane is one of those plants that has been cosmopolitan for so long that botanists remain unsure of its origins or native residency status. Various sources claim it as native to South America, North Africa, or the Middle East. Herbalist Euell Gibbons called it "India's gift to the world," but archaeological research into native tribal cultures indicates its presence in North America long before Columbus sailed; purslane has dwelled here at least 2,500 to 3,000 years. If it is an alien, it's a very old one indeed (at some prehistoric point, the native/alien distinction becomes meaningless).

Purslane has also proven itself a useful archaeological index. American natives often raised purslane along with corn for food, and the association of its pollen and seeds with corn pollen, which the wind does not disperse for any appreciable distance, has helped identify Indian garden sites. In some Ontario archaeological sites, the presence of corn pollen in lakes, indicating Indian agriculture, may owe to the native practice of washing purslane that collected large amounts of pollen on its foliage from adjacent cornstalks.

Pussytoes, Field *(Antennaria neglecta)*. Aster family. A cluster of dense, woolly tufts surmount the solitary stem of pussytoes, a native perennial and one of the earliest spring flowers. The sparsely leaved stem rises 8 to 12 inches from a ground-hugging rosette of spoon-shaped basal leaves, often forming dense mats that last over winter.

Other names: Dwarf, spring, or early everlasting, cat's paw, mouse-ear, white plantain, ladies' tobacco.

Close relatives: The number of *Antennaria* species that exist depends upon which taxonomist one consults this week. Thirty or so mostly North American species have been classified and named, but only about half a dozen of these reside in the East, according to Gleason and Cronquist's *Manual* (see Bibliography). The most common species after *A. neglecta* is probably plantain-leaved pussytoes *(A. plantaginifolia)*, a larger plant. Near aster family kin include pearly everlasting *(q.v.)*, cudweeds *(Gnaphalium)*, and joe-pye-weeds *(Eupatorium)*.

Lifestyle: The unisexual floral biology of *Antennaria* closely resembles that of its close relative, pearly everlasting. Unlike the sexual arrangement in most wildflowers, male and female *Antennaria* flowers occur separately on different plants, not on the same one, and one must inspect the flower closely to identify the sex. Female plants, more abundant than males, show tubular pistils elevated over the bristles *(pappi)* of the flowerhead, whereas the male plants have broader stamens submerged within the pappus hairs—sunken, as it were, into the visible flowerhead surface. Female flowerheads continue to elongate after pollination, elevating their pappi to the wind.

Pussytoes usually grows in unisexual clonal patches, with cross-pollination (by insects) virtually guaranteed as a result (many *Antennaria* species other than *A. neglecta* are *apomictic*—that is, they reproduce without a fusion of sex cells or even a need for male plants, which indeed are rarely or never seen in these populations). Occasionally male and female plants mingle their clones by intruding *stolons* (aboveground, creeping, horizontal stems) among their separate stands.

The 1-seeded achenes, each encircled by long hairs of the pappus, are dispersed by wind. Pussytoes reproduces both by seed and by stolons that extend from a plant and sprout a new clone at their ends. Sprouting plants produce a leafy basal rosette, from which rise solitary flowering stems, each of which may produce 3 to 10 clustered flowerheads. The 1-ribbed, wedge-shaped, basal leaves have pointed tips, are densely silvery-woolly beneath (as is the entire grayish green plant to a lesser extent); these rosettes remain green beneath the snow in winter. Crowded rosettes often form a matlike growth on the ground. Pussytoes roots are shallow and fibrous.

Associates: Field pussytoes favors dry, sandy ground in open fields, grassy hillsides, often in woodlands, since they flower before the canopy shade develops. Not as spectacular a wildflower as the colorful spring ephemeral wildflowers, their silver-gray, silken tufts may clothe acres of open ground alongside trout-lilies *(Erythronium americanum)* and spring-beauties *(Claytonia virginica).* Field pussytoes resides across the continent from Quebec and the Yukon south to the middle tier of states.

The only insect of note that feeds on pussytoes is the American lady or painted beauty butterfly caterpillar *(Vanessa virginiensis),* velvety black with spines and yellow crossbands; sometimes it builds a webbed nest on the plant.

One of spring's earliest wildflowers, field pussytoes' woolly flowerheads and downy foliage cover open, unshaded land in many habitats.

Pussytoes pollinators usually consist of the smaller bees (Halictidae, Andrenidae) and flies.

"Their seeds are too minute to be significant as wildlife food," as one manual states, "but several kinds of birds and mammals relish the tender rosettes of leaves." These include ruffed grouse, northern bobwhites, cottontail rabbits, snowshoe hares, and white-tailed deer.

Lore: One division of plant endeavor common in English-speaking countries may be labeled "the botany of cute." It finds greatest expression in the vernacular naming of plants, especially wildflowers. It is related to the antique doctrine of signatures belief (see Blueweed), which attempted to correlate plant shapes and forms with their human usages. The botany of cute endeavors to correspond plants with human sentiments (forget-me-not), with names of persons or other creatures, or with anatomical portions thereof—as in ladies'-tresses, jack-in-the-pulpit, blue-eyed Mary, and many others. Once primarily a garden botany and associated mainly with maiden aunts and Sunday school outings, the botany of cute has long since crashed those borders. Thus flowers named after feet, a subdivision of this weird anatomical botany, are not uncommon—rabbit's-foot clover, birdsfoot violet and trefoil, coltsfoot, and turkey foot (if not pawpaw)—are only a few. Pussytoes is, of course, a standard bearer in the botany of foot-cute, a plant so named from the woolly floral branches that supposedly resemble furry cat digits. Although it really has nothing to do with science or scientific nomenclature, the botany of cute has provided handy labels, many from folklore, by which to identify and remember given plants, and its contributions to botanical nomenclature are widely accepted in most current plant manuals. An alternative to such nomenclature would, of course, be English names that were helpfully, straightforwardly descriptive. But then a vivid (if often affected) imagery would be gone from our botany, gaps that maybe only other (and worse) metaphors might fill.

Like most aster family plants, *Antennaria* has no gastronomic palatability or value for humans. These plants found some usage as a treatment for diarrhea and lung ailments by herbal practitioners, also as a poultice for sprains, festers, and snakebite. In an early example of frontier showbiz, "Indians will for a trifle allow themselves to be bitten," reported American naturalist Constantine Rafinesque in 1828, "and cure themselves at once," reputedly by using a pussytoes potion.

The name *Antennaria* derives from a Latin word meaning "like [insects'] antennae," referring to features of the female flowerhead.

Queen Anne's Lace *(Daucus carota)*. Carrot family. An alien biennial or short-lived perennial and one of our most familiar summer wildflowers, Queen Anne's lace stands 2 or 3 feet tall. Its white, umbrellalike flower clusters form a lacy pattern, often centered by a tiny, dark purple floret. Flower clusters curl up into a nestlike cup shape as they age. Leaves are lacy, fernlike, finely subdivided.

Other names: Wild carrot, bird's-nest, devil's-plague.

Close relatives: Some 60 *Daucus* species range worldwide. Only 2 (including *D. carota)* reside in eastern North America—*D. pusillus* is the other. The familiar garden carrot, with its enlarged orange taproot, is a race of *D. carota*. Family kin include poison hemlock *(Conium maculatum)*, golden alexanders *(Zizia)*, parsnip *(Pastinaca sativa)*, angelicas *(Angelica)*, celery *(Apium graveolens)*, parsley *(Petroselinum crispum)*, caraway *(Carum carvi)*, anise *(Pimpinella anisum)*, and dill *(Anethum graveolens)*.

Lifestyle: Flowering stages of Queen Anne's lace can be easily traced by noting the progressively varying shapes of the flowerhead *(umbel)*. A flowering plant may produce 5 to 10 umbels at once, up to 100 umbels from July to September. Each umbel flowers from 10 to 15 days, has a slightly pungent odor. The disklike umbels, 2 to 4 inches in diameter, consist of numerous smaller clusters *(umbellets)*, each of which terminates a stalk that rises from a central point atop the main stem. Stiff, 3-forked bracts or rays underlie the umbel, clasp it closed during later phases of development. As the florets (usually 10 to 20 in an umbellet, more than 1,000 in an umbel) mature, the umbel assumes a flat-topped or convex shape. When fertilization occurs and seeds begin developing, the umbel sinks in the center, becomes concave, saucer-shaped. Soon it closes, the cupped bracts bending upward to form the closed seedhead "nest," inside which the green fruits ripen. The double-seeded fruits (called *schizocarps)* ripen first on the outer edges of the terminal umbels. They soon split apart, forming 1-seeded *mericarps*. As the mericarps mature and become dry, the cup opens outward again, flattens, and empties the seeds (which may number 1,000 to 40,000 per plant). Or mericarps may remain in the dry umbel until winter winds shake them loose or they attach to a passing coat or pelt by means of their tiny hooked spines.

Inspecting closer, one may observe that each white floret has 5 petals. Each floret is bisexual but *protandrous* (that is, the male parts develop and decline before the female parts mature), making it sequentially unisexual—a system that enhances the likelihood of cross-fertilization. Lacking insects to pollinate the florets (owing to weather conditions or low insect populations), they are also capable of self-fertilization via the long anthers of adjacent florets.

Botanists have long puzzled the significance of the red or purple central floret (occasionally more than one) in Queen Anne's lacy umbel. Many have assumed that the color contrast of the white-backed floret provides a long-distance visual signal that attracts pollinating insects. Experiments do not corroborate this assumption, however; a 1996 study confirmed earlier findings that most insects do not show a preference for umbels with a purple central floret over those with none. Thus the floret's function, if any, remains a puzzle. Observers will note that not all of the umbels possess these dark central florets—some 20 percent of umbels lack them. In these cases, botanists believe, the plant's production of anthocyanins, chemical source of the color, may have mistimed.

Flushes of seed germination often occur following rainy periods, not only in spring but also in summer and fall. Queen Anne's lace can and often does occur as an annual, flowering 6 weeks after spring germination and completing its life cycle within a single growing season. In shady conditions, the plant can also linger as a short-lived perennial, not flowering until its third or fourth year after germination. Typically, however, these plants are biennials, germinating in summer or fall, then wintering as a 6- to 8-inch-long whitish taproot surmounted by a leafy, ground-level rosette. Once having flowered (however long it takes), the plant dies, a system called *semelparous*. All reproduction is by seed—Queen Anne's lace does not extend itself by adventitious sprouts or rhizomes.

Associates: A worldwide resident of temperate regions in both Northern and Southern Hemispheres, Queen Anne's lace probably originated in Afghanistan and adjacent areas. It had spread to Mediterranean Europe before the Christian era. Highly adaptable to many soil types and moisture conditions, it favors clay and limy soils and open, sunny locales but is not limited to them. Almost every weedy field and roadside displays abundant *Daucus* populations. In some areas, the plant competes with native grasses and forbs.

Queen Anne's lace, as well as domesticated garden carrot, may host some 40 fungous parasites, often identical in both plants. Two common leaf-spot fungi exclusive to *Daucus* are cercospora blight *(Cercospora carotae)*, mainly affecting younger leaves; and alternaria blight *(Alternaria dauci)*. Both cause lesions on leaves and browning of foliage. Numerous blights, molds, rusts, mildews, and other fungi also find a frequent host in *Daucus*.

Probably the plant's most destructive parasite is aster yellows disease (see Aster), transmitted by *Macrosteles* leafhoppers; Queen Anne's lace, along with many other weedy plants, provides a reservoir for the toxic mycoplasm that affects many garden crops.

Protylenchus and *Meloidogyne* nematodes (roundworms) attack the roots of *Daucus*, as well as those of many other plants. Larvae of the carrot rust fly *(Psila rosae)* also feed on the roots; the adult flies are small and shiny black.

Relatively few foliage feeders or insect parasites exist on this plant. Probably the commonest is the caterpillar of the black swallowtail butterfly *(Papilio polyxenes)*, green and well camouflaged, also called parsleyworm.

Some 200 to 300 insects are said to pollinate Queen Anne's lace. These include a large variety of flies (including mosquitoes and gnats), beetles, bees, wasps, and ants, also butterflies and moths. Bumblebee *(Bombus)* pollen collectors apparently feed *Daucus* pollen to their

larvae, since it has been found in the larval meconia (intestinal contents). Pennsylvania or goldenrod soldier beetles
(Chauliognathus pennsylvanicus), orange-
yellow and black, frequent the flowerheads, as do banded long-horned beetles
(Typocerus velutinus) and *Gasteruption
assectator* wasps, resembling ichneumons with long ovipositors. Owners of
red pine *(Pinus resinosa)* plantations
don't mind seeing weedy fields of Queen
Anne's lace, for the latter hosts the parasite of a red pine pest, the European pine

*The convex, aggregate flowerhead of Queen Anne's lace usu-
ally consists of more than 1,000 individual florets. Banded
long-horned beetles* (Typocerus velutinus), *as shown here,
are common visitors.*

shoot moth *(Rhyacionia buoliana),* a tortricid moth caterpillar. Its parasite, an adult braconid
wasp *(Orgilus obscurator),* feeds in *Daucus* flowerheads.

Other common insects often seen on the flowers include syrphus or hover flies (Syrphidae) and tachinid flies (Tachinidae). Tiphiid wasps *(Tiphia intermedia)* are also common. Brownish yellow stinkbugs *(Trichopepla semivittata)* commonly suck the sap. *Lygus*
plant bugs, in nymph stage, consume many developing *Daucus* seeds in the umbel, especially in late summer and fall.

Predators of insects also abound on the umbels—especially crab spiders *(Misumena
vatia),* often camouflaged in color, and jumping spiders (Salticidae). Both are "sit and wait"
predators, but jumping spiders usually lurk on the undersides of umbels. Green lacewings
(Chrysopidae) plus ladybird beetles (Coccinellidae), ambush bugs (Phymatidae), and sphecid wasps *(Chalybion, Sceliphron, Sphex, Isodontia, Podalonia,* and *Ammophila* species) also
attack other insect visitors.

I have often seen dormant ladybird beetles and other insects hibernating inside the
seedhead thickets of *Daucus* during winter.

Though not a favored forage, Queen Anne's lace is grazed by cattle, sheep, and
horses. In digestibility and nutritive value, it resembles legumes. Relatively few birds ingest
the seeds, probably because of their spiny hooks; ruffed grouse, ring-necked pheasants,
and American goldfinches consume them to some extent, as do pine mice. Birds also occasionally cache seeds from other plants in the dried seedheads.

Lore: Accounts vary regarding the name of this plant. Some sources say it all began in
Elizabethan England, where the lately introduced plant's delicate leaves served as a head-
dress adornment for noble ladies. Queen Anne, arriving on the throne 99 years after Eliza-
beth, brought the plant to legendary status—the purple floret centering the flowerhead was

said to symbolize a drop of royal finger blood while she tatted lace. Other accounts state that Queen Anne liked to wear lacy medallion patterns resembling the flowerhead disk of *Daucus*, thence the flower's name. Whatever the name's origin, in America, at least, it remains almost the sole reminder of this queen's long reign. The irony is that the plant became an alien in Britain (brought by the Dutch, it is said) only shortly before it arrived with English colonists in America—probably only decades before Queen Anne's birth in 1665.

Nobody knows, at this date, what kind of carrots the colonists imported. Although Queen Anne's lace and the domestic garden carrot are the same species, they differ much in appearance, mainly of the roots; their *phenotypes* (physical appearances), in other words, show much more variety than their almost identical *genotypes* (genetic makeup). The Queen Anne's lace taproot more closely resembles a parsnip than a carrot. Current consensus among researchers is that the modern cultivated carrot is a hybrid cross between *Daucus carota* and the giant carrot *(D. maximus)* of the Mediterranean region. Queen Anne's lace and garden carrot can and do hybridize where they grow in proximity. The former can also host pests of the latter, so commercial carrot farmers do not relish the sight of Anne's medallions decorating any field near their crop rows.

Several carrot family plants (most notably poison hemlock, fool's parsley, and water-hemlock) are deadly toxic, and the leaves of some look similar to those of *Daucus*, so food harvesters of the wild carrot need to carry awareness along with the trowel; the wrong root dug for lunch from this tribe is likely to be a last repast. Only the first-year roots of *Daucus* are tender enough for cooking like regular carrots—older ones become too woody and fibrous.

The root tea of Queen Anne's lace, herbalists discovered, has beneficial effects. Scientists have confirmed its properties as an antiseptic, diuretic, and vermicide. It also enjoys some repute as a remedy for flatulence. Almost any health benefit to be derived from carrots can likewise be had from Queen Anne's lace. Both are rich sources of vitamin A. Experimental evidence indicates that seed extracts may inhibit implantation of fertilized ova in the womb, suggesting a possible role in birth control.

Picked before they fully open, the flowers make durable winter bouquets.

Ragweeds (*Ambrosia* species). Aster family. The 2 most abundant ragweeds, both native annuals with greenish flowers on long spikes *(racemes),* differ mainly in size and leaf shape. Common ragweed *(A. artemisiifolia)* stands 1 to 5 feet tall, has dissected, fernlike leaves. Giant ragweed *(A. trifida),* with a woody, bamboolike stem, grows up to 15 feet tall, has large, 3-lobed leaves. Both ragweeds flower in summer and fall.

Other names: Short or small ragweed, Roman or wild wormwood, bitterweed, hog-weed, hayfever-weed, many others *(A. artemisiifolia);* great or tall ragweed, kinghead, horseweed, others *(A. trifida).*

Close relatives: About 40 *Ambrosia* species, all in the Western Hemisphere, include 6 that reside in eastern North America: skeletonleaf-bursage *(A. tomentosa)*, annual bursage or bur-ragweed *(A. acanthicarpa)*, western or perennial ragweed *(A. psilostachya)*, and lanceleaf ragweed *(A. bidenta)*, plus the 2 aforementioned. Near kin include rosin-weeds *(Silphium)*, marsh-elders *(Iva)*, cockleburs *(Xanthium)*, and common yarrow *(q.v.)*.

Lifestyle: Male and female flowers occupy separate sites on the same plant in both species. The conspicuous racemes seen at the ends of stems and branches consist of all male flowers; female flowers, much more sparse and inconspicuous, occur singly or in small clusters at the bases and forks of upper branches. Female flowers are probably *protogynous* (maturing before the male flowers), thus increasing chances of cross-pollination. Ragweed flowers are wind-pollinated, can also self-pollinate. They produce 2-seeded *achenes*.

Common ragweed flowers, the bane of hay-fever sufferers, occur as separate sexes on the same plant (monoecious); male, pollen-producing flowers (top) are most conspicuous, whereas the small female flowers appear at branch bases (bottom).

These plants reproduce only by seed. Seeds of common ragweed number from 3,000 on a small plant to more than 50,000 on a large one. Common ragweed seeds that do not germinate in the spring following their production may enter a secondary dormancy period that can last for 40 years or more; some botanists call the plant a "buried seed strategist" for this reason. Giant ragweed produces fewer seeds, 300 or less per plant. Both plants have fibrous roots and relatively short taproots.

Ragweeds are known as short-day plants because they begin flowering only after day length begins to shorten in midsummer. Common and giant ragweeds sometimes hybridize, producing a plant with intermediate characteristics.

A 1973 study discovered a common ragweed adaptation that could account in some degree for its success. Experiments demonstrated that the plant collects and channels rainfall and nightly dew condensation down its slightly grooved stem to its root system, providing "a competitive advantage," wrote the researchers.

Associates: Common ragweed grows in open, disturbed sites of almost any sort—roadsides, railroad embankments, fields, vacant lots, and erosion channels and gulleys. It favors loamy, low-acid soils, grows less vigorously on acid soils. Land clearing and agricul-

Giant ragweed's large, 3-lobed leaf differs considerably from common ragweed's finely cut leaves.

tural settlement brought episodes of abundant ragweed growth called *ambrosia rises,* which followed the farmer's plow throughout the East and Midwest.

Giant ragweed favors moister disturbed ground— river floodplains are among its foremost habitats. It often grows in dense stands along ditches and stream-banks and in lowland fields. Its early emergence in spring and its height usually make it the dominant plant where it grows.

A frequent summer roadside strip association I have noted in the Midwest includes common ragweed, chicory *(q.v.),* and foxtail grass *(Setaria).* Common dod-der *(Cuscuta gronovii)* grows parasitically on ragweeds, its twining yellow stems tapping into the plant tissue.

Numerous parasitic fungi attack ragweeds. Common kinds include powdery mildew *(Erisiphe cichoracearum),* a downy mildew *(Plasmopara), Albugo* and *Puccinia* rusts, and spot or blister smuts *(Entyloma).* Root rot fungi *(Ophiobolus)* occur on giant ragweed. Aster yellows disease (see Asters) sometimes stunts common ragweeds.

Botanist Jan E. Mikesell, researching another aspect of ragweeds, discovered "assem-blages of pennate [feather-shaped] diatoms" on the male flower spikes of both common and giant ragweeds. Some 8 species of these microscopic golden brown algae (Chrysophyta), presumably windblown onto the plants, survived on the dried racemes long after they had been collected and stored; *Navicula* species were especially prevalent. (Mikesell, when queried, could provide no details of diatom association and their frequency on ragweeds.)

The mite *Eriophyes boycei* commonly infests ragweed plants.

Although insects play no role in ragweed pollination, they feed on the plants in abun-dance; some 220 species were listed by one research team. (Except as noted, all of the fol-lowing items refer to common ragweed.)

Foliage feeders include the gorgone checkerspot butterfly caterpillar *(Chlosyne gor-gone),* yellowish and striped with barbed spines. An olive green caterpillar with yellowish granulations may be that of the common sootywing *(Pholisora catullus),* a skipper.

Moth caterpillar feeders include the following noctuids: the common pinkband *(Ogdo-conta cinereola);* the ragweed flower moth *(Schinia rivulosa);* the olive-shaded bird-dropping moth *(Tarachidia candefacta);* and the small bird-dropping moth *(T. erastrioides).* Giant rag-weed hosts the first-named caterpillar plus the black-barred brown *(Plagiomimicus pityochro-mus),* Thoreau's flower moth *(Schinia thoreaui),* and the forage looper *(Caenurgina erechthea).*

Larvae of the treehopper *Publilia concava*, humped insects that suck sap, feed on giant ragweed, as do stinkbugs *(Cosmopepla bimaculata)*, red striped and spotted.

Broad-bodied leaf beetles *(Caligrapha similis, C. elegans, C. californica)* and the ragweed leaf beetle *(Zygogramma suturalis)*, oval-shaped, often with spots or lines, also feed on ragweed, as does the skeletonizing leaf beetle *Galerucella notulata* and the predaceous ragweed plant bug *(Chlamydatus associatus)*. *Zygogramma* as well as the aforementioned *Tarachidia* moth and *Eriophyes* mite were imported to Russia for the biological control of ragweed some 25 years ago, with undetermined results.

The bidens borer *(Epiblema otiosana)*, a tortricid moth caterpillar, invades and feeds in ragweed stems, as does the stalk borer *(Papaipema nebris)*, a noctuid pest of corn and garden plants, often migrating to them from ragweeds. Other tortricid stem borers include *Epiblema cataclystiana* and the related ragweed borer *(E. strenuana)*, which creates long, narrow galls in ragweed stems. An ichneumon wasp *(Glypta rufiscutellaris)* parasitizes the latter insect. The smartweed borer (see Knotweeds) also feeds in the stems of both ragweed species.

Chionedes mediofuscella, a tiny gelechiid moth caterpillar, feeds on seeds of giant ragweed. Other seed feeders on both species include the tephritid fly larvae *Euaresta bella* and *E. festiva*, which might qualify as biocontrol agents.

The pith of dead ragweed stems often hosts larvae of *Acropteroxys gracilis*, called lizard beetles. *Dectes spinosus*, a long-horned beetle larva, also hibernates in the stems. Larvae of flat-faced long-horned beetles *(Hippopsis lemniscata)* feed on the living plants, as do the adult beetles—long and narrow, they have back-swept antennae that extend twice as long as the body.

Among predatory insects, the spined assassin bug *(Sinea diadema)* often lies in wait for other insects on ragweed racemes.

The 2 ragweed species of this account differ markedly in their seed use by wildlife. Common ragweed, for all of its despised reputation among farmers, gardeners, and allergy sufferers, is bird manna, sustaining resident bird populations over winter and helping fuel many a fall migration. It provides a major food resource for gamebirds and songbirds alike. Major users include ring-necked pheasants, greater prairie-chickens, northern bobwhites, wild turkeys, mourning doves, horned larks, and red-winged blackbirds—plus almost every ground sparrow, finch, junco, bunting, redpoll, and towhee, all of which feed on the seeds, sometimes lavishly. Giant ragweed, by contrast—with its tough seed coats—is relatively little used. Birds that feed on it to some extent include house sparrows, northern cardinals, purple finches, and red-winged blackbirds.

Mammal seedeaters of common ragweed include least chipmunks, ground squirrels, deer mice, and voles. Cottontail rabbits and white-tailed deer feed at times on the foliage.

Lore: Although common ragweed ranks as one of North America's most valuable wildlife food plants, its allergenic effects on humans are well known. It is probably the dominant hay-fever plant, operant as such during its flowering season from mid-August sometimes to October frost. Each plant, it is said, can produce a billion pollen grains during this period, and the microscopic, windblown grains can travel up to 400 miles. What makes ragweed pollen such an insidious enemy of human respiratory membranes is not a pollen chemical but the simple fact of mechanical abrasion—these grains are ragged and spiny, can hook into and irritate sensitive nasal passages like fine-ground glass, evoking defensive responses from the tissues, swellings and histamines that produce the allergic reactions. Smooth pollen grains, such as most flowering plants produce, do not set off such reactive events. Some persons (35 million Americans, at least) seem much more sensitive than others to ground glass up the nose, as it were.

"Perchance some poet likened this yellow dust to the ambrosia of the gods," speculated Thoreau on ragweeds' generic name, which signifies immortality (or the food of the gods who gave it). The "rag" in ragweed is said to derive from the ragged pattern of the leaves in some species.

Windblown ragweed pollen in archaeological sites has proven a useful tool and indicator for dating and analyzing regional environmental conditions of the past. Since ragweeds so often accompany agricultural plantings, a ragweed pollen deposit can and often does indicate a historic or prehistoric tribal settlement site—as well as records of later pioneer settlement.

Reindeer Lichens (*Cladina* species). Reindeer lichen family. Recognize these ground lichens by their bushy, branching form of growth. The most common species include soft lichen (*C. mitis*), yellowish green, subdividing into 3- and 4-parted branchlets, the entire plants forming large, loaflike mounds; reindeer moss (*C. rangiferina*), gray and bushy with a feltlike surface; and starry lichen (*C. stellaris*), yellowish green with radiating, cauliflowerlike heads in billowing mats and tight, 4-parted branching with a fuzzy surface.

Other names: Reindeer moss, caribou lichen, shrub lichen, green or yellow reindeer lichen (*C. mitis*); gray or true reindeer lichen (*C. rangiferina*); northern reindeer lichen (*C. stellaris*).

The generic name *Cladina* is contested among botanists; most regional floras thus classify this group, but older, more conservative taxonomies still list these lichens as a subgenus of *Cladonia*, by which reindeer lichens were long labeled. Also, since lichens are compound organisms—an association of an alga and a fungus—some botanists believe that these components should bear separate generic names (in the case of the algae components, many already do, since they also survive and occur apart from the fungus associate).

Close relatives: Some 14 *Cladina* species, as presently classified, exist in northern and alpine climates worldwide. Much resembling *C. mitis* is *C. arbuscula,* the tree reindeer lichen, also yellowish green. The closely related *Cladonia* lichens, many of them with club-like, hornlike, or cuplike stalks, include pixie-cup lichen *(C. chlorophaea),* British soldiers *(C. cristatella),* and golf tee lichen *(C. fimbriata),* among many others.

Lifestyle: The lichen, wrote specialist J. Mackenzie Lamb, is "a fungus that imitates a green plant by using another plant [an alga] to make up for its own inability to conduct photosynthesis." The alga part *(phycobiont)* of the lichen symbiosis can survive without the fungus partner *(mycobiont),* but the fungus cannot survive on its own. The fungus probably benefits most in this relationship, gaining nutritionally from photosynthesis and other compounds produced by the alga component. Despite the popular conception of lichens as symbiotic partnerships, "all available evidence," wrote Lamb, "indicates that the fungus is a controlled parasite of the alga." Yet the alga may benefit to some extent from the sheltered structure provided by the fungus component and from the dispersal mechanism of the *soredia* (asexual surface granules—actually lichens in miniature—containing a cluster of phycobiont with a few strands of mycobiont; these powdery particles are wind dispersed).

Reindeer lichens, also called shrub lichens because of their bushy, upright growth form (though they stand only a few inches tall), are a type of *fruticose* lichen, all of which grow erect or suspended, as distinct from crustose (flat, crustlike, cracking) and foliose (leaflike) lichens. Details of lichen structure differ among the 3 growth forms mentioned. Reindeer lichens consist of stalklike, densely branched, fungal structures called *podetia,* in which the single-celled algae exist in a separate layer of tissue close to the outer surface. Reindeer lichen podetia are hollow, and they lack a *cortex* (protective outer covering), making the lichen surface look dull, sometimes cottony, in appearance. Maximum growth occurs in spring and fall.

The algae in reindeer lichens are *Trebouxia* species. Fungus components of reindeer lichens consist of *ascomycetes* (sac fungi) that produce an abundance of spores from *apothecia,* open, dark, disklike structures at the branch tips. However, in order to give rise to another reindeer lichen (since the fungus cannot survive apart from its alga host), the spores must encounter free-living *Trebouxia* algae, an encounter never observed in nature and unlikely (given the rarity of these algae outside of the lichen relationship) to occur. Thus *Cladina* as well as other lichens probably reproduce mainly by fragmentation and the aforementioned soredia; the spores and apothecia may well be vestigial organs that play little if any part in lichen reproduction. "The biology of lichens," as Lamb wrote, "abounds in unsolved problems of deep significance."

Reindeer lichens not only grow slowly but survive long; stable-habitat colonies may often exceed several centuries in age. Three growth stages typically occur: In the growth-accumulation period, lasting 5 to 25 years, the plant adds to its biomass, annually producing new growth at the tips of podetia, increasing their length; in the growth-renewal period, often exceeding 100 years, tip growth and die-off of basal podetia occur at equal rates, maintaining size of the lichen plant; in the final degeneration period, which may also last 100 years or more, die-off occurs faster than growth. The age of a lichen clump can often be roughly estimated by counting back through its major branchings.

Reindeer lichens, adapted for survival in the harshest northern climates, absorb moisture from the air, thriving on constant conditions of alternate wetting and drying. All reindeer lichens form extensive patches, mats, and carpets on the ground. Their soft, springy surface after a rain dries to a crisp upper layer that crunches and crumbles when stepped upon, but the plant retains much moisture in the inner layers of the podetia.

Associates: Winter is an arid season in the North, and reindeer lichens are well adapted for survival in the cold deserts of boreal and permafrost regions. Yet they also require periods of high relative humidity in order to thrive. They primarily reside in northern regions worldwide. In North America, they grow throughout Alaska, Canada, and the northern United States, occurring southward in boggy and montane areas to the Gulf. In the subarctic "lichen steppes" of Eurasia, they grow most abundantly on glacial drift.

Typical habitats include sterile sandy and acid soils in open spruce or jack-pine forests, oak savannas, dry hummocks of lowland bogs, arctic tundra, and mountainous areas. Avoiding limy soils, they grow on bare ground, also on rocks, stumps, and (very often) on decaying logs and logging debris. In Michigan's northern stump prairies, once the domain of white pine forests, I have observed how the ground patterns of reindeer lichen often outline the shapes of coniferous logs that have completely decayed away; only the lichens remain to mark, like linear graves, where they once lay. Such lichen markers probably represent the final decay phase of a pine log. In some areas, the gray *C. rangiferina* typically grows closely adjacent to puffy pillows of the yellow-green *C. mitis* or *C. arbuscola,* giving a 2-tone cast to the lichen flora. Reindeer lichens quickly die out in tree canopy shade, to become replaced

Last remnant of a tree: Reindeer lichens populate the decayed residues of white pine logs in the bracken fern plains.

by shade-tolerant mosses such as mountain fern moss *(Hylocomium splendens)* and Schreber's feathermoss *(Pleurozium schreberi).* Despite their adaptations to dry soils and the arid cold, reindeer lichens require ample moisture during the warmer seasons. They favor a combination of humid climates and sufficiently low annual temperatures, which inhibit competitive plant growth.

The lichen mats can and do restrict invasion by other plants; a seedling that germinates on or beneath the lichen mat hasn't much chance of surviving amid the repeated expansions and contractions of the lichens in response to changing humidity. Typical plant associates include white and black spruces, jack-pines, white birches, and sphagnum mosses. A 1979 study found that reindeer lichens retarded the root development of white spruce and jack-pine seedlings though did not inhibit their seed germination. Reindeer lichens also undergo a plant succession of their own species (see Lore).

Although many insects and other invertebrates are labeled as generalized lichen feeders—for example, oribatid mites (also called beetle or moss mites—tiny, dark, hard-shelled, spiderlike creatures); collembolans or springtails (Collembola), minute jumping insects; and lichen moth caterpillars (Lithosiinae), including *Crambida, Cisthene, Lycomorpha,* and *Hypoprepia* species, among others—little information exists about invertebrate associations with reindeer lichen species. One research report accounted for this astonishing paucity thus: "(1) Few biologists possess a detailed knowledge of both lichens and invertebrates, (2) lichenologists have seldom been interested in the microfauna present in their samples, and (3) zoologists have rarely bothered to get the lichens in their samples identified." Most faunal research in which lichens are involved refers simply to "lichens"—as if, in studying bees, one should refer simply to "flowers." To date, any invertebrates that may be exclusive to reindeer lichens remain unknown.

The only creatures known to feed frequently on reindeer lichens are woodland and barren-ground caribou and musk-oxen. In some northern areas, these plants make up more than half the caribou winter diet, in others the almost exclusive winter food intake. The reindeer of Scandinavia (a caribou subspecies) likewise consume it as a winter staple. These deer of both continents find reindeer lichens highly palatable, though their low protein, vitamin, and crude fat levels often result in loss of weight for the animals. In many areas, however, the caribou may balance the protein deficiency by also consuming relatively high-protein foliose dog lichens *(Peltigera)* and fruticose lattice lichens *(Stereocaulon).* The caribou rumen (stomach) seems well adapted, with specialized bacteria and protozoa, for digesting the crude fiber and complex carbohydrates of *Cladina.*

Willow ptarmigans often use dense beds of reindeer lichen for nesting cover.

Lore: Reindeer lichens become questionably fit for human consumption only by soaking, powdering, and mixing with edible cornstarch or flour. Our digestive tracts are simply not equipped to break down their compounds into usable energy. The only way in which they can become somewhat edible is by being predigested, say by a caribou. Inuit hunters relished partially digested lichens from the stomachs of freshly killed caribou, sometimes mixing the contents with meat scraps to make a pudding and eating it uncooked.

Yet various native peoples, including the Cree, used medicinal teas brewed from reindeer lichens for expelling intestinal worms as well as for treating, in both tea and poultice form, aches, fevers, and other ailments.

Aside from their iffy edibility for humans, reindeer lichens provide an interesting dating indicator on the ground. The plants can survive light ground fires, but they are highly flammable, and a severe wildfire erases them for years. Recovery of reindeer lichens is slow, requires at least 40 to 50 years. Often fire begins a lichen succession. *C. mitis* usually reappears first, gradually succeeded by the other two. *C. rangiferina* and *C. stellaris* may require almost a century to resume their prefire abundance. Thus anyplace where reindeer lichens abound can be estimated as having been free of fire for several decades, at least. Some studies, however, indicate that infrequent fire, at least, may induce a heavy growth of reindeer lichens. The passage of severe fire in some boreal forest areas may generate "an almost solid reindeer lichen stand in some 40 to 50 years," according to one study.

Reindeer lichens "resemble dead litter more than live tissue in their susceptibility to fire," as one report states. They dry out rapidly during periods of low atmospheric humidity, yet in early morning or evening may burn poorly owing to higher moisture at these times. "Atmospheric vapor alone," according to one report, "can raise lichen moisture by 15 percent." At hot midday, however, the lichens may "flare up with almost incredible heat and flame." Continuous mats of the lichens collect tree and shrub litter, presenting a more or less uniform surface along which a fire spreads. As campfire tinder, dry reindeer lichens rival the kindling capacities of birch bark (though only the latter is good for rainy-day ignition). Wet or damp reindeer lichens can pliably withstand much trampling by caribou and other mammals; when dry, however, the lichens readily crumble and fragment if stepped upon.

One harsh environment exists wherein even the hardiest lichens cannot reside—the urban environment of smog and air pollution. Since lichens have ample take-up mechanisms for air and moisture but few means of excretion, they readily absorb all gaseous and liquid toxic elements present, and these substances kill them. They also absorb, and cannot survive, what is termed acid rain, the sulfuric and nitric acids formed from the oxides produced by fossil fuels. Fruticose lichens such as *Cladina* are the most vulnerable and the first to disappear, followed by the foliose, then the crustose lichens. Lichens thus provide a readily observable monitor—"miners' canaries," as it were—on the quality of the air we breathe, of the rain in our yards. A city lacking lichens on its stone walls and sidewalks is not a great place for one's health.

Lichens not only serve as poison sinks and indicators; they also accumulate radioactivity, especially in the form of strontium 90 and cesium 137. One of the first indications of the 1986 nuclear accident at Chernobyl was the accumulation of radioactive fallout in the milk and meat of reindeer, which were feeding as usual on *Cladina*. Air currents brought the radioactive scourge to Scandinavia as well, where thousands of reindeer had to be destroyed.

The yellowish color of soft and starry reindeer lichens, among other species, comes from usnic acid, which causes allergenic reactions in some people. The gray-colored *C. rangiferina* contains another kind of acid (fumarprotocetaric) that has no ill effects (unless taken into a noncaribou stomach). Dense mats of this and other light-colored fruticose lichens produce an *albedo effect,* reflecting radiant energy from sunlight, thus helping maintain cooler soil temperatures or permafrost in tundra areas. Layers of "white peat"—centuries of decay-resistant reindeer lichen accumulations—exist in some northern areas. Ground surface microclimates change drastically when a fire passage destroys the lichens.

C. stellaris has long been popular with landscape architects and model railroaders for re-creating lifelike miniature trees and shrubs for fake landscapes. A million-dollar Scandinavian industry thrives on exporting glycerine-treated reindeer lichen for such uses. In Germany, this lichen species is widely used for making Christmas and grave wreaths.

A familiar plant in the moors of Scotland, *C. rangiferina* is prided as the official badge of the clan McKenzie.

Reindeer lichens are so named from their antlerlike branching as well as from their chief (Eurasian) forager.

Rocket, Yellow *(Barbarea vulgaris).* Mustard family. One of the most common mustards, this yellow-flowered alien biennial populates fields and roadsides in spring. Standing 1 to 2 feet tall, it has branching stems surmounted by end clusters of 4-petaled flowers. The lobe-toothed leaves and inch-long seedpods *(siliques)* hug the distinctively ridged stem. Basal leaves, glossy and dark green, have a large, egg-shaped terminal lobe.

Other names: Winter-cress, wild mustard, bitter cress, rocket-cress, yellow weed.

Close relatives: About 20 *Barbarea* species occupy north temperate regions worldwide. North American generic residents include northern winter-cress *(B. orthoceras)* and early winter-cress *(B. verna).* Yellow rocket resembles *Brassica* mustards as well as other *Barbarea* species, but this species grows more abundantly than most of them. Family relatives include hoary alyssum *(q.v.),* garlic mustard *(q.v.),* water-cress *(Rorippa nasturtium-aquaticum),* dame's rocket *(Hesperis matronalis),* rock-cresses *(Arabis),* and many others.

Lifestyle: One of the "early yellows" along with dandelions—in contrast to most early-spring flowers, which are white or purplish—yellow rocket continues blooming into sum-

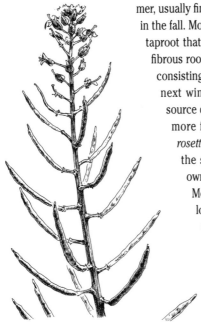

mer, usually finishes by late June but occasionally flowers again later in the fall. Most of the plants germinate in early spring, producing a taproot that may extend more than a foot deep plus a secondary fibrous root system. They also produce a ground-hugging rosette consisting of about 5 leaves that remain green throughout the next winter. If the rosette survives frost-heaving (a major source of plant mortality) in the early spring, from it rise 1 or more flowering stems that may also sprout leafy *cauline rosettes* on the stems before they die off in the fall. When the stems fall, these cauline rosettes may develop their own root systems and, the next spring, flowering stems. Most cauline rosettes fail to survive winter, however. Yellow rocket's root crown and root branches also generate buds and rosettes in late summer and fall, and these may also sprout flowering stems the next spring. Unless a rosette root separates from its parent root branch, it usually does not survive more than 3 growing seasons.

Yellow rocket flowers, insect-pollinated, require cross-fertilization in order to produce seed. Bisexual, they project 4 long, prominent (male) stamens and 2 shorter ones plus a single, central (female) stigma.

Like most mustard plants, yellow rocket erects siliques, or seedpods, which progressively develop up the ridged stem behind the flowerheads.

Each seedpod, or *silique,* holds an average of 13 seeds, and each plant may produce 40,000 to 116,000 seeds—though sometimes much less, depending upon habitat quality. Seeds remain viable for at least 10 to 20 years, breaking dormancy and germinating when moisture, temperature, and light conditions near the soil surface become optimal. New seeds require a several-week period of cold stratification at about 20 degrees F or less in order to break dormancy.

Associates: Yellow rocket probably originated in Mediterranean regions. Today it grows throughout most of North America from 51 degrees N latitude south to Arkansas. Its most abundant populations reside in the Northeast, with increasingly heavy invasion, since the 1950s, of the Midwest. Although it thrives as an opportunist in a variety of soils and open habitats, it favors moist, rich, recently disturbed soils. It often becomes a dominant plant in early spring, but does not compete well against such grasses as quack-grass *(Elytrigia repens)* and bluegrasses *(q.v.).* It does, however, invade clover, alfalfa, and wheat fields in America and abroad, becoming a particular pest in legume hay, which livestock may refuse to consume if too many stems of *Barbarea* are present.

Many fungi parasitize this plant. Probably the most important is *Sclerotinia* crown rot, which may account for most mortality of 2-year-old yellow rocket plants. Other fungi include leaf spots *(Alternaria, Ramularia barbareae)*, downy mildew *(Peronospora parasitica)*, stem rot *(Sclerotium rolfsii)*, clubroot *(Plasmodiophora brassicae)*, and others. The plant hosts cucumber mosaic virus *(Marmor cucumeris)* in its roots over winter.

A climbing plant parasite of yellow rocket, as well as of many other plants, is common dodder *(Cuscuta gronovii)*.

Plants of the mustard family attract a distinctive invertebrate fauna, probably via a complex array of mustard oils and glycosides. Many insects and other organisms of this group become pests of such crop mustards as radishes, collards, and turnips, the parasites using yellow rocket and other wild mustards as temporary hosts. Because of yellow rocket's "vegetative growth in late autumn, its early resumption of growth in spring, and its abundance in open fields," wrote a Cornell University research team, many mustard insects "are able to utilize this plant during adverse seasons when most other hosts are not available."

Insect sap suckers and foliage eaters on yellow rocket include powdery white colonies of cabbage aphids *(Brevicoryne brassicae)* and buckthorn aphids *(Aphis nasturtii)*. *Pegomyia affinis*, a larval fly, mines the leaves, and meadow spittlebugs *(Philaenus spumarius)*, their sap-sucking nymphs encased in froth, are also common.

Caterpillars of the black or greasy cutworm moth *(Agrotis ipsilon)*, also called ipsilon dart, a noctuid, appear dark with a broken yellow line on the back; they feed on many cultivated plants. Two of yellow rocket's foremost feeders include 2 green caterpillars: the imported cabbageworm, also known as the cabbage butterfly *(Pieris rapae)*; and the mustard white *(P. napi)*. Related butterfly caterpillar feeders include the falcate orangetip *(Anthocharis midea)*, dull green and finely striped; and the olympia marble *(Euchloe olympia)*.

Root feeders include the cabbage maggot *(Hylemya brassicae)*, a fly larva; poplar petiole gall aphids *(Pemphigus populitransversus)*; and several flea beetle larvae, mainly striped flea beetles *(Phyllotreta striolata)* and hop flea beetles *(Psylliodes punctulata)*. Adult flea beetles chew shotholelike perforations in the leaves. Striped flea beetles move to garden plants and other weeds in late spring. Root-knot nematodes *(Meloidogyne)*, tiny roundworms, also attack the roots.

Seed weevils *(Ceutorhynchus americanus)* feed in the siliques as adult insects, in the stems as larvae.

Calling yellow rocket "a critical link" for mustard family fauna, "it seems likely," wrote the Cornell researchers, that the population densities of these organisms—and even the species composition—"would be greatly altered if *B. vulgaris* were not an abundant member of our flora."

Foremost pollinators include native bees *(Andrena, Halictus, Dialictus)* and honeybees *(Apis mellifera)*—all forage on the flowers, mainly for pollen. Other flower visitors and possible pollinators include several braconid wasps. Lady beetles *(Coccinella),* aphid predators, also frequent the plants.

A common nocturnal foliage feeder is the gray garden slug *(Deroceras reticulatum).* Another mollusk, the glossy pillar snail *(Cionella lubrica),* a shiny, brownish, cigar-shaped land snail, also feeds on the plant.

Mourning doves and pine grosbeaks have been observed feeding on yellow rocket seeds. Probably several ground finches and sparrows also consume them, since the plant is so ubiquitous. Livestock readily consume the early, high-protein sprouts but reject the fibrous mature plants.

Lore: This plant's generic name *Barbarea* reveals its reputed connection to the early December feast day of St. Barbara, third-century virgin martyr and patron saint of architects, grave diggers, and others; for medieval farmers, fresh green rosettes of yellow rocket provided a winter taste treat, loaded with much-needed vitamin C. A mustard oil called sinigrin accounts for the leaves' tangy flavor. As the season progresses, the leaves become bitter, less edible unless boiled to shreds. The plant should be cautiously sampled, if at all; recent research indicates that sinigrin may cause kidney problems.

Yellow rocket apparently entered North America about 1800 by unknown means but did not reach official noxious weed status for another 150 years. Homeopathic healers and, later, even some native tribes brewed teas for common ailments, also used the plant for skin poultices.

Rose, Multiflora *(Rosa multiflora).* Rose family. Recognize this widely escaped thicket-forming alien shrub by its pyramidal clusters of small white flowers; its compound leaves consisting of 7 to 9 oblong, toothed leaflets; and its fringed or comblike *stipules* (small leaflike appendages at the leafstalk base). It stands 7 to 10 feet tall, with spiny stems and branches that arch and droop to the ground. Pea-size, reddish orange fruits called *hips* develop in late summer and fall.

Other names: Rambler rose, Japanese rose.

Close relatives: About 20 rose species—many of which hybridize—reside in northeastern North America, of about 100 or more worldwide. Native roses include climbing prairie-rose *(R. setigera),* which closely resembles multiflora rose; pasture-rose *(R. carolina);* and swamp-rose *(R. palustris).* Family relatives include wild strawberry, common cinquefoil, apple, hawthorns (all *q.v.*), and many others.

Lifestyle: Multiflora rose begins flowering and producing prolific seed at age two to five. The name multiflora derives from the 5-petaled flowers, 6 to 30 occurring in each cluster, or *panicle.* The fragrant and spectacular bisexual flower has a thick central cluster of pollen-bearing stamens turned slightly outward from the (female) pistils, which are united into a protruding central column. This arrangement hinders self-fertilization, also guides an incoming, presumably pollen-laden insect to the prominent, sticky stigma on the pistil first. Flowering occurs in May and June.

The clustered, orange-red rose hips, enclosing the 1-seeded *achenes,* do not split and release them to the wind, but dry on the shrub to form a leathery capsule relished by many birds, multiflora's primary dispersal agents. Uneaten hips remain on the plant over winter. Most birds regurgitate the seeds, others deposit them in droppings; studies show that the seeds in droppings germinate at a higher rate than the others. A single medium-size bush can produce upward of 500,000 seeds per year.

Seeds require a period of freezing or cold stratification, usually 30 to 120 days, in order to germinate. They may remain viable in the soil for a decade or longer. Seedlings often remain low, trailing, and inconspicuous during their first year or so.

Multiflora rose also reproduces vegetatively by *layering*—that is, by rooting at the tips of its drooping canes where they touch the ground. The plant's distinctive sprawling, arching appearance, similar to that of blackberry canes, results from this habit. New clonal stems also rise from root sprouts and from horizontal underground stems *(rhizomes).* A deep root anchors the plant firmly.

Spines are short, stout, and recurved in this species.

Associates: Native to Japan, Korea, and portions of China, multiflora rose engaged wide attention as another panacea of wildlife and conservation experts, similar to campaigns they launched on behalf of autumn olive *(q.v.)* and the Sichuan pheasant. Not so long afterward, it was noted with some astonishment that alien multiflora rose tended to take over entire pastures, hedges, power line corridors, and roadsides, creating dense, thorny, impenetrable thickets in hugely diverse habitats. Widely tolerant of soil types from clay to sand, both acid and alkaline, multiflora rose is limited in distribution mainly by moisture and temperature. It favors drier over wetter sites, regions of long summers and short winters, moderate shade to full sunlight, and previously plowed (11 to 15 years ago), disturbed ground. It occurs generally throughout North America except in mountain and desert areas, along the southeastern coastal plain, and above latitude 45 degrees N. It thrives most abundantly in the central and southern states, probably resides in most counties of the Midwest. It rises vigorously in seed deposit sites beneath such bird perches as power lines and tree limbs.

Probably the most destructive organism to afflict multiflora rose, as well as some cultivated roses and other rose family members, is a viruslike mycoplasm called rose rosette.

Rose rosette disease (RRD) causes *witches' brooms*—abnormal bushy growths along the stem—plus deformation and bright red mosaic pigmentation of leaflets. RRD usually kills the plant within a year or two. Although the specific causative agent remains unknown, it is apparently transmitted by an eriophyid mite *(Phyllocoptes fructiphilus)*, which first infests the roots, then moves to the canes. Because of RRD's proclivity to attack ornamental and garden roses as well as *R. multiflora,* its use for biocontrol of the latter species appears unwise. Some researchers disagree, however; since the mite is a relatively sedentary creature that rarely travels from its home rosebush, it offers minimal chance, they say, of spreading the disease except where roses occur in dense stands.

Numerous insects feed on rose species. Few if any are exclusive to multiflora rose (see Wild Roses account in *The Book of Forest and Thicket*), and probably the abundance of *R. multiflora* as an insect host has increased pest problems for ornamental rose growers. Only those insects especially prominent on or relevant to multiflora rose are noted here.

Larvae of the rose stem girdler *(Agrilus aurichalceus),* a buprestid beetle, hatch inside multiflora rose canes and eventually girdle the stems, causing them to die and appear as brown "flags" on the bushes. The larvae overwinter in the girdled canes, emerging as adult beetles in May; metallic golden or bronze in color, they can be seen on the foliage in spring. Raspberry cane borers *(Oberea bimaculata),* cerambycid beetles, also feed as larvae inside the canes. In this case, however, the adult female—a slender, striped and dotted beetle— girdles the stem above and below the egg puncture; the larva eats downward in the cane, overwintering in the subsurface root crown.

The rose seed chalcid *(Megastigmus aculeatus),* a chalcid wasp, feeds on the developing achenes, overwintering in the rose hips. When the rose petals fall (usually in June or July), the adult wasps emerge, leaving round exit holes. The adult wasps have distinctively swollen hind femorae (upper leg segments). The rose hip borer *(Grapholita packardi),* a tortricid moth caterpillar also called the cherry fruitworm, also feeds on rose hips as well as cherry fruits.

All of these insects have been proposed as candidates for biocontrol programs. Yet since none of them feed exclusively upon multiflora rose but attack other fruit-bearing trees and shrubs as well, their usage for such purposes appears limited at best.

Other common herbivores on multiflora rose include the rose curculio *(Merhynchites bicolor).* This beetle larva also feeds in the hips; the adult beetles eat holes in the flower buds, which die or produce hole-ridden petals. The European earwig *(Forficula auricularia),* blackish brown insects with forcep tails, feeds on the petals as well. Roseslug sawfly larvae *(Endelomyia aethiops),* resembling sluglike, yellow-green caterpillars, feed colonially, skeletonizing the leaves.

Many aphids, beetles, moth caterpillars, and bees frequent roses. Bees collect more pollen than nectar from roses; they typically shake the anthers, dusting themselves with the pollen "rainfall."

Dense, thorny multiflora rose thickets provide wildlife food and shelter but also invade fields and pastures. The rose hips (inset) feed many birds during winter.

Gamebirds and songbirds feed extensively on multiflora rose hips. Ruffed and sharp-tailed grouse, greater prairie-chickens, ring-necked pheasants, wild turkeys, and northern bobwhites consume and disperse the seeds, as do a number of passerine (songbird) species. In many areas, multiflora's main bird associate is the northern mockingbird; this bird's range expansion into northern states since the 1950s has, in fact, closely paralleled the spread of multiflora rose. Multiflora hips have become its chief winter food in these areas—and because mockingbirds also nest in the rose thickets, the association extends year-round. Cedar waxwings find multiflora rose hips a choice food as well. Other bird feeders include eastern bluebirds, American robins, Swainson's thrushes, brown thrashers, American goldfinches, northern cardinals, evening grosbeaks, and fox, song, and American tree sparrows. Mammal seed and hip eaters include black bears, striped skunks, red squirrels, and white-footed mice. White-tailed deer and cottontail rabbits browse the canes, as do beavers to some extent. Among livestock, goats browse the plant, but cattle generally avoid it.

Birds and mammals also use multiflora rose as nesting and escape cover. The hedges frequently host northern cardinal and gray catbird nests; and white-footed mice often adopt the vacated nests of these birds for their own nests, which they pile with plant down. Networks of sheltered rabbit and vole trails often thread beneath these thickets.

As early as 1956, however, Illinois wildlife biologist Willard D. Klimstra, after researching the plant thoroughly, concluded that little evidence existed for its value to wildlife except in circumstances where little other food or cover was available.

Lore: "Plain old Charlie Deam," legendary Indiana state forester and botanist, was among the few who strongly opposed the use of multiflora rose for landscaping purposes in 1948. Responding to proposals that cemeteries be planted with it, he wrote that "when Gabriel sounds his horn, I am afraid some will be stranded and not be able to get thru the roses." Deam himself recommended multiflora rose "for the bonfire."

Petals and hips of all roses are humanly edible and vitamin rich. Since those of multiflora rose are smaller than analogous parts of most rose species, however, their consumption may require more energy than they provide.

Multiflora rose was first imported to North America in 1886 to provide rootstocks for ornamental roses, a function it admirably served. Highway engineers also planted hedges of it for crash barriers and to reduce headlight glare in medians. The plant is no longer used or commercially available for such purposes. Not until the 1930s, when the U.S. Soil Conservation Service began hyping multiflora rose hedges for usage as "living fences" to confine livestock and for soil erosion projects—and also began distributing thousands of seedlings to farmers and ranchers—did the plant begin achieving pest status. As recently as the 1960s, certain state conservation departments were still donating rooted cuttings to property owners. Today, however, multiflora rose is designated a noxious weed in many states.

Rush, Path *(Juncus tenuis)*. Rush family. Recognize rushes by their smooth, round, spirelike stems and 3-parted flowers and fruit capsules. This common little dry-land rush, a native perennial, grows in scraggly, grasslike clumps. Its curly bracts extend beyond the small flowerheads atop the tough, wiry, unjointed stems. The plants grow up to a foot tall.

Path rush, which thrives in roadways and trodden habitats, is grasslike and inconspicuous but very common wherever people or animals move.

Other names: Poverty rush, yard rush, field rush, slender rush, wiregrass.

Close relatives: Most of the almost 50 *Juncus* residents in eastern North America are wetland plants, as are the 200 or so total species worldwide. Common wetland rushes include wire-rush *(J. arcticus)*, soft rush *(J. effusus)*, and Canada rush *(J. canadensis)*. (See *The Book of Swamp and Bog*.) Wood-rushes *(Luzula)* belong in the same family.

Lifestyle: One of the few rushes that one can seek, find, and inspect without wearing boots or wetting feet, path rush is also one of the smallest. It becomes most conspicuous in late summer and fall, when the long primary bracts twist like curled ribbons atop the stems.

The greenish brown flower clusters, appearing in spring and early summer, occur at the tips of the branches, which divide from the stem near its top. Each tuft or cluster consists of 5 to 40 bisexual, wind-pollinated flowers that produce tan seed capsules, each splitting into 3 sections. According to one source, the flowers "are very slightly protogynous" (that is, the female parts maturing before male parts), with (female) stigmas ripened even before the flower bud opens; the (male) anthers ripen soon after the flower appears.

Seeds, which spill from split capsules during rains, number from about 100 to 300 per capsule. The orange-brown seeds become sticky when wet, often attaching to pelts, pants, or wheels. The "large slimy transparent masses of seeds," wrote botanist P. W. Richards, resemble "frog's spawn." They remain viable for at least 2 years, probably longer.

This plant's flat, grasslike leaves, shorter by half or two-thirds than the flowering stems, remain fairly inconspicuous. The fibrous, tufted roots, though shallow, grip the ground tightly, making the plant difficult to pull up. Besides reproducing by seed, this plant raises shoots from densely branching underground stems *(rhizomes),* producing cloned clumps near the parent plant. Erect stems die back in winter, leaving green leaf rosettes. Individual plants apparently survive only a few years at most.

Associates: Path rush, especially abundant in the Northeast, resides throughout North America, also ranges globally where introduced. It frequents dry to moist open ground, favors the compacted earth of roadsides, cracks in concrete, gravel pits, fields, human and game trails. Path rush thrives where people do, where footsteps and wheels have packed the ground, creating *anthropophilic* (human-originated) habitats for these whiskery little stems. Path rush tolerates heavy traffic, its wiry stems springing back rapidly after trampling or tire roll-over.

A few insects favor rushes (see *The Book of Swamp and Bog),* but scant research exists on the invertebrate fauna of this rush species.

Although rabbits and deer probably graze path rush, and its seeds may be sampled by gamebirds and songbirds on the ground, its small size and scattered distribution make it a relatively insignificant food source for wildlife.

Lore: Few human uses are recorded for rushes. They supply no food or materials to serve for building or craft.

Path rush, probably introduced from North America into Europe in cattle fodder, appeared in England by 1795, in Belgium by 1824. It has since spread throughout Eurasia, also in China, Australia, and other places. Outside North America, it seems to occupy more restricted habitats, adhering more exclusively to the compacted soils of paths and roadways. "The greatly accelerated spread of the species in Britain," wrote a researcher in England, "may be largely due to the development of motor transport, the 'tread' of the tyres being very suitable for the dispersal of the seeds."

St. John's-wort, Common *(Hypericum perforatum)*. Mangosteen family. Recognize this alien perennial, one of our most common summer wildflowers, by its 5-petaled, inch-broad, yellow flowers, the fringed petals margined by black glandular dots. Held up to the light, its small, opposite, untoothed leaves show translucent dots. Stems are 2-ridged, extending down each side, making them seem flattened. (Ridges also run down branches from the base of each leaf.) Form of the plant is often bushy and unkempt, the flowers numerous and showy on many top branches.

Other names: Goatweed, klamathweed, amber, rosin-rose, tipton weed.

Close relatives: Almost 30 *Hypericum* species, most of them native perennials, annuals, and shrubs, reside in eastern North America. These include St. Peter's-wort *(H. stans)*, St. Andrew's cross *(H. hypericoides)*, spotted St. John's-wort *(H. punctatum)*, dwarf St. John's-wort *(H. mutilum)*, shrubby St. John's-wort *(H. prolificum)*, Aaron's beard *(H. calycinum)*, and orange-grass *(H. gentianoides)*. Marsh St. John's-worts *(Triadenum)*, a closely related genus, are wetland plants. About 400 *Hypericum* species exist worldwide, mainly in north temperate climates. Family relatives include the autograph tree or pitch apple *(Clusia rosa)* and the mangosteen *(Garcinia mangostana)*, a tropical fruit tree.

Lifestyle: St. John's-wort flowers occur in rounded or flattened clusters called *cymes*, in which the terminal flower of each cluster develops and opens first. Each flower, a regular 5-petaled radiating form, is bisexual, showing 3 bushy clumps of (male) stamens in the center surrounding a 3-parted (female) style. Although they are insect-pollinated, these flowers do not rely exclusively upon cross-pollination for reproduction; they can also reproduce asexually *(apomixis)* and by *pseudogamy*, whereby a male gamete merely "knocks at the door," thereby initiating growth of an embryo, but does not fuse with the egg—a mimicry of sexual reproduction without the genetic contribution. Flowering usually begins in June, lasts until September. Withered flowers usually remain on the plant, giving it an increasingly scrubby appearance as the season advances. Soil moisture determines the flowering duration in these plants.

Seeds vary in number from less than 100 to 500 per 3-celled capsule; a typical plant may produce some 15,000 to 30,000 seeds. The sticky seed coats attach to passing animals, shoes, and clothing. One study found that the first expansion of St. John's-worts into an area reflected animal trails and movements. To germinate, seeds generally require a period of 4 to 6 months afterripening; hence few of them germinate the same year they develop. A passage of fire often produces a growth flush of St. John's-wort; the brief heat exposure seems to increase germination of seeds lingering dormant in the soil seed bank. Seeds in the soil may remain viable for 6 to 10 years or longer.

Seedlings may require several years to produce flowering stems (though most plants flower by age two), a period in which they become highly vulnerable to plant competition.

After their first year or so, they become well equipped to compete with other plants by means of a woody taproot that may penetrate the soil to 4 or 5 feet, finding moisture at levels beneath the summer drought-depleted higher levels. One or more root crowns per mature plant may produce up to 30 flowering stems each year. The crowns, spaced apart along *rhizomes* (underground stems), produce colonies of the plant. The horizontal, clone-budding rhizomes, 2 or 3 inches deep, may extend 3 feet or so, but usually only a few inches. Rhizomes may later decay, leaving disconnected clones.

The black glandular dots on petal margins, stems, and underside leaf margins, and the translucent dots in the leaves, contain a fluorescent phototoxic chemical called hypericin, which causes abnormal sensitivity to sunlight (hypericism or erythema) if ingested by insects and mammals. These defensive adaptations to *herbivory* (plant eating) by organisms also give St. John's-wort a competitive edge.

Flowering stems die back to the perennial root crowns in the fall but often remain dead and erect for a year or so. The root crowns may produce numerous branched, prostrate rosettes in the fall. These last over winter, dying before the flowering shoots arise in spring.

St. John's-wort thus reveals a number of competitive survival strategies: its versatile reproductive systems (sexual, asexual, and vegetative); its prolific seed production, dispersal mechanisms, and long viability; its root anatomy, enabling it to access moisture where other plants can't; and its phototoxic defenses. All account for this plant's widespread abundance across much of the continent.

Associates: Fields, roadsides, just about any moderately moist, open, sunny spot within its range hosts St. John's-wort. Its North American range includes the eastern and central continent from southern Canada west to Minnesota and Texas, also the Pacific Northwest. A large midcontinental gap in distribution exists in the prairie states and provinces, where the stress of cold winters has prevented the plant's long-term establishment. Native to Eurasia and North Africa, St. John's-wort now occurs as a weed in 21 countries worldwide. Fairly shade-intolerant, it does not thrive in wet soils. It rapidly responds, however, to the invitations represented by overgrazed or disturbed (including recently burned) landscapes.

Dotted margins of St. John's-wort petals plus translucent dots in the leaves contain a substance that causes phototoxic reactions in insect or mammal herbivores.

St. John's-wort frequently invades fruit crops—especially orchards and lowbush blueberry and strawberry plantations. Spotted knapweed, ox-eye daisy, Queen Anne's lace, and common mullein (all *q.v.*) are common weed associates.

One of the fungi imperfecti, *Colletotrichum gloeosporioides,* causes sunken anthracnose lesions on the stems; infected plants often show red or yellowish foliage, and lesions eventually girdle stems and branches, killing the plant. This disease, endemic in eastern Canada, often appears in blueberry fields where St. John's-wort is present. Other fungi on St. John's-wort include the mildew *Erysiphe communis* and *Uromyces* rusts.

Insect feeders on common St. John's-wort number some 44 in its native lands. Studies indicate that the amounts of hypericin produced in the plant may increase when the plant is attacked by herbivorous insects. Successful foragers have evolved defenses or strategies of their own to counter the light sensitivity created by the plant's chemical defenses. Most foraging insects either avoid the chemical, avoid sunlight, or have a cuticle that screens out the harmful wavelengths.

Several insect species, all exclusive feeders on *Hypericum,* have been imported into North America from the plant's native regions for biocontrol purposes, with varying degrees of success. Two of them—the St. John's-wort beetle *(Chrysolina hyperici)* and the klamath beetle *(C. quadrigemina)*—provide one of America's foremost biocontrol success stories to date. *C. hyperici,* a broad-bodied leaf beetle shaped like a ladybird beetle, is a shiny gold foliage feeder that defoliates entire plants. Its *elytra* (protective wing covers) transmit hardly any light, thus not activating the hypericin that the insect has ingested. Also, the adult beetles seldom fly from plant to plant, not opening their elytra to sunlight exposure. They usually drop quickly from the plant when disturbed. In July, these insects go into a resting phase called *summer diapause,* burrowing into the soil for several weeks and becoming vulnerable to ground beetle (Carabidae) predation. Survivors emerge in late summer to mate and lay eggs that overwinter in St. John's-wort stems and roots. Hatching in spring, the larvae feed only at night, hiding in terminal leaf buds or in the soil during daylight, also pupating in the soil beneath the plants. They emerge as adult insects in early June. *C. hyperici* also transmits the aforementioned *Colletotrichum* anthracnose on its feet and mouthparts, making it an even more effective biocontrol. *C. hyperici,* imported from Atlantic coastal regions of Europe, requires moist sites, whereas *C. quadrigemina,* imported from Mediterranean Europe, favors drier summer habitats. The latter insect, metallic bronze or blue, also feeds extensively on the leaves, has a similar lifestyle pattern. Following the initial introduction of these beetles to western North America via Australia in the late 1940s, researchers found that 3 years of heavy feeding by them could effectively destroy St. John's-wort invasions, opening up thousands of formerly weed-grown acres to new forage capacity and increased plant diversity. It must also be noted, however, that some of the beetle-cleared areas were immediately replaced by invasions of spotted knap-weed *(q.v.)* and tansy-ragwort *(Senecio jacobaea)*, indicating more basic problems, such as overgrazing and erosion, that could not be fixed by biocontrol alone.

Several other insects introduced for biocontrol of St. John's-wort have proven not as effective as the two *Chrysolina* beetles. They include a buprestid beetle *(Agrilus hyperici)*, whose long, white larvae bore into the roots and tapered, reddish bronze adults feed on the foliage in summer; a green aphid *(Aphis chloris)* that sucks sap from leaves and stems; the St. John's-wort inchworm moth *(Anaitis plagiata)*, a reddish brown defoliating caterpillar that mimics a dead twig and feeds on the plant both day and night and whose fall generation feeds on the flowers; and reddish larvae of the klamath weed midge *(Zeuxidiplosis giardi)*. A tiny imported eriophyid mite, *Aculus hyperici,* also feeds on the plant, stunting its growth.

Many moth and butterfly caterpillars feed nonexclusively on St. John's-wort. More than 50 percent of them, one study showed, have concealed feeding habits (rolling or tying leaves, boring into stems or seeds, mining leaves, feeding at night), presumably as defenses from the plant's phototoxin. The velvety green, sluglike caterpillar of the gray or common hairstreak butterfly *(Strymon melinus)* bores into the seed capsules. Gray half-spot moth caterpillars *(Nedra ramosula)*, noctuids, colonies of which prey on the leaf buds, cause leaves to join and form a hollow gall in which they feed. The oval leaf beetle *Graphops curtipennis* feeds on the foliage, as do several leaf tier caterpillars: the spotted fireworm *(Choristoneura parallela)*, the sparganothis fruitworm *(Sparganothis sulfureana)*, and the variegated leafroller *(Platynota flavedana)*, all tortricid moths. Soldier beetles *(Chauliognathus)*, yellow-orange with black striping, are common pollen feeders.

Pollinating insects include bees and butterflies. Among the latter may be seen monarchs *(Danaus plexippus)*, red admirals *(Vanessa atalanta)*, sulphurs (Coliadinae), and skippers (Hesperiidae). Since the flower doesn't produce much nectar, much pollinator activity consists of pollen foraging.

Few records of seed eating by birds or small mammals occur for this plant. Livestock as well as wildlife grazers tend to avoid the grown plants, though the young, succulent plants are readily grazed. If they do ingest it in hay or forage, light-skinned animals may develop severe skin lesions from sunlight sensitivity caused by phototoxic reaction.

Lore: Used at least since the Greek classical age as remedies for a long list of human disorders—including liver and bowel ailments plus hysteria, obesity, and insomnia—St. John's-wort was primarily applied as a wound poultice for the relief of contusions, burns, and sprains, also to soothe the aching feet of Roman soldiers. The plant's pinhole perforations in the leaves (also its red, bloodlike juice when flower buds are squeezed) suggested to medieval physicians via the doctrine of signatures (see Blue-weed) that God intended the plant as a cure for skin punctures or cuts. St. John's-wort remains a favorite plant of modern herbalists, who continue to prescribe it for an astonishing variety of human aches and pains. Without question, *Hypericum* extracts contain beneficial antibiotics and antivirals. The plant came into the limelight most recently in 1984, when German researchers claimed beneficial effects of the plant extract as a mild antidepressant. Sales boomed through the 1980s–90s, with more than a million Americans eventually ingesting the tablets on a regular basis to ease their psychic pain. More recent and rigorous scientific work, however, has called into question the former findings, concluding that the extract is essentially useless as the highly promoted "nature's Prozac."

St. John's-wort has no food potential for humans.

Hypericum's sunlight-sensitive effects are seen mainly in light-skinned animals that have eaten the plant. Animals rarely die from the toxic effects, but they may suffer severe skin irritations and loss of weight.

The plant's namesake is St. John the Baptist, whose feast (birth) day is celebrated on June 24. The summer solstice brings the peak of the flower's bloom in some of its native areas, but the exact origin of its association with the saint remains shrouded in mythology and the use of symbols—including the red hypericin representing his shed blood and the translucent leaf dots depicting the tears of his followers. Perhaps because of its name and curative reputation, St. John's-wort achieved notable usage as a talisman for spiritual protection. Hung in windows and doorways and above icons in loose or wreath form, it reputedly warded off evil demons and poltergeists. Farmers collected and burned the plants on the saint's day to protect their property from devils and witches. Indeed, few other plants figure so prominently in European folklore. Its magical powers were said to extend to rats—the Pied Piper supposedly used sprigs of St. John's-wort to lure the vermin from Hamelin in 1284.

Since St. John's-wort became the subject of possibly the first biocontrol projects in North America, the phenomenal success of that early experiment provided much impetus for subsequent biocontrol efforts against many kinds of invasive weeds, resulting in greater or lesser degrees of success (most often the latter).

In most places where it exists today as an alien, the plant was apparently deliberately imported as a medicinal herb. Pioneer botanist John Bartram not only recorded its presence as "a very pernicious weed" in 1758 Pennsylvania, but also noted its phototoxic effects. Some sources, however, say that the plant arrived accidentally in grass and grain seeds of colonists and was first recorded about 30 years later, in Massachusetts.

Wort is the old English term for "plant"; *Hypericum,* derived from the Greek, means "above a picture," that is, power over an apparition.

Sandbur, Common *(Cenchrus longispinus).* Grass family. This native annual grass sprawls in mats, erecting spiny-clustered stems up to 3 feet tall. The burs, about 1/8 inch long, stiff and sharp, "hurt bad when you pull them out of your shoelaces," as one observer noted—they hurt even worse when stepped on by bare feet. Leaves, 2 to 5 inches long, are smooth and twisted. This grass flowers and seeds in summer and fall.

Other names: Longspine, mat, or field sandbur, burgrass, bear grass, sandspur, grass-bur, innocent-weed.

Close relatives: About 20 *Cenchrus* species range globally, most in warm regions. Other North American species include hedgehog-grass *(C. echinatus)* and dune-sandbur *(C. tribuloides).* Several unrelated spiny or burred, grasslike sedges exist, most in wetland habitats.

Lifestyle: Sandbur floral biology resembles that of most grasses (see Bluegrasses). Flower spikelets, as in many grasses, consist of only 2 florets—a single, fertile, bisexual floret topping a neuter or staminate (male) floret. Look closely and you will see that these spikelets or earlets are enclosed by the spiny bur, which actually forms a thorny, protective fence. Ten to 30 of these pea-size burs, each projecting 45 to 75 long, stiffly recurved barbs, cluster along each flower spike *(raceme).* Later, each fiercely spined bur encloses 1 to 3 seeds. Each bur apparently contains 2 types of seed that vary in length of dormancy; the seeds from the upper parts of spikelets can usually germinate within a year, whereas seeds from the lower parts require a longer dormancy.

Light apparently inhibits the germination of sandbur seeds—most seedlings emerge from soil burial of an inch or less, but seeds can germinate from depths of 4 inches or so. Seeds seldom remain viable longer than 3 years. Sandbur also reproduces vegetatively, by rooting at stem nodes where they touch the ground, sometimes producing large mats of cloned plants. Roots are shallow and fibrous.

Associates: Sandbur frequents open, dry, sandy soil—fields, roadsides, beaches, disturbed habitats. It can withstand drought but not much plant competition. Thus, like many annuals, it tends to pioneer early plant succession, often becomes a pest in newly seeded pastures. Widespread throughout the continent, sandbur apparently originated in the West, spreading eastward as invited by land disturbance.

This plant's foremost fungal parasite, sandbur smut *(Sporisorium syntherisimae),* produces windblown spores

A bare foot that trods on common sandbur will not walk that way again; this grass favors sandy areas and beaches, exactly where bare feet abound.

that invade those spiny fences lined along the racemes, destroying every bur in severe infesta-tions. "A similar undescribed species," reported one researcher, infects "only the seed, leaving the bur intact, and hence has evolved to utilize the long distance dissemination mechanism (us mammals) of the host." Other fungi may include *Ustilago* smut and *Puccinia* rusts.

Sandbur is one of the grass hosts for the wheat curl mite *(Aceria tosichella)*, a vector of wheat streak mosaic and high plains viruses, destructive diseases of corn and wheat. The mites, visible with a pocket magnifier, lie in protected crevices of the plant or in depressions between leaf veins, float like dust particles on air currents. Infected plants may show distorted leaves.

Being annuals, sandburs must rely on seed dispersion for population survival, estab-lishing new colonies in areas of scant competition. Probably the spiny bur functions as much for dispersion as for flower and seed protection. Burs efficiently cling to animal fur, clothing, shoes, even tires, thereby making associates of all adherent passers-by.

Sandburs have scant food value. The only bird recorded as feeding on the seeds to any extent is the pyrrhuloxia, a grayish southwestern cardinal. Probably some other ground finches consume them also.

Livestock avoid the mature plants, which can injure mouths, noses, and eyes, but they readily graze the young, burless seedlings, as do white-tailed deer.

Lore: The name *Cenchrus* derives from the Greek word *kegchros,* apparently a general-ized term for "millet."

Sandbur has no known history of medicinal or other uses in folk or tribal cultures.

Self-heal *(Prunella vulgaris).* Mint family. Recognize this blue-flowered native perennial mint by its square stems; its opposite, almost toothless leaves; and its violet, hooded flow-ers with fringed lower lips crowded among densely leafy bracts. (Pinkish or white-flowered plants also occasionally appear.) The square-shaped or oblong spike surmounts a 3- to 12-inch-tall stem. Flowering from early summer into fall, the plant tends to sprawl on the ground, raising only its flowering branches erect. Unlike most mints, self-heal has no aroma.

Other names: Heal-all, allheal, blue curls, blue lucy, brownwort, carpenter weed.

Close relatives: Only 4 *Prunella* species exist worldwide. Cut-leaved self-heal *(P. lacini-ata),* a white-flowered, much hairier herb, occasionally appears as a waif plant. Self-heal somewhat resembles the related wood-mints *(Blephilia).* North American family relatives include mints *(Mentha),* catnip *(q.v.),* wild bergamot *(q.v.),* sages *(Salvia),* and many others.

Lifestyle: Mint family flowers usually appear in one of 2 distinct forms—in leaf angles along the stem, or atop the plant. Self-heal exhibits one of the latter forms. It produces 1 to 10 flowering stems from a root, each stem bearing up to 6 paired, flowering branches. Self-heal's blue flowers appear closely packed in tiers or whorls on the thick flower spike. Each tier—some 6 to 12 total—consists of sets displaying 3 stalkless flowers that emerge in the angles of green, hairy, closely set bracts. Flowering on the spike is irregular, with entire tiers seldom blooming all at once, so the spike usually looks somewhat ragged and only partially flowered. Tiers begin flowering from the apex toward the base, however, and on any given spike, flowers may occur in all stages of development—in bud, in bloom, or setting seed. The spikes continue to elongate as flower tiers develop, may finally extend more than 3 inches.

Each flower consists of 5 petals fused into 2 lips. The upper lip forms a wide, flat hood with a peaked roof that shelters 2 pairs of (male) stamens and a long (female) pistil extending between them. The lower lip, shorter and 3-lobed, forms a landing platform for visitors to this bisexual,

Self-heal's short, thick spike produces blue flowers at irregular intervals, progressing downward from the top.

insect-pollinated flower. In entering the corolla tube, at the bottom of which pools the sought-after nectar, the furry heads and thoraxes of bees become dusted with pollen that, in flowers of subsequent visits, rubs off onto the jostled stigmas, thus effecting cross-pollination. Self-heal flowers are also self-compatible, can produce abundant seed without cross-pollination.

Four 1-sided nutlets develop from each flower; the spike now somewhat resembles a stubby ear of corn. Seeds usually remain viable no longer than a year. In the meantime, the plant extends prostrate leafy stems in every direction. These stems produce new roots at their nodes, often forming clonal colonies, the green rosettes of which survive over winter and raise new flowering stems in the spring.

Self-heal roots are shallow and fibrous.

Associates: Adaptable to just about any habitat—wet or dry, disturbed or pristine, along streams and roadsides, in shaded woods, open fields, and suburban lawns—self-heal adds a touch of blue almost everywhere. In my own observation, it favors low-lying, dampish spots along forest roads or in fields. Native forms of the plant grow in both Eurasia and North America (the alien European variety also grows in North America). Self-heal ranges globally, aggressive but not as much so as many invasive alien weeds.

Few fungi or insects parasitize this plant. Most insect activity focuses on the flowers. Bumblebees *(Bombus)* are probably its chief pollinators; they also collect large quantities of pollen from this plant, combing it from their fur and packing it into their enlarged hind tarsi or pollen baskets. Other bees plus butterflies—clouded or common sulphurs *(Colias philodice)*, swallowtails *(Papilio)*, American painted ladies *(Vanessa virginiensis)*, among others—also pollinate the plant.

Among birds, common redpolls are known to feed on the seeds in winter, and ruffed grouse devour leaves and seeds. Probably some other ground-feeding birds consume the seeds as well, but self-heal is not an important wildlife food source.

Lore: "It always suggests freshness and coolness, from the places where it grows," wrote Thoreau of the plant he called prunella. Many botanists over the years have labeled self-heal an alien, imported to American gardens as a medicinal herb. Although Eurasian forms of the plant have certainly invaded and today exist in America, credible evidence shows that the native variety, *P. v. lanceolata* (identified by its narrower leaves), dwelled here long before colonial settlement.

Chippewa, Mohegan, and Delaware tribes, among others, brewed teas from self-heal to treat fevers and dysentery. "There is not a better wound herb in the world," wrote English herbalist John Gerard in 1633. "It is an especial remedy for all green wounds to close the lips of them," wrote physician Nicholas Culpeper in 1652. Between its functions of chemistry and suture, self-heal was truly viewed as a miracle plant, according to all the old herbalists (not to say hyperbolists), literally a cure-all for just about any human pain or unpleasantness. But "these uses have not withstood the rigorous testing of modern medicine," according to researcher Laurence J. Crockett. Its popular name heal-all reflected the plant's ample uses in Europe for a roster of human ailments. According to the doctrine of signatures belief (see Blue-weed), self-heal's throatlike corollas suggested it as a remedy for mouth sores and sore throat (quinsy). Today the plant's main recognized medicinal benefit is probably as an effective astringent, useful for stopping blood flow from a cut or wound as well as for poulticing sores and, taken internally, for treating diarrhea. It contains ursolic acid, an antitumor and diuretic compound, and the plant also possesses astringent antibiotic qualities plus possible capacities of lowering blood pressure and blocking genetic mutations.

This plant, lacking the strongly aromatic character of most mints, is humanly palatable as neither food nor flavoring.

The name *Prunella* apparently stems from the German label *Brunella* for this plant, in turn deriving from the word *bruen,* "brown," the plant's final color in the fall.

Soapwort *(Saponaria officinalis).* Pink family. This common alien perennial spreads 5 scallop-tipped, slightly notched, white or pinkish petals, bent slightly backward (reflexed), from a 3/4-inch-long floral tube (the *calyx,* consisting of the fused sepals). The dark green leaves are smooth, untoothed, and opposite, their bases forming a collar around the stem, giving stem joints a swollen appearance. Flowering from July into fall, the plant stands 1 to 2 feet tall, often in large colonies.

Other names: Bouncing Bet, hedge pink, bruisewort, fuller's herb, scourwort, many others.

Close relatives: About 30 *Saponaria* species exist, all natives of temperate Eurasian regions. Soapwort somewhat resembles the related genera of campions and catchflies *(Lychnis, Silene).* Other family relatives include common chickweed *(q.v.),* corn-cockle *(Agrostemma githago),* baby's breaths *(Gypsophila),* pinks *(Dianthus),* carnation *(D. caryophyllus),* plus many others.

Lifestyle: Spicy-scented soapwort flowers occur in tight clusters *(panicles)* on short stems at and near the top of the plant. Both double flowers and double petals may commonly be seen, indicating that this species is probably in a current state of evolutionary flux. Each insect-pollinated flower projects from its center of 10 (male) stamens in 2 sequential sets and 1 (female) pistil divided into 2 stalks, or *styles.* Indeed, the reflexed petals surrounding the sexual organs give the impression of flagrant thrust—this is a gaudy, unshy flower. The entire plant appears somewhat coarse in form and feature, ranking low in the consensus qualities of beauty and grace.

Soapwort's flower, about an inch across, is sequentially unisexual, or *protandrous* (the male parts developing and declining before female parts mature); its pistil remains hidden until the flower's abundant pollen is gone, then opens up, exposing itself and exhaling fragrance, luring insects from younger, still-pollinating flowers, and thus averting self-pollination. Soapwort's fragrance tends to increase at sundown, attracting night-flying moths (see Associates). The sexual stages sometimes overlap, however, and individual soapwort flowers can and do self-pollinate. Seeds develop and spill numerously from oval capsules.

Soapwort projects its floral organs forward in a petals-bent-back display, attracting moth pollinators at night; its floral tubes become the long seed capsules shown.

This plant also reproduces vegetatively, cloning itself into colonies by sprouting from short, branched, almost woody underground stems *(rhizomes)*.

Associates: Some of the first American colonists brought soapwort from Europe as a medicinal and useful household herb (see Lore). The plant rapidly escaped colonial kitchen gardens and yard strips, now ranges throughout most temperate regions of North America and the globe. It favors disturbed, desolate spots—vacant lots, roadsides, railroads, ditch banks, sometimes fields and pastures. ("It's surprising," wrote researcher Laurence J. Crockett, "that no one has called *Saponaria officinalis* railroad weed.") Although it thrives best in moist, sandy soil, it is also drought-tolerant, thus widely adaptive to many habitats. In most areas, the plant seems quite thoroughly *naturalized* (that is, not extremely competitive with native vegetation).

Several parasitic fungi widely affect plants of the pink family. *Alternaria* leaf spot or blight *(Alternaria saponariae)* appears fairly often.

Insect foliage feeders appear uncommon on this plant, perhaps owing to its chemistry (see Lore). One common leaf feeder is the twice-stabbed stink bug *(Cosmopepla bimaculata)*, so-named from the 2 red spots on its black back. Another is an alien leaf-eating lady beetle called Jacques' beetle or alfalfa ladybird *(Subcoccinella vigintiquatuorpunctata)*.

Soapwort's chief pollinators are probably night-flying moths. A patch of soapwort at dusk is an excellent place to watch for sphinx or hawk moths, which include some of the larger, more spectacular lepidopterans. Among these may be seen the five-spotted hawk moth *(Manduca quinquemaculata)*, the pawpaw sphinx *(Dolba hyloeus)*, the hermit sphinx *(Sphinx eremitus)*, the laurel sphinx *(S. kalmiae)*, the apple sphinx *(S. gordius)*, the ello sphinx *(Erinnyis ello)*, the hummingbird or common clearwing sphinx *(Hemaris thysbe)*, the slender clearwing *(H. gracilis)*, the pandorus sphinx *(Eumorpha pandorus)*, the white-lined sphinx *(Hyles lineata)*, the galium sphinx *(H. gallii)*—and possibly others as well. (A moth field guide will help an observer identify these species.) Other frequent pollinators include halictid bees (Halictidae), colonial ground nesters.

A few ground-feeding birds, such as vesper sparrows, probably consume the seeds, though data are slim. Unpalatable to grazers, the plant seems generally avoided by mammals. Eaten in any quantity, it can poison horses, cattle, and poultry.

Soapwort's most important associate—as is true of most plants we label weeds—is undoubtedly humankind, without whose helpful interventions the plant would surely be much rarer than it is.

Lore: Romans of 2,000 years ago called this plant *herba lanaria*, "wool herb," for its usage in washing and shrinking wool. Though long used by many peoples and cultures as an important, gentle substitute for soap, this plant does not contain or produce real soap, though it duplicates wash day lathers in its foamy suds and detergent (grease-cutting) effects. The soapy substance is a glycoside called saponin, brought forth by crushing the stems, leaves, and roots in water. Native to Eurasia, soapwort arrived in England during the Middle Ages. The plant decorated most European cottage gardens, was especially used for washing delicate linens, silks, woolens, and fragile fabrics such as old curtains and tapestries; it still finds occasional use for these purposes. It is said that Londoners, in presewer days, planted soapworts to deodorize their streets and alleys, calling the flower "London pride." Owners of textile mills during the early Industrial Revolution often planted adjacent fields of soapwort as a ready source of detergent. Even today, a soapwort solution can clean and polish glass and china as well as or better than most commercial formulas.

Probably soapwort's rapid spread in North America owes to "the aid of thrifty settlers fond of clean laundry," as one observer wrote. Along with its sink-and-basin utility, however, soapwort has a roster of remedies for everything from leprosy to liver ailments, with coughs and kidney stones between. Saponin, anti-inflammatory, encourages bile flow, is not only laxative but purgative. Herbalists have widely recommended it as a poultice for boils and skin rashes, including poison ivy. Saponins are also mildly toxic; all parts of the plant, especially the seeds, may cause gastric distress to people and livestock, which may accidentally ingest it in feed and hay. Drying and storage do not dispel the toxin. Thus soapwort has no food value, even in direst emergency. Yet old-time brewers, noting its suds, used its saponins to produce a frothy head on beer (probably one's hangover hurt only slightly worse for the foam topping).

The plant's generic name *Saponaria* derives from the Latin *sapo,* "soap." *Officina,* the species name, means "workshop," denoting a plant for practical uses. Bouncing Bet, one of the plant's common names, is said to stem from an old term for a vigorous washwoman, "bouncing Betty." "The inflated calyx and scalloped petals of the flower," according to one folklorist, "suggested the rear view of a laundress, her numerous petticoats pinned up."

Saponins exist in hundreds of plants, but the proportion in soapwort (some 5 percent) measures more than in most.

Sorrel, Sheep *(Rumex acetosella).* Smartweed family. Identify this slim, 4- to 12-inch-tall alien perennial by its halberd-shaped leaves with lobed, pointed bases, and by its loose, spikelike clusters *(racemes)* of tiny greenish flowers that turn to brownish red seed stalks.

Other names: Common, red, field, or wild sorrel, sour dock, sourgrass.

Close relatives: See Dock, Curly. Garden or green sorrel *(R. acetosa),* another alien, is often cultivated for greens. *Rumex* plants are unrelated to wood sorrels *(Oxalis).*

Lifestyle: A thin, reddish ground cover on poor land in summer is probably sheep sorrel, which often colonizes large tracts that other plants don't want. Sexes occur separately on different plants *(dioecious)* in this species (with occasional instances of male, female,

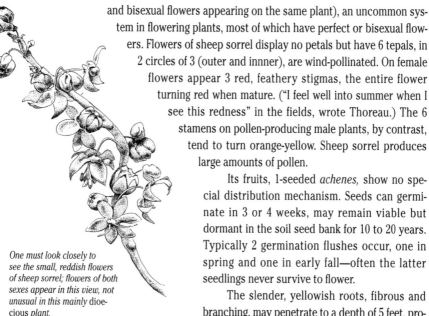

and bisexual flowers appearing on the same plant), an uncommon system in flowering plants, most of which have perfect or bisexual flowers. Flowers of sheep sorrel display no petals but have 6 tepals, in 2 circles of 3 (outer and innner), are wind-pollinated. On female flowers appear 3 red, feathery stigmas, the entire flower turning red when mature. ("I feel well into summer when I see this redness" in the fields, wrote Thoreau.) The 6 stamens on pollen-producing male plants, by contrast, tend to turn orange-yellow. Sheep sorrel produces large amounts of pollen.

One must look closely to see the small, reddish flowers of sheep sorrel; flowers of both sexes appear in this view, not unusual in this mainly dioecious plant.

Its fruits, 1-seeded *achenes,* show no special distribution mechanism. Seeds can germinate in 3 or 4 weeks, may remain viable but dormant in the soil seed bank for 10 to 20 years. Typically 2 germination flushes occur, one in spring and one in early fall—often the latter seedlings never survive to flower.

The slender, yellowish roots, fibrous and branching, may penetrate to a depth of 5 feet, producing an underground tangle that "can be a gardener's nightmare," wrote one busy weeder. The entire root system can produce buds; even a 1/2-inch fragment can regenerate a new shoot, and unless every particle of the easily broken root is weeded, the plant will likely sprout again. The roots also extend horizontally and rhizomelike (true *rhizomes,* or underground stems, bud from the roots but are not themselves roots), sending up erect clones from their tips. Sheep sorrel's root extensions, rather than its seeding, probably account for most of its colonial spread. Both seedlings and root sprouts produce leafy rosettes, from which may arise several flowering stems. Individual root crowns probably last about 18 months, by which time their creeping roots have produced several other crowns. Thus a given patch or clonal group of sheep sorrel may be decades old.

Associates: Sheep sorrel favors deprived ground—that is, dry, sandy, disturbed soil in open areas. It thrives on acidic soils of low fertility. Although long regarded as an acid-soil indicator, sheep sorrel hardly restricts itself to such soils. Its presence there may not necessarily owe to its inherent preference for low pH, but—as some researchers and studies suggest—being acid-tolerant, it may simply encounter less plant competition in such sites.

"What a wholesome red!" exclaimed Thoreau, seeing the June sheep sorrel in Concord fields. "It is densest," he noted, "in parallel lines according to the plowing or cultivation." Sheep sorrel also frequently occurs in flood- and fire-disturbed sites. The plant adapts to less ravaged habitats as well, however, sometimes invades woodlands and undisturbed soils. A native of Eurasia, sheep sorrel occurs throughout most of North America and in temperate regions worldwide.

Probably sheep sorrel's most common fungal parasite is a leaf spot *(Cercospora acetosella)*, one of the fungi imperfecti. Sheep sorrel is also the most common winter host for *Botrytis cinerea*, gray mold fungus, which spreads to lowbush blueberry *(Vaccinium angustifolium)* flowers in spring, producing blight and tip dieback of the shrubs.

Sheep sorrel, though usually not highly competitive with other plants in areas of medium or high soil fertility, does compete in some areas with wild strawberry *(q.v.)*, also in cultivated strawberry plantations.

Probably the plant's only major insect forager is the downy, slug-shaped, reddish or bright green caterpillar of the American copper butterfly *(Lycaena phlaeas)*. This butterfly produces spring and summer broods. The adult males, showing black-spotted, copper-colored forewings, defend small territories centered on sunny patches of sheep sorrel, often darting at other butterflies, also at birds and even persons who dare to intrude. Some other *Lycaena* caterpillars may also feed on this *Rumex*.

Ants frequently harvest mature seeds of sheep sorrel, dispersing them to their mounds. Probably many clonal patches of sheep sorrel have started from anthills.

Bumblebees *(Bombus)*, honeybees *(Apis mellifera)*, and some of the smaller butterflies visit the male plants, collecting or feeding on the abundant pollen.

Sheep sorrel provides a major food resource for many birds, mainly ground-feeding seedeaters. Ruffed and sharp-tailed grouse, ring-necked pheasants, greater prairie-chickens, northern bobwhites, wild turkeys, and American woodcocks consume the seeds—as do horned larks, red-winged blackbirds, bobolinks, hoary redpolls, and many sparrows (field, fox, grasshopper, savannah, song, American tree, vesper, and white-crowned). Meadow voles and white-footed mice also eat the seeds. Poultry, cottontail rabbits, and deer readily graze the plant. This plant is, however, potentially toxic to livestock, which do not feed on it if other forage is available. Sheep sorrel's nutritional values as well as energy and protein contents are generally ranked poor to fair.

Lore: Sheep sorrel's sour, pungent taste, similar to that of the unrelated wood sorrels, emanates from potassium oxalate acid crystals in the foliage. The leaves make a pleasant-tasting salad, cooked green, or trail-nibble, but its oxalates make it toxic to mammals in large quantity.

Despite its poor forage ranking, sheep sorrel is rich in vitamin C and several other vitamins, as well as carotinoids. Herbalists and practitioners of folk medicine have long cherished the plant for its reputed curative qualities—in poultices for tumors and as teas for diarrhea, fevers, and other ailments. It "sharpens the appetite, assuages heat, cools the

liver and strengthens the heart," maintained English diarist John Evelyn in 1720. The profuse pollen, on the other hand, can bother hay-fever sufferers.

Although of Eurasian origin, sheep sorrel has apparently resided in North America for
a very long time; for, as Cree writer-historian Bernard Assiniwi wrote of this plant, "No
Algonquin Ojibway child can ever forget 'jiwisi' the sour leaf." Many native tribes readily
adopted the plant into their medicinal troves and lore.

Classified as a noxious weed in 23 states, sheep sorrel proves difficult to eradicate,
once established, owing to its perennial creeping rootstocks, any fragment of which may
readily produce a new plant. Heavy grazing and land abuse invites its presence; fertile,
well-treated land seldom hosts sheep sorrel.

This plant still plays a large part in commemorative rites of the Irish, celebrating their
victory at County Meath over Norse invaders in the year 980. The blood red hue of sorrel
on midsummer's Tara Hill, it is said, symbolizes the graves of the patriot defenders.

The word *sorrel* stems from the French *sur,* meaning "sour." The sheep association
probably refers to the plant's usage as forage in poor pastures. *Rumex* is the Latin word for
docks; *acetosella,* the species name, means "slightly acid" or "vinegar salts."

This plant metaphorized a values decision by 19th-century English poet Algernon
Charles Swinburne: "Shall I strew on thee rose or rue or laurel. . . . Or simplest growth of
meadow-sweet or sorrel?"

Speedwells (*Veronica* species). Figwort family. Recognize these low, creeping,
mostly alien perennials by their opposite leaves and tiny, 4-petaled, violet or lavender flowers (the bottom petal smaller than the 3 others) on loose spikes *(racemes)* atop branching
stems. Some species display solitary flowers in leaf angles.

The most familiar species include common speedwell *(V. officinalis),* downy with shal-
low-toothed, stalked leaves; germander or bird's-eye speedwell *(V. chamedrys),* also woolly
with unstalked, toothed leaves and a widely spaced raceme; and creeping or slender speedwell *(V. filiformis),* with larger flowers on threadlike stalks.

Other names: Fluellin, ground-hale, gypsy-weed, Paul's-betony.

Close relatives: Some 20 *Veronica* species, of about 300 worldwide, reside in North
America, but few are native. Several wetland species exist. Others in addition to the aforementioned species include thyme-leaved speedwell *(V. serpyllifolia),* with small, oval,
toothless leaves; purslane-speedwell *(V. peregrina),* a native annual with linear leaves; corn
or field speedwell *(V. arvensis);* and brooklime *(V. beccabunga).* Family relatives include
common mullein, beard-tongues, butter-and-eggs, and painted cup (all *q.v.*), among others.

Lifestyle: Speedwells form dense patches and mats, erecting their flower stalks only a few inches above their prostrate creeping stems. Floral biology of all the species is similar except that several of the less common species are annuals, completing their life cycles within a year.

Inconspicuous in the grass, speedwells' tiny flowers attract attention only when masses of them appear from spring through summer. Colorwise, naturalist John Burroughs called *Veronica* "a small and delicate edition of our hepatica, done in indigo blue"—the shade of blue known to some Chinese artists as "the sky after rain." The plant's colonial habit plus its clustered racemes help make it visible. Its insect-pollinated flowers are *protogynous* (sequentially unisexual, the female parts maturing and declining before the male parts, thus aiding chances of cross-pollination). Two hornlike (male) stamens stretch outward from either side of the top petal. Grasped by an insect visitor probing for nectar, they dust the visitor's underside with pollen, thus furbishing the insect for a subsequent visit to a flower still in female phase, the flower's sticky (female) stigma projecting over its dwarf lower petal, its stamens not yet ready. The flower's *corolla* (all the petals collectively) "is so lightly attached," wrote one observer, "that the least jarring causes it to drop." Speedwell flowers close at night and remain closed in the rain. At least some speedwell species can self-fertilize inside the closed flower (a process called *cleistogamy*) during lengthy periods of wet weather.

Flattened, heart-shaped capsules contain numerous seeds. Speedwells reproduce not only by seed, but also by rooting where the prostrate stems touch the ground. The stems of germander speedwell show 2 fuzzy lines of long hairs descending from each pair of leaves, perhaps defensive barriers against crawling insect herbivores.

Associates: Speedwells occupy north temperate regions worldwide, generally favoring open areas, though habitat preferences exist among species. Common speedwell favors dry fields and upland woods, especially along trails or in clearings. Germander speedwell invades woodland as well, also resides along roadsides and trails and in lawns. Creeping speedwell often appears in lawns and gardens. Thoreau noted speedwells growing in pasture hollows "where perchance a rock has formerly been taken out," also in grassy ruts of old cart paths.

Common fungal parasites include downy and powdery mildews plus septoria leaf spot *(Septoria veronicae),* the latter causing small, circular spots that eventually coalesce on the leaves, causing defoliation. *Sorosphaera veronicae,* a plasmodiophorid fungus, causes swollen, oblong stem galls on speedwells. *Sclerotium rolfsii,* a blight fungus, kills the plant, causing brown patches in infested areas.

Darker blue striping on the flower of most *Veronica* species ("a pretty little blue-veined face," wrote Thoreau) probably serve as *nectar guides* for landing insects. Few data exist, however, regarding insect (or any other) feeders on speedwells. Chief pollinators

Recognize ground-hugging speedwells by their small, 4-petaled, assymetrical flowers, pollinated mainly by syrphid or hover flies.

include syrphid flies (Syrphidae) such as the drone fly *(Eristalis tenax)*, resembling the honeybee. Bees and small butterflies also visit the flowers.

Probably ground birds consume the seeds, but again, data are lacking. The plants' smallness and inconspicuous occurrence probably render them inconsequential food plants. One of the speedwells' glycoside components, aucubin (also found in plantains and common mullein, both *q.v.*) can be toxic to grazers.

Lore: Some sources claim that common speedwell may indeed be a native North American as well as European resident. The Cherokee, it is said, used it for treating various ailments. Most sources, however, identify this species as an alien import, one that probably arrived in grains and hay forage with the first colonists. Also, many a settler's shoe boarded ship, no doubt, with a speedwell seed stuck to its sole. Indeed, the sister ship of the *Mayflower* was christened the *Speedwell*, reflecting a tradition of handing bouquets of the blue flowers to departing travelers with the blessing "Speed well."

The plants' English name, apparently associated with farewells, may also refer to the flower's easy dislodgment, or to its familiar presence along roadways and paths, its color bidding travelers a cheery "Godspeed." But "the most entertaining explanation," wrote one observer, is that English peasants brewed an expectorant from the plant's leaves to treat colds, earning it the good name "spit-well." The genus name *Veronica* stems from St. Veronica (Greek words *veron* and *ikon,* meaning "true image"), a Jewish maiden who, in Roman Catholic hagiography, wiped the face of a cross-bearing Jesus with her towel, thus preserving the sacred image on the linen relic and naming herself thereby. "Medieval flower lovers, whose piety seems to have been eclipsed only by their imaginations," wrote botanist Neltje Blanchan, "named this little flower from a fancied resemblance to the relic."

Too insubstantial and too bitter to use as food plants, speedwells have a long history of usage in "the-bitterer-the-better" folk medicine. Stems, leaves, and roots, boiled for tea or packed into poultices, treated coughs, stomach and urinary ailments, gout, rheumatism, and skin diseases, among other ills. As astringents and tonics, they "purified the blood," also eased breathing for asthmatics. Speedwell herbal remedies apparently found particular usage among Welsh peasantry. Modern herbalists still prescribe the plant. Common speedwell, used in the manufacture of some vermouths, also adds some bite to absinthe.

Popular greenhouse varieties of *Veronica* (usually *V. gentianoides*) rarely need replacement as border plantings once established. Of *V. filiformis,* one botanist wrote that "if a person once puts it on his property, he will always have something growing there." This species may completely take over a lawn—which may not be all bad if one seeks a colorful ground cover or erosion control on a terrace or bank.

Spurges *(Euphorbia* species). Spurge family. Recognize these plants, which bloom in spring and summer, by their small flowers that, in common species, occur in branched, flat-topped clusters *(umbels)* atop the leafy stems, and by their milky sap. Species otherwise vary to such an extent that a completely inclusive generic description is difficult.

Three of our most common spurges are leafy spurge *(E. esula),* an alien, green-flowered perennial with pairs of yellow-green bracts and linear leaves, and with few lateral branches, standing up to 2 feet tall; cypress spurge *(E. cyparissias),* an alien perennial with small, densely crowded, cypresslike leaves on many lateral branches, also green-flowered, but with paired floral bracts, a smaller plant standing 6 to 12 inches high; and flowering spurge *(E. corollata),* a white-flowered native perennial with 5 petal-like bracts, standing 1 to 3 feet tall.

Other names: Wolf's-milk, Faitour's grass *(E. esula);* graveyard spurge *(E. cyparissias);* prairie baby's breath *(E. corollata).*

Close relatives: More than 30 *Euphorbia* species—of about 1,500 globally—reside in northeastern North America. Some of these include wartweed *(E. helioscopia),* fire-on-the-mountain *(E. cyathophora),* ipecac spurge *(E. ipecacuanhae,* a widely used emetic), snow-on-the-mountain *(E. marginata),* and milk-purslane *(E. maculata).* The poinsettia *(E. pulcherrima),* a popular Christmas plant, is native to Mexico. Spurges, one of the world's largest plant families, number some 7,500 species. Members include 3 economically important natives of Brazil: the rubber tree *(Hevea brasiliensis),* source of natural rubber latex; the cassava or manioc *(Manihot esculenta),* vital starch and tapioca source; and the castor bean *(Ricinus communis),* source of castor oil.

Lifestyle: Carpeting open country with canopies of bright yellow-green in early summer, leafy spurge gleams with shiny nectar droplets in its flowers and a sweet fragrance that bathes the air around its colonies. Cypress spurge emits likewise, its denser foliage and branches identifying it. The 2 species seldom occur together; where they do, hybrids often occur.

Spurges share with aster family plants (composites) some optical illusions and mimicry (though not a similar form) concerning the "flower." What appears to be a tiny flower arranged in a cluster of them is actually a structure called a *cyathium,* consisting of a cup-shaped *involucre.* Inside the involucre, some 11 to 20 male flowers surround each 3-part (female) pistil, producing orange, sticky pollen masses that clump together. The pistillate stalk elongates as it ages; male flowers last only 2 to 5 days. Around the involucral rim lie 4 large, crescent-shaped glands that secrete copious nectar. The central cyathium, which is oldest and usually aborts, stands surrounded by 25 to 60 other ciathia; the entire mock inflorescence, mimicking a cluster of single flowers, is termed the *pseudocyme.* Each apparent entire flower, in other words, actually consists of separate arrangements of several unisexual flowers that, together, form numerous bisexual groupings. (The apparent petals are really heart-shaped bracts that support the small central flowers.) Such groups within groups illustrate the fact that variations on the sexual theme abound in the plant kingdom; as one country botanist expressed it, "There ain't just one way." The aspect of entire flowers condensing in form to the sexual structures of the typical flowers displayed by most species—and then displaying these structures in the gross form of a conventional flower—makes spurge flowers some of the most botanically complex that exist, also represents an evolutionary option unique in North America to this genus.

A whorl of small leaves circles the base of the stem-top floral branches. All of the tiny unisexual flowers crowded together at the tips of radiating branches are insect-pollinated, though leafy spurge—and probably others—can also self-pollinate. Female flowers in the centers of the cyathia usually mature and invert themselves on their stalks before male flowers develop, hindering chances of self-pollination.

Seeds ripen about 30 days after pollination occurs. Spurge fruits are 3-chambered capsules *(regmas),* each chamber producing a seed with a yellowish *caruncle,* a fleshy outgrowth, at one end. These seed capsules are audibly explosive; when mature, they shoot their contents outward with great force, up to 15 feet away. Once hurled, the seeds may be further dispersed by birds, mammals, insects, or farm machinery, or in hay and fodder. Look for seedling plants mainly on the outer edges of a colony; a patch of spurge in optimal habitat may expand almost 3 feet in a year. Seeds may remain viable for 5 to 8 years, germinating best after a period of freezing or cold stratification (winter). Individual plants of leafy spurge may produce up to 300 seeds; cypress spurge plants may shoot 900 or more.

Cypress spurge, however, presents some special reproductive circumstances, based upon 2 different North American chromosomal populations: Those with diploid (double) chromosomes have sterile pollen, thus cannot produce or reproduce by seed, whereas the tetraploid (with 4 sets of chromosomes) populations are fertile and produce seed. The 2 cypress spurge types also present somewhat different colonial aspects: Whereas both forms create colonies by means of vegetative reproduction, the sterile diploid plants, which must rely solely on this means, tend to occur in a continuous, uniform spread; the tetraploid populations tend to form circular clusters, expanding in diameter as they vegetatively reproduce from a single-seedling origin. The tetraploid patches "may eventually coalesce to form stands many square yards in extent," wrote one research team, "in which case they can be mistaken for sterile diploid stands."

Also complex are spurge root systems, consisting of vertical plus long and short horizontal roots. Taproots, with thick, corky bark, contain abundant starch reserves. They commonly extend 6 feet downward but sometimes more than twice as far, enabling the plants to survive long periods of drought. The horizontal short or feeder root system usually lasts only a single growing season, but the long, lateral, rhizomelike roots produce buds that give rise to cloning shoots in spring. Spurge colonies more frequently expand by these spreading roots rather than by seed. Root fragments, such as plows and harrows create—even as small as 1/2 inch long—can also bud and produce new plants. Root buds, whether from the root crown, a horizontal extension, or a fragment, develop most readily in the spring; they slow when the plants flower in June and July, increase development again in late summer, and virtually cease by fall. Spurge stems all die back to the soil surface in the fall. Leafy spurge leaves often redden before dropping.

Spurges' white sap or latex, sticky and caustic, helps deter insect herbivores. Chemically it consists of an irritating ingenane ester known as 13-hydroxyinginol.

Leafy and cypress spurges often hybridize with each other; the hybrid plant, showing intermediate characters, is known as *E. xpseudoesula.*

Associates: A true Caucasian, apparently originating in the Caucasus steppes of Eurasia, leafy spurge first arrived in North America about 1827, probably as a contaminant in ship ballast. It was subsequently reintroduced many times from different regions of its native range, probably accounting for the variability it shows. Today in North America, it occurs within latitudes 36 to 58 degrees N, most abundantly in the West. Globally, it occurs in dry to humid and subtropical to subarctic habitats.

Cypress spurge, more uniform in physical appearance but with varying chromosomal makeup as aforementioned, originated in Mediterranean and western European regions. The sterile diploid form probably arose as a mutant in England between 1768 and 1818, apparently came to North America as a garden ornamental. Tetraploid plants probably arrived as accidental contaminants about the same time as leafy spurge. Today cypress spurge ranges throughout temperate Eurasia; in North America, it resides most commonly in the Northeast.

Both spurge species occur in dry to moderately moist, disturbed, open sites—old fields, roadsides, woodland clearings. They often favor light, sandy soils. Leafy spurge appears more aggressive than cypress spurge in cultivated crop fields, can become a dominant plant in mixed-grass prairies and the main source of pollen and nectar for local insect populations. Root secretions and the decayed litter of spurge plants apparently exert *allelopathic* (chemically inhibiting) effects on the germination and growth of certain other plants, thereby increasing spurges' own competitive edge. Leafy spurge threatens endangered populations of prairie or western spiderwort *(Tradescantia occidentalis)*, the western prairie fringed orchid *(Habenaria leucophaea)*, and the northern prairie skink, a ground lizard. Leafy spurge also inhibits the growth of tomatoes, quack-grass *(Elytrigia repens)*, and common ragweed *(q.v.)*, among others. Yet neither spurge species is noted as an aggressive weed in its native lands. No well-developed plant communities are associated with these species in North America, though cypress spurge often occurs with poison ivy *(Toxicodendron radicans)* and staghorn-sumac *(Rhus typhina)* on railroad embankments. In some areas, grass species intensely compete with spurges, can inhibit their spread. I have noted the close occurrence of leafy spurge with timothy *(q.v.)* in certain midwestern areas. Spurges need sunlight, tend to die out beneath a shade canopy.

The native flowering spurge, common throughout the continent, appears much less invasive than the 2 alien spurges. It favors sandy plains and dry woodlands.

Some researchers suggest that the vigor of invasive spurges owes much to the plants' mycorrhizal fungi, which penetrate the root cells and facilitate the uptake of nutrients into the roots. Mycorrhizal species consist (among others) of *Glomus constrictum*.

One of the main fungous parasites on spurges is a rust *(Uromyces striatus)*, which also parasitizes alfalfa *(q.v.)*, clovers *(q.v.)*, and other legumes. Spurges act as alternate hosts for this fungus, which causes enlargement and eventual death of leaves and stems.

Uromyces also extends interactions with insect pollinators; J. A. Parmelee's research in 1962 showed that spurges' honey-sweet fragrance probably emanates not from the flower nectar but from the *pycnia* (fruiting bodies) of the *Uromyces* rust—an interesting case of a destructive parasite luring insects that facilitate spurges' reproduction. A related rust *(U. scutellatus)* has shown potential as a biocontrol agent of leafy and cypress spurges. Other fungi reported on spurges include an imported Chinese rust *(Melampsora euphorbiae)*, leaf spots *(Cercospora, Alternaria)*, and the root rots *Phymatotrichum omnivorum* and *Rhizoctonia solani*.

Broom-rape *(Orobanche)*, a spikelike, scaly-stemmed, blue wildflower, parasitizes flowering spurge roots.

Despite spurges' off-putting latex, which inhibits and prevents many insect would-be foragers from chewing and sucking, these plants nevertheless display numerous associations with insects—about 200 species, in one leafy spurge study. These consist mainly of pollen and nectar seekers and predators of other insects, however, not foliage herbivores. Exceptions occur—certain insects have evolved chemical adaptations to the plants and feed on them harmlessly. Some 40 of these—most of them imported from the plants' native areas—have been suggested or tried, with varying success, as biological control agents. They include the following.

Horned caterpillars of the spurge hawk moth *(Hyles euphorbiae)* defoliate spurges, but the pupae succumb to cold American winters, and ants also attack the larvae. The spurge leafroller *(Lobesia euphorbiana)*, a tortricid moth caterpillar, rolls and ties bracts around the umbel, preventing flowering and seed set. An inchworm caterpillar called the drab looper *(Minoa murinata)* feeds on the flowers and floral bracts. Two noctuid moth caterpillars, *Simyra dentinosa* and *Oxicesta geographica*, actively defoliate spurges in Eurasia, have also been released for that purpose in North America. The most successful biocontrol agents—reducing spurge cover from 100 to 10 percent in certain study areas—are tiny jumping insects that forage on the roots. These spurge flea beetles *(Aphthona)*, some 5 species established in North America, feed as larvae on the roots; the adult beetles forage on stems, leaves, and flowers. Flea beetle attack typically creates an expanding circle of nonflowering spurge stems that dies out and becomes replaced by grass over the next 2 years. "The flea beetles and spurge have reached a natural balance," reported one researcher in 1999; "if the spurge increases, the flea beetle populations will increase and keep it under control."

A flat-faced long-horned beetle that bores into stems and roots is the red-headed spurge stem borer *Oberea erythrocephala;* larvae feed in the root crown, and the slate gray, reddish-headed, slender adults consume spurge leaves and flowers.

Two spurge shoot-tip gall midges *(Spurgia capitigena* on cypress spurge, and *S. esulae* on leafy spurge), plus other gall midges *(Dasineura)*, have had minimal biocontrol effect on spurge densities.

None of these biocontrol imports have become widely established as yet, thus are unlikely to be seen in most areas. Other host-specific insects have also been introduced but have failed to become established.

The ello sphinx moth *(Erinnyis ello)*, native to Florida and Texas, feeds as a caterpillar on spurges. The adult moths, showing orange hindwings, sometimes stray in summer and fall, may occasionally lay eggs on the plants in the Northeast.

A *Meloidogyne* root-boring nematode (roundworm) also feeds on spurge belowground. Native flea beetles that feed on the roots include *Glyptina* species.

Grasshoppers may defoliate spurges in drought years when choicer plant species are gone.

By far the largest number and variety of insects on spurges are attracted by the plants' abundant nectar and pollen, as well as by the insects that seek them. Flies (including mosquitoes), bees, wasps, and beetles are spurges' most numerous visitors. Among the adult butterflies I have observed on leafy spurge are American coppers *(Lycaena phlaeas)* and great spangled fritillaries *(Speyeria cybele)*. Ants (especially *Lasius* species) also feed on the nectar and presumably pollinate the flowers.

Ants also act as one of spurges' main seed dispersers; this ant-plant mutualism is called *myrmechochory*. The caruncles on the seeds contain oily *elaiosomes* that ants eat. They carry the seeds to their nests or deposit them nearby after consuming the oil bodies.

American copper butterflies (Lycaena phlaeas) *are among the many insects attracted to leafy spurge by this plant's copious nectar.*

Ant dispersers include *Lasius* ground ants and *Formica* mound ants; the latter may also use stems of the plant in construction of their mounds. Leafy spurge seedlings often sprout on or near ant mounds.

Birds also disperse spurge seeds. Among seedeaters are greater prairie-chickens, northern bobwhites, horned larks, American pipits, chipping sparrows, and likely others. Probably most feeding occurs from the ground, where the expelled seeds lie. One study suggested that mourning doves, which are major spurge seed feeders, may account for much of the plants' dispersal. Spurge may, in fact, qualify as something of a dove indicator. Although the doves thoroughly digest the seeds they eat, they also regurgitate undigested seeds for their nestlings, which leave viable seeds in their feces. Since mourning doves do not keep sanitary nests, many of the seeds finally end on the ground where the old nests fall, soon to begin a new patch of spurge.

Cattle and horses cannot eat spurges—the acid latex blisters their mouths, also causes scours (acute diarrhea), which may kill the animals. Sheep and goats, however, seem usually unaffected by the plants' chemistry, even come to relish spurges and thus provide an important—perhaps the most important—means of biocontrol in some areas. These livestock can also disperse the plant, however, via their droppings.

Lore: Leafy spurge (and probably cypress spurge as well) "appears to be a serious problem only in the continental climate of North America," reported one research team. Leafy spurge currently infests at least 5 million acres of prairie rangeland. North Dakota is said to be its area of heaviest concentration. The vast amount of American research attention focused on how to "purge spurge" reflects the dire economic effects of these plants upon agriculture. Spurge not only "eats up" land quickly, but once established, it does not easily relinquish hold; it resists fire, flood, drought, mowing, and herbicides. Pulling up spurges by hand or spade only fragments and increases their abundance (as with many weeds). Biocontrol appears the only cost-effective means of eliminating or controlling these plants, and even these procedures require large investments of money, time, and experimentation. Spurges' almost sole benefitters are nectar- and pollen-feeding insects, upon which the plants depend for seed production, and sheep and goat foragers.

Aside from the competitive advantages bestowed by their prolific seed dispersal, aggressive root systems, allelopathy, and resistance to cow, plow, fire, and herbicide, spurges show another "one-up" character. Their tremendous genetic variability increases their adaptability in many habitats. This variability also extends to the plants' *phenotypes* (physical appearances), "which do not lend themselves to clear-cut taxonomic division," as one researcher wrote. Spurges, in short, provide major headaches for botanical classifiers, who cherish clear-cut distinctions and among whom spurges fuel disagreements as prolific as the plants themselves. European taxonomists have tended to subdivide the leafy spurge complex into a roster of several species, subspecies, and hybrid varieties to reflect its differences, whereas most North American botanists favor lumping these different forms under the rubric of a single, highly variable species. "Part of the variation observed in North American populations," suggested a Canadian research team, "is the result of the plant having been introduced many times from its wide native range."

Spurges' acrid latex sap can cause rashes and irritations on human skin. Even a small amount in the eyes produces extreme pain. Flowering spurge latex is so skin-caustic that it has even been used to brand cattle.

Any plant that tastes bitter is likely to have found numerous medicinal usages, and the spurges are no exceptions. The latex, though harsh on the skin, astonishingly was used to treat and supposedly alleviate skin irritations, one more apparent spurge paradox. Known for its purgative effects on cattle, spurges were also widely used as strong laxatives (an Indian name for flowering spurge translated as "go-quick"). Sixth-century exterminators used spurges mixed with barley and honey for rodent poison.

Cypress spurge achieved wide popularity in Europe and America as a dense ground cover, especially in cemeteries, resembling a thick but miniature pine forest. Diploid varieties were once used as ornamentals in landscaping.

The genus name *Euphorbia,* "of Euphorbus," refers to a royal physician of ancient Numidia. The word *spurge* derives from the Latin *expurgare,* meaning "to purge," indicating the plants' laxative nature. Wolf's-milk, a folk name for leafy spurge, refers to the plant's white latex, indeed a biting experience.

Strawberry, Wild *(Fragaria virginiana)*. Rose family. Recognize wild strawberry, a native perennial, by its low growth (3 to 6 inches high); its hairy, dark green leaves
divided into 3 leaflets; its 5-petaled white flowers in flat clusters on a separate stalk; its
long, reddish runners *(stolons)* threading over the ground surface; and its red fruits with 1-
seeded *achenes* embedded in surface pits.

Other names: Common, scarlet, meadow, or Virginia strawberry, thick-leaved wild
strawberry.

Close relatives: About 30 *Fragaria* species exist in north temperate regions and in
South America. Only 2 species—*F. virginiana* and *F. vesca,* the woodland strawberry—
reside as wild plants in eastern North America. Related species include barren strawberry
(Waldsteinea fragaroides), as well as common cinquefoil, multiflora rose, apple, hawthorns
(all *q.v.*), and many others.

Lifestyle: The white, insect-pollinated flowers of wild strawberry, one of the most
familiar and conspicuous low plants of April and May, seem almost as common as dandelions, especially in open, grassy areas. I always wondered at the fact that the abundance of
strawberry flowers in April seemed to outnumber by far the plants that held actual fruits in
June. Perhaps part of the answer is that some wild strawberry populations are *gynodioe-
cious*—that is, they consist of both bisexual and unisexual (mainly female) plants. The
female flowers, which produce most strawberry fruits in wild populations, have 20 to 30
vestigial (male) stamens but produce no pollen. Cultivated strawberry varieties (see Lore)
are mostly bisexual, but original native wild strawberry populations produced mainly unisexual flowers. Of the minority bisexual flowers, "on the average not one in 10 flowers set
fruit," according to an 1854 observer. Today exclusively male flowers are rare, perhaps
extirpated by the selection pressures of cultivation and genetic migration from cultivated
hybrids to wild strawberry populations. Only bisexual flowers produce pollen, but the fre-
quencies of female and bisexual forms vary among populations. Several studies have
revealed a west-to-east gradient of increasing bisexuality in wild strawberry. Wild strawberry thus exhibits what researchers call "a transitional breeding system." Strawberry's
sexual schematics appear among our native flora's most complex, though crop genetics
has reduced these variations to a large extent. In addition to the variable sexual expressions in this species, pollination sometimes occurs unevenly or not at all; also, some flowers are sterile, and frost, fungi, and insects often damage flowers. All of these causes may
help account for my impression that flowers vastly outnumber fruits in wild strawberry.

Flower clusters are *cymes,* in which the primary or terminal flower matures first, is
likeliest to set fruit, and produces the earliest, largest fruit. Two secondary and up to 4 ter-
tial (plus sometimes more) flowers produce smaller, later-ripening fruits. Typically about
10 flowers occur in each cyme, with usually only a single one opening at a time and lasting

about a day. Many of the later flowers never develop fruits. Primary fruits may hold 100 or more achenes. Wild strawberry ripens about June 12 in southern Michigan.

Typical bisexual flowers of wild strawberry exhibit numerous yellow stamens encircling the tiny, greenish yellow, spirally arranged pistils ("like pins protruding from a pincushion," wrote one observer) on the conelike *receptacle* (end of the stem). The receptacle becomes increasingly fleshy as it matures. Red strawberries are actually the swollen stem ends, the fruit holders (of achenes) rather than true fruits themselves. In common with apple and some other actual fruits, however, the strawberry may function as a nutrient sink or collector for other parts of the plant, a vitamin-rich microhabitat for achene development. Insects as well as wind pollinate strawberry flowers, and self-pollination readily occurs. Pistils remain receptive for several days. Thus, between its variably sexed flowers and its mimic fruits, strawberry is a plant whose most conspicuous structures are both more and less than they seem, all apparently adaptive to its own survival.

Wild strawberry also reproduces vegetatively, cloning itself by means of its horizontal stolons. One to 4 stolons per rooted plant shallowly arch 1 to 3 feet along the ground surface, rooting *(pegging)* new strawberry plants where they touch soil. By means of this "guerilla strategy" (so-called by strawberry researchers), large, genetically identical strawberry populations may cover many yards of ground, the entire spread basically consisting of one plant with many separate stems, roots, and flowers. In the stolons, "food and water may be carried freely in either direction," wrote strawberry scholar George M. Darrow, "and the parent plant may support, or be supported by, a large clone of runner plants for months." Stolons wither and die in winter, after cloned plants have rooted.

Strawberry's dense, fan-shaped networks of fibrous roots tend to turn woody and dark with age. Many roots are biennial, dying at fruiting time, though some may survive

Wild strawberry spreads by stolons, its aboveground surface runners producing genetically identical stands (clones) of a single plant.

many years. They remain fairly shallow, seldom penetrating more than a foot, making the plant vulnerable to drought. Lengthwise curled strawberry leaves are familiar sights during such periods.

Like violets and a few other spring-blooming plants, wild strawberry often flowers again in September, when day-length hours match those of spring day length. Leaves on the plant often redden as the fruits mature, "as if Nature meant thus to conceal the fruit," wrote Thoreau.

Associates: Strawberry's versatile reproduction, life cycles, and adaptiveness render its presence possible and its survivability assured in just about any land habitat except extremes of drought or wetness. Regional populations develop special tolerances; far northern populations, for example, can withstand cold below –40 degrees F, whereas southern plants are much less cold-hardy. And wild strawberry proves much more adaptable to various habitats than cultivated varieties, ranging from woodlands to fields, roadsides, lawns, shores. Although shade-tolerant, it favors open, sunny clearings where competing vegetation is not dense. Sheep sorrel *(q.v.)* is a frequent associate and competitor, and wild strawberry roots also become foremost hemiparasitic hosts for painted cup *(q.v.)*. Wild strawberry begins the year's fruiting season; as strawberry fruits decline in summer, blueberries begin to ripen. Wild strawberry ranges throughout the continent from Alaska and Canada southward, in South America, and as an alien in Eurasia.

Cultivated strawberries may host numerous viral and fungal parasites, most of which can also infect wild strawberries. These parasites, however, seem much less invasive in wild populations, which apparently have evolved effective genetic defenses against them. Wild strawberries may, however, act as reservoirs for various plant viruses that severely affect strawberry crops, which is why strawberry growers try to avoid planting new stocks where the wild plants abound. Virus diseases include various types: June yellows, leaf-crinkle, witches'-broom, leaf-roll, and others, most of which produce stunted and deformed plants. A common fungus is gray mold *(Botrytis cinerea)*, which produces brown, wilting flowers and a gray, fuzzy rot on the ripening fruit. Powdery mildew *(Sphaerotheca macularis)* appears as a grayish coating on leaf undersides. Other fungi may include verticillium wilt *(Verticillium albo-atrum)*, causing leaf wilting; leaf scorch *(Diplocarpon earliana)*, causing dark, scorchlike spotting on leaves; leaf blight *(Dendrophoma obscurans)*, marked by V-shaped dead areas in the leaves, also rotting the fruit; leaf spot *(Mycosphaerella fragariae)*, also causing spots; and leather rot *(Phytophthora cactorum)*, making the fruit soft and mushy, then dry and leathery. Root fungi include red stele *(P. fragariae)*, stunting and discoloring the plant; and black root rot, caused by a complex of fungi with similar effects. Some 50 other parasitic fungi may infect leaves, fruits, or roots. In warm, wet weather, slime molds *(Diachea, Physarum)*, cream or tan jellylike masses, may move from the soil onto the leaves; though not parasitic on the plants, they may smother leaves or fruits.

Other fungi, which reside in the roots and may be *mycorrhizal* (aiding uptake of nourishment by plant roots), are *Endogone* and *Glomus* species.

Slime trails on fruit or leaf surfaces indicate the presence of slugs *(Deroceras, Arion)*, which may eat deep, ragged holes into the fruits.

Strawberry spider mites *(Tetranychus turkestani)*, two-spotted spider mites *(T. urticae)*, and cyclamen or strawberry crown mites *(Stenotarsonemus pallidus)* are almost microscopic in size; they suck sap, causing wrinkled leaves.

As with fungi, numerous insects that afflict cultivated strawberries, finding a uniform crop laid out, also occur less invasively on the wild plants. Strawberry aphids *(Chaetosiphon fragaefolii)*, pale yellow and often densely clustered, are more prevalent in the West, can transmit several viruses. Several other aphid species—*Myzus* and *Macrosiphum*, among others—may also be vectors of these diseases.

Flower or strawberry thrips *(Frankliniella tritici)*, tiny, slender, yellowish brown sap suckers, feed in flowers and fruit, cause fruit stunting and discoloration. In the upper Northeast and Midwest, they arrive each spring as long-distance migrants from the South, carried on high-level winds.

Other sap suckers include the tarnished plant bug *(Lygus lineolaris)*, of coppery brown color—look for a characteristic yellow triangle behind its head; nymphs of the meadow spittlebug *(Philaenus spumarius)*, which produce frothy masses on stems; and potato leafhoppers *(Empoasca fabae)*, the green nymphs of which feed on leaf undersides, causing yellowing and distortion. Thoreau, who had scant use for cultivated strawberries but devoted pages of his journal to wild strawberries, deplored that an unidentified species of stink bug (Pentatomidae) usually got to the fruits before he did, leaving its rancid odor and taste; "like the dog in the manger, he spoils a whole mouthful for you, without enjoying them himself."

Spined caterpillars of several lesser fritillary butterfly species *(Boloria)* sometimes feed on wild strawberry leaves. Moth caterpillar foragers on strawberry leaves include the strawberry leafroller *(Ancylis comptana)*, a brownish or greenish tortricid. Another tortricid caterpillar feeder is the garden tortrix *(Ptycholoma peritana)*.

Cultivated bisexual plants appear especially vulnerable to damage by the strawberry bud weevil, also called strawberry clipper *(Anthonomus signatus)*. This small, brownish beetle punctures mature flower buds, feeding on the new pollen, then lays an egg in the bud and girdles the stem so that the loaded bud falls off—so much for that strawberry.

Strawberry sap beetles *(Stelidota geminata)*, flat, oval, and mottled brown, feed on ripe berries, often in groups, dropping to the ground when disturbed.

Strawberry rootworms *(Paria fragariae)*, dark, shiny, oval leaf beetles, feed at night. They riddle the leaves in summer with small holes; as larvae, they feed on the plant roots. Adult strawberry root weevils *(Otiorhyncus ovatus)*, also called crown girdlers and also larval root feeders, munch notches around leaf margins as adults, and perforate strawberry fruits.

Other strawberry root feeders include strawberry root aphids *(Aphis forbesi)*, which in some areas are attended by cornfield ants *(Lasius alienus);* the ants carry new-hatched aphids to the roots from stems and foliage, and spread aphid colonies from plant to plant. Strawberry crown borers *(Tyloderma fragariae)*, larval weevils, gouge out root crowns and the larger roots. Strawberry crown moths *(Synanthedon bibionipennis)*, thick-bodied white or yellowish clear-winged moth caterpillars, also feed in the root crowns, as do strawberry crown miners *(Monochroa fragariae)*, tiny gelechiid moth caterpillars. Tiny nematodes (roundworms) that parasitize strawberry roots and wilt and stunt the plants include *Xiphenema, Pratylenchus,* and *Aphelenchoides* species. Root-knot nematodes *(Meloidogyne)* cause knots or galls on the roots.

Strawberry's most reliably effective pollinators consist of bees and flies. A 1987 study found that of 32 pollinating visitors, the most abundant were honeybees *(Apis mellifera)*, halictid bees (Halictidae), and syrphid flies (Syrphidae). Other bee pollinators include small carpenter bees *(Ceratina)*, cuckoo bees *(Nomada)*, andrenid bees (Andrenidae), and leaf-cutting bees (Megachilidae). Other fly pollinators include bee flies (Bombyliidae) and thick-headed flies *(Thecophora occidensis).* Sphecid thread-waisted wasps such as the cutworm wasp *(Podalonia luctosa)* may also effect pollination while foraging on the flowers. One study indicated that bees, seeking nectar and pollen, accounted for about 80 percent of visits to wild strawberry flowers, whereas ants *(Formica, Lasius)*, seeking nectar only, registered only 5 to 10 percent of visits. Bees and flies exhibit a preference for bisexual strawberry flowers rather than unisexual female flowers, perhaps attracted by the pollen odor. The bisexual flowers have longer, wider petals and provide nectar as well.

Butterflies may also pollinate strawberry. Common visitors include eastern tailed-blues *(Everes comyntas)*, silvery blues *(Glaucopsyche lygdamus)*, European cabbage butterflies *(Pieris rapae)*, West Virginia whites *(P. virginiensis)*, olympia marbles *(Euchloe olympia)*, and clouded sulphurs *(Colias philodice).*

Strawberry fruits are, of course, relished by many birds, which also disperse the plant in their droppings. Foremost fruit eaters include ruffed grouse, ring-necked pheasants, greater prairie-chickens, wild turkeys, red-bellied and red-headed woodpeckers, yellow-bellied sapsuckers, northern flickers, eastern kingbirds, American crows, blue jays, northern mockingbirds, gray catbirds, brown thrashers, European starlings, cedar waxwings, wood thrushes, veeries, American robins (often pests in strawberry crop fields), eastern towhees, northern cardinals, swamp and white-throated sparrows, and rose-breasted and evening grosbeaks. Grouse, pheasants, and probably other upland gamebirds consume the leaves of young plants as well. Mammal foliage and fruit eaters include opossums, ground squirrels, eastern chipmunks, meadow voles, white-footed mice, striped skunks, fox and red squirrels, cottontail rabbits, and snowshoe hares. White-tailed deer also graze the plants.

Lore: The wild strawberry invariably "makes up in flavor what it lacks in size," as botanist Edward G. Voss wrote; "its wild crop is first in the hearts of many of us." "What beautiful and palatable bread!" waxed Thoreau. London physician William Butler agreed: "Doubtless God could have made, but doubtless God never did make, a better berry." Yet the unique tang of its flavor, unduplicated by any cultivated strawberry, does not last long once plucked off the plant; it rapidly turns "red delicious," a rubric sweet, and loses its distinctive soul. Wild strawberries are best consumed, aficionados agree, in a single motion from plant to hand to mouth. Eaters who defer their gratification to a later mealtime will seldom know this flavor. Although native Americans commonly dried and preserved them for winter food, these fruits do not refrigerate or freeze well.

The cultivated strawberry, usually considered a separate species *(F. ananassa),* is a fertile hybrid derived from 2 wild species: the beach strawberry *(F. chiloensis),* native to Pacific North America, Argentina, and Chile; and *F. virginiana,* the topic of this account. Today the number of *F. ananassa* cultivated varieties almost equals that of apple *(q.v.),* its family relative, though the culture methodology is not the same (apple varieties result from grafting, whereas strawberry types owe to constant interbreeding of racial hybrids). Today's *F. ananassa* is actually a bioengineered crop; gene flow via pollen from its hybrid varieties into native strawberry populations may account in part for the aforementioned shifts in gender prevalence among wild strawberries.

Our wild strawberry, exported to Europe in the early 1600s, did not become popular there until hybrid varieties developed more than a century later increased its acceptance. European strawberries cultivated in gardens since the 1300s, mainly small-fruited species, included the wood strawberry *(F. vesca)* and the musky strawberry *(F. moschata).* Before that period, the ancient writers (Virgil, Ovid) mentioned the plants only casually in their bucolic verses. Commercial strawberry production, using *F. virginiana,* began in the United States about 1800.

Before planting, commercial strawberry growers (80 percent of the crop comes from California) zap their soil with methyl bromide, a fumigant that kills almost every possible competing or parasitic organism—bacteria, fungi, weeds—and produces large, "perfect" strawberries. The technique is currently being phased out by most growers, however, since discovery that methyl bromide is a major planetary ozone depleter and possible health hazard.

In addition to wild strawberry's long usage as a food by native cultures (Iroquois tribes celebrated its June ripening by special longhouse ceremonies), root and leaf teas of the plant were commonly dosed medicines. The mildly astringent teas, sometimes steeped with thimbleberry *(Rubus parviflorus)* leaves, treated gout, bowel disorders, sore throat, bladder and kidney problems, and was also used as a nerve tonic. The fresh leaves, high in vitamin C, as are the fruits, also make a satisfactory tea.

The name *strawberry* supposedly derives from the European practice of bedding the plants with straw, in which they sprouted. Botanist Neltje Blanchan, however, suggested another theory: "In earliest Anglo-Saxon it was called streowberie and later straberry, from the peculiarity of its *straying* suckers lying as if strewn on the ground." *Fragaria* comes from the Latin *fraga,* "frequent."

Sunflower, Common *(Helianthus annus).* Aster family. Recognize this native annual by its golden yellow ray flowers radiating from a central brownish pad of disk flowers, blooming summer to fall. Its stems, often branched with several flowerheads and with toothed, heart-shaped, alternate leaves, stand 3 to 12 feet tall.

Other names: American Mary-gold.

Close relatives: Resembling coneflowers *(q.v.),* ox-eye daisy *(q.v.),* and many other aster family plants, some 50 *Helianthus* species all reside in North America, about half of them in the East. Species identification is notoriously difficult, since hybrids abound, and probably few taxonomists agree on the same *Helianthus* roster. Other eastern sunflowers include the divaricate or woodland sunflower *(H. divaricatus),* the stiff or prairie sunflower *(H. pauciflorus),* the Jerusalem-artichoke *(H. tuberosus),* and the swamp, tall, or giant sunflower *(H. giganteus);* the last 2 species frequently dwell in wetlands. Almost all sunflowers (this species, *H. annus,* being an exception) are perennials. Aster family relatives abound throughout this book.

Lifestyle: Sunflowers exist as prototypical members of the aster or composite family; that is, their flowerheads consist of multiple disk and 10 to 20 ray florets. Disk florets, which make up the crowded central mass, are the bisexual and prolific seed producers, whereas the yellow, radiating ray florets, vestigially female and sterile, flag insect pollinators. A close look at a disk floret reveals the pollination mechanism. (Male) anthers form a tube enclosing the (female) *style* or pistillate stalk; lengthening growth of the latter pushes pollen out the top of the tube, exposing it for random pickup by foraging insects. The style then ruptures, exposing the stigma surface ready to receive incoming pollen brought by an insect visitor from another sunflower head. Such flowers, producing mature pollen before mature stigmas, are called *protandrous.* Although disk florets can also self-pollinate, the self-produced pollen seldom germinates; thus individual florets are functionally self-incompatible, or obligate *outcrossers* (that is, they require cross-pollination in order to set seed). The disk florets, arranged in 2 spirals on the disk, appear as concentric whorls. The outside ring of florets on the disk matures first; the central ones develop last. From pollination to the existence of mature, 1-seeded *achenes*—up to 600 on a seedhead—requires about a month. Total florets in the bouquet of a sunflower head number 1,000 to 2,000.

Flowerheads range from several inches up to a foot or more across. They exhibit a marked directional *phototropism* (orientation toward sunlight) only before they open. "The heliotropic movement of the sunflower's head results from a bending of the stem," as sunflower specialist Benjamin H. Beard wrote, "and is termed nutation. After sunset the stem gradually straightens, so that by dawn the head is again facing east. When the plant reaches the stage of anthesis [the opening of the flower], nutation ceases; therefter the head faces only eastward." This directional orientation, though not invariable, occurs often enough that sunflowers may serve

The outside ring of disk florets in common sunflower matures first, progressing inward toward the center, eventually producing hundreds of achenes; the bright ray flowers produce no seed but attract insect pollinators.

as useful compass indicators in the field. Contrary to many if not most accounts about sunflowers—that the flowers are solar trackers *(heliotropic),* following the sun from dawn to eve throughout the day—sunflowers, once in bloom, do no such thing. "Once the flower head opens, it no longer bends toward the source of light," and the bent stem beneath the head becomes rigid, as botanist Charles B. Heiser, Jr., wrote. The error, sanctified by egregious repetition, apparently results from an astonishing failure of simple observation.

Common sunflowers hybridize widely, but only with other annual sunflowers, never with perennial species, often making species identification difficult (perennial sunflower species, being more numerous, hybridize among themselves even more rampantly). Yet, contrary to logical expectation, such intermixture of genes does not lead to a breakdown or fusion of species, but results "only in a slight blurring of the species boundaries," as Heiser wrote. The stunted reproductive capacity of hybrids plus different habitat adaptations and blooming schedules of species (albeit with much overlap) all work toward keeping the genetic lines intact if not impervious.

Wild sunflower species exhibit more *trichomes* (plant hairs) on stems and leaves than cultivated varieties. Some of the trichomes are glandular, containing and secreting lactones, sticky oils or resins; others are nonglandular. All, however, apparently deter, to some extent, insect climbers and foragers on the plants.

Sunflower roots consist of a fibrous lateral network and a taproot that may extend 5 or 6 feet deep. Root secretions of chlorogenic acids are apparently *allelopathic* (chemically inhibiting) to the germination of other plants, including even sunflower seedlings. Allelopathy appears most active in sites or conditions of nutrient stress, as in a worn-out field, where it may hold back the advance of plant succession.

Associates: Gaudy resident of roadsides, dry fields, vacant lots, even trash dumps, common sunflower ranges throughout North America from about 55 degrees N latitude to northern Mexico, as well as in temperate regions globally. It does not tolerate heavy shade or acidic or waterlogged soils. From its original range, the western Great Plains states, clearing, settlement, and cultivation helped establish it continentally, and colonial explorers and traders also imported this economically important plant to Old World lands and peoples. Wild sunflowers often pioneer younger stages of plant succession.

Numerous bacterial, fungal, and viral intruders parasitize sunflowers. Most seem inconsequential in wild sunflower populations, but the farmer who raises sunflowers as a uniform crop must do constant battle with these infections. Some of the prominent bacterial parasites include leaf spots and wilt *(Pseudomonas)* and *Erwina* stalk and head rots. Fungous parasites include *Alternaria* blights, stem spot, and rots; gray mold *(Botrytis cinerea);* downy mildew *(Plasmopara);* powdery mildews *(Erysiphecichoracearum* and others); *Fusarium* stalk rots and wilts; *Phomopsis* brown stem cankers; *Sclerotinia* rots and wilts; plus several rusts *(Uromyces, Coleosporium,* others). Sunflowers may host at least 60 fungi. Just about any individual fungous species of garden or cropland (most of them fungi imperfecti and sac fungi) can, in fact, be found in sunflower fields unless the fields have been soaked in fungicides. Fungi less commonly invade wild sunflower stands. "To develop new sunflower breeding lines with disease resistance, we rely heavily on genetic resources from wild sunflowers that evolved in their native North America," according to one plant pathologist.

Herbal plants that parasitize sunflowers include broom-rapes *(Orobanche)* and dodders *(Cuscuta,* especially rope-dodder, *C. glomerata).* Sunflowers can compete with soybean crops; compounding the problem may be invasion of the soybean stem borer (see below), which also bores into sunflowers. One plant apparently resistant to sunflower allelopathy is prairie three-awn grass *(Aristida oligantha),* which in some areas tends to outlast and replace sunflower growth in old-field plant succession.

Insect feeders, like fungi, tend to be more numerous in uniform crop fields than in wild sunflower stands.

Stem and foliage feeders include the following. Dogwood aphids *(Aphis cornifoliae),* brown, black, or dark green, migrate to sunflower in summer from dogwoods *(Cornus),* sucking sap. Olive green *A. helianthi,* sunflower aphids, may also be seen. Nymphs of sunflower spittlebugs *(Clastoptera xanthocephala)* also suck sap, enclosing themselves in frothy masses along leaves and stem; treehoppers (Membracidae) frequent the plants as well. Southern armyworms *(Spodoptera eridania),* destructive noctuid moth caterpillars, often migrate to sunflowers from amaranths *(q.v.),* their primary hosts.

Larval stem borers include several beetle, fly, and moth species. Sunflower stem weevils *(Cylindrocopturus adspersus)* feed in the pith of lower stems, where they construct chambers, often causing stem breakage; the creamy white larvae often lie in curled or C-shaped positions. Black sunflower stem weevils *(Apion occidentale),* as larvae, also mine stems. Sunflower maggots *(Strauzia longipennis),* gall gnats, feed as white, legless grubs in the stalk, and can cause breakage. Sunflower bud moths *(Suleima helianthana),* smooth, cream-colored tortricid caterpillars, hatch outside the stem but tunnel in, leaving characteristic entrance holes surrounded by *frass* (excrement); they also exit as adult moths from these holes. *Eucosma womonana,* another tortricid caterpillar, bores into stalks as well. The bumble flower beetle *(Euphoria inda),* a scarab that mimics a bumblebee in sound and flight, bores holes into sunflower stalks, feeding on the sap; the sap flow attracts many other insects both day and night—moths, butterflies, long-horned beetles, flies, and wasps. Long-horned beetle stem-feeding larvae include *Megacyllene decora* and the soybean stem borer *(Dectes texanus),* plus *Ataxia hubbardi* and *Mecas* species. Other larval borers in the sunflower stalk guild: rhubarb curculios *(Lixus concavus)* and caterpillars of the sunflower borer moth *(Papaipema necopina)* and of the rigid sunflower borer moth *(P. rigida),* both noctuids.

As many if not more larval insects bore into the flowerheads, feeding on fleshy tissues and developing seeds. One of crop sunflower's major pests is the sunflower head-clipping weevil *(Haplorhynchites aeneus);* the shiny black female weevil feeds on pollen and nectar, then punctures holes around the stalk beneath the flowerhead, thereafter laying eggs in the flowerhead; the girdled head eventually falls to the ground, where the grublike larvae continue to feed inside it. Fly larvae that feed in the flowerhead include sunflower midges *(Contarinia schulzi),* creamy yellowish grubs; they begin feeding on flowerhead margins, move to the center as the head develops, and finally drop to the ground, where they pupate. Resembling them are sunflower maggots *(Gymnocarena diffusa),* larvae that emerge by an exit hole on the underside of the flowerhead (some also pupate inside the head); the green-eyed adult flies may often be seen on leaf undersides. *Neotephritis finalis,* the sunflower seed maggot, has 2 generations: The first, after a 2-week feeding period in the flowerhead, pupates there; the second generations overwinter as pupae in the soil. The aforementioned black sunflower stem weevils and sunflower bud moth caterpillars also attack pith areas of the flowerhead. Another caterpillar, the banded sunflower moth *(Cochylis hospes),* a pinkish tortricid, feeds in the florets, then tunnels into the developing seed; small areas of silken webbing on mature flowerheads indicate its presence. Trashy-appearing flowerheads and banded caterpillars may also indicate feeding of sunflower moths *(Homoeosoma electellum)*; these pyralid moths migrate in summer from the south-central states, their caterpillars consuming pollen and florets. Caterpillars of the frothy moth *(Stibadium spumosum)*, a noctuid, likewise tunnel in the flowerheads. Sunflower beetles *(Zygogramma exclamationis)*, resembling Colorado potato beetles, feed as reddish-headed adult leaf beetles in the bracts of the flowerhead.

Seedeaters in the flowerhead, also numerous, include seed weevils. The red sunflower seed weevil *(Smicronyx fulvus)* and gray sunflower seed weevil *(S. sordidus)* feed as larvae inside the achenes, hollowing them out, and the adults feed on floral buds and pollen. The aforementioned sunflower moth caterpillars also consume developing seeds.

Sunflower leaf eaters, likewise numerous, include the yellowish green, hump-backed larvae of the aforementioned sunflower beetles; if numerous, they can defoliate a plant. Small, circular holes in leaves may indicate feeding of the aforementioned stem weevils. Cutworms *(Euxoa, Feltia)*, the noctuid caterpillars of dart moths, cut off stems near the soil line and chew leaves. The June beetle *Phyllophaga lanceolata* feeds on the leaves, as do red-legged grasshoppers *(Melanoplus femurrubrum)* and adult sunflower root weevils (see next paragraph). Yellowish green, hairy caterpillars of the painted lady or cosmopolite *(Vanessa cardui)* and striped and spined caterpillars of gorgone checkerspots *(Chlosyne gorgone)* are the main butterfly feeders.

Sunflower root weevils *(Baris strenua)*, oval, robust, and dull black, attack root tissue near the soil line, causing plants to wilt and lodge (tip over against other plants). Carrot beetles *(Ligyrus gibbosus)* also feed as larvae in sunflower roots, as reddish brown adult beetles on the foliage. Parasitic nemodes (roundworms) also thrive in sunflower roots. They include *Rotylenchulus* and *Meloidogyne* species, among others.

Pollinating insects of sunflower probably number into the hundreds. Foremost are bees, including honeybees *(Apis mellifera)* and the so-called sunflower bee *(Megachile pugnata)*, a leaf-cutting bee. In sunflower crop fields, a hive of honeybees per acre is considered adequate for pollination coverage. Other bees that frequent sunflowers include several plasterer bee species *(Colletes)*, andrenids (Andrenidae), and digger bees *(Melissodes)*. The long-horned beetle *Batyle suturalis* is also a common pollinator. Butterflies frequently visit sunflowers—among them eastern tiger swallowtails *(Papilio glaucus)* and monarchs *(Danaus plexippus)*.

Sunflowers rank among the most important bird and mammal food plants, both for availability and nutritional qualities. Many birds relish the seeds, as any backyard bird-feeding platform will reveal. Almost any seed-eating bird, including most gamebird and songbird species (exclusive insect and fruit eaters excepted), devour the seeds where they find them, on the sunflower seedhead itself or in a bird feeder. On the seedheads, birds typically feed from the edge toward the center, perhaps favoring the oldest achenes. Blackbirds (mainly red-winged and yellow-headed) have probably become the major pests of crop sunflowers. The large seedheads, serving as ready perches, seem apt as feeding stations, and growers employ many deterrents against bird raiders. It is ironic that while the enormous birdseed market (some 52 million Americans in 1996) provides sunflower growers with major income, those same growers are often besieged by bird invasions before the crop can be harvested and sold. It's a matter of birds being in the right place at the wrong time. Woodpeckers, nuthatches, blue jays, and a few others also cache the seeds in bark, crevices, or the ground; these cachers probably account for much wild sunflower distribution.

Mammal seedeaters include chipmunks; ground squirrels; red, gray, and fox squirrels; voles; white-footed mice; and pocket gophers. Several grazers, including livestock, relish sunflower stems and foliage, especially those of younger plants. Muskrats, white-tailed deer, and rabbits are probably sunflower's foremost mammal herbivores.

Lore: Argentina currently leads the world in the production of sunflower seed, Russia ranks second, and the United States, native land of the sunflower, holds third place. American production did not become significant, however, until the 1960s. More than 30 other countries also raise the plant commercially. The chief products of value are the oil extracted from the seeds, second only to soybeans as a source of vegetable oil; and the seeds themselves, used as snack and confectionery foods, bird feed, and (ground into meal) as protein supplement for livestock. Seeds contain some 40 percent protein and a like percentage of oil. They rank high in polyunsaturated fat, starch, pectin, and calories, contain no cholesterol. Sunflower oil, used in cooking, also goes into many food products such as margarines, salad dressings, and mayonnaise—and, in nonfood products, into soaps, lubricants, paints, and varnishes; it even offers some potential value as a diesel fuel. The current center of commercial sunflower growth in America is North Dakota.

Nonseed uses for sunflower have included manufacture of a yellow dye from the ray florets, fiberboard from the shredded stalks, and storage of the entire plant as silage fodder, ranking almost equal to corn silage in nutrient value. Sunflower harvesting for silage, though largely discontinued in America, is still widely practiced in Europe.

In art and design, the sunflower has achieved notable popularity. In America, it decorates everything from greeting cards and T-shirts to pottery and dishes, lampshades, pillows, and neckties—almost a national identity marker, in league with bald eagles and ballparks. "Sunflowers are pure, undistilled summer," wrote one gardener. "May it not stand for the character of August?" Thoreau queried. Overseas, the sunflower (an alien there) came to symbolize Oscar Wilde's "art for art's sake" aesthetic movement, also became the subject of a van Gogh masterpiece as well as a highly stylized motif in architecture.

The long route of the sunflower from America to the world and back home has been an intricate passage. Archaeological evidence exists that southwestern tribes—the Hopis and their precursors—cultivated sunflowers some 5,000 years ago. Many other tribes collected the seeds as food. Champlain, Lewis and Clark, and other explorers recorded wide usage of both cultivated and wild sunflowers among American tribes east and west. Apparently natives first domesticated the wild sunflower by selecting and planting single-stem (the modern crop type) rather than branched-stem plants (grown today mainly as ornamentals). Paleobotanists believe that the epicenter of prehistoric sunflower cultivation was probably the North American Midwest. Spanish explorers brought sunflowers (probably from Mexico) to Europe in 1581. Sunflowers, becoming popular garden ornamentals there, eventually arrived in Russia. Russian farmers and plant breeders developed the crop sunflower about 1915, and from there it was reintroduced to North America. "Practically all the sunflowers now cultivated in the Americas," as Charles Heiser wrote, are "of Russian origin." The same route was not traveled, of course, by the wild common sunflower, which stayed home and remains a weedy opportunist of our old fields and roadsides.

Although primarily a food plant for native tribes, sunflower also provided herbal medicine for many North American peoples. Its main medicinal value, from earliest times to the present, has been claimed for pulmonary ailments—coughs, colds, bronchitis. Sufferers drank leaf teas for fevers and malaria, and poulticed leaves treated snakebite and spider bites. The plant also served decorative and ceremonial tribal uses.

Kansas adopted the sunflower as its state flower in 1903. In 1969, neighboring Iowa verged on declaring sunflower a noxious weed, infesting too many of its soybean fields—until Kansas threatened to retaliate by declaring Iowa's state bird, the American goldfinch, a public nuisance. "The governor of Iowa offered a solution to the 'flower-feather fracas' . . . when he offered to exchange all of Iowa's sunflowers for Kansas' supply of goldfinches," according to one report. Neither proposal finally survived common sense.

Fields of dried sunflower stalks in winter make excellent traps for blowing snow, almost as effective as hedges or snow fences.

Sweet Clovers (*Melilotus* species). Pea family. Recognize these alien legumes by their size (2 to 8 feet tall), their *trifoliate* (3-part) leaves with only the middle leaflet stalked, and their small, pealike flowers in terminal, slender, tapering clusters *(racemes)*. Both flowers and foliage are honey-fragrant.

Most commonly seen are white sweet clover *(M. alba)*, with white flowers; and yellow sweet clover *(M. officinalis)*, yellow flowered; other minor differences also exist between them.

Other names: White or sweet melilot, bokhara, tree or honey clover, honey lotus *(M. alba)*; yellow melilot, balsam-flower, hay flower, hart's or king's clover, sweet lucerne *(M. officinalis)*.

Close relatives: About 20 *Melilotus* species exist, all Old World natives. Less common than white and yellow sweet clovers in eastern North America are the 2 aliens *M. indica* and *M. altissima*. Alfalfa is a near relative, and other family kin include lupine, birdsfoot-trefoil, clovers, vetches, tick-trefoils, and bush-clovers (all *q.v.*), plus many others.

Lifestyle: Visibly obvious differences exist between clovers and sweet clovers, despite their similarity in names. The pollinating mechanism of sweet clovers closely resembles that of clovers and legumes generally. "Slight weight depresses the keel, releasing the stigma and anthers," as one naturalist wrote; "so soon as a bee alights and opens the flower [it] is hit below the belt by the projecting stigma." Then, when the insect departs, "the floret springs back to its closed condition."

The 2 species, white-flowered and yellow-flowered, differ somewhat in their sexual biology. Flowers of both are bisexual and insect-pollinated, but the length of white sweet clover's sex organs *(pistil* and *stamens)* is variable. Sometimes they extend to equal length, in which case self-pollination often occurs; but sometimes pistils extend longer than stamens, in which case the flower rarely self-pollinates. Yellow sweet clover operates differently; it is pollen protective, its pollen germinating very slowly, if at all, on its own stigma; thus the flower rarely self-fertilizes.

Most sweet clover populations exhibit a biennial (2-year) life cycle, though annual plants also exist, the difference accounted for by the presence of a single gene pair. In a 1981 study, researchers Kenneth M. Klemow and Dudley J. Raynal demonstrated the uniqueness of sweet clovers' biennialism. Whereas most biennials such as Queen Anne's lace *(q.v.)* are *semelparous* or *facultative* (that is, biennial if conditions are right for flowering, but if not, able to survive in rosette form for several years until they are), sweet clovers are *obligate* (that is, necessary or invariable) biennials—they complete their life cycle in 2 years regardless of stress or competitive factors that may cause flowering delay in facultative biennials.

Sweet clover seedlings typically emerge in 2 main growth flushes—in March–April and September–October. Some may germinate from seeds that have lain for years in the soil, since the hard seed coats sometimes require a lengthy period to lose dormancy and become permeable to moisture. Seeds may also germinate during winter thaws of 3 days or more. The seedling forms a leafy stem 10 or 12 inches high; it produces no flowering stems the first year (except in annual plants), but develops a thick, carrotlike taproot that holds food reserves and may penetrate 4 feet deep. The root is also contractile, pulling the budded root crown 2 inches or more below the soil line in the fall, protecting it from surface freezing. This first-year

root growth supports flower and seed production in the plant's second year, when buds on the root crown produce 1 to 10 erect, fast-growing stems. The plants die after producing seed. Almost all seedlings that sprout during late summer and fall also die before spring. Most survivor plants are those that first appear from March to May.

On the raceme, flowering proceeds from the bottom up, with the progression much faster in yellow sweet clover. Racemes, often longer in *M. alba* plants, typically hold 40 to 80 individual flowers, each flower lasting for about 2 days. Yellow sweet clover, with slightly smaller flowers, usually begins flowering a few days or weeks earlier in June than white sweet clover.

In his book *The Power of Movement in Plants,* Charles Darwin described the "sleep of leaves," a nighttime movement of sweet clover's trifoliate leaflets: They twist in a 90-degree turn, the longer terminal leaflet bending to touch upper sides with one of the side leaflets, apparently a protective, heat-conserving adaptation. (Leaves of many legumes are likewise sensitive to atmospheric pressure, temperature, and humidity.)

Sweet-smelling sweet clover racemes flower in acropetal style, from the bottom up; in this view, all flowering stages, from buds to seedpods, may be seen.

Seedpods, holding 1 or 2 seeds, appear highly variable in number—sometimes more than 200,000 in white sweet clover, often less than 100,000 in yellow. The first seedpods usually ripen by late July or early August in the Northeast. Not firmly attached (though some may remain on the plant over winter), the pods typically release their seeds as soon as they mature. Rainwash disperses many of them. The hard seed coats require *scarification* or abrasion of the seed coat—usually accomplished by natural freezing and thawing, sometimes by ground fire—before they can germinate. Seeds may remain viable for 40 years or longer in the soil. Sweet clovers reproduce only by seed—no vegetative cloning occurs.

Source of sweet clovers' vanilla fragrance, mainly emanating from the flowers but also from the young leaves, is a substance called coumarin, a compound that occurs in many plants, including bedstraws, lavender, woodruff, strawberries, and cinnamon. Though sweet smelling, coumarin tastes bitter; it probably evolved as a defense against insect (and possibly vertebrate) herbivores. (See Lore.)

These 2 common sweet clover species often occur together, but despite their many similarities, they rarely hybridize under natural conditions. In some such areas, each biennial species tends to flower in alternate years.

   Associates: Intolerant of shade, flooding, and acid soils, sweet clovers frequent disturbed areas, fields, gravel pits, and roadsides almost worldwide. They are *calciphiles,*
favoring limy soils. Pioneering plant colonizers of disturbed or eroded sites, they quickly
germinate in bare ground but cannot long maintain large populations in competition
against perennials that become established. White sweet clover shows somewhat wider
geographical distribution than yellow, probably because of its greater frequency as a crop
planting. It also produces more nectar and extends farther north into arctic Canada. Yellow
sweet clover may occupy somewhat drier soils, though the deep taproot of both species
makes them highly adaptable to drought conditions.

   Sweet clovers' chief associates are the nitrogen-fixing bacteria that inhabit root nodules in all legumes, a true mutualism. *Rhizobium meliloti* bacteria convert atmospheric
nitrogen into ammonia, a form of nitrogen usable to the plant. "The legume gets a plentiful
supply of ammonia from the bacterium for protein production," as ecologist Richard
Brewer wrote, and "from the plant, the bacterium receives photosynthate [carbohydrate
food manufactured by photosynthesis] and a suitable microhabitat."

   Numerous fungi parasitize sweet clovers, but few are widespread or a serious mortality factor. They include root rot *(Phytophthora cactorum),* crown rot *(Sclerotinia trifoliorum),* black stem *(Ascochyta meliloti, Cercospora davisii),* stem canker or gooseneck *(A.
caulicola,* causing stunted, bent stems), and pepper spot *(Leptosphaerulina trifolii),* which
causes pepperlike lesions on the leaves, eventually withering them.

   Many if not most insect herbivores that frequent alfalfa *(q.v.)* may also be found on
sweet clovers. White sweet clover seems to attract a larger variety of insects than yellow.
Probably these plants' most common insect foliage eater and destructive pest is the sweetclover weevil *(Sitona cylindricollis),* which defoliates seedlings, chewing crescent-shaped
notches in leaf margins. Other leaf feeders include grasshoppers, cutworm (dart moth)
caterpillars *(Agrotis, Feltia,* others), a pyralid moth caterpillar *(Nomophila nearctica),* and
green cloverworms *(Hypena scabra),* noctuid moth caterpillars. Caterpillars of eastern tailed
blue butterflies *(Everes comyntas),* downy and dark green, feed on many legumes, including
sweet clovers (mainly yellow). *Epicauta* blister beetles, exuding caustic cantharidin, sometimes feed on young, low-coumarin plants, as do clover leaf weevils *(Hypera punctata).*
Sweetclover aphids *(Therioaphis riehmi),* pea aphids *(Acyrthosiphon pisum),* and spittlebug
nymphs *(Philaenus leucophthalmus),* hidden in froth, suck sap from the plants. Transverse
or 3-banded ladybird beetles *(Coccinella trifasciata),* among others, attack the aphids. Alfalfa
plant bugs *(Adelphocoris lineolatus),* light green sap suckers, also commonly feed.

   Foremost pollinators and nectar seekers are honeybees *(Apis mellifera;* see Lore), but
sweet clovers' fragrance and copious nectar attract many other visitors as well. These
include alfalfa leaf-cutting bees *(Megachile rotundata);* halictid bees (Halictidae); butterflies

such as small blues (Polyommatinae); moths such as the Virginia ctenucha *(Ctenucha virginica)*, a spectacular wasp moth; plus soldier beetles *(Chauliognathus pennsylvanicus)*, syrphid or hover flies *(Sphaerophoria)*, and parasitic eulophid wasps *(Tetrastichus)*.

Root feeders include the sweetclover root borer *(Walshia miscecolorella)*, a cosmopterigid moth caterpillar, and larvae of the aforementioned sweetclover weevils and the clover root curculio *(Sitona hispidulus)*. Tiny soybean cyst nematodes or roundworms *(Heterodera glycines)* create galls or cysts on the roots.

Moderately valuable as wildlife food plants, sweet clovers provide both seeds and leaves for upland gamebirds such as sharp-tailed grouse, ring-necked pheasants, greater prairie-chickens, and gray partridges. One recent study, however, found that northern bobwhites, dark-eyed juncos, and Harris's sparrows, given a choice, favored seeds of yellow foxtail grass *(Setaria glauca)* over those of yellow sweet clover. Ring-necked pheasants sometimes nest in white sweet clover stands along roadsides. Deer mice store sweet clover seeds, muskrats sometimes feed on the roots, and cottontail rabbits, ground squirrels, elk, and white-tailed deer forage on leaves and stems. Deer and livestock grazers also relish the flowers.

Lore: Both as widespread weeds and soil-improving forage crops, sweet clovers produce not only abundant flowers and seeds, but also mixed feelings in the minds of conservationists and farmers. In North America, as one account reports, they "have been the subject of a love-hate relationship with humans." Natives of central Eurasia but long resident in North America (first reported in 1664), sweet clovers rarely underwent cultivation until about 1900, when agronomists discovered that "they have no equal as a soil-improving crop," as one research team wrote. Not only do the nitrogen-processing root nodules (see Associates) increase soil fertility, but the strong taproots aerate the subsoil, and the ultimate decay of roots and plant parts improves the soil's physical condition *(tilth)*. Often planted and plowed under as green manure, sweet clovers also provide quality forage, both as hay and pasturage. Second-year plants make less palatable forage owing to their coarse stems but can be used for silage and straw. The problem of sweet clovers' coumarin component—which may cause a fatal anticlotting reaction ("bleeding disease") in cattle—has been largely eliminated in crop sweet clovers by genetic development of low-coumarin cultivars. (Coumarin itself is harmless, but its fungal conversion to dicoumerol, the toxic substance, occurs in improperly cured plants.) Coumarin content tends to rise as the plants age, making late-summer growth less palatable for livestock than spring and early-summer plants.

One of sweet clovers' foremost commercial uses occurs as "bee pasture." Most honey marketed today comes from alfalfa and sweet clovers (white sweet clover produces more nectar than yellow). Light in color and mild in fragrance and flavor, sweet clover honey has achieved renown as the highest-quality honey available.

Beekeepers probably hastened the continentwide dispersal of sweet clovers. Before 1900, when the plants were almost universally despised as intrusive weeds, beekeepers would stealthily sow the seeds along roadsides, were often blamed whenever the plants appeared in a new area. New England and some of the central states still class sweet clovers as noxious weeds, invading wheat and barley fields. Yet farmers frequently plant them as companion crops with oats, and sweet clovers often prove a mainstay of regular crop-rotation programs owing to their soil-improvement utility. Sweet clovers' effects are not totally beneficial, however, even to farmers who raise them as crops. These plants draw calcium, phosphate, and potassium from the soil in much larger amounts than do hay crops of grass—"great enough to cast doubt on the over-all soil improving future of legumes in the rotation," as one agricultural source noted, despite their nitrogen-adding capacities. America's love-hate reactions toward these plants are well illustrated by the current contradictory research efforts involving these plants: In some areas, researchers are actively pursuing biocontrol options using the aforementioned sweetclover weevils—at the same time that in other, sweet clover–kindlier areas, pesticidal and biocontrol efforts proceed against the same weevils.

Probably the greatest stimulant to sweet clover germination and rejuvenation is spring or fall burning. Fire scarifies (abrades) the hard exteriors of long-dormant seeds in the soil, resulting in a new, pioneering ground cover and bee pasture. Successive summer burns can also be used to suppress and reduce sweet clover during its critical growth periods.

Homeopathic practitioners have prescribed teas made of dried sweet clover flowers and plants for everything from nervous headaches to flatulence, and poultices for every sort of wound and fester—even, smoked in a pipe, for asthma. Coumarin, used for manufacture of the compound warfarin, a rodenticide and anticoagulant, is processed from sweet clovers and other plants.

Young leaves of sweet clover, high in protein, can be added to salads or eaten as cooked greens; dried and crushed, they add a vanillalike flavor to pastries. The seeds can also flavor soups and stews.

Teasel, Common *(Dipsacus sylvestris).* Teasel family. Standing 2 to 6 feet tall, this alien biennial has long, paired leaves that embrace the ridged, prickly stem at their bases; a spiny, egg-shaped flowerhead with lavender florets atop the solitary stem or branch; and a densely spined seedhead.

Other names: Teazel, wild or card teasel, gypsy combs, church-broom, clothier's-brush, shepherd's-thistle, Venus-cup.

Close relatives: Almost 15 teasel species exist, all native to Eurasia and north Africa. Botanists disagree on the nomenclature, but other alien teasels present in the Northeast include fullers' teasel (*D. fullonum,* a name used by some botanists for the common teasel) and cut-leaf teasel (*D. laciniatus*). Other teasel family plants, some 10 genera, also originated in the Old World; they include devil's bits *(Succisella, Succisa),* pincushion-flowers *(Scabiosa),* and blue buttons or field scabious *(Knautia).* Teasel flowerheads much resemble those of the aster or composite family in appearance.

Lifestyle: "The old teasel stalks standing gaunt and gray in the fields," wrote naturalist Anna Botsford Comstock, "seem like old suits of armor." What an imposing piece of architecture is the domed seedpod of teasel, a mound of sharp minarets, spined as a porcupine, "a panoply of spears," in Comstock's words. The flowerhead *(inflorescence)* that produces it is no less spectacular. Inflorescences typically number 3 to 9 per plant but may range from only 1 up to 35. Usually 3 or 4 inches in length, the inflorescence stands surrounded by upcurved, pronged bracts, some of which extend above it. Flowers do not appear all at once. The first ones open in a ring about midway up the oval head; thence rings of flowers move both upward and downward from the middle over a period of weeks from July to September. The top and bottom of the inflorescence become the last areas to produce flowers and seed.

The flowers themselves, consisting of 4 fused lilac or dark pink petals, 4 (male) stamens, and 1 (female) pistil, are *protandrous* (stamens maturing before the pistil), thus making them sequentially unisexual and promoting cross-pollination (by insects) from teasels with flowers in other time phases. Self-pollination and self-fertilization occasionally occur, but the resulting seeds often show low viability.

A single plant may produce 3,000 or more 1-seeded *achenes,* which mature on the head and simply drop off in the fall. Teasel's seeds float in water; the plant's dispersal in North America has mainly proceeded along creeks and rivers. Most of the seeds germinate from April to June, producing ground-hugging rosettes of crinkled leaves that increase in size until late fall, then overwinter (though rosette leaves may turn brownish green and portions of them die off). If, by autumn, the rosette reaches a critical size of about a foot in diameter, it produces a flowering stem from its center the next May; then the entire plant dies after producing seeds. Teasel exhibits this 2-year (biennial) life cycle, however, only in optimal conditions and habitats. It is a *semelparous* plant,

Teasel's large, spiny seedpod is this plant's dominant feature, presenting a formidable defense against herbivores.

often surviving 3 or more years until the rosette achieves the critical size for flowering. Thus some botanists prefer to call this plant a *monocarpic perennial* (that is, a plant that lives until it bears seed only once) rather than a biennial.

Teasel's taproot, often exceeding 2 feet in length, gives it a drought-competitive edge over shorter-rooted plants found in its habitats. The plant reproduces only by seed, does not sprout vegetative clones. Yet despite its noncloning habit, common teasel often forms dense, slow-spreading colonies and thickets. Teasel's habit of providing its own optimal seedling sites—relatively large patches of bare ground, formerly covered by a teasel plant's basal leaves and newly exposed when an old plant dies—probably accounts for its often populous colonies.

Teasel leaves, a study unto themselves, occur in pairs, spaced at 90-degree angles to each other down the stem, thus receiving maximum sunlight. Often spiny on their under-side midribs, the leaves and prickly stems discourage munchers. Also, the united opposite leaf bases form small receptacles or cups next to the stem itself; these hold rainwater, act-ing as traps and providing microhabitats for various organisms (see Associates). Some botanists believe that teasel shows us the evolutionary beginnings of plant insectivory, as seen in pitcher-plants (*Sarracenia;* see *The Book of Swamp and Bog*).

Associates: Widely adapted to many sorts of soils, common teasel favors moist, open, low-lying ground, as along drainage ditches and in floodplain meadows. It also resides in old fields, vacant lots, dumps, and other disturbed-soil areas. A prominent roadside weed, in recent decades it has colonized many areas along interstate highways. The plant is a *halo-phyte,* tolerating road salt. Its large leaf rosettes shade out many competing seedlings such as grasses, though it emits no known *allelopathic* (plant-inhibiting) chemicals. Teasel ranges across the continent in areas of local abundance, perhaps reflecting multiple introductions from its native Eurasia (see Lore). It does not inhabit arctic or subarctic regions, also shuns the northern Great Plains, presumably because of cold climate or lack of adequate moisture.

Teasel seems relatively free of both fungous and insect parasites. Occasional fungi found on the plant include leaf and stem spots *(Cercospora elongata, Mycosphaerella asteri-noides, Phoma oleracea);* downy mildews *(Peronospora dipsaci, Phyllactinia corylea);* and the root rot *Phymatotrichum omnivorum.*

The plant's spines and downward-pointing prickles discourage most insect and mam-mal herbivores. Any stem crawlers the barbs don't deter, the water pools (called *phytotel-mata,* meaning "plant ponds") cupped by the leaf bases do; "there is no drawbridge over this moat," as one naturalist wrote. Phytotelmata probably defend mainly against ants climbing toward the flower. Often, however, such insects tumble into the rainwater cis-terns. These so-called teasel or axil waters form one of the most intriguing microhabitats among plants, akin to the aquatic reservoirs of pitcher-plants, bromeliads, some angelicas, and more than 70 other plants worldwide. In addition to the creatures that drown in the pools, creating a nutrient "soup," a roster of living organisms—many of them protozoa and ciliate fauna—inhabit these waters. Zoologist Bassett Maguire, Jr., analyzed the axil waters of 113 teasel plants in 1956 and found a minute biota consisting of hypotrichs, the ciliates *Colpoda, Cyclidium,* and holotrich species, rotifers, nematodes (roundworms), rhabdocoels (turbellarian flatworms), *Aeolosoma* annelid (segmented) bristle worms, and tardigrades (water bears), plus green, spherical, one-celled algae and strands of filamentous algae—a surfeit of life. Yet "the surface area of the water in teasel axils seldom exceeds about 25 square centimeters and is commonly less than 1 square centimeter," reported Maguire. Also, the time available for biotic colonization of these isolated bodies of water does "not persist much longer than 2 months." The puzzling question remains: How do these organisms get there? For, as Maguire pointed out, they "must not only have been transported overland to the teasel axil, but also must have entered the teasel axil community . . . against pressures such as competition and predation." In addition, they are able to survive and reproduce in the high temperature and low oxygen content of the axil waters. Their unknown "mechanisms of passive dispersal," as Maguire wrote, "must be very effective."

Sources have named "unidentified stem-boring lepidoteran [moth] larvae"—probably noctuid caterpillars similar to those found in sunflower and common burdock (both *q.v.*)—in teasel that sometimes weaken the stem.

Foremost teasel pollinators are bumblebees *(Bombus)* and smaller bees. The flowerhead spines prevent "body pollination" by flower crawlers; the bees pollinate mainly by picking up and depositing pollen in their head fur as they forage. Butterflies, including pipevine swallowtails *(Battus philenor),* also visit.

Teasel seed is said to be eaten by ants; presumably they harvest it from the ground rather than from seedheads.

Probably several seed-eating birds, in addition to observed white-winged crossbills and American goldfinches, forage on the seedhead. Teasel thickets along pasture edges also provide cover for many birds; such thickets have been cited as frequent migration and winter habitats for Lincoln's sparrows.

No mammals are known to graze on these tongue-ripping plants.

Lore: Teasel has no widely known human medicinal or food usages (except for its tasty honey), but its spiny seedheads once served admirably as combs for carding wool and making mohair fabric, both in the home and in textile factories. Some of the latter industries grew their own fields of teasel—specifically fullers' teasel, differing from common teasel in its larger seedheads—for such purposes. Thoreau noted frequent teasel heads floating in Concord River "from factories above," the currents thus distributing the plant along New England watercourses. From its nap-teasing function for wool fabric comes the plant's English name. The men who cut the teasel heads in Somerset and Yorkshire "wore a kind of waterproof smock," wrote F. Martin Duncan, "to prevent their clothes being drenched with water from the teasel cups," and they also wore thick leather gloves. The heads, set in a frame, carded the wool fabric that passed beneath the combs. "Although all sorts of methods have been tried for this particular kind of work," reported Duncan, "nothing quite so good as teasel heads" has ever been found. Their value apparently resides in the fact that they break at any obstruction in the fabric rather than snag and tear the cloth, as metal combs do.

Teasel seedheads have long been popular in flower or dried bouquets, wreaths, and decorations. It is said that teasel's frequent spread in cemeteries owes to such arrangements placed on graves.

Whether or how much the plant benefits from its cuplike leaf cisterns remains unknown. Naturalist Francis Darwin said he observed protoplasmic filaments extending from plant tissue into the water, but these may have been strands of filamentous algae. "You would not care to drink the water standing in the teasel cups," wrote Duncan, "for it looks and smells most unpleasant." Yet old sources state that teasel waters were once considered a wayfarer's thirst quencher, and the genus name *Dipsacus* (from the Greek *dipsa*, meaning "thirst") refers exactly to this wayside quaff. Washing in the water also provided a certain cure for warts, it was said.

Teasel probably arrived in North America with early settlers who brought it as an ornamental or for carding wool.

Thistle, Canada *(Cirsium arvense)*. Aster family. This colonial alien perennial, common almost everywhere, has small, pale lilac to rose-purple or pinkish, brushlike flowerheads. Extremely fragrant, they occur in branching, somewhat flat-topped clusters atop the plant. The crinkled, lobed, and very prickly leaves are gray-green. Degrees of leaf lobing and spininess differ among individuals and varieties of this plant. Unlike many thistles, this species has smooth, unspined stems. It stands 1 to 5 feet tall.

Other names: Field, cursed, creeping, corn, hard, prickly, or way thistle.

Close relatives: Some 200 *Cirsium* species exist worldwide, some of them native to North America. Among the latter are the pasture thistle *(C. pumilum)*, the field thistle *(C. discolor)*, the tall thistle *(C. altissimum)*, the dune thistle *(C. pitcheri)*, and the swamp thistle *(C. muticum)*. The bull thistle *(C. vulgare)*, another common alien, is one of the largest. *Carduus* or plumeless thistles—among them the musk or nodding thistle *(C. nutans)*—closely resemble the *Cirsium* thistles. Other near kin include common burdock *(q.v.)*, milk-thistles *(Silybum)*, and spotted knapweed *(q.v.)*, among numerous family genera.

Lifestyle: Canada thistle, the most abundant thistle on our continent, is also the only *dioecious* North American thistle (that is, with male and female flowers occurring on separate plants). "Occasionally," as botanist Arnold Appleby noted, "a male flower will produce a seed, so separation is not absolute." Indeed, some studies indicate that up to a quarter of all "male" plants can self-pollinate and produce seed. Actually, all the flowers are *perfect* (bisexual), but female pistils are vestigial or abort in some flowers and male stamens do likewise in others, producing functionally unisexual flowers. The functionally male flowerheads appear rounder in shape and somewhat smaller than the female flowerheads, which look more flask-shaped.

This "long-day" plant requires 15 hours of day length in order to begin flowering, usually in middle June or early July, lasting into September. Thistle flowerheads consist exclusively of tubular disk flowers; no ray flowers, as seen in daisies or sunflowers, are present. The shaving brush–like purple heads, massive in some thistle species, appear modest in size, less than an inch across, but emit a very sweet-smelling aroma in Canada thistle. The flowerheads typically contain about 100 florets. Healthy plants may produce 30 to 60 flowerheads in clusters of 1 to 5 per branch atop the plant.

The insect-pollinated flowers produce 1-seeded *achenes*. An average plant may develop 30 to 70 achenes per flowerhead some 10 days or so after flowering; a single plant typically produces about 1,500. Seeding success depends upon the extent of pollination, hence nearness of a male thistle clone. Studies have shown that female clones separated by only 50 to 100 feet from a male clone produce much larger amounts of seed than clonal colonies sited 500 feet or farther apart. The feathery plume or *pappus* (thistledown) attached to the achene, existing in many aster family plants, aids in wind dispersal up to a mile or more. Many observers have noted the tendency of thistle plumes to float free, however, leaving their achenes back in the seedhead; those little wisps of fluff so often seen riding the breezes in late summer and fall are parachutes gone astray. Thistle seeds can germinate immediately, sprouting best at temperatures of 70 degrees F and above. Seedlings form leafy rosettes in the fall, and flowering stems emerge the following spring. Unsprouted seeds, dormant in the soil until spring or later, may remain viable for 20 years.

In order to produce seed (left), female Canada thistle plants must reside within several hundred feet of a male stand of the plants; thistle flowerheads consist solely of disk florets.

But Canada thistle reproduces most successfully not by seed, but by vegetative means. The plant lacks *rhizomes* (horizontal underground stems), despite assertions otherwise in various plant manuals, but it buds extensively from creeping roots. New plants can develop from root fragments as small as 1/4 inch in size. A single plant, which may extend 13 to 20 feet laterally in a season, sprouting genetically identical clones, may produce a 60-foot-diameter clonal thicket in 3 seasons, eventually spanning more than 100 feet. The subsurface root connections last only about 2 years before decaying, eventually isolating clones or clonal groups from the parent, but each individual also proceeds to send out its own budding roots. Seed production depends upon the proximity of both male and female plants in an area. Thistle's aerial stems die back to the roots in the fall.

In addition to its wide-spreading horizontal roots, thistle also sinks slender, vertical taproots, often down to the water table; root depths of 6 to 9 feet are common, occasionally extending much deeper. Root secretions may inhibit germination *(allelopathy)* of thistle seed in the vicinity as well as seeds of clovers *(q.v.)*, wheat, flax, and certain other plants. Thistle's deep roots and allelopathy, as well as its spiny foliage, probably give these plants a competitive edge over shallower-rooted, less drought-resistant, and more mammal-palatable plants, including many crop species.

Associates: Canada thistle—not a native of Canada, where it ranges widely, but of southeastern Europe and the eastern Mediterranean region—has long gone worldwide, today occupying almost every continent. Northward, it extends to 59 degrees N latitude in Canada, south to about 35 degrees N latitude. It also resides in temperate regions of the Southern Hemisphere. Adaptable to numerous soils and habitats, Canada thistle thrives best in open, sunny, fairly moist locales where soil has been disturbed—roadsides, old fields, overgrazed pastures, fencerows, campgrounds, recent burns, often in marshy ground or ditches (these last may provide invasion corridors). It favors clay soil or silt loams but can grow on almost any soil except peat and in waterlogged sites. Although it often invades cropland (infesting at least 27 crops in 37 countries) and native vegetation, Canada thistle rapidly declines in shade. Certain so-called "smother crops," planted to choke and shade out weeds, are sometimes planted by farmers in defense. "To be effective against Canada thistle," one report states, "the crop must come up first, grow rapidly during the early summer, and retain vigor until frost." Two of the most effective thistle smother crops are alfalfa and sweet clovers (both *q.v.*).

At least a dozen fungi parasitize Canada thistle, but none to serious extent. A rust fungus, *Puccinia punctiformis,* and a leaf-spot fungus, *Septoria cirsii,* are specific to Canada thistle, weakening both seed and vegetative reproduction. *Sclerotinia sclerotiorum,* a wilt fungus that attacks crown and roots, is not a host-specific parasite. These fungi may, in combination with certain insect parasites (mentioned below), provide a measure of thistle biocontrol. Other nonspecific thistle fungi include powdery mildew *(Erysiphe cichoracearum)*, root rots *(Fusarium)*, sclerotial blight *(Sclerotium rolfsii)*, and several others. Buttonbush-dodder *(Cuscuta cephalanthi)*, a parasitic vine, sometimes climbs and taps into thistle stems.

Despite Canada thistle's formidable foliage defenses—its prickly spines—this plant hosts some 84 insect feeders, plus about 45 occasional visitors and insect predators. Hardly any of these insects are exclusive to thistles, however. Plainly this plant's defensive armory aims mainly at mammal grazers.

Sap suckers (heteropterans) on leaves and stems are numerous. Plant bug sap suckers include four-lined plant bugs *(Poecilocapsus lineatus)*, rapid plant bugs *(Adelphocoris rapidus)*, tarnished plant bugs *(Lygus lineolaris)* plus other *Lygus* species, black bugs *(Corimelaena pulicaria)*, and one-spotted and two-spotted stink bugs *(Euschistus variolarius, Cosmopepla bimaculata)*. Among homopterans, spittlebug (froghopper) nymphs *(Philaenus spumarius)* feed beneath the froth they excrete. Treehoppers, humped or thorn-shaped, include *Campylenchia latipes, Entylia carinata,* and *Stictocephala* species. Leafhoppers, elongate jumpers, include a dozen or so genera; common ones include clover leafhoppers *(Aceratagallia sanguinolenta)* plus *Erythroneura aspera, Helochara communis,* and others. Thistle aphids *(Brachycaudus cardui)* plus artichoke aphids *(Capitophorus elaeagni)* and green peach or spinach aphids *(Myzus persicae)* reside commonly on thistles; most of them winter on other plants, feeding on thistle (and other plants) only in summer. A common aphid predator on thistles is the insidious flower bug *(Orius insidiosus)*, also called the minute pirate bug.

Thistle leaf munchers include several grasshoppers; the differential and migratory grasshoppers *(Melanoplus differentialis, M. sanguinipes)*, plus other *Melanoplus* thistle feeders, are known as spur-throated short-horned grasshoppers. Look for leaf beetles: *Pyrrhalta, Psylliodes, Hydrothassa vittata.* The tortoise beetle *(Cassida rubiginosa)*, a defoliator, and shining leaf beetles *(Lema cyanella)* are fairly common. Flea beetles, small jumpers, include *Disonycha* and *Longitarsus* species plus *Altica carduorum*, a possible biocontrol insect. Alfalfa weevils (see Alfalfa) skeletonize the leaves as adult insects.

Moth caterpillars include noctuids: the subgothic dart or dingy cutworm *(Feltia subgothica)*, other darts *(Agrotis)*, the variegated cutworm *(Peridroma saucia)*, and the clover looper *(Caenurgina crassiuscula)*. Caterpillars of the painted lady butterfly *(Vanessa cardui)*, hairy and yellowish green, construct webbed nests on the plants. Mainly resident in southern states, painted lady populations irrupt every 8 to 11 years and the butterflies migrate northward; according to one report, "they can be very effective biocontrol agents" of thistle.

Feeders in the flowerhead include flower thrips *(Frankliniella tritici)*, tiny amber-yellow insects with fringed wings; flower weevils *(Baris subsimilis);* the scythridid moth caterpillar *Scythris eboracensis,* which forms webs on the flowerheads; and the aforementioned *Altica* flea beetle. Seedhead feeders may also be seen: the small milkweed bug (see Milkweed, Common); several seed weevils *(Acanthoscelides fraterculus, Gymnetron antirrhini, Larinus planus, Miccotrogus* species); and fruit fly (tephritid) larvae of *Orellia* species. Thistle midge larvae *(Dasineura gibsoni)* also consume the seed.

Thistle stem feeders and borers also dwell numerously: alfalfa weevils (see Alfalfa), rhubarb curculios *(Lixus concavus)*, the stem weevil *Centorhynchus litura* (which mines leaves as larvae and transmits the aforementioned *Puccinia* rust), and several moth caterpillar borers—mainly noctuids *(Papaipema* species), pyralids *(Dicymolomia julianis, Pyrausta subsequalis)*, and the artichoke plume moth *Platyptilia carduidactyla*. Larvae of the thistle stem gall fly *(Urophora cardui)* attack young shoots of the plant; this insect creates hard, round, woody galls beneath flowerheads, is said to be thistle's most promising biocontrol agent.

Thistle root feeders include larvae of strawberry root weevils (see Strawberry, Wild), the root weevil *Cleonus piger*, sweetclover root borers (see Clovers, Sweet), and the aforementioned stem weevil and flower weevils. Root knot nematodes or roundworms *(Meloidogyne)* also infest the roots.

Probably thistle's foremost pollinators are honeybees *(Apis mellifera)*, but many other bees plus wasps, beetles, and butterflies visit the flowers seeking their abundant nectar. An entire genus of butterflies *(Vanessa)* is labeled thistle butterflies because of their frequent presence at thistle flowers: American lady and painted lady *(V. virginiensis, V. cardui)* and red admiral *(V. atalanta)*. Other butterflies that frequent thistles include tiger swallowtails *(Papilio)*, black swallowtails *(P. polyxenes)*, great spangled fritillaries *(Speyeria cybele)*, regal fritillaries *(S. idalia)*, gulf fritillaries *(Agraulis vanillae)*, pearl crescents *(Phyciodes tharos)*, viceroys *(Limenitis archippus)*, and silver-spotted skippers *(Epargyreus clarus)*.

Many predatory and parasitic insects also visit thistles, capturing insect prey or parasitizing insect eggs and larvae. Familiar ones include ambush bugs *(Phymata)*, soldier beetles *(Chauliognathus pennsylvanicus)*, and ladybird beetles (Coccinellidae), plus many small parasitic wasps.

Not a wide variety of birds consume thistle seed. Best-known feeders are American goldfinches. This native bird and its alien plant resource exhibit other coactions as well. Goldfinches (being summer nesters) raid the seedheads for fluffy nesting materials as well as food; a ring of thistledown seen on the ground beneath the plant usually means that goldfinches have been pillaging. Thoreau attributed the wide occurrence of floating thistledown in August to the rummaging of goldfinches on the thistle heads. "The thistle seed would oftener remain attached to its receptacle," he wrote, "if this bird did not come like a midwife . . . to launch it in the atmosphere." The white thistledown nests of goldfinches, easily visible in shrubs after leaves drop in the fall, remain compact, so tightly woven that they hold rainwater, yet so flexible that they expand as nestlings grow. After the birds vacate, white-footed mice often adopt them for their own nests, piling on heaps of cattail down.

Goldfinch thistledown also turns up in other nests, such as those of yellow warblers, which sometimes raid last summer's goldfinch nests for spring nesting materials of their own. Goldfinches often nest within 100 yards of thistle-seed food sources (that is, stands of female plants). The birds probably disperse the plant to some extent, both by collecting thistledown and in their droppings. Clay-colored sparrows, inhabiting open, brushy areas, also forage heavily on thistle seeds. Ruby-throated hummingbirds often visit the flowers for nectar food.

Mammal feeders include pocket gophers, which store root cuttings in underground caches, sometimes establishing new thistle populations thereby. Probably other rodents collect root fragments and seeds as well. The earthen mounds of pocket gophers, badgers, and woodchucks in the Midwest often sprout thistles.

Cattle and horses avoid thistle foliage (which is more highly nutritious than alfalfa) because of its spines and prickles. In some national parks, Canada thistle has invaded along horse trails, apparently as a result of horses consuming unprocessed hay containing thistle seeds. Sheep and goats, however, relish the tender rosette leaves in spring. Both mule and white-tailed deer may occasionally forage on the plant, and grizzly bears are said to consume it (probably the roots) also.

Lore: To the thistle (perhaps the dwarf thistle, *C. acaule*), Scots claim, they owe their rescue from Norse invaders in 1263 (some accounts date the event in the 11th century)—specifically, when a Dane stepped on a thistle in the dark, cried out, and thereby alerted the sleeping Scots, who drove off the invaders. Thus the thistle, after a time, became Scotland's national emblem, bearing the Latin motto *Nemo me impune lacessit* ("No one provokes me with impunity"). Thus, not only the scourge of herbivores, thistle became, to the Scots, a Viking repellent and an emblem of independence and retaliation—also a symbol of Scots stereotypes, the burr in the dialect and supposedly prickly manners.

Canada thistle probably arrived in New France sometime in the early 1600s as a contaminant in crop seed or ship's ballast. It is said to have entered the American colonies via the hay for British general Burgoyne's horses during the Revolution. The plant did not appear west of the Alleghenies until after 1835, but by 1900 it resided in all the northern states.

Owing to its deep taproots and propensity to reproduce clonally and from root fragments, Canada thistle is not easily eliminated once it is established, especially in cropland. Not only do the plant roots survive ground fire, but no consistently effective biocontrols have been established to date; also, herbicide or mowing operations must be repeated for years to get rid of it. "Most weeds have some virtue," according to one exasperated gardener, "this outlaw has none."

Wrong, of course (and no Scotsman he). Thistles produce a fine honey, and beekeepers are never sorry to see them (unless they begin taking over clover fields). The plants, mainly the peeled young stems, are not only edible but highly nourishing, making a fine survival food, cooked or raw. Young leaves with spines removed can be served as salad or cooked greens. Removing thistle spines is not a simple job, however; it requires thick-gloved hands. Thistle's astringent properties were well known to herbalists from ancient times. Leaf teas, prescribed as tonics, also treated dysentery and diarrhea; externally (and ironically, given the thistle armory), thistle brews poulticed skin sores and rashes. American tribal healers quickly adopted the alien plant, especially its root, for treating mouth sores and upset innards.

The word *thistle* derives from various similar names meaning "something sharp" in old European languages. *Cirsium* apparently stems from *kirsos,* Greek word for a swollen vein, which a thistle poultice may have remedied; and *arvense* refers to "cultivated fields," where this weed seems most at home.

Tick-trefoil, Canadian *(Desmodium canadense).* Pea family. Tick-trefoil, a native perennial standing 2 to 6 feet tall, bears loose spikes of magenta, pink, or lavender (rarely white) pealike flowers above cloverlike trifoliate leaves (divided into 3 leaflets). Hairy, flat, jointed seedpods consisting of 3 to 5 segments ("sticktights") adhere to clothing or fur.

Other names: Showy or Canada tick-trefoil, sticktights, beggar's-lice, beggar ticks, devil's-thistle, tick-clover.

Close relatives: About 300 *Desmodium* species exist globally, most in warm regions. Northeastern tick-trefoils number about 22 species, many of them woodland residents. Some include naked tick-trefoil *(D. nudiflorum),* marked by a tall, leafless flower stalk; hoary tick-trefoil *(D. canescens),* branched and sticky; and panicled tick-trefoil *(D. paniculatum),* with long leafstalks and horizontal branchlets on flower stalks. Related genera include bush-clovers, vetches, alfalfa, clovers, birdsfoot-trefoil, lupine (all *q.v.*), and many others. Beggar-ticks *(q.v.)* are unrelated aster family plants.

Lifestyle: Canadian tick-trefoil, the showiest and commonest of this colorful spindly genus, attracts attention both in flower—a spectacular, elongated plume or *raceme,* progressively flowering up the stalk in July and August—and in its adherent seed, matted souvenirs stuck on one's clothing after a walk in the autumn fields. When not in flower or seed, however, this plant is easily overlooked.

Bisexual *Desmodium* flowers, irregular in form as are the flowers of most legumes, consist of a rooflike banner or *standard* petal, 2 oblong wing petals at the sides, and a keel of 2 fused petals that enfold 10 (male) stamens and a (female) pistil in its horizontal length. When an insect probes between the wing petals, the motion snaps down the keel, jerking the stamens loose and exploding a puff of pollen on the insect's underside. Those wing-petal triggers only function once—the flower dusts but a single time—which usually proves more than enough to paste ample seeds onto any passerby.

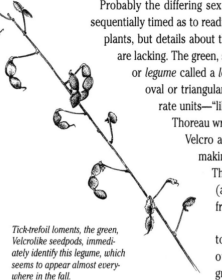

Probably the differing sex organs of individual *Desmodium* flowers are sequentially timed as to readiness, thus promoting cross-pollination among plants, but details about this, as about the frequency of self-pollination, are lacking. The green, slightly curved, inch-long fruit, a modified pod or *legume* called a *loment*, consists of a chain of several 1-seeded oval or triangular segments that ultimately tear apart as separate units—"like a piece of a saw blade with three teeth," as Thoreau wrote. Tiny, hooked hairs on the loment give it a Velcro adherence; hairs also cover the ridged stems, making insect approach via lower routes difficult. The hard seed coats require time or *scarification* (a scratch, break, or cut), often by means of freezing or fire, in order to germinate.

Tick-trefoil loments, the green, Velcrolike seedpods, immediately identify this legume, which seems to appear almost everywhere in the fall.

Tick-trefoil stems, as they lengthen, tend to *lodge*—that is, tilt over, sometimes against other plants, sometimes almost to the ground—"like raking masts with countless guys slanted far over the neighboring plants," as Thoreau wrote. Perhaps such lodging is an adaptation that brings seeds down to the pelt level of passing mammals. It's why loments often encrust one's socks after an autumn hike.

Associates: Canadian tick-trefoil favors open, sandy ground, dry or moist. Common sites include fields, clearings, roadsides, even wet prairies and fen edges. These plants often sprout quickly after a ground fire, which scarifies the seed, enabling it to germinate. "They love dry hillsides," wrote one observer; in some areas, tick-trefoil growth seems to favor north-facing slopes. This species resides across the continent but mainly north of the central states into southern Canada.

Like most legumes (see Alfalfa), tick-trefoil exists by means of a vital symbiosis. It creates nitrogen in a form available for its own and other plant use by means of root nodules containing nitrogen-fixing bacteria *(Rhizobium).*

Organisms exclusive to this plant are few if any. Many fungal and insect parasites that live on bush-clovers *(q.v.)* may also be found on *Desmodium.* A *Uromyces* rust is sometimes seen on the plant.

Among aphid sap suckers are *Microparsus variabilis* and *Aphis glycines,* the soybean aphid. Leaf miners include buprestid beetle larvae *(Pachyschelus confusus),* which feed between leaf layers; look for a little pocket on leaf undersides where the oval, black adult beetle inserts an egg. The related *P. laevigatus* also make broadly linear tracks beneath the leaf epidermis. Leaf-mining moth caterpillars include a nepticulid species *(Nepticula),* which etches winding mines around leaf margins; and a gracillariid *Phyllonorycter* species, which creates blotch mines in the leaf center. Other leaf miners include larvae of *Atomocera,* an argid sawfly.

Leaf feeders include the Mexican bean beetle *(Epilachna varivestis),* a leaf-eating lady beetle; both the spiny, yellow-orange larvae and the adults, yellow with black spots, skeletonize leaves from the underside.

Several butterfly caterpillars feed on *Desmodium,* among them silver-spotted skippers *(Epigyreus clarus),* yellow with 2 eyelike orange spots; the northern cloudy wing *(Thorybes pylades),* green with stripes and haired wartlets; and sometimes orange and clouded sulphurs *(Colias eurytheme, C. philodice),* grass green caterpillars. Butterfly caterpillars of the eastern tailed blue *(Everes comyntas),* sluglike and dark green, often feed in the flowerheads, as do hoary edge or frosted skippers *(Achalarus lyciades),* dark green caterpillars with orange spots.

Many adult butterflies visit the flowers as well: American coppers *(Lycaena phlaeas)* and gray hairstreaks *(Strymon melinus),* among others. Long-tongued bees (mainly bumblebees, *Bombus),* however, are tick-trefoil's chief pollinators.

Tick-trefoil depends upon animal mobility for seed dispersal, a stratagem known as *epizoochory.*

Although tick-trefoil seeds do not rank as an important wildlife food, several bird species consume them, most notably northern bobwhites. Ring-necked pheasants, wild turkeys, ruffed grouse, eastern towhees, and dark-eyed juncos also eat them. Among mammals, opossums and white-footed mice ingest the seeds, and elk and white-tailed deer relish the foliage.

Lore: Wearing corduroy trousers when walking afield is probably the best defense against acquiring a thick armor of the clinging loments. A small pocket comb can strip these hitchhikers from clothing.

Despite making its presence thickly "felt" in the fall, this native tick-trefoil is not much of an invasive or noxious weed. Moreover, it improves the soil wherever it grows, and it feeds a few creatures besides. Some *Desmodium* species, though not this one, are indeed planted as forage crops in some parts of the world. Like most legumes, the plant ranks high in protein and palatability.

No part of *Desmodium* is humanly edible, though people chewed the roots as a treatment for mouth sores in some tribal cultures.

The name *tick-trefoil* originated from the loment's ticklike adherence and from the 3-part form of the leaf. The Greek word *desmos* denotes "chain," again descriptive of the linear loment.

Timothy *(Phleum pratense).* Grass family. One of our most common hay forages and roadside grasses, timothy easily identifies itself by its narrow cylinder of a flower spike *(panicle),* which appears in early summer atop a stem 1 to 3 feet tall. Although an alien perennial, it has become thoroughly naturalized in North America.

Other names: Herd grass or Herd's-grass, cat's-tail.

Close relatives: About 10 *Phleum* species exist in temperate and cool regions worldwide. Mountain-timothy *(P. alpinum)* also resides globally but in wet meadows and bogs of colder regions; turf timothy *(P. bertolonii),* a smaller species, is sometimes planted as a pasture or turf grass. Grass kin includes foxtails *(Alopecurus),* brome-grasses *(q.v.),* and wild ryes *(Elymus),* plus all other grasses in this book and, totally, more than 100 northeastern genera.

Lifestyle: When timothy flowers, purple anthers coat the 2- to 6-inch-long, bristly cylinder atop the stem, a subtle coloration that hues the fields in mauve mist. Inspected closely, this spike seems one of the most attractive flowers of summer. Soon the anthers load with yellow pollen, producing a bright puff when flicked with a finger. These flowers, bisexual as in most grasses (see Bluegrasses) and both wind- and insect-pollinated, produce small, hard seeds enclosed in awned (bristled), urn-shaped husks. The prolific seeds, scattered by wind and livestock, often germinate soon after ripening in the fall, producing roots and shoots that remain over winter. Seeds may remain viable 4 to 5 years in the soil.

Individual timothy shoots are usually biennial, germinate one year, produce flower and seeds the next, then die. It is vegetative reproduction that makes this grass a perennial: *Tillers* (shoots) bud from stem bases, producing annual or biennial stems, essentially clones of the parent stem. In time, such growth gives the plant a bunch-grass form, with many stems rising densely from the original root mass, most of which is shallow and fibrous (though parts of it can extend 4 feet deep), thus maintaining the plant as a perennial. An entire cloning mass or tuft typically survives 4 to 5 (sometimes to 7) years. Not a sod-forming grass, shallow-rooted timothy extends no *rhizomes* (subsurface stems) and does not spread laterally.

Distinctive to timothy are its bulbous *corms* (sometimes called *haplocorms*)—swollen, thickened areas of the subsurface stem that store carbohydrates, enabling the plants to survive winter. Corms

Timothy in flower, its purplish, pollen-loaded anthers projecting from the flower spike, is not only a popular hay and forage crop, but also an important wildlife food resource.

develop in spring and early summer, giving rise to the tillers (often called *aftermath* or *rowen*). The corms die off with the individual stems.

Timothy leaves, flat, about 1/4 inch wide and 4 to 12 inches long, taper to a fine point. *Cilia* (small hairs) fringe the leaf margins. The topmost or *flag leaf,* beneath the flower spike and shorter than the others, extends upward alongside the stem. Unlike some forage grasses, timothy stems stand firm, seldom *lodge* (that is, become bent over by wind), thus are easily mowed and harvested for hay.

Associates: Residing in cool, humid climates, timothy occupies its native Eurasia from northern Norway and Scotland into the Baltic states and Russia. South, it extends into Algeria, also growing in temperate regions of South America. Its North American range spans central Alaska and southern Canada, residing south to the central tier of states. As a crop, it thrives mainly east of the Great Plains. Shallow-rooted timothy tolerates neither drought nor wet, acidic, or highly alkaline soils. It favors fertile loam and clay soils, also prefers open sunlight to moderate shade. It is a plant of few extremes. Its restrained vegetative reproduction makes it a so-called intermediate competitor in early to middle stages of plant succession after fire or other land disturbance. Although usually regarded as a nonaggressive grass, timothy can sometimes establish domination over other plants, colonizing by seed and forming self-sustaining grassland. It can strongly compete, in seedling stage, with conifer seedlings in pine, fir, or spruce plantations. Later, timothy growth may aid conifer plantings by excluding shrub competition.

Important fungal associates of timothy include *endomycorrhizae,* which penetrate the root cells and aid nutrient uptake of the roots.

More than 70 fungi (many of them classified as fungi imperfecti) parasitize timothy, but most do minimal damage and are relatively insignificant. One of the commonest is stem rust *(Puccinia graminis),* identified by reddish (later black) pustules on stems. Other fungi on timothy include eyespot or purple spot *(Heterosporium phlei),* causing oval, brown spots on leaves; brown stripe *(Scolecotrichum graminis),* showing spotted and streaked leaves; seedling blight *(Pythium graminicola);* and several others.

Timothy hosts relatively few insect foliage feeders. Most are stem-boring moth caterpillars that also occur on other grasses. False wainscots *(Leucania pseudargyria),* bordered apameas *(Apamea finitima),* and glassy cutworms *(A. devastator)* usually feed on stems and crown at or below the soil surface; all are noctuids. A tiny elachistid moth caterpillar *(Cosmistes illectella)* mines the leaves of timothy and other grasses. Broken-lined brocades *(Oligia fractilinea),* noctuids also called lined stalkborers, tunnel into stems, as do smartweed borers (see Knotweeds) and wheat stem maggots *(Meromyza americana),* which develop into frit flies. Meadow plant bugs *(Leptopterma dolabrata),* reddish brown or greenish white (depending on sex), suck the sap, as do chinch bugs *(Blissus leucopterus),* which hibernate over winter in the subsurface root crowns. Armyworms *(Pseudaletia unipuncta)* also feed on timothy. The stem suckers and borers mentioned probably inflict the most damage upon timothy. These insects often produce a visible effect known as *silvertop,* consisting of empty or dead seedheads resulting from stem damage and consequent loss of nutrients above the damage. The dead seedheads look silvery white scattered among the normal green heads.

Caterpillars of the European skipper *(Thymelicus lineola),* a grass skipper and relatively recent pest of timothy, feed at night on the flag leaf, then work down the stem. Other skipper caterpillars, identified as such by the necklike constriction behind the head, may also be found on timothy and other grasses.

The "soft cats' tails of timothy," as one naturalist called the flower and seed spikes, also attract guilds of pollen feeders and seedeaters. Along with wind, timothy visitors probably pollinate the plant as well. Pollen collectors include many bees, which easily gather it from the projecting anthers; "a bee simply scrambles up an inflorescence," as zoologist Bernd Heinrich noted, working much less hard for its larder than it must in collecting pollen from other flower types. Syrphid or hover flies such as *Melanostoma mellinum* also feed on the pollen. Very frequently in July, I observe four-lined plant bugs *(Poecilocapsus lineatus)* clustered on the heads, apparently feeding on the flower parts and residual pollen. Wheathead armyworms *(Faronata diffusa),* striped noctuid moth caterpillars, feed mainly on timothy and wheat heads at night. Swollen galls in the seedhead indicate the presence of grass seed nematodes or roundworms *(Anguina agrostis).*

Burrower bugs *(Sehirus cinctus)* sometimes forage among timothy roots. At least 15 species of nematodes also parasitize timothy roots; *Meloidogyne, Pratylenchus,* and *Tylenchus* are common species.

Many birds relish timothy seed. As one research team noted, "Probably songbirds feed on the seeds of roadside and fence-row timothy as least as much as on the hayfield plants," owing to this grass's common use as escape cover by birds. In one study area, greater white-fronted geese favored seedling timothy's youngest, tenderest leaf blades for food; researchers noted that this favoritism apparently increased leafy growth on the plant. Canada geese and sandhill cranes eat the corms, while northern bobwhites and horned larks frequently consume the seed. Songbird seedeaters include chipping, field, fox, song, vesper, American tree, and house sparrows; common and hoary redpolls; dark-eyed juncos, snow buntings, and American goldfinches; red-winged blackbirds, bobolinks, and brown-headed cowbirds. Roadside timothy stands also provide nesting and brood-rearing cover for blue-winged teal, sharp-tailed grouse, and prairie-chickens.

Among mammals, chipmunks consume the seeds, as do meadow voles. Naturalist Edwin Way Teale described signs of vole feeding on timothy as "little piles of crisscrossed, match-length sections of timothy stems." A vole, "intent on gaining the seedhead at the top . . . snips off a stem near its base," continuing to shorten the still-erect stem supported by adjacent stems "until the seed head has been lowered within reach." What's left is the pile of stem sections "almost uniform in length." Voles also store timothy corms in their underground burrows.

White-tailed deer, elk, and moose readily consume this grass. As livestock forage, timothy is considered as prime hay for horses. Farmers often plant it with clover and alfalfa as pasture mixture.

Lore: Found growing by one John Herd near Portsmouth, New Hampshire, about 1711—hence named Herd grass—timothy probably first arrived from England as a contaminant in hay, litter, and ship's ballast. The grass, cultivated here in North America before being recognized as a useful forage back in England (about 1763), was early promoted as a good hay and pasture resource by farmer Timothy Hanson. (Benjamin Franklin was the first recorded user of the name timothy in a 1747 letter, recognizing a Herd grass sample sent to him as "mere timothy," a label presumably adopted from Hanson's given name.) Hanson carried seed from New England to Maryland about 1720, later to North Carolina and Virginia. By 1747, timothy had become well known in eastern North America; by 1807, it had become the most important hay grass in the United States. Timothy production declined after 1900, partly because of declining numbers of horses on farms, also because improved cultivars of other pasture and hay grasses became available. Today farmers plant some 25 varieties or cultivars of timothy as hay and pasture forages, crops that rank second only to ryegrass *(Lolium perenne)* in planting frequency. As one report stated, "Its energy storage pattern" (that is, the corms) makes it a better crop for hay than for pasture forage owing to its high amount of dry matter. Timothy in its early flowering stages, or even before, appears more nutritious and fragrant than in later phases; its quality decreases after flowering. Early mowing, however, increases yield and causes a flush of aftermath growth, which makes good pasturage. In addition to livestock forage, timothy hay is widely recommended as food and bedding for rabbits, guinea pigs, chinchillas, and other caged mammal herbivores. Industry also uses timothy as a raw material for chlorophyll extraction.

Timothy provides a frequently used cover for land rehabilitation and erosion control after clear-cutting, burning, overgrazing, or construction of highways, railroads, and canals. Human food or medicinal uses for the plant are few if any.

For berrying afield, Thoreau recommended timothy stems for stringing together black raspberries, "the most convenient way of bringing them home if you have no dish."

Vetches *(Vicia* species). Pea family. Vetch leaves, divided into numerous oblong, opposite leaflets along the midrib, terminate in tendrils, by which these plants climb and sprawl upon other plants or supports. Flower stalks and color, as well as life cycle duration, vary among the species.

The 3 most familiar vetches in the Northeast are common vetch *(V. sativa),* an alien annual with 4 to 8 pairs of notched leaflets and pink or purple flowers that are single or paired; hairy vetch *(V. villosa),* an alien annual or biennial with hairy stems and leaves and 6 to 8 leaflet pairs with 10 to 40 usually bicolored (blue and white) flowers on densely crowded spikes; and bird-vetch *(V. cracca),* perennial natives and aliens with 8 to 12 leaflets, each with a pronounced spiny tip, and 20 to 50 blue-violet flowers crowded on one side of long-stalked flower spikes. All 3 species may stand 1 to 3 feet tall, but they often sprawl horizontally over surrounding vegetation.

Other names: Spring or pebble vetch, tare *(V. sativa);* sand, winter, woolly or woolypod, Russian, or Siberian vetch *(V. villosa);* blue, tufted, or cow vetch, cat pea, tinegrass *(V. cracca).*

Close relatives: Some 140 vetches exist worldwide. About 15 species, many of them alien, reside in northeastern North America. American or purple vetch *(V. americana)* is the only widespread native vetch. Crown-vetch *(Coronilla varia),* widely planted along highways for erosion control, has become an invasive alien nuisance in some areas. Legume relatives include clovers, sweet clovers, alfalfa (all *q.v.),* vetchling or wild pea *(Lathyrus),* milk-vetches *(Astragalus),* and tick-trefoils *(q.v.).* Other family plants include lupine, birdsfoot-trefoil, and bush-clovers (all *q.v.).*

Lifestyle: Resembling small, sprawling locust trees, vetches mat over the ground and upon other plants in summer, their flowers producing colorful hues of blue in fields and along roadsides. Most vetches bear *racemes,* long spikes with flowers that open in sequence from the bottom up; an exception is common vetch, which typically bears no raceme but only a pair of flowers in the upper leaf angles. Vetch racemes and leafstalks often curve, unlike those in similar pea family plants.

Form of the 3 species differs somewhat. Common vetch straggles or climbs, attaining tallest height (3 to 5 feet) only if supported by a tall grass such as rye or another tall plant; its taproots typically extend more than 2 feet down. Hairy vetch stems may reach 12 feet in length, but the plant's viny, sprawling habit seldom lets it rise more than 3 or 4 feet; it has a fibrous root mass with a taproot that extends to a depth of 1 to 3 feet. Bird-vetch, most distinctive because of its 1-sided flower and seed stalk, may form twining mats and tangled patches; it has wiry, spreading roots.

The vetch flower exemplifies the classic pea family type of 5 irregular petals: the topmost *banner* or *standard,* a wing petal at either side, and 2 fused keel petals that enclose the *sexual column* consisting of 10 (male) stamens and a (female) pistil. Keel parts slip aside as an insect lands to forage nectar at the base of the stamens, which dust the insect's underside with pollen at the same time that the top of the pistil, a sticky tongue *(stigma),* "licks" an arriving insect's belly for incoming pollen. This mechanisim adapts the flowers for cross-pollination. Vetch species differ in sexual strategies, however. Common vetch produces both aerial and

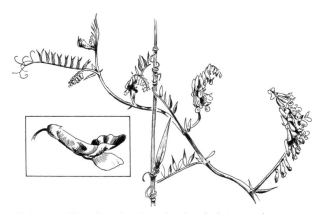

Vetches exemplify epiphytes that rely on other plants for their support by means of tendrils. Bird-vetch, as shown with flowers in characteristic 1-sided racemes, displays a typical pea family flower (inset profile).

cleistogamous (self-pollinating in the bud) flowers, creating most of its seed by self-fertilization *(autogamy).* Hairy vetch is often *protogynous* (sequentially unisexual, maturing its stigma before its anthers). It can also self-pollinate but requires insects to rupture the stigmatic membrane, releasing its stickiness; insect pollination thus produces much more seed than self-pollination in this species. Bird-vetch is mainly cross-pollinated. Much remains unknown and uncertain about vetch pollination, however; it is a subject "badly in need of clarification," according to one government agricultural handbook. Vetches typically flower from June into September.

Vetch fruits, called *legumes,* are flat pods an inch or more long that split into 2 twisted halves, releasing several seeds. At the right time, as one walks through a stand of vetches, the rustling explosions of rupturing pods, expelling their seeds, are audible. Common vetch germinates in spring, dies in fall; hairy vetch germinates in the fall, overwinters as a seedling, flowering and dying the next summer; bird-vetch may germinate in either spring or fall, with individual stems dying after they flower, but this species can also reproduce vegetatively by budding clones from its spreading roots.

Vetches' hard, impermeable seed coats require a period of freezing or chemical abrasion (as achieved in passage through animal intestines) in order to germinate. All vetch reproduction, except in the perennial bird-vetch, is by seed only.

At the base of each compound leaf in common vetch projects a pair of small *stipules,* each of which bears on its underside a reddish purple nectary, which secretes a thick, sugary fluid said to be more attractive to bees than the floral nectaries (see Associates). A few other vetches (but neither hairy vetch nor bird-vetch) also bear stipular nectaries.

Associates: All 3 vetches occupy similar habitats throughout most of North America—roadsides, vacant lots, old fields, pastures, cropland. Hairy vetch, probably the most widespread, is also resistant to drought, is shade-tolerant and the most adaptable to cold climates. Like most legumes, vetches improve the soil by means of a symbiotic relationship with nitrogen-fixing bacteria *(Rhizobium)*, which occupy nodules in the roots (see Alfalfa). Some studies indicate that vetch roots may release *allelopathic* compounds into the soil, inhibiting the growth of various grasses, but apparent effects are slight.

Vetches, via their curling tendrils at the ends of their compound leaves, are *epiphytes*—that is, they grow nonparasitically on other plants. Those tendrils indicate their reliance on plant species with taller, stronger stems—often cereal grasses—a coaction known as a *commensal* relationship, in which the vetches benefit (by acquiring greater access to light) and the host plants neither suffer nor benefit.

Vetches themselves host several parasitic fungi. These include *Ascochyta* species, causing a blight that creates spots on the leaves and lesions on stems and seedpods. *Botrytis* leaf-spot fungi produce dark red spots on foliage and stems of common vetch, while *Colletotrichum* anthracnose also produces spots and lesions. *Uromyces* rusts also affect all 3 vetches.

Hairy vetch hosts pea seed-borne mosaic virus, transmitted from vetches to pea fields by aphids. Bacterial brown-spot disease *(Pseudomonas syringae)* also resides harmlessly on hairy vetch, can cause disease outbreaks in adjacent bean fields. Bean and pea farmers try to eliminate nearby vetches, which can harbor disease-carrying legume viruses and bacteria.

Vetch sap suckers include pea aphids *(Acyrthosiphum pisum),* blue alfalfa aphids *(A. kondoi),* and cowpea aphids *(Aphis craccivora),* among others. Aphids attract aphid predators, especially convergent lady beetles *(Hippodamia convergens)* and seven-spotted lady beetles *(Coccinella septempunctata).* The insidious flower bug *(Orius insidiosus),* oval and black with white wing patches and one of agriculture's most valuable allies, is a small, active predator of aphids, thrips, insect eggs, and mites on many plants. Big-eyed bugs *(Geocoris punctipes),* with large eyes and a black-dotted pronotum (upper thorax plate), also attack plant-eating insects.

Other sap suckers include clover leafhoppers *(Aceratagallia sanguinolenta)* and potato leafhoppers *(Empoasca fabae).* Tarnished plant bugs *(Lygus lineolaris),* oval and flattened with mottled patterns, also suck sap as well as stipular nectar; other *Lygus* bugs are also common on vetches. Thrips *(Frankliniella),* minute black, sucking insects, often infest vetch flowers.

The stipular nectaries of common vetch attract many insects, including plant bugs *(Lygus),* bees, ants, and wasps (Vespidae, icheneumons). Studies indicate that an ant-plant mutualism may exist, whereby ants *(Formica, Solenopsis,* and the Argentine ant *Iridomyrmex humilis,* possibly others) attracted to the nectaries also attack insect foliage eaters, thereby protecting the plant from herbivore damage.

Caterpillars of the vetch looper moth *(Caenurgia chloropha)*, a noctuid, feed on the foliage, as do other legume-feeding moths (see Alfalfa, Clover). American grasshoppers *(Schistocerca americana)* also chew on vetches.

Vetches attract many butterflies, both as caterpillars and winged adults. A slug-shaped, light green caterpillar may be the silvery blue butterfly *(Glaucopsyche lygdamus)*. Eastern tailed blues *(Everes comyntas)*, downy, dark green caterpillars, often feed in the flower racemes as well as on the leaves. Common or clouded sulphur butterfly caterpillars *(Colias philodice)*, green with stripes, also feed on vetches, as do gray hairstreak caterpillars *(Strymon melinus)*, reddish brown. Adult butterflies seen at the flowers include the clouded sulphurs as well as eastern tiger swallowtails *(Papilio glaucus)*, great spangled frit-illaries *(Speyeria cybele)*, cabbage whites *(Pieris rapae)*, European skippers *(Thymelicus lineola)*, and others. Also look for hummingbird clearwings *(Hemaris thysbe)*, large, reddish brown sphinx moths that hover as they sip nectar.

Vetches' main seed pest is the vetch bruchid *(Bruchus brachialis)*, a seed beetle larva that bores into pods, consumes seeds, and completes its development there.

Pollinating insects include both nectar and pollen seekers. Foremost pollinators are honeybees *(Apis mellifera)*, many species of bumblebees *(Bombus)*, *Andrena* bee species, and small carpenter bees *(Ceratina)*. Bumblebees often bite holes at the base of the flow-ers, thereby tapping into the nectaries without entering the front-door pollination route, and other bees also exploit these holes. "The same bee always acts in the same manner," claimed anthropomorphic botanist Neltje Blanchan, "one sucking the nectar legitimately, another always biting a hole to obtain it surreptitiously, the natural inference . . . being that some bees, like small boys, are naturally depraved."

Many kinds of nematodes (roundworms) infest vetch roots, especially those of hairy vetch, which hosts some 30 species. *Belonolaimus, Heterodera,* and *Meloidogyne* are among the common genera.

Several gamebird species consume vetch leaves and seeds. These include ruffed and sharp-tailed grouse, ring-necked pheasants, greater prairie-chickens, wild turkeys, and northern bobwhites. Mourning doves also consume both items. Song sparrows and proba-bly other ground-feeding finches forage on the seeds, as do ground squirrels and possibly other rodents. Deer graze the plants to an unknown extent. Seeds of common and hairy vetches, containing cyanogenic glycosides, are toxic to cattle if ingested in quantity. Some reports ascribe toxic effects to aphids associated with the plant. Plainly a lot remains unknown about these plants and their associates.

Vetches also provide cover habitat for rabbits and mice.

Lore: Like their sweet clover *(q.v.)* relatives, vetches provide mixed blessings to farm-ers. On the one hand, they produce a soil-improving green manure and cover crop as well as nourishing, palatable hay, silage, and pasture forage for livestock. Many cultivars of hairy and common vetches exist; farmers often plant them in vetch-rye, wheat, or oat combinations for pasturage. On the other hand, vetches may infest cereal crops, their twining growth causing *lodging* (leaning) of grass stalks, increasing likelihood of disease and difficulty of harvest. Hairy vetch can be a serious pest weed in wheat. Bird-vetch, the perennial, appears the most persistent and difficult to control in grain and berry crops.

Common and hairy vetches produce excellent honey, the only humanly edible product of most vetches (except for fava or broad beans, the seeds of *V. faba,* an imported vetch raised for food in many areas).

Hairy vetch plantings have been found useful for highway medians and borders. The thick growth stabilizes the soil, needs scant mowing and maintenance, also provides a cost-effective, attractive alternative to spraying with herbicides.

Long grown in their native Europe as forage and cover crops, vetches probably originated in the Near East and arrived in the New World repeatedly at unknown dates; some came as seed contaminants in grain, some as crop seed. Bird-vetch, according to some authorities, may be a North American as well as Eurasian native, but most local populations appear alien in origin.

The word *vetch* stems from the Latin *vencire,* "to tie" or "bind," referring to the tendrils of these plants.

Wormwood, Common *(Artemisia absinthium).* Aster family. Recognize this alien perennial by its upswept branches lined with small, yellow-green flowerheads; its silky, gray-green, lobed and finely cut leaves; and its strong aroma when cut or bruised. Its several stems rising erect from a single woody crown and its 2- to 5-foot height often give it a coarse, shrubby appearance.

Other names: Absinthium, absinth, absinthe wormwood, wormwood sage, madderwort, varmit, warmut, green-ginger.

Close relatives: More than 100 *Artemisia* species range globally in the Northern Hemisphere and in South America. About a dozen reside in eastern North America, many though not all of them aliens. These include Roman wormwood *(A. pontica),* mugwort or sagewort *(A. vulgaris),* white sage or western mugwort *(A. ludoviciana),* biennial wormwood *(A. biennis),* and wild wormwood *(A. campestris).* Big sagebrush *(A. tridentata)* is the common bushy sagebrush of the West; another wormwood is the seasoning herb terragon *(A. dracunculus).* Near kin include tansies *(Tanacetum),* pineapple-weed *(Matricaria matricaioides),* and ragworts *(Senecio),* plus all of the many aster family plants in this book.

Lifestyle: This common weed, often seen growing in barren, unfertile land, flowers in summer, but its abundant flowers appear inconspicuous, crowded into the small, round heads *(inflorescences)* that, in this species, are hairy and tend to nod over. Like many aster family flowers, each consists of ray florets, which surround the central disk florets. Ray flowers are *pistillate* (female) with long stigmas, and the tubular disk flowers are bisexual. Wind-pollinated wormwood flowers produce abundant light, dry pollen that travels far on the breezes, but they produce no nectar. Inflorescences occur on the upper erect, leafy branches in July, but the number of flowerheads per stem varies inversely with the number of flowering stems. Plants consisting of 2 flowering stems, for example, may produce an average of 1,500 flowerheads per stem, while those with 4 stems may produce many less; a large plant with a dozen or so stems may produce only 700 flowerheads per stem. The fewer the stems, in other words, the more flowers appear in a sort of nature's-balance equation. Long-lived, vigorous wormwood plants may erect 20 or more flowering stems from a single crown, spanning a ground area of 4 feet.

Tall and coarse, common wormwood produces numerous small flowerheads that shed abundant pollen to the wind.

The 1-seeded *achene* matures in late summer. Unlike those of most aster family plants, it bears no *pappus,* or feathery plume. Number of achenes per flowerhead apparently varies with the flowerhead's location on the stem; more achenes (typically about 40) develop from the upper flowerheads than from middle (about 15) and lower (about 7) flowerheads. Thus the mathematics of stem number and flowerhead placement seems to govern much of this plant's reproductive capacity.

Dispersed by wind and water, many seeds spread long distances when stems break off and blow like tumbleweeds in the fall. Many also germinate along watercourses. Wormwood reproduces only by seed, though uprooted plants and root fragments may reroot. Seeds may remain viable 3 or 4 years. They may germinate anytime from spring to fall, forming leafy rosettes, which hug the ground and last over winter, then produce 1 or more flowering stems the next spring. In the fall, stems die back to the woody root crown, which may span more than 2 inches across in older plants. New stems emerge from crown buds in the spring, rising amid last year's dead stalks.

Wormwood roots, extending to 6 feet horizontally in all directions, become strongly fibrous, even woody, but their generally shallow depth makes the plant vulnerable to drought conditions.

Fernlike foliage of the plant resembles miniature, blunt-tipped, deeply lobed oak leaves.

Associates: A native of Eurasia and North Africa and resident in temperate regions north to Lapland and Siberia, common wormwood now grows across North America, mainly in the northern states and all Canadian provinces. It favors areas of abundant moisture, is shade-tolerant and salt-intolerant, occurs most often in solid stands along roadsides and fencerows. It also frequents gravel pits, vacant lots, and other open areas. Plants growing in well-watered sites appear greener than those in gravel pits or other drier areas, where they exhibit a gray-green hue. Wormwood seedlings compete poorly against grasses, do not readily establish where other plant growth is dense. Various reports of *allelopathy* (chemical inhibition of germination and growth of nearby plants) have appeared for this species, but much of the experimental evidence remains inconclusive. Wormwood roots do, however, extract large amounts of soil nitrogen, which could account, in some cases, for apparent allelopathic effects.

Roots of broom-rapes *(Orobanche),* fleshy, yellowish, parasitic plants, often attach to the roots of wormwoods; clustered broom-rape *(O. fasciculata)* and prairie broom-rape *(O. ludoviciana)* seem to favor wormwood hosts.

Parasitic fungi on common wormwood include powdery mildew *(Erysiphe cichoracearum),* the leaf spot *Cercospora ferruginea,* and the leaf blight *C. olivacea.* The orange rust *Puccinia atrofusca* may also appear on the plant.

Almost 300 insect species are known to frequent common wormwood—but not all at the same time—and their effects seem relatively minor. "Most of the insects," as one research team wrote, "are attracted to absinth for pollen, are predaceous or parasitic on other insects or are seeking shelter from wind or sun."

Most actual feeding on wormwood foliage occurs in early spring, when the plants are young and other plant sources are sparse; as the season advances, these feeders tend to abandon wormwoods. Such consumers include several leafhopper species (Cicadellidae), leaf beetles (Chrysomelidae), and a few moth caterpillars, such as some unidentified casebearers *(Coleophora)* and inchworms or geometers *(Xanthotype).* Painted lady butterfly caterpillars *(Vanessa cardui),* yellowish green and hairy, sometimes feed on wormwoods, tenting in a compact nest of leaf fragments and silk.

Some 92 species of adult flies, some of them pollen eaters, visit or inhabit wormwoods. Perhaps some are attracted by the plant's strong odor. These include anthomyiids such as *Hylemya,* frit flies such as *Meromyza* and *Olcella,* long-legged flies *(Dolichopus),* and *Rhopalomyia* gall gnats, which form 1 or more galls on the flowerheads, sometimes displacing up to 50 percent of the seeds.

Although wildlife users are numerous for the western *Artemisia* sagebrush species, which provide food and cover for desert birds and small mammals plus forage for antelope, deer, elk, and mountain sheep, data for users of common wormwood are scarce. Almost alone among the plants in this book, this plant virtually lacks recorded vertebrate feeders. No doubt rabbits, rodents, and possibly deer graze to some extent on the young rosettes, but not enough to give common wormwood any ranking as a resource. The characteristic acrid odor and bitter taste probably make it unpalatable to most grazers. Livestock generally avoid the plant.

Lore: Several substances account for wormwood odor and taste. These include absinthin, anabsinthin, and thujone, a toxic terpenoid compound also present in resins of cedar *(Thuja)*, tansies *(Tanacetum)*, and sages *(Salvia)*, among others. It is thujone, a psychotropic substance, that accounts for the major human uses of this plant. Distilled wormwood oil became the major flavoring of absinthe liqueur, a green, bitter quaff popular from the 16th century until the early 20th, when most nations (including the United States) banned it because of its severely addictive and cumulative psychoactive effects, also its high alcoholic content (85 percent) and its toxic adulterants and colorants (copper sulfate, turmeric, indigo). "Absinthe makes the heart grow fonder" was apparently more of a desired than actual effect of this libation. It is said that not only did artist Vincent van Gogh, an absinthe addict, undergo numerous personality changes that may have led to his suicide, but also that absinthe overdoses may have caused him to experience yellow-tinged vision, explaining his lavish yellows in his last paintings—a highly speculative suggestion at best. Indeed, many of the reputed effects of absinthe remain somewhat in the realm of esoteric anecdote, have never been subject to modern laboratory analysis. Today absinthe can still be imbibed in a few European countries (Spain, Portugal, Denmark, Czech Republic), but sale remains illegal in most nations.

Any plant as forbiddingly bitter as wormwood—next to rue *(Ruta)* the bitterest herb known, according to some sources—was bound to become a popular herbal medication, and wormwood's medicinal usages go back to ancient Greece and Rome. Wormwood infused popular recipes for everything from vermifuges (worm-expelling potions, source of the name wormwood) and potions for aborting pregnancy to healing balms for "a pain in the anus of demonic origin." Wormwood also treated less exotic problems—liver and gallbladder ailments, fevers, indigestion, bruises and muscular strains, infections of every sort.

Biblical imagery used wormwood as the symbol of bitterness and bile. Wormwood originally "sprang up in the track of the serpent as it writhed along the ground when driven out of Paradise," according to one tradition. Burning the plant could call up spirits, either protective or malicious; wearing it in amulets could evoke love charms and powerful magic, plus doses of fear in goodly measure. Mothers once used wormwood for weaning babies, making the nipple taste bitter. In the American South, backwoods distillery operators would add wormwood to the batch, giving white lightning "the kick of a mule," according to one folklorist. Like numerous Old World herbs of vast repute, the blessings and curses of wormwood seem to balance out fairly evenly—thus this plant of our fencerows and roadsides.

English colonists brought common wormwood to their North American herb gardens. They used it not only for home-brewed tonics and sagelike flavoring, but also as an apparently effective pesticide against household rodents and moths. English herbalist John Parkinson had noted in 1640 that books written in ink containing wormwood remained untouched by hungry mice. Gardeners have long claimed wormwood's powers as an effective repellent against insect herbivores when planted in the vicinity of vegetables. Today the plant is still cultivated in some parts of Europe as a pharmaceutical resource. In North America, it had established itself as a roadside weed by 1840.

The French word *vermouth* derives from the German *wermuth*, and wormwood slightly flavors some vermouths. *Artemisia* derives from Artemis, virgin goddess of the hunt and the moon in Greek mythology (equated with the goddess Diana in Roman lore); it was she who discovered these plants, in ancient tradition, and made them available to humankind.

"It is time," wrote Thoreau on a slow day in Concord, "we had a little wormwood to flavor the somewhat tasteless or cloying summer, which palls upon the taste." In our northeastern outdoors, the change of seasons and the smell of wormwood rescue us from ennui.

Yarrow, Common *(Achillea millefolium)*. Aster family. This perennial, both alien and native races, stands 1 to 3 feet tall and exhibits a dense, flat-topped, usually white (sometimes pinkish) flower cluster and soft, finely cut, fernlike leaves ("like the wispy feathers of young birds," wrote one observer) that alternately ascend the somewhat hairy stem. Yarrow smells pungently aromatic when crushed or bruised.

Other names: Milfoil, western yarrow, yarroway, old-man's-pepper, nosebleed, sneezefoil, staunchweed, soldier's-woundwort, green arrow, thousand-weed, many others.

Close relatives: About 75 *Achillea* species, mainly Eurasian natives, exist in the Northern Hemisphere. Besides common yarrow, which shows many variations in color and chromosomal identity, a few others also reside in North America. Sneezeweed *(A. ptarmica)*, fern-leaf yarrow *(A. filipendulina)*, and woolly yarrow *(A. tomentosa)*, the last two yellow-flowered, are the chief ones. Closely related aster family genera include chamomiles *(Anthemis)*, ox-eye daisy *(q.v.)*, tansies *(Tanacetum)*, and common wormwood *(q.v.)*. Yarrow in flower superficially resembles Queen Anne's lace *(q.v.)*, an unrelated carrot family plant.

Lifestyle: Probably as common as dandelions in many areas, but taller, common yarrow is one of those ubiquitous weedy wildflowers that define summer in North America. Most American yarrow populations are probably native, being distinguished from historical European introductions of the plant by their difference in chromosome number. The entire species consists of many hybrid variations of both native and alien forms. Some sources say that native varieties show rounder-topped flowerheads than the aliens.

As in some other aster family plants, the flowers of yarrow are deceptive in appearance. What looks like a small individual flower in the flat-topped cluster atop the stem—a regular, radially symmetrical flower complete with 5 petals radiating from a central hub—is actually an aggregate flowerhead made up of many flowers. Clusters may contain several hundred flowerheads. A flowerhead's 3-toothed "petals," 5 in number, are actually pistillate (female) ray flowers; the 10 to 30 tubular disk flowers in the center are bisexual. Self-incompatible and producing a sucrose-rich nectar, flowers must be cross-fertilized and insect-pollinated to produce the 1-seeded, nonplumed *achenes.* Typically, about 12 or 13 achenes per flowerhead develop, and each plant may produce 500 to 2,000 achenes (many of the flowers remain unpollinated). Simply blown off the seedhead in fall and winter, yarrow seeds may remain viable for years.

Many seeds, however, germinate the following spring, most forming only leafy rosettes that dormantly survive the next winter and produce flowering stems the second year; a few, however, may flower in their first year. The plants typically flower in July and August, producing seed in August and September. Yarrow stems die back to new-grown rosettes in the fall. Yarrow rosettes may, however, be seen at almost any time of year, since the seeds may germinate in any season except winter.

Yarrow usually occurs in colonial stands owing to its extensively branched stems *(rhizomes)* below ground surface, which may spread horizontally up to 8 inches per year, producing clonal aerial stems. But unlike many clonal groups, which soon decay their subsurface connections, yarrow rhizomes apparently remain intact, leading botanists to assess that "vegetative growth would appear to be exploitive [for the parent plant] rather than reproductive," as one report stated.

Yet, as studies demonstrate, dense clonal stands produce many fewer seeds than thinner stands, also less flowering, less seed production from flowering stems, and more plant die-off. The limiting density appears about 300 stems per square meter.

Yarrow has a shallow but extensive fibrous root system, enabling the plant to survive dry spells. Roots typically extend 2 to 5 inches deep.

Common yarrow's flattish, aggregate flowerhead somewhat resembles that of unrelated Queen Anne's lace, but yarrow's flowers do not occur in umbrellalike umbels.

Root and rhizome fragments do not readily propagate this species. Yarrow's finely cut leaves, with their small surface area, result in relatively modest transpiration rates, further conserving available moisture.

Associates: Common yarrow resides almost everywhere throughout the Northern Hemisphere, has also been introduced into temperate regions of the Southern Hemisphere. In North America, it extends from the Canadian provinces into Mexico. Favoring open land (high or low) and abundant sunlight, it also tolerates shade and can persist on many soil types, including sandy and unfertile sites. Rare is the North American roadside, old field, or vacant lot without a stand of yarrow. Of all the many plants in this book that have widely adapted to numerous sites and conditions, yarrow ranks among the most versatile and ubiquitous. And unlike most comparable plants, it is primarily a native resident, not an alien invader. Yet yarrow can at times invade and compete with other plants, especially in gardens and cropland. Generally the plant's presence indicates poor soil, overgrazing, or land abuse or disturbance.

Two fairly common plant parasites on yarrow are buttonbush-dodder *(Cuscuta cephalanthi)*, a yellow-orange climbing vine; and yarrow or purple broom-rape *(Orobanche purpurea)*, a yellowish, blue-flowered root parasite with scalelike leaves.

Many parasitic fungi attack common yarrow, though most are fairly insignificant. They include spot smut *(Entyloma compositarum)*, powdery mildew *(Erysiphe polygoni)*, leaf spots *(Leptosphaeria, Pleospora)*, black stem *(Mycosphaerella)*, yarrow rust *(Puccinia millefolii)*, and several others.

Both Old and New World yarrow populations host extensive and distinctive fauna—sap suckers, flower feeders, stem borers, root parasites.

Aphid sap suckers include *Microsiphum* and other species. Meadow spittlebug nymphs *(Philaenus spumarius)*, covered in froth, also tap into the stems.

Foliage feeders on yarrow are scarce—apparently the plant's pungent sesquiterpenes provide a strong chemical defense against munching creatures. Also, the small, fernlike leaves offer little substance.

The flowers, rich in nectar, apparently offer much more. Moth caterpillar flower feeders include the blackberry looper *(Chlorochlamys chloroleucaria)*, an inchworm that feeds on yarrow's ray flowers; and *Eupithecia nimbicolor*, another inchworm. The bronze leaf beetle *(Diachus auratus)*, metallic blue, green, or bronze colored, relishes yarrow flowers; and *Megalocoleus molliculus*, a plant bug, also breeds and feeds in yarrow flowers.

Mosquitoes raid yarrow flowers for the nectar—among them, *Anopheles earlei;* several *Aedes* species, including the floodwater mosquito *(A. sticticus)* and the vexans mosquito *(A. vexans);* and the northern house mosquito *(Culex pipiens).*

Stem-boring moth caterpillars on yarrow include *Platyptilia pallidactyla*, a plume moth; and the stalk borer *(Papaipema nebris)*, a noctuid. Larvae of leaf miner flies *Phytomyza matricariae* also tunnel into stems.

Parasitic root nematodes (roundworms) on yarrow consist mainly of *Meloidogyne* and *Heterodera* species.

Pollinating insects include bees and butterflies. Commonly seen on the flowers are American copper butterflies *(Lycaena phlaeas)*. American lady or painted beauty butterflies *(Vanessa virginiensis)* also frequent the plant. Syrphid or hover flies (Syrphidae), also attracted to nectar, include *Eristalis arbustorum, Syritta pipiens, Toxomerus germinatus*, and several *Sphaerophoria* species. Other flies seen on the flowers include March flies *(Dilophus stigmaterus)*, green bottle flies *(Phaenicia sericata)*, and tachinids such as *Peleteria iterans.* Wasps also sip nectar at yarrow: predatory thread-waisted sphecine wasps such as *Podalonia luctosa* and the very common *Ammophila urnaria*, plus smaller braconid wasps such as *Agathis metzneriae*. Also attracted to aphids and other insects on yarrow are predators— crab spiders *(Misumena)*, ladybird beetles (Coccinellidae), and ambush bugs (Phymatidae), among others.

Yarrow seedeaters, if any, are uncommon; the seed bug *Ligyrocoris sylvestris* has been seen on the flowerheads and probably consumes seedheads.

Several birds and mammals, however, relish yarrow's bitter leaves—ruffed and sharp-tailed grouse, cottontail rabbits, and pine mice. White-tailed deer graze the flowerheads; in some areas, yarrow apparently provides an important deer forage in the autumn diet. Cattle and horses generally avoid the plant, though sheep and goats consume it readily. When cows do graze it, the plant may taint their milk with an unpalatable flavor.

Lore: Remnants of yarrow, its bitterness beloved from ancient times as medicine and magic for almost any physical or spiritual ailment that human flesh bears, have been found in 60,000-year-old Neanderthal burial caves. Yarrow was one of 4 plants so universally dosed that English herbalists labeled each of them "allheal" (the others: garden valerian or heliotrope, *Valeriana officinalis;* self-heal, *q.v.;* and European mistletoe, *Viscum album*). Yarrow, tansy *(Tanacetum)*, and lovage *(Levisticum)* were once the staple herbs of traditional herb and kitchen gardens. Some gardeners call yarrow the "herb's herb."

This plant contains more than 100 biologically active compounds—among them, thujone, the alkaloid achilleine, lactones, ethanol, resins, tannins, gums, and the essential oil known as oleum millefolii. Medicinally, yarrow teas and tonics have been used as antispasmodics, astringents, hemostats, gas-relieving carminatives, analgesics, antiseptics, antibiotics, sweat-inducing diaphoretics, menses-inducing emmenagogues, and stimulants. Yarrow, stranger to few of our ills through history, has treated colds, fevers, indigestion, cramps, kidney disorders, toothache, internal bleeding, and infections of every sort, both as decoction and poultice. One unorthodox use recorded by English herbalist John Gerard was to relieve a young man's embarrassing "swelling of those secret parts," the yarrow leaves in lard applied warm "into the privie parts." Yet the name old-man's-pepper for the plant derived from its supposed aphrodisiac powers. In ancient battles—and up to the American Civil War—yarrow served as standard medical treatment for stopping bleeding, thus one of its names, soldier's-woundwort. The centaur Charon, it is said, gave this plant to Achilles, who first used it as field medication for his wounded comrades during the Trojan War; from Achilles comes the plant's generic name. Roman warriors called the plant *herba militaris,* and Anglo-Saxons and Crusaders all knew it as a useful wound dressing and healing herb.

American colonists and some 46 native tribes, at least, applied yarrow to more than 25 ailments. For many tribes, the plant served as a sacred sweat lodge herb. Modern medicine uses a yarrow compound in the treatment of acute viral hepatitis and *Staphylococcus* bacterial infections. Chamazulene, found in the flowerheads, is apparently the main therapeutic substance.

Yarrow's reputed magical powers as witch, demon, and evil-power repellent also experienced ample workouts through history. Not to be outdone, at different times and places, were its devil-conjuring powers. Yarrow stalks are the traditional tools for consulting the *I Ching* or *Chinese Book of Changes* divination oracles; the spontaneous synchronicity of 50 stalks tossed on the ground—how they land—refers the tosser to an exceedingly abstruse entry in the book.

Planted in gardens, yarrow is said to repel destructive insects; and fleas and lice reputedly go away when they find it as a dried plant in animal bedding. Other uses of yarrow have included yellow and olive green dyes made from the flowers, hair shampoos, tobacco substitute, refreshing herbal baths, and dried floral bouquets. Horticulturists have developed pink, red, purple, and yellow varieties of yarrow, some of which occasionally escape to the countryside.

Foodwise, yarrow offers not much to humans, the leaves being too bitter and unpalatable for most salads, even. In Sweden, yarrow once served as a substitute for hops in brewing. "The differences between food, medicine, and poison," as one naturalist wrote, "are a matter of dosage," a statement that certainly applies to yarrow. As an exceedingly bitter tea or tonic, it is harmless, perhaps even beneficial, if not precisely refreshing. Large or frequent doses, however, should be avoided; the toxic substance, though less than in common wormwood *(q.v.),* is thujone. Yarrow's lactones make the plant allergenic to some individuals, causing skin irritations and rashes if handled.

The word *yarrow* derives from the Anglo-Saxon name of the plant, gearwe. *Gordolobo* is the appealing Spanish name for this plant.

Yucca *(Yucca filamentosa)*. Agave family. Recognize this coarse, evergreen, native perennial by its tussocks or rosettes of stiff, straplike, sharp-tipped leaves and its large, pendent, somewhat bulbous and bell-like, greenish white flowers that rise on a separate woody stalk. Another identification feature: the loose, stringy threads and fibers on leaf margins.

Other names: Spanish bayonet, Adam's needle, beargrass, soapweed.

Close relatives: Some 35 *Yucca* species reside mainly in western North America. The soap-plant *(Y. glauca)* is the only other *Yucca* that occurs eastward to the midwestern states. Foremost in southwestern deserts is the blue or banana yucca or amole *(Y. baccata)*, which Navaho and Hopi tribes, among others, value for food and fibers. The Joshua tree *(Y. brevifolia)* is also a well-known desert resident. Family members include the agave or century-plant *(Agave utahensis)*, false aloe *(A. virginica)*, sisal hemp *(A. sisalana)*, bowstring hemp *(Sansevieria trifasciata)*, cabbage palms *(Cordyline terminalis, C. indivisa)*, and corn plant *(Dracaena fragrans)*.

Lifestyle: Rising 3 to 6 feet or more in height by early summer, yucca's central woody flower stalk, or *raceme* (sometimes called Our Lord's candle), bears up to several dozen of the white, 2-inch-long flowers. Flowers develop and appear in progressive sequence from the bottom of the raceme upward. Each pendent flower consists of 3 sepals, 3 petals (both look alike, hence are called *tepals)*, 6 (male) stamens that produce a heavy, sticky pollen, and 1 (female) pistil. The stamens, shorter than the pistil, bend away from it, thus hindering self-fertilization. This bisexual flower has evolved a codependency *(mutualism)* upon a single insect genus, the yucca moths (see Associates), for flower pollination and seed production. The moths, active only at night, respond to the flower's *nyctinasty* (night movements), which consists of turning upward, opening wide, and emitting a sweet, soapy fragrance. Without the moths, yuccas cannot sexually reproduce.

They can and do, however, reproduce by vegetative cloning from the roots and root fragments, producing adjacent clumps and rosettes but never spreading far. The plant's system of deep taproots gives it drought resistance, also makes it extremely difficult to eliminate once it is established.

Yucca seedpods, developing only from moth-infested flowers, consist of 3 chambers called *carpels,* each carpel holding 2 rows or stacks of black, waferlike seeds. The pods dry out and blacken by late summer, splitting and spilling their seed loads like pepper shakers. The stacked seeds leave parallel markings on the inside walls of the carpels, a bit of artistry easily visible in winter when the dried, split-open pods dangle. A very high percentage of yucca seeds are viable and readily germinate.

Yucca's leaf clump may stand about 3 feet tall, spanning a similar width. The swordlike leaves are perennial—only the vertical flower stalk dies each year. A new one rises each spring from the thick, woody crown *(caudex)* just beneath ground surface.

Associates: Yucca favors sandy, open, unshaded sites, including dunes and barrens. Although its succulent leaves identify it as a desert-adapted plant, this yucca's center of distribution is the humid Southeast. It appears tolerant of dry urban environments, also of road salt. Native to most of eastern North America, it primarily resides from North Carolina to the Gulf and westward to the Mississippi; disjunct populations, however—some but not all of them garden escapes—appear fairly commonly northward into New England and southern Canada. In some of those places, a frequent associate is eastern prickly pear *(q.v.)*, a cactus.

Fungi on wild-growing yucca seem relatively rare and insignificant. Some *Yucca* species host brown leaf spot *(Coniothyrium)* and *Fusarium* stem rot.

Sap-sucking insects may include thrips (Thysanoptera); armored scale insects (Diaspididae), such as the oleander scale *(Aspidiotus nerii)* and oystershell scale *(Lepidosaphes ulmi);* and aphids (Aphididae). The yucca plant bug *(Halticotoma valida),* a colorful, oval, orange-red and blue-black hemipteran, specializes in sucking yucca, causing yellow stippling on leaves.

Among occasional insects that tunnel into the flower stalk are stalk borers *(Papaipema nebris),* noctuid moth caterpillars. Caterpillars of yucca giant-skippers *(Megathymus yuccae),* mothlike lepidopterans, also bore into stems and leaf bases. The large, dark, yellow-spotted adult skippers may be seen flying around yucca plants in late afternoon or evening. They mainly range from South Carolina south and westward.

The ornate checkered beetle *(Trichodes ornatus),* red and yellow, sometimes feeds on yucca flower pollen.

Vital to this yucca's reproduction and survival is its specialized relationship with the yucca moth *(Tegeticula yuccasella),* a prodoxid. The adult female, with pure white forewings and gray, white-edged hindwings, bears 2 long, curved tentacles or palps on the mouthparts; with these, it gathers the sticky pollen, forms it into a ball, tucks it between head and thorax, then moves to another flower, where it pushes the pollen ball into the funnel end of the stigmatic (female) organ, thus pollinating the flower. "It's as if the moths are farming the plants," as one researcher remarked. At the same time, the insect inserts eggs into various portions of the flower base *(Tegeticula* means "little concealer"). As the seeds develop inside the green pods, so do the gray or pinkish moth caterpillars—2 or 3 in most pods, sometimes 6 to 12. The caterpillars feed on the seeds, boring into a neighboring carpel if they run out of seeds in the first. Often a caved-in portion of the pod reveals the caterpillar's internal consumption of the seeds, which the larvae hollow out. Although some pods carry an oversupply of moth eggs and caterpillars—probably because of egg deposition by more than 1 female moth—most pods shelter only a few caterpillars, which consume only modest amounts (about 18 to 20, no more than a third of the seeds) on average. In 1984, biologist Robert Kingsolver suggested a possible "lottery" mechanism regulating the number of eggs with the available flowers: The plant produces, then drops, many of its flowers, including pollinated ones; the moth that places "smaller bets" (fewer eggs) in more flowers, rather than more eggs in fewer flowers, increases chances that more caterpillars will hatch and survive among the flowers that have remained on the plant. "In this way," as one report stated, "a plant might force moths to lay eggs 'thin and wide.'"

When the caterpillars mature, they tunnel exit burrows from the pod (the number of exit holes reveals the number of caterpillars a pod held), holes that remain visible in the dry pods seen in winter. The caterpillars drop to the ground, crawl for a period, then burrow into the soil and pupate. Sometimes they emerge as adult moths the next spring, sometimes not for 2 or more years. Emergent moths, as the flowers begin blooming, immediately enter the flowers, where they remain hidden during daytime and where mating occurs. "The yucca moths are so secure inside the flowers," stated one report, "that a researcher has to batter a flower considerably to encourage the moth to leave."

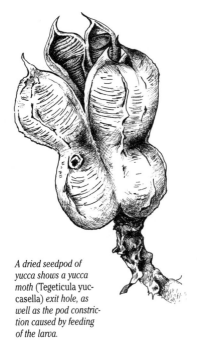

A dried seedpod of yucca shows a yucca moth (Tegeticula yuccasella) *exit hole, as well as the pod constriction caused by feeding of the larva.*

Pollinating flights occur between dusk and midnight, and flowers also become most fragrant at these hours. The moths do not range far from their home plants, and they remain active for only a few days.

Closely related to the yucca moth, and similar in appearance but smaller, is the so-called bogus or false yucca moth *(Prodoxus quinquepunctellus)*. These caterpillars develop inside the flower stalk and in the green, fleshy pods, where females deposit their eggs. Pupation also occurs there, and the insects emerge as adults, often feeding inside the flower. This insect appears entirely parasitic on the plant.

The extent to which bee and other moth pollinators are attracted to these flowers remains unknown. Some accounts state that they never are, but other observers indicate their sometime presence.

Although western yucca species provide important wildlife resources—food, nesting cavities and materials, perching sites—our eastern species seems relatively scant in vertebrate associates. Seed feeders on *Y. filamentosa,* besides the aforementioned moths, are unrecorded. Apparently few if any birds take seeds from this plant, and mammal grazers avoid its formidable foliage.

Lore: So tightly have the yucca plant and the yucca moth coevolved that should either of them disappear, so too would its counterpart organism. This so-called textbook example of coevolution, similar to that of the termite and its gut protozoans, actually reveals the evolution of an entire system that incorporates changes in each separate organism. A Missouri entomologist, Charles V. Riley, first researched and published details of this plant-moth relationship in 1892, work that ultimately led to many more discoveries in the entire subject realm of mutualism. Yucca and moth apparently coevolved in the southwestern region of this continent. "Ancestors of the yucca moth," one research team concluded, "almost certainly began as harmful feeders on yucca tissues but converted to feeding on seeds and eventually took over the pollination duties."

A few observers, however, have questioned this simplified, idealized "textbook example." "In fact," wrote researcher Herbert G. Baker in 1986, "the interaction is probably more complicated than any single account has implied." Questions exist as to the frequency of self-fertilization in the absence of pollinating moths, also as to the roster of other insects—bees, wasps, beetles—that may on occasion be attracted to, and pollinate, the flowers. Observation is needed to fill in some of the blanks about this intriguing plant.

Yuccas, especially southwestern species, were amply utilized by native tribes. The plants' strong fibers helped create cordage, bowstrings, matting, cloth, baskets, nets, and footwear. Tribal healers used yucca roots for a variety of poultice treatments and salves for skin sores and sprains. Also from the roots came mild, frothy, soaplike saponins (hence the name soapweed), useful for cleaning and applying to skin irritations. Some commercial soaps and shampoos use yucca substances today. The same saponins in the form of mashed roots tossed into a fish pond had a toxic, stupefying effect on the fish, causing them to float so they could be easily collected.

Yucca's edible flower tepals are said to taste like Belgian endive, may be eaten raw or cooked.

Probably the spread of *Y. filamentosa* into northern areas during the past 150 years owes much to its popularity as a yard and garden plant. It has also been widely used in cemetery plantings. The extent of its presettlement distribution in the North remains unknown.

The name *yucca* is said to derive from *yuca,* Spanish for the Caribbean manihot, manioc, or cassava plant, a word that itself stemmed from a Taino Indian word for the latter plant (spurge family). Hence the name *yucca* was a misnomer at the outset and remains so. *Filamentosa* refers to the loose, threadlike fibers on the leaf margins.

New Mexico claims soap-plant *(Y. glauca)* as its state flower.

Glossary

Achene. A dry fruit, usually 1-seeded, that does not split open along suture lines; the typical fruiting form of aster family plants as well as some others.

Acropetal. Refers to progressive ascending development of flowers or leaves toward an apex or summit.

Adaptation. An evolved process, structure, or activity by which an organism becomes apparently better suited to its habitat or environment, or for particular functions.

Adaptive. Refers to any feature or characteristic of an organism that aids its ability to survive in its environment.

Allelopathy. One plant's inhibition of another by secreted chemicals, often from roots.

Alternation of generations. The reproductive scheme of nonflowering plants (mosses, ferns, horsetails), whereby the sexual generation alternates with an asexual generation.

Annual. A plant that completes its entire life cycle within a year or single growing season.

Anther. The pollen-bearing part of a stamen.

Apomixis. The development of fruit or seed without the fusion of sex cells; parthenogenesis. Also called *apogamy.*

Biennial. A plant that completes its entire life cycle within a 2-year period, flowering and producing seed in its second year.

Bisexual flower. A flower having both male and female sex organs; also called a *perfect flower.*

Calciphile. A plant favoring soil or water high in calcium.

Cleistogamy. The process of self-pollination in flowers that remain closed in the bud, a reproductive alternative in certain species.

Clone. A plant or group of plants produced by vegetative reproduction or apomixis and carrying the same genetic makeup as the parent.

Coaction. An interaction between 2 or more organisms.

Commensalism. A form of symbiosis in which one partner benefits and neither is harmed.

Cultivar. A strain, variety, form, or race of a plant species developed and maintained as a cultivated or crop growth.

Cyme. A flower stalk bearing flowers that develop and mature from the stalk tip downward.

Diapause. An insect resting period or stage, in which growth and activity cease, resuming later; usually occurs in midsumer and winter.

Dioecious. See *Unisexual flower.*

Dormancy. A state or condition of inactive metabolism, as in many seeds and insects, lasting in some cases for years, in others for only weeks or a season.

Drupe. A stone fruit with a fleshy outer layer surrounding a hard seed cover, as in autumn olive.

Epiphyte. A plant growing on another plant, using it as support but deriving no nourishment from it, as vetches on surrounding stems.

Floret. A small flower, especially on an aggregate flowerhead, as in aster family plants.

Forb. Any herbaceous plant other than a grass, sedge, or rush.

Gall. A localized growth on a plant induced by a fungus or by egg-laying or feeding of certain mites or insect larvae, especially aphids, gall gnats, or gall wasps.

Gametophyte. In plants exhibiting alternation of generations, the plant produced by a spore and giving rise to male and female sex cells, which produce an asexual spore-bearing plant.

Germination. The sprouting of a seed or spore, resulting in a seedling or gametophyte, respectively.

Guild. A group of species that share a common resource in a community, as stem borers or pollen feeders.

Habitat. A total set of environmental conditions in which an organism exists.

Herb. Any nonwoody plant (excluding fungi) whose aboveground parts die back each year.

Herbivore. Any animal that feeds on plants.

Hybrid. The offspring of a cross between 2 different though closely related species; often this offspring cannot itself reproduce.

Inflorescence. An individual flowerhead or cluster of floral parts.

Irruption. A sudden, temporary increase in population abundance and size, as in periodic outbreaks of certain insects.

Lodging. Bending or leaning of stems against other plants or the ground, usually caused by wind, rain, or insect attack upon stems.

Microhabitat. A subdivision of a habitat, such as a stump, small pool, or teasel axil, to which certain organisms may become specifically adapted.

Mimicry. The evolved adaptive resemblance of a species to an unrelated species or to organic material (as in resemblance of certain moths to bird droppings or leaves).

Monoecious. See *Unisexual flower.*

Mutualism. An interaction between 2 species from which both derive benefit.

Mycorrhiza. The symbiotic relationship of a subsurface fungus with vascular plant roots; the fungus aids, and in many cases is vital to, nutrient absorption by the roots.

Naturalized. Refers to an alien plant of long residence that is not extremely competitve with native plants.

Nectar guides. Colored lines or markings on flower petals or sepals, believed to aid alighting insects in finding the flower nectaries.

Parasite. Any organism living on or in another living organism from which it derives nourishment, as dodder on various plant hosts.

Perennial. A plant that lives for 3 or more years, its aboveground parts often dying back to the roots in autumn; short-lived perennials usually die after 3 or 4 years.

Photosynthesis. The process by which green plants manufacture sugars from carbon dioxide, water, and light energy.

Pistil. The female seed-bearing flower organ, consisting of ovary, style, and stigma.

Pome. A fleshy fruit with a papery core, as in apples, hawthorns.

Protandry. Sex sequencing in a bisexual flower in which the male parts mature and decline before the female parts mature.

Protogyny. Sex sequencing in a bisexual flower in which the female parts mature and decline before the male parts mature.

Raceme. A flower stalk bearing flowers that develop and mature from the stalk base upward.

Rhizome. A horizontal, underground, rootlike stem that produces roots and cloning aerial stems.

Rosette. A cluster of leaves at the base of a stem; in perennials and biennials, the typical wintering form of the plant.

Seed bank. The accumulation of viable seeds in the soil.

Semelparous. Refers to the frequent tendency of some biennial plants, as common burdock, to delay flowering for 1 or more years, often depending upon the size of the basal rosette; semelparous plants are also called *monocarpic* (one-time flowering) *perennials* or *facultative biennials.*

Sepal. A modified leaf underlying the sexual parts of a flowerhead.

Spore. A 1-celled, asexual, reproductive organ borne on sporophytes; spores germinate to produce sexual gametophytes.

Sporophyte. In plants exhibiting alternation of generations, the spore-producing plant that grows from a gametophyte.

Stamen. The male pollen-bearing organ of a flower, consisting of anther and filament.

Stigma. The pollen-receiving part of the female flower pistil.

Stolon. A horizontal stem on the ground surface, giving rise to roots and shoots along its length, as in wild strawberry and many grasses.

Stratification. The period requirement of some seeds to undergo freezing in the soil before germination can occur; often *cold stratification.*

Succession. Natural replacement of one plant community by another.

Symbiosis. Any intimate coaction between different organisms; includes parasitism, commensalism, and mutualism.

Tepal. A sepal or petal, labeled as tepal when the 2 parts appear visually similar.

Tussock. A compact, densely tufted growth form bearing many stems from a matlike crown, as in yuccas.

Umbel. An umbrellalike flower cluster with flower stalks radiating from a single point, as in Queen Anne's lace.

Unisexual flower. A flower having either male or female sex organs, but not both. *Dioecious plants* bear each sex on different individuals; *monoecious plants* bear each sex separately on the same individual.

Utricle. A 1-seeded, bladderlike fruit, as in amaranths.

Vector. An organism, usually an insect, that transmits disease pathogens.

Vegetative reproduction. Any replication of a plant not directly resulting from seed or spore germination, as in fragmentation, cloning, or sprouting from roots, stolons, or rhizomes; the dominant form of reproduction in many plants.

Selected
Bibliography

In addition to the following listed references and others, basic sources have included relevant research monographs and articles in *American Journal of Botany, American Midland Naturalist, Canadian Field Naturalist, Canadian Journal of Botany, Canadian Journal of Plant Science,* and *Ecology,* among other professional biological journals. Internet resources included the *USDA Forest Service Federal U.S. Database* and the *Element Stewardship Abstracts of the Nature Conservancy.* I have used many older as well as recent references, finding that materials long out of print offer some of the best, most valuable, and descriptive basic knowledge about the plants concerned.

Arnett, Ross H., Jr. *American Insects.* 2nd ed. New York: CRC Press, 2000.

Benchley, Winifred E. *Weeds of Farm Land.* London: Longmans, Green, 1920.

Blanchan, Neltje. *Nature's Garden.* Garden City, NY: Garden City Publishing, 1900.

Bolton, J. L. *Alfalfa: Botany, Cultivation, and Utilization.* London: Leonard Hill, 1962.

Borror, Donald J., and Richard E. White. *A Field Guide to the Insects.* Boston: Houghton Mifflin, 1970.

Bosik, Joseph J., ed. *Common Names of Insects and Related Organisms 1997.* Lanham, MD: Entomological Society of America, 1997.

Brewer, Richard. *The Science of Ecology.* 2nd ed. New York: Saunders, 1994.

Brown, Lauren. *Grasses: An Identification Guide.* Boston: Houghton Mifflin, 1979.

Brown, Tom, Jr. *Tom Brown's Guide to Wild Edible and Medicinal Plants.* New York: Berkley, 1985.

Browning, Frank. *Apples.* New York: North Point Press, 1998.

Burroughs, John. *Winter Sunshine.* Boston: Houghton, Mifflin, 1894.

Clewell, Andre F. *I. Identification of the Lespedezas in North America. II. A Selected Bibliography on Lespedeza.* Number 7. Tallahassee, FL: Tall Timbers Research Station, 1966.

———. *Natural History, Cytology, and Isolating Mechanisms of the Native American Lespedezas.* Number 6. Tallahassee, FL: Tall Timbers Research Station, 1966.

Coffey, Timothy. *The History and Folklore of North American Wildflowers.* Boston: Houghton Mifflin, 1993.

Comstock, Anna Botsford. *Handbook of Nature-Study.* Ithaca, NY: Comstock, 1939.

Covell, Charles V., Jr. *A Field Guide to the Moths.* Boston: Houghton Mifflin, 1984.

Darrow, George M. *The Strawberry: History, Breeding and Physiology.* New York: Holt, Rinehart and Winston, 1966.

Darwin, Charles, and Francis Darwin. *The Power of Movement in Plants.* London: John Murray, 1880.

Davison, Verne E. *Attracting Birds: From the Prairies to the Atlantic.* New York: Crowell, 1967.

Dunn, Gary A. *Insects of the Great Lakes Region.* Ann Arbor, MI: University of Michigan Press, 1996.

Eastman, John. *The Book of Forest and Thicket.* Harrisburg, PA: Stackpole Books, 1992.

———. *The Book of Swamp and Bog.* Mechanicsburg, PA: Stackpole Books, 1995.

Elbroch, Mark, and Eleanor Marks. *Bird Tracks and Sign: A Guide to North American Species.* Mechanicsburg, PA: Stackpole Books, 2001.

Erichsen-Brown, Charlotte. *Medicinal and Other Uses of North American Plants.* New York: Dover, 1989.

Felt, Ephraim Porter. *Plant Galls and Gall Makers.* New York: Hafner, 1965.

Foster, Steven, and James A. Duke. *A Field Guide to Medicinal Plants.* Boston: Houghton Mifflin, 1990.

Frankton, Clarence, and Gerald A. Mulligan. *Weeds of Canada.* Ottawa: Canada Department of Agriculture, 1971.

Gleason, Henry A., and Arthur Cronquist. *Manual of Vascular Plants of Northeastern United States and Adjacent Canada.* 2nd ed. Bronx, NY: New York Botanical Garden, 1991.

Hanson, Herbert C. *Dictionary of Ecology.* New York: Bonanza Books, 1962.

Heath, Maurice E., Darrel S. Metcalfe, and Robert F. Barnes, eds. *Forages: The Science of Grassland Agriculture.* 3rd ed. Ames, IA: Iowa State University Press, 1973.

Heinrich, Bernd. *Bumblebee Economics.* Cambridge, MA: Harvard University Press, 1979.

Jones, Pamela. *Just Weeds: History, Myths and Uses.* Shelburne, VT: Chapters, 1994.

Klots, Alexander B. *A Field Guide to the Butterflies.* Boston: Houghton Mifflin, 1951.

Leopold, Aldo. *A Sand County Almanac.* London: Oxford University Press, 1949.

Lutz, Frank E. *Field Book of Insects.* 3rd ed. New York: G. P. Putnam's Sons, 1948.

Martin, Alexander C., Herbert S. Zim, and Arnold L. Nelson. *American Wildlife and Plants.* New York: Dover, 1961.

Medlin, Julie Jones. *Michigan Lichens.* Bulletin 60. Bloomfield Hills, MI: Cranbrook Institute of Science, 1996.

Newcomb, Lawrence. *Newcomb's Wildflower Guide.* Boston: Little, Brown. 1977.

Pasture and Range Plants. Parts 1–6. Bartlesville, OK: Phillips Petroleum Company, 1959.

Peairs, Leonard Marion. *Insect Pests of Farm, Garden, and Orchard.* 4th ed. New York: John Wiley & Sons, 1941.

Peattie, Donald Culross. *Flowering Earth.* New York: G. P. Putnam's Sons, 1939.

Peterson, Lee Allen. *A Field Guide to Edible Wild Plants.* Boston: Houghton Mifflin, 1977.

Peterson, Roger Tory, and Margaret McKenny. *A Field Guide to Wildflowers.* Boston: Houghton Mifflin, 1968.

Pond, Barbara. *A Sampler of Wayside Herbs.* Riverside, CT: Chatham Press, 1974.

Reice, Seth R. *The Silver Lining: The Benefits of Natural Disasters.* Princeton, NJ: Princeton University Press, 2001.

Semple, John C., and Gordon S. Ringius. *The Goldenrods of Ontario.* Waterloo, Ontario: University of Waterloo, 1992.

Sheley, Roger L., and Janet K. Petroff, eds. *Biology and Management of Noxious Rangeland Weeds.* Corvallis, OR: Oregon State University Press, 1999.

Smith, James Payne, Jr. *Vascular Plant Families.* Eureka, CA: Mad River Press, 1977.

Steen, Edwin B. *Dictionary of Biology.* New York: Barnes & Noble, 1971.

Sternberg, Guy. *Autumn Olive in Illinois Conservation Practice.* Springfield, IL: Illinois Department of Conservation, 1982.

Stokes, Donald W., and Lillian Q. Stokes. *A Guide to Enjoying Wildflowers.* New York: Little, Brown, 1985.

Taylor, Raymond L. *Plants of Colonial Days.* Mineola, NY: Dover, 1996.

Thoreau, Henry D. *Excursions.* New York: Corinth, 1962.

———. *Faith in a Seed.* Bradley P. Dean, ed. Washington, DC: Island Press, 1993.

———. *The Journal of Henry D. Thoreau.* Bradford Torrey and Francis H. Allen, eds. Vols. 1–14. New York: Dover, 1962.

———. *Wild Fruits.* Bradley P. Dean, ed. New York: W. W. Norton, 2000.

Underwood, Lucien Marcus. *Moulds Mildews and Mushrooms.* New York: Henry Holt, 1899.

United States Department of Agriculture. *Insects: The Yearbook of Agriculture 1952.* Washington, DC: U.S. Government Printing Office, 1952.

———. *Plant Diseases: The Yearbook of Agriculture 1953.* Washington, DC: U.S. Government Printing Office, 1953.

Vander Wall, Stephen B. *Food Hoarding in Animals.* Chicago: University of Chicago Press, 1990.

Voss, Edward G. *Michigan Flora. Part I, Gymnosperms and Monocots.* Bulletin 55. Bloomfield Hills, MI: Cranbrook Institute, 1972.

————. *Michigan Flora. Part II, Dicots.* Bulletin 59. Bloomfield Hills, MI: Cranbrook Institute, 1985.

————. *Michigan Flora. Part III, Dicots.* Bulletin 61. Bloomfield Hills, MI: Cranbrook Institute, 1996.

Weeds of the North Central States. Urbana, IL: University of Illinois Agricultural Experiment Station, 1960.

Westcott, Cynthia. *The Gardener's Bug Book.* New York: American Garden Guild, 1946.

White, Richard E. *A Field Guide to the Beetles.* Boston: Houghton Mifflin, 1983.

Index